Learning Rails

Learning Rails

Simon St.Laurent and Edd Dumbill

O'REILLY®

Beijing · Cambridge · Farnham · Köln · Sebastopol · Taipei · Tokyo

Learning Rails
by Simon St.Laurent and Edd Dumbill

Published by O'Reilly Media, Inc., 1005 Gravenstein Highway North, Sebastopol, CA 95472.

O'Reilly books may be purchased for educational, business, or sales promotional use. Online editions are also available for most titles (*http://safari.oreilly.com*). For more information, contact our corporate/institutional sales department: 800-998-9938 or *corporate@oreilly.com*.

Editor: Mike Loukides
Production Editor: Sarah Schneider
Production Services: Appingo, Inc.

Indexer: Seth Maislin
Cover Designer: Karen Montgomery
Interior Designer: David Futato
Illustrator: Jessamyn Read

Printing History:
November 2008:   First Edition.

ISBN: 978-0-596-51877-6

[LSI]   [07/10]

1280258816

Table of Contents

Preface

Everyone cool seems to agree: Ruby on Rails is an amazing way to build web (or heck, Web 2.0) applications. Ruby is a powerful and flexible programming language, and Rails takes advantage of that flexibility to build a web application framework that takes care of a tremendous amount of work for the developer. Everything sounds great!

Except, well... all the Ruby on Rails books talk about this "Model-View-Controller" thing, and they start deep inside the application, close to the database, most of the time. From an experienced Rails developer's perspective, this makes sense—the framework's power lies largely in making it easy for developers to create a data model quickly, layer controller logic on top of that, and then, once all the hard work is done, put a thin layer of interface view on the very top. It's good programming style, and it makes for more robust applications. Advanced Ajax functionality seems to come almost for free!

From the point of view of someone learning Ruby on Rails, however, that race to show off Rails' power can be extremely painful. There's a lot of seemingly magical behavior in Rails that works wonderfully—until one of the incantations isn't quite right and figuring out what happened means unraveling all that work Rails did. Rails certainly makes it easier to work with databases and objects without spending forever thinking about them, but there are a lot of things to figure out before that ease becomes obvious.

If you'd rather learn Ruby on Rails more slowly, starting from pieces that are more familiar to the average web developer and then moving slowly into controllers and models, you're in the right place. You can start from the HTML you already likely know, and then move more deeply into Rails' many interlinked components.

This updated version of Learning Rails covers version 2.x up through version 2.3.5, but will mention places where Rails 3.0 will be different. The Rails 3.0 beta arrived recently, and while we can't encourage learning Rails on beta software, being ready for the future is important too.

Who This Book Is For

You've probably been working with the Web for long enough to know that writing web applications always seems more complicated than it should be. There are lots of parts to manage, along with lots of people to manage, and hopefully lots of visitors to please. Ruby on Rails has intrigued you as one possible solution to that situation.

You may be a designer who's moving toward application development or a developer who combines some design skills with some programming skills. You may be a programmer who's familiar with HTML but who lacks the sense of grace needed to create beautiful design—that's a fair description of one of the authors of this book, anyway. Wherever you're from, whatever you do, you know the Web well and would like to learn how Rails can make your life easier.

The only mandatory technical prerequisite for reading this book is direct familiarity with HTML and a general sense of how programming works. You'll be inserting Ruby code into that HTML as a first step toward writing Ruby code directly, so understanding HTML is a key foundation. (If you don't know Ruby at all, you probably want to look over Appendix A or at least keep it handy for reference.)

Cascading Style Sheets (CSS) will help you make that HTML look a lot nicer, but it's not necessary for this book. Similarly, a sense of how JavaScript works may help. Experience with other templating languages (like PHP, ASP, and ASP.NET) can also help, but it isn't required.

You also need to be willing to work from the command line sometimes. The commands aren't terribly complicated, but they aren't (yet) completely hidden behind a graphical interface. Even Heroku Garden, an online integrated development environment (IDE) for Rails, still has some necessary command-line features.

Who This Book Is Not For

We don't really want to cut anyone out of the possibility of reading this book, but there are some groups of people who aren't likely to enjoy it. Model-View-

Controller purists will probably grind their teeth through the first few chapters, and people who insist that data structures are at the heart of a good application are going to have to wait an even longer time to see their hopes realized. If you consider HTML just a nuisance that programmers have to put up with, odds are good that this book isn't for you. Most of the other Ruby on Rails books, though, are written for people who want to start from the model!

Also, people who are convinced that Ruby and Rails are the one true way may have some problems with this book, which spends a fair amount of time warning readers about potential problems and confusions they need to avoid. Yes, once you've worked with Ruby and Rails for a while, their elegance is obvious. However, reaching that level of comfort and familiarity is often a difficult road. This book attempts to ease as many of those challenges as possible by describing them clearly.

What You'll Learn

Building a Ruby on Rails application requires mastering a complicated set of skills. You may find that—depending on how you're working with it, and who you're working with—you only need part of this tour. That's fine. Just go as far as you think you'll need.

At the beginning, you'll need to install Ruby on Rails. We'll explore different ways of doing this, with an emphasis on easier approaches to getting Ruby and Rails operational.

Next, we'll create a very simple Ruby on Rails application, with only a basic view and then a controller that does a very few things. From this foundation we'll explore ways to create a more sophisticated layout using a variety of tools, learning more about Ruby along the way.

Once we've learned how to present information, we'll take a closer look at controllers and what they can do. Forms processing is critical to most web applications, so we'll build a few forms and process their results, moving from the simple to the complex.

Forms can do interesting things without storing data, but after a while it's a lot more fun to have data that lasts for more than just a few moments. The next step is setting up a database to store information and figuring out how the magic of Rails' ActiveRecord makes it easy to create code that maps directly to database structures—without having to think too hard about database structures or SQL.

Once we have ActiveRecord up and running, we'll explore scaffolding and its possibilities. Rails scaffolding not only helps you build applications quickly, it helps you learn to build them well. The RESTful approach that Rails 2.0 chose to emphasize will make it simpler for you to create applications that are both attractive and maintainable. For purposes of illustration, using scaffolding also makes it easier to demonstrate one task at a time, which we hope will make it easier for you to understand what's happening.

Ideally, at this point you'll feel comfortable with slightly more complicated data models, and we'll take a look at applications that need to combine data in multiple tables. Mixing and matching data is at the heart of most web applications.

We'll also take a look at testing and debugging Rails code, a key factor in the framework's success. Migrations, which make it easy to modify your underlying data structures (and even roll back those changes if necessary), are another key part of Rails' approach to application maintainability.

The next step will be to add some common web applications elements like sessions and cookies, as well as authentication. Rails (sometimes with the help of plug-ins) can manage a lot of this work for you.

We'll also let Rails stretch its legs a bit, building more exciting Ajax applications and sending email messages. Finally, we'll show you one approach to bringing your Rails application to a wider public, deploying it with MySQL and Phusion Passenger, as well as exploring some other possibilities.

By the end of this tour, you should be comfortable with working in Ruby on Rails. You may not be a Rails guru yet, but you'll be ready to take advantage of all of the other resources out there for becoming one.

Ruby and Rails Style

It's definitely possible to write Ruby on Rails code in ways that look familiar to programmers from other languages. However, that code often isn't really idiomatic Ruby, as Ruby programmers have chosen other paths. In general, this book will always try to introduce new concepts using syntax that's likely to be familiar to developers from other environments, and then explain what the local idiom does. You'll learn to write idiomatic Ruby that way (if you want to), and at the same time you'll figure out how to read code from the Ruby pros.

We've tried to make sure that the code we present is understandable to those without a strong background in Ruby. Ruby itself is worth an introductory book (or several), but the Ruby code in a lot of Rails applications is simple, thanks to the hard work the framework's creators have already put into it. You may want to install Rails in Chapter 1, and then explore Appendix A, "A Quick Guide to Ruby," if you want some background before diving in.

Other Options

There are lots of different ways to learn Rails. Some people want to learn Ruby in detail before jumping into a framework that uses it. That's a perfectly good option, and if you want to start that way, you should explore:

- *Learning Ruby* (O'Reilly, 2007)
- *The Ruby Programming Language* (O'Reilly, 2008)
- *Ruby Pocket Reference* (O'Reilly, 2007)
- *Programming Ruby,* Third Edition (Pragmatic Programmers, 2008)

You may also want to supplement (or replace) this book with other books on Rails. If you want some other resources, you can explore:

- *Head First Rails* (O'Reilly, 2008), for a much more visual approach with exercises
- *Up and Running with Rails*, Second Edition (O'Reilly, 2008), for a very quick start
- *Simply Rails 2* (SitePoint, 2008) takes a similar approach to *Learning Rails*, but with different opinions and details
- *http://www.learningrails.com*, a site with free podcasts and screencasts for getting started in Rails
- *The Rails Way* (Addison-Wesley, 2007), a big-book reference approach for developers who already know their way
- *Rails Pocket Reference* (O'Reilly, 2008), a small-book reference
- *Agile Web Development with Rails*, Third Edition (Pragmatic Programmers, 2008), for a detailed explanation of a wide range of features.
- *Enterprise Rails* (O'Reilly, 2008), for building large-scale applications with a strict relational database foundation
- *Advanced Rails* (O'Reilly, 2008), for when you want to move to the next level

You'll want to make sure that whatever books or online documentation you use covers Rails 2.0 or later. Rails' perpetual evolution has unfortunately made it dangerous to use a lot of formerly great but now dated material. (Some of it works, some of it doesn't.)

Rails Versions

The Rails team is perpetually improving Rails and releasing new versions. This book was originally written using Rails 2.0 and 2.1, and all examples have been tested in 2.1 and 2.2. 2.3 will be out soon, and while it has more changes than 2.1 or 2.2, most of them don't look likely to affect the examples here. There are notes in a few places pointing out where things may look a little different in different versions. We'll post updates in new versions of this electronic book and at *http://www.excursionsonrails.com*.

If You Have Problems Making Examples Work

When you're starting to use a new framework, error messages can be hard, even impossible, to decipher. We've included occasional notes in the book about particular errors you might see, but it seems very normal for different people to encounter different errors as they work through examples. Sometimes it's the result of skipping a step or entering code just a little differently than it was in the book. It's probably not the result of a problem in Rails itself, even if the error message seems to come from deep in the framework. That isn't likely an error in the framework, but much more likely a problem the framework is having in figuring out how to deal with the unexpected code it just encountered.

If you find yourself stuck, here are a few things you should check:

What version of Ruby are you running?
> You can check by entering `ruby -v`. All of the examples in this book were written with Ruby 1.8.6. Older versions of Ruby may cause problems for Rails, and the 1.9 versions add features, but may create new issues as well. Chapter 1 explores how to install Ruby, but you may need to find documentation specific to your specific operating system and environment.

What version of Rails are you running?
> You can check by running `rails -v`. While you should be able to use the examples here with any version of Rails 2.*x*, the examples, including the ones you can download from the book's site, were built on Rails 2.1.0. If you're running a different version, especially an earlier version, you may encounter problems. (While a few of the examples here may run on versions of Rails older than 2.0, most of them will encounter major problems quickly.)

Are you calling the program the right way?
> Linux and Mac OS X both use a forward slash, /, as a directory separator, whereas Windows uses a backslash, \. This book uses the forward slash, but if you're in Windows, you may need to use the backslash.

Is the database connected?
> By default, Rails expects you to have SQLite up and running, though some installations use MySQL or other databases. If you're getting errors that

have "sql" in them somewhere, it's probably the database. For simple applications that aren't calling a database, check the instructions at the end of Chapter 1 for telling Rails not to look for a database. For more complex applications where your application expects a database, check that the database is installed and running, that the settings in *database.yml* are correct, and that the permissions, if any, are set correctly.

Are all of the pieces there?

Most of the time, assembling a Rails application, even a simple one, requires modifying multiple files—at least a view and a controller. If you've only built a controller, you're missing a key piece you need to see your results; if you've only built a view, you need a controller to call it. As you build more and more complex applications, you'll need to make sure you've considered routing, models, and maybe even configuration and plug-ins. What looks like a simple call in one part of the application may depend on pieces elsewhere.

Eventually, you'll know what kinds of problems specific missing pieces cause, but at least at first, try to make sure you've entered complete examples before running them.

It's also possible to have files present but with the wrong permissions set. If you know a file is there, but Rails can't seem to get to it, check to make sure that permissions are set correctly.

Is everything named correctly?

Rails depends on naming conventions to establish connections between data and code without you having to specify them explicitly. This works wonderfully, until you have a typo somewhere obscure. Rails also relies on a number of Ruby conventions for variables, prefacing instance variables with @ or symbols with :. These special characters make a big difference, so make sure they're correct.

Is the Ruby syntax right?

If you get syntax errors, or sometimes even if you get a `nil` object error, you may have an extra space, missing bracket, or similar issue. Ruby syntax is extremely flexible, so you can usually ignore the discipline of brackets, parentheses, or spaces—but sometimes it really does matter.

Are you running the right program?

Yes, this sounds weird. When you're developing real programs, it makes sense to leave the server running to check back and forth with your changes. If you're testing out a lot of small application examples quickly, though, you may have problems. Definitely leave the server running while you're working within a given example, but stop it when you change chapters or set off to create a new application with the `rails` command.

Did the authors just plain screw up?

Obviously, we're working hard to ensure that all of the code in this book runs smoothly the first time, but it's possible that an error crept through. You'll want to check the errata, described in the next section, and download sample code, which will be updated for errata.

It's tempting to try Googling errors to find a quick fix. Unfortunately, the issues just described are more likely to be the problem than something else that has clear documentation. The Rails API documentation might be helpful at times, especially if you're experimenting with extending an example. There shouldn't be much out there, though, beyond the book example files themselves that you can download to fix an example.

If You Like (or Don't Like) This Book

If you like—or don't like—this book, by all means, please let people know. Amazon reviews are one popular way to share your happiness (or lack of happiness), or you can leave reviews on the site for this book:

http://www.oreilly.com/catalog/9780596518776/

There's also a link to errata there. Errata gives readers a way to let us know about typos, errors, and other problems with the book. The errata will be visible on the page immediately, and we'll confirm it after checking it out. O'Reilly can also fix errata in future printings of the book and on Safari, making for a better reader experience pretty quickly.

We hope to keep this book updated for future versions of Rails and will also incorporate suggestions and complaints into future editions.

Conventions Used in This Book

The following font conventions are used in this book:

Italic

Indicates pathnames, filenames, and program names; Internet addresses, such as domain names and URLs; and new items where they are defined.

`Constant width`

Indicates command lines and options that should be typed verbatim; names and keywords in programs, including method names, variable names, and class names; and HTML element tags.

`Constant width bold`

Indicates emphasis in program code lines.

Constant width italic

Indicates text that should be replaced with user-supplied values.

This icon signifies a tip, suggestion, or general note.

This icon indicates a warning or caution.

Using Code Examples

The code examples for this book, which are available from *http://oreilly.com/ catalog/9780596518776/*, come in two forms. One is a set of examples, organized by chapter, with each example numbered and named. These examples are referenced from the relevant chapter. The other form is a dump of all the code from the book, in the order it was presented in the book. That can be helpful if you need a line that didn't make it into the final example, or if you want to cut and paste pieces as you walk through the examples. Hopefully, the code will help you learn.

So far, the code examples for this electronic version of the book have stayed in sync with the code examples for the print book, updated for errata.

This book is here to help you get your job done. In general, you may use the code in this book in your programs and documentation. You do not need to contact us for permission unless you're reproducing a significant portion of the code. For example, writing a program that uses several chunks of code from this book does not require permission. Selling or distributing a CD-ROM of examples from O'Reilly books *does* require permission. Answering a question by citing this book and quoting example code does not require permission. Incorporating a significant amount of example code from this book into your product's documentation *does* require permission.

We appreciate, but do not require, attribution. An attribution usually includes the title, author, publisher, and ISBN. For example: "*Learning Rails* by Simon St.Laurent and Edd Dumbill. Copyright 2009 Simon St.Laurent and Edd Dumbill, 978-0-596-51877-6."

If you feel your use of code examples falls outside fair use or the permission given above, feel free to contact us at *permissions@oreilly.com*.

How to Contact Us

We have tested and verified the information in this book to the best of our ability, but you may find that features have changed (or even that we have made a few mistakes!). Please let us know about any errors you find, as well as your suggestions for future editions, by writing to:

O'Reilly Media, Inc.
1005 Gravenstein Highway North
Sebastopol, CA 95472
800-998-9938 (in the U.S. or Canada)
707-829-0515 (international/local)
707-829-0104 (fax)

We have a web page for this book, including links to the forum, examples, and the errata list. (If you report errata, please note that it came from the updated electronic edition!) You can access this page at:

http://oreilly.com/catalog/9780596518776/

There is also a supporting page for the book, including screencasts, installation help, and more, at:

http://excursionsonrails.com/

To comment or ask technical questions about this book, send email to:

bookquestions@oreilly.com

or visit the forum for this book at:

http://forums.oreilly.com/category/40/Learning-Rails/

For more information about O'Reilly books, conferences, Resource Centers, and the O'Reilly Network, see our website at:

http://www.oreilly.com

Acknowledgments

Thanks to Mike Loukides for thinking that Rails could use a new and different approach, and for supporting this project along the way. Tech reviewers Gregg Pollack, Shelley Powers, Mike Fitzgerald, Eric Berry, David Schruth, Mike Hendrickson, and Mark Levitt all helped improve the book tremendously. The rubyonrails-talk group provided regular inspiration, as did the screencasts and podcasts at *http://railscasts.com* and *http://railsenvy.com*.

Thanks to Andrew Savikas and Keith Fahlgren for giving us the opportunity to present this as an updated electronic book.

Edd Dumbill wishes to thank his lovely children, Thomas, Katherine and Peter, for bashing earnestly on the keyboard, and his coauthor, Simon St.Laurent, for his patient encouragement in writing this book.

Simon St.Laurent wants to thank Angelika St.Laurent for her support over the course of writing this, even when it interfered with dinner, and Sungiva St.Laurent for her loudly shouted suggestions. Simon would also like to thank Edd Dumbill for his initial encouragement and for making this book possible.

We'd like to thank Sarah Schneider, for seeing this book through production, as well as Mark Jewett and Virginia Ogozalek at Appingo for their work on it. Jessamyn Read made the figures much more appealing, and Seth Maislin created the index.

## CHAPTER 1

Starting Up Ruby on Rails

Before you can use Rails, you have to install it. Even if it's already installed on your computer, or you opt to use a web-based development environment, there are a few things you'll need to do to make it actually do something visible. In this chapter, we'll take a look at some ways of installing Ruby, Rails, and the supporting infrastructure, and get a first, rather trivial project up and running.

Feel very welcome to jump to whatever pieces of this section interest you and skip past those that don't. Once the software is working, we'll generate the basic Rails application, which will at least let you know if Rails is working.

There used to be a few options for installing Rails without battling the details involved in its installation. Heroku Garden was a web-based approach that has since disappeared, and Instant Rails offers a simple (though growingly obsolete) installation for Windows users. For more on Instant Rails, see the screencast at *http://broadcast.oreilly.com/2008/12/installing-instant-rails-on-wi.html*. However you decide to set up Rails, in the end you're going to need to install a structure like that shown in Figure 1-1.

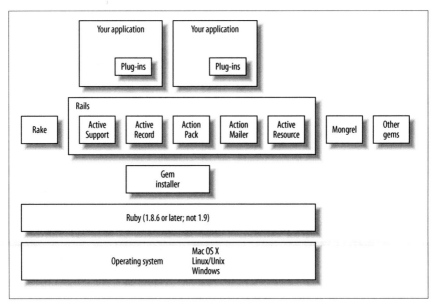

Figure 1-1. The many components of a Rails installation

 All of these options are free. You don't need to spend any money to use Rails, unless maybe you feel like buying a nice text editor.

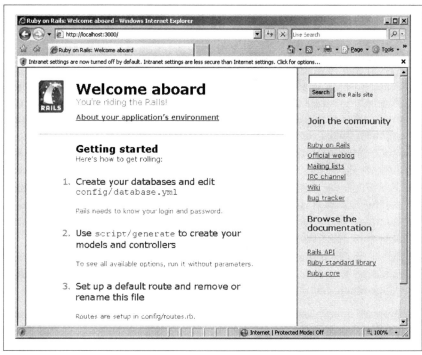

Figure 1-2. The Rails welcome page

Getting Started at the Command Line

Installing Rails by hand requires installing Ruby, installing Gems, and then installing Rails. You will eventually also need to install SQLite, MySQL, or another relational database, though SQLite is already present on the Mac and in many Linux distributions.

 If you're wondering how to find this "command line," you need to find a terminal application. On the Mac, it's called Terminal, and it's in the *Utilities* folder of *Applications*. Linux terminals vary, but it's probably gnome-terminal or kterm. On Windows, it's the Command Prompt, *cmd.exe*. If you've never used a command line, you may want to get a quick reference guide for your operating system that covers it.

Ruby comes standard on a number of Linux and Macintosh platforms. To see whether it's there, and what version it has, enter `ruby -v` at the command prompt. You'll want Ruby 1.8.6 or later, so you may need to update it to a more recent version:

- On Mac OS X, Snow Leopard (10.6) includes Ruby 1.8.7, and Leopard (10.5) includes Ruby 1.8.6, but the previous version of OS X included Ruby 1.8.2. If you're on Tiger (10.4) or an earlier version of OS X, you'll need to update Ruby itself, a challenge that's beyond the scope of this book. You may want to investigate MacPorts, and the directions at *http: //nowiknow.wordpress.com/2007/10/07/install-ruby-on-rails-for-mac/.* For a more comprehensive installation, explore *http://paulsturgess.co.uk/ articles/show/46.*

- For Windows, the One-Click Ruby Installer (*http://rubyinstaller.rubyforge .org/wiki/wiki.pl*) is probably your easiest option, though there are other alternatives, including Cygwin (*http://www.cygwin.com/*), which brings a lot of the Unix environment to Windows.

- Most distributions of Linux include Ruby, but you'll want to use your package manager to make sure it's updated to 1.8.6. Some, notably Ubuntu and Debian, will name the gem command gem1.8.

For more on how to install Ruby on a variety of platforms, see *http://www.ruby -lang.org/en/downloads/.*

> For screencasts that shows how to get started with Rails on Ubuntu, see *http://broadcast.oreilly.com/2008/11/installing -rails-on-hardy-hero.html* for the desktop version and *http:// broadcast.oreilly.com/2008/11/installing-rails-on-ubuntu-har .html* for the server version. There's also a first steps for using Rails on Mac OS X 10.5 at *http://broadcast.oreilly.com/2008/ 11/first-steps-into-rails-on-the.html.*

> You don't need to update Ruby to version 1.9—indeed, it's better if you don't, at this point.

Gems is also starting to come standard on a number of platforms, most recently on Mac OS X Leopard and Snow Leopard, but if you need to install Gems, see the RubyGems User Guide's instructions at *http://www.rubygems.org/read/ chapter/3.*

If you use MacPorts, apt-get, or a similar package installer, you may want to use it only to install Ruby, and then proceed from the command line. You certainly can install Gems and Rails with these tools, but Gems can update itself, which can make for very confusing package update issues.

Once you have Gems installed, Rails is just a command away:

```
~ simonstl$ sudo gem install rails
Password:
Successfully installed activesupport-2.3.5
Successfully installed activerecord-2.3.5
Successfully installed actionpack-2.3.5
Successfully installed actionmailer-2.3.5
Successfully installed activeresource-2.3.5
Successfully installed rails-2.3.5
6 gems installed
Installing ri documentation for activesupport-2.3.5...
Installing ri documentation for activerecord-2.3.5...
Installing ri documentation for actionpack-2.3.5...
Installing ri documentation for actionmailer-2.3.5...
Installing ri documentation for activeresource-2.3.5...
Installing RDoc documentation for activesupport-2.3.5...
Installing RDoc documentation for activerecord-2.3.5...
Installing RDoc documentation for actionpack-2.3.5...
Installing RDoc documentation for actionmailer-2.3.5...
Installing RDoc documentation for activeresource-2.3.5...
```

 gem install rails will install the latest official release of Rails, which at present is 2.3.5. It will not install the Rails 3.0 beta. If you want to install the Rails 3.0 beta - studying the latest and greatest, but wandering away from the version covered here - see *http://weblog.rubyonrails.org/2010/2/5/rails-3-0 -beta-release*.

You only need to use sudo, which gives your command the power of the root (administrative) account, if you're working in an environment that requires root access for the installation—otherwise, you can just type gem install rails. That will install the latest version of Rails, which may be more recent than 2.3.4, as well as all of its dependencies. (To see which version of Rails is installed, enter rails -v at the command line.)

Mac OS X Snow Leopard (10.6) includes Rails 2.2.2 installed, which, though a little behind, will work well with the examples in this book. If you'd like more control over how Rails is installed, though, take a look at *http://eddorre.com/posts/in stalling-ruby-on-rails-postgresql-mysql-on-snow-leopard.*

However, Mac OS X Leopard (10.5) comes with Rails 1.2.3 installed. You'll definitely need to update Rails to version 2.1, as shown earlier, to work with the rest of this book. You'll also probably need to keep an eye on future updates from Apple that could change Rails on you, and maybe even lock down Rails versions in your critical applications with the rake tool's freeze task.

If you're ever wondering which gems (and which versions of gems) are installed, type gem list --local. For more information on gems, just type gem, or visit *http://rubygems.rubyforge.org.*

There are a few gems you may want to install, though these come preinstalled on Mac OS X 10.5 and later. To install the Mongrel app server, run sudo gem install mongrel. To install the Ruby bindings for SQLite, run sudo gem install sqlite3-ruby. (You'll still need to install SQLite 3.)

You can see the documentation that gems have installed by running the command gem server, and visiting the URL (usually *http://localhost:8808*) that command reports. When you're done, you can turn off the server with Ctrl-C.

Starting Up Rails

Once you have Rails installed, you can create a Rails application easily from the command line:

```
~ $ rails hello
      create
      create  app/controllers
      create  app/helpers
      create  app/models
      create  app/views/layouts
      create  config/environments
...
      create  public/images/rails.png
      create  public/javascripts/prototype.js
      create  public/javascripts/effects.js
      create  public/javascripts/dragdrop.js
      create  public/javascripts/controls.js
      create  public/javascripts/application.js
      create  doc/README_FOR_APP
```

```
create  log/server.log
create  log/production.log
create  log/development.log
create  log/test.log
```

Rails application directories are just ordinary directories. You can move them, obliterate them and start over, or do whatever you need to do with ordinary file-management tools. Each application directory is also completely independent—the general "Rails environment" just generates these applications.

To start Rails, you'll need to move into the directory you just created—cd hello—and then issue your first command to get the Mongrel server busy running your application:

```
~ $ ruby script/server
=> Booting Mongrel (use 'script/server webrick' to force WEBrick)
=> Rails application starting on http://0.0.0.0:3000
=> Call with -d to detach
=> Ctrl-C to shutdown server
** Starting Mongrel listening at 0.0.0.0:3000
** Starting Rails with development environment...
** Rails loaded.
** Loading any Rails specific GemPlugins
** Signals ready.  TERM => stop.  USR2 => restart.  INT => stop (no restart).
** Rails signals registered.  HUP => reload (without restart).  It might not work
well.
** Mongrel available at 0.0.0.0:3000
** Use CTRL-C to stop.
```

Rails is now running, and you can watch any errors it encounters through the extensive logging you'll see in this window.

On most Linux and Mac systems, you can leave off the ruby part—script/server will do. And you should note that by default, script/server binds only to localhost, and the application isn't visible from other computers. Normally, that's a security feature, not a bug, though you can specify an address for the server to use with the -b option (and -p for a specific port) if you want to make it visible.

For more details on options for using script/server, just enter ruby script/server -h.

If you now visit *http://localhost:3000*, you'll see the same welcome screen shown previously in Figure 1-2. When you're ready to stop Rails, you can just press Ctrl-C.

You really only need to stop Rails when you're done developing, if then. In development mode, you can make all the
changes you want to your application with the server running,
and you won't have to restart the server to see them.

Dodging Database Issues

By default, Rails 2.0 and later expects every application to have a database
behind it. (That's why Figure 1-2 refers to configuring databases at the start.)
That expectation makes it a little difficult to get started with Rails, so it can be
a good idea to either make sure that SQLite is installed or turn off the features
that will call a database, at least at first.

Rails 2.0.2 and later versions use SQLite as the default database, and connects
to it much more automatically. If you're running an operating system that
includes SQLite—such as many versions of Linux and Mac OS X 10.4 or later
—you can skip this section.

To check that it's available, you can run `sqlite3 -help`. If that returns a friendly
help message, you're set. You can just run `rake db:create` or `rake
db:migrate` from the command line before running your application, and that
will perform the necessary database setup. If the help message doesn't come
up, installing SQLite would be a good idea. (For more on SQLite, see *http://
www.sqlite.org/*.)

If you decide to postpone database installation and get weird errors that look
like your application can't find a database, and you weren't expecting it to
need one, then you should turn off the database connection. The key to doing
this is the *environment.rb* file, which you'll find in the *config* directory. About
halfway down the file, you'll find:

```
# Skip frameworks you're not going to use (only works if using vendor/rails).
# To use Rails without a database, you must remove the ActiveRecord framework
# config.frameworks -= [ :active_record, :active_resource, :action_mailer ]
```

To turn off Rails' demand for a database, just remove the highlighted # symbol
in front of `config.frameworks`. You need to do this *before* you start up Rails
with `script/server`.

In development mode (which is where you start), you can
change code on the fly and Rails will immediately reflect your
changes, but this doesn't apply to configuration files. They
only get loaded when Rails starts up. If you need to change
any configuration files, stop your application and then start it
again after you've saved the change.

We'll come back to Rails' powerful database-centric core after taking a closer look at how it interacts with the Web.

What Server Is That?

You might wonder what server is running your Rails application—after all, nothing so far has required any configuration, despite the fairly complicated usual installs needed to get web programming environments to run. You can continue without knowing (until it's time for real deployment), but if you're curious, here are the details.

You may be familiar with Apache or Microsoft's Internet Information Server (IIS), but neither of those web servers is probably running these Rails programs. (They can run Rails, but unless you took a very different path for installation, they're not running yet.) Instead, your programs are probably running in Mongrel. The Rails 2.x command line uses Mongrel. (In earlier versions of Rails, running the application from the command line in the usual way started up an instance of WEBrick.) Instant Rails uses Apache with Mongrel actually interacting with Rails behind it. WEBrick and Mongrel come with slightly different priorities:

WEBrick (http://www.webrick.org/)
> WEBrick is written in Ruby and bundled with recent releases of Ruby. It's very convenient for Ruby development, with or without Rails. It's an excellent testing server, but not designed for large scale deployment.

Mongrel (http://mongrel.rubyforge.org/)
> Mongrel is a highly optimized server written in Ruby that "does the bare minimum necessary to serve a Ruby application." It's designed to be as absolutely fast as possible and is often used in conjunction with Apache on production web servers.

> For development work, you'll likely run at least one of these servers on your local machine, probably on an odd port, like 3000, instead of the traditional default web server port of 80. For deployment, as described in Chapter 18, you'll probably use Apache (with Mongrel or Passenger behind it) or lighttpd. (You can deploy Rails on Windows with Mongrel or IIS, but it's rarely the most efficient approach.)

 If you've never used Ruby before, now would be a good time to explore Appendix A, which teaches some key components of the language inside of a very simple Rails application.

Test Your Knowledge

Quiz

1. What's the name of the Ruby application packaging utility and how do you install Rails with it?
2. In what instances would you avoid WEBrick?
3. Why should you install a particular version of Ruby on your platform when Ruby already comes installed?

Answers

1. RubyGems, or just "gems," which is run with the gem command, is Ruby's application packager. To install the latest version of Rails and all its dependencies, just type gem install rails.
2. WEBrick is great for testing your Rails applications, but definitely not the best choice for deployments where performance matters.
3. Rails is still running on version 1.8 of Ruby, not the latest 1.9, but it requires features in the more recent versions of 1.8, notably 1.8.6.

## CHAPTER 2

Rails on the Web

Now that you have Rails installed, it's time to make Rails do something—not necessarily very much yet, but enough to show you what happens when you make a call to a Rails application, and enough to let you do something to respond when those calls come in. There's a long tradition in computer books of starting out with a program that says "hello" to the programmer. We'll follow that tradition and pursue it a bit further to make clear how Rails can work with HTML. You're welcome, of course, to make Rails say whatever you'd like.

 The work in this chapter depends on the *hello* application created in Chapter 1. If you didn't create one, go back and explore the directions given there. You can also find the files for the first demonstration in *ch02/hello001* of the downloadable code.

Creating Your Own View

Saying "hello" is a simple thing, focused exclusively on putting a message on a screen. To get started, we can post that message using a view including HTML that will get sent to the browser.

Rails actually won't let you create views directly. Its controller-centric perspective requires that views be associated with controllers. While that might seem like a bit of an imposition, it's not too hard to work around.

Creating anything in Rails requires going to the command line. Open a terminal or command window and go to the home directory of your Rails application.

Then type:

```
ruby script/generate controller Hello index
```

The script/generate part of this command is calling a program, generate, in the *script* directory of the application. The first argument, controller, specifies that it should generate code for a controller, in this case named Hello, the second argument. Finally, including index at the end requests a view named index, bound to the hello controller.

 On Linux and the Mac, you can generally leave off the ruby at the start of script/generate and similar commands.

Model-View-Controller

"You keep talking about views, controllers, and models. What is all that?"

It's a bit of programmer-speak: Model-View-Controller, or MVC, is an old idea that got its start in the Smalltalk programming world of the 1970s. The *model* is the underlying data structure, specific to the task the program is addressing; *controllers* manage the flow of data into and out of those objects; and *views* present the information provided by those controllers to users.

MVC is an excellent approach for building maintainable applications, as each layer keeps its logic to itself. Views might include a bit of code for presenting the data from the controller, but most of the logic for moving information around should be kept in the controller, and logic about data structures should be kept in the model. If you want to change how something looks, but not change the logic or the data structures, you can just create a new view, without disrupting everything underneath it.

As you see more of Rails, in this book and elsewhere, you'll probably come to appreciate MVC's virtues, though it can seem confusing and constraining at first. Chapter 4 will explain how Rails uses MVC in more detail.

You'll see something like:

```
1       exists   app/controllers/
2       exists   app/helpers/
3       create   app/views/hello
4       exists   test/functional/
5       create   app/controllers/hello_controller.rb
6       create   test/functional/hello_controller_test.rb
7       create   app/helpers/hello_helper.rb
8       create   app/views/hello/index.html.erb
```

The lines starting with exists reflect directories or files that the generator could have created, but that were already there. The create entries identify directories and files that the generator created itself. You'll see a new *views* directory in line 3, a controller in line 5, a template for creating tests for that controller in line 6, a helper in line 7, and the index file (*index.html.erb*) we requested in line 8. (The *.rb* file extension is the conventional extension for Ruby files; *.erb* is the common extension for Embedded Ruby files.)

 If you foul up a `script/generate` command, you can issue `script/destroy` to have Rails try to fix your mistakes.

That index file is now available to the application. Run `ruby script/server` to get it going, and then take a look at *hello* in the application. Figure 2-1 shows what Rails created to start with.

Figure 2-1. The generated index file identifies its home

This isn't pretty, but there's already something to learn here. Note that the URL that brought up this page is *http://localhost:3000/hello/*. As the page itself says, though, the file is in *app/views/hello/index.html.erb*. There's a web server running and it's serving files out of the application's directory, but Rails uses its own rules, not the file structure, to decide what gets presented at what URL. For right now, it's enough to know that the name of the controller, hello, will bring up its associated view, which is defined by the *index.html.erb* file.

The initial contents of that file are fairly simple, like those of Example 2-1.

Example 2-1. The default contents of index.html.erb

```
<h1>Hello#index</h1>
<p>Find me in app/views/hello/index.html.erb</p>
```

The Rails designers didn't even give these generated pieces a full HTML document structure. Since the generated code will get replaced anyway, it doesn't matter very much. It's not that Rails doesn't care about the surrounding markup, but rather that the surrounding markup usually comes from layouts, which are covered later in this chapter. If you had generated scaffolding (a larger set of pieces) and not just a view, Rails would also have generated a layout itself. For this chapter's purposes, however, the view is all there is to work with.

For starters, we'll just modify the file a little bit so that it presents a complete HTML document with a slightly friendlier hello, as shown in Example 2-2.

Example 2-2. The new contents of index.html.erb

```
<html>
<head><title>Hello!</title></head>
<body>
<h1>Hello!</h1>
<p>This is a greeting from app/views/hello/index.html.erb</p>
</body>
</html>
```

If you save that file and then reload, you'll see something like Figure 2-2.

Figure 2-2. A revised greeting

Putting one simple HTML page in the slightly obscure location of a generated HTML page isn't incredibly exciting, but it's a start.

What Are All Those Folders?

The examples in this chapter have called programs in the *script* folder and modified files in the *app* and *public* folders. You might have noticed the large set of folders Rails created for an application. We'll explore most of these in detail over the course of this book, but for now, here's a quick guide to what's there:

app

> Where you build your application's core. It includes subfolders for controllers, helpers, models, and views.

config

> Hosts database configuration, URL routing rules, and the Rails environment structures for development, testing, and deployment.

db

> Provides a home to scripts used to manage relational database tables.

doc

> Collects documentation generated from Ruby code using RubyDoc. RubyDoc is a documentation generator for Ruby, much like JavaDoc. For a lot more information, see *http://www.ruby-doc.org/*.

lib

> Holds code that doesn't quite fit into the model, view, or controller classifications, typically code that's shared by these components or plug-ins you install. The *tasks* subdirectory contains Rake tasks for your application.

log

> Gathers log data—not just errors, but very rich information on requests, how they were processed, how long it took to process them, and session data from the request.

public

> Contains things like stylesheets, images, JavaScript, and things like 404 Not Found error reporting pages.

script

> The home for the prebuilt code you'll be using to generate, run, and interact with large portions of your Rails application.

test

> Contains code—generated at first, but updated by you—for testing your Rails application.

tmp

Rails' internal home for session variables, temporary files, cached data, etc.

vendor

Houses plug-ins and gems from outside of Rails itself. Also, if the application has been frozen to a particular version of Rails, that version may be stored here.

Most of the time you'll work in *app* or *test*, with some ventures into *public* to work on the parts of your application (like stylesheets, JavaScript, or images) that Rails doesn't control directly.

Adding Some Data

As pretty much every piece of Rails documentation will suggest, views are really meant to provide users with a perspective on data managed by a controller. It's a little strange to run through all this generation and layers of folders just to create an HTML file. To start taking advantage of a little more of Rails' power, we'll put some data into the controller for *hello*, *hello_controller.rb*, and then incorporate that data into the view.

If you open *app/controllers/hello_controller.rb*, you'll see the default code that Rails generated, like that in Example 2-3.

Example 2-3. A very, very basic controller that does nothing

```
class HelloController < ApplicationController

  def index
  end
end
```

This is the first real Ruby code we've encountered, so it's worth explaining a bit. The name of the class, `HelloController`, was created by the script generator based on the name we gave, Hello. Rails chose this name to indicate the name and type of the class, using its normal convention for controllers. Controllers are defined as Ruby classes, which inherit (`<`) most of their functionality from the `ApplicationController` class. (You don't need to know anything about `ApplicationControllers`, or even classes—at least not yet—so if you don't understand at this point, just enjoy the generated code and keep reading.)

 If you need to learn more about Ruby to be comfortable proceeding, take a look at Appendix A, "An Incredibly Brief Guide to Ruby."

`def index` is the start of the `index` method, which Rails will call by default when it's asked for a Hello. As you can see, it comes to a nearly immediate `end`, which is followed by the `end` for the class as a whole. If we want to make the `index` method do anything, we'll have to add some logic. For our current purposes, that logic can stay extremely simple. Defining a few variables, as shown in Example 2-4, will let us play with the basic interactions between controllers and views, and allow the view to do a few more interesting things. (Example 2-4 is part of the code in *ch02/hello002*.)

Example 2-4. A basic controller that sets some variables

```
class HelloController < ApplicationController

  def index
    @message="Hello!"

    @count=3

    @bonus="This message came from the controller."
  end
end
```

Variables whose names start with @ are called instance variables. They belong to the class that defines them and have the convenient property of being accessible from the associated view.

When choosing variable names, always be very careful to avoid the enormous list of reserved words presented at *http://wiki.rubyonrails.org/rails/pages/ReservedWords*.

If you use those names, you may find not only that your programs don't run correctly, but also that the supporting development environment misbehaves in strange and annoying ways.

To actually use those variables, make some changes to the view as in Example 2-5.

Example 2-5. Modifying index.html.erb to use instance variables from the controller

```
<html>
<head><title><%= @message%> </title></head>
<body>
<h1><%= @message %></h1>
<p>This is a greeting from app/views/hello/index.html.erb</p>
<p><%= @bonus %></p>
</body>
</html>
```

There are three new pieces here, highlighted in bold. Each contains the name of one of the instance variables from *hello_controller.rb*, surrounded by the <%= and %> tags. When Rails processes this document, it will replace the <%= ... %> with the value inside. You can, of course, create those values from much more complex sources than just a simple variable, but it's easier to see what's happening here in a simple example.

> The <% and %> tags are delimiters used by ERb, Embedded Ruby. ERb is part of Ruby and is used extensively in Rails. ERb isn't the only way to generate result views with Rails, but it's definitely the most common.

The result, shown in Figure 2-3, incorporates the variables from HelloControl ler into the resulting document.

Figure 2-3. Resulting document incorporating instance variables from the controller

Looking at the HTML in Example 2-6, the ERb markup has completely disappeared, replaced by the instance variable values.

Example 2-6. HTML that Rails generated based on Examples 2-4 and 2-5

```
<html>
<head><title>Hello! </title></head>
<body>
<h1>Hello!</h1>
<p>This is a greeting from app/views/hello/index.html.erb</p>

<p>This message came from the controller.</p>
</body>
</html>
```

How Hello World Works

The Hello World programs are actually doing a lot of work, as shown in Figure 2-4, though most of it happens transparently.

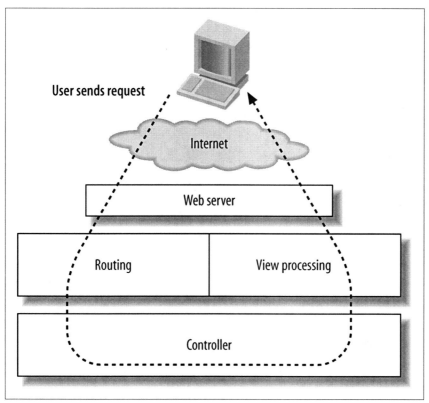

Figure 2-4. Simplified processing path for the Hello World programs

When the code runs, Rails interprets the request for *http://localhost:3000/ hello/* as a call to the Hello controller. It has a list of routing rules, managed through a *config/routes.rb* file you can edit—this is just the default behavior. Controllers can have multiple methods, but the default method (just like when you request an HTML file) is index. Rails routing functionality then calls the index method, which sets up some basic variables.

When the controller is done, Rails passes its data to the view in the *app/views/ hello* directory. How does it know to go there? Thanks to the magic of naming conventions, that view processing (possibly including layouts) generates an HTML result, which gets sent to the browser.

Rails applications have lots of moving parts, but you can usually look at the parts and guess (or control) what Rails is going to do with them. As you'll see in later chapters, the connections between controllers and models and models and databases rely heavily on such naming conventions and default behaviors. The connections that Rails creates in this way won't solve all of your problems all of the time, but they do make it easy to solve a wide variety of problems most of the time. Figure 2-5 shows the pathways Rails built on naming conventions in the view and controller.

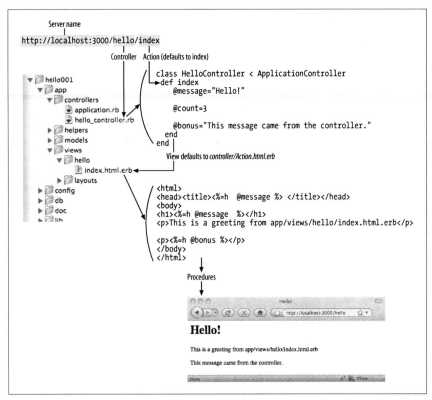

Figure 2-5. Paths Rails follows through naming conventions

Protecting Your View from the Controller

There's already a danger in Example 2-4, called *HTML injection*. While the source of `@message` and `@bonus` is clear at the moment—the controller code is stupidly simple and receives no user input—more complicated programs offer opportunities for malicious users to send their own HTML through parameters or form fields. To reduce their odds of causing a problem, wrap values that you know aren't supposed to contain HTML in an h function, short for html_escape(). Example 2-7 shows a safer version of the code from Example 2-5.

Example 2-7. Modifying index.html.erb to use instance variables from the controller

```
<html>
<head><title><%= h(@message) %> </title></head>
<body>
<h1><%= h(@message) %></h1>
<p>This is a greeting from app/views/hello/index.html.erb</p>

<p><%= h(@bonus) %></p>
</body>
</html>
```

Using h() isn't always appropriate because there will be times when you want to include HTML directly, without turning "this is **bold**" into "this is bold." Sometimes applications need to be able to say **bold** instead of bold. For these cases, you can use sanitize() instead of h(). The sanitize function escapes form and script tags and removes event handling attributes whose names start with on, as well as links starting with java script:. Using the h() and sanitize() functions does take more typing, but it can spare you considerable pain later on, for security reasons that Chapter 18 will explore in more depth. (You can, of course, leave them off in the rare cases where you're really intending to include everything, even the dangerous parts, when you know you've managed the dangers within the controller code.)

 If sanitize() isn't strong enough for you, you can explore the white_list plug-in at *http://weblog.techno-weenie.net/2006/9/ 3/white-listing-plugin-for-rails.*

Parentheses Are (Usually) Optional

Example 2-7 works perfectly well, but experienced Rails developers will look at it and wonder why we typed so much. Why? The parentheses around the arguments to h() are (usually) optional. You can produce the same result with the version shown in Example 2-8.

Example 2-8. Escaping instance variables without using the parentheses

```
<html>
<head><title><%=h @message %> </title></head>
<body>
<h1><%=h @message %></h1>
<p>This is a greeting from app/views/hello/index.html.erb</p>
```

```
<p><%=h @bonus %></p>
</body>
</html>
```

A lot of developers just think of <%=h as the opening to escaped content, and when you're just dropping an instance variable into the content, this works beautifully.

It doesn't work, however, when Ruby needs to know where the parentheses are for more complex or ambiguous expressions, such as:

```
<%=h if @foo.length > 1 then "Sausages" else "Mash" end %>
```

which will produce the unwanted and mysterious:

```
>> "syntax error, unexpected kTHEN, expecting $end"
```

You'll have to choose for yourself which approach is easiest for you—the idiomatic Ruby approach or the safer but more cluttered approach of making parentheses explicit.

 If you want to comment out ERb lines, you can just insert a # symbol after the <%. For example, <%#=h @message %> would do nothing, because of the #.

Adding Logic to the View

You can also put more sophisticated logic into the views, thanks to the <% and %> tags. (The opening tag lacks the = sign.) These tags let you put Ruby code directly into your ERb files. We'll start with a very simple example, shown in Example 2-9, that takes advantage of the count variable in the controller. (This example is part of the *ch02/hello003* code sample.)

Example 2-9. Modifying index.html.erb to present the @bonus message as many times as @count specifies

```
<html>
<head><title><%=h @message %> </title></head>
<body>
<h1><%=h @message %></h1>
<p>This is a greeting from app/views/hello/index.html.erb</p>

<% for i in 1..@count %>
  <p><%=h @bonus %></p>
<% end %>

</body>
</html>
```

The count variable now controls the number of times the bonus message appears because of the for...end loop, which will simply count from 1 to the value of the count variable.

The for loop is familiar to developers from a wide variety of programming languages, but it's not especially idiomatic Ruby. Ruby developers would likely use a times construct instead, such as:

```
<% @count.times do %>
<p><%=h @bonus %></p>
<% end %>
```

Depending on your fondness for punctuation, you can also replace the do and end with curly braces, as in:

```
<% @count.times { %>
<p><%=h @bonus %></p>
<% } %>
```

As always, you can choose the approach you find most comfortable.

The loop will run three times, counting up to the value the controller set for the count variable. As a result, "This message came from the controller." will appear three times, as shown in Figure 2-6.

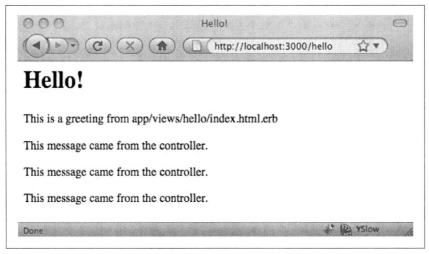

Figure 2-6. The Hello page after the loop executes

It's not the most exciting page, but it's the foundation for a lot more work to come.

If you're picky about the amount of whitespace you put into documents, perhaps because you're generating text files or emails, you may also want to know how to suppress the extra whitespace created by the loop's markup. It's easy—just replace the closing %> with -%>. Any trailing newlines will be stripped. (It won't look any different in the HTML, though.)

Test Your Knowledge

Quiz

1. What is the difference between <% and <%=?
2. How much logic should you put in your ERb files?
3. How does Rails know what controller goes with what view, if you don't tell it?
4. Which methods should you use to protect yourself against potential insertions of unwanted HTML?

Answers

1. When you use <%=, Rails will insert the return value of the code you've used into the document. If you use <%, nothing will be added to the document.
2. In general, you should put as little logic into your ERb files as possible. You may need to put some logic there to make sure that users get the right presentation of the information you're sharing, or to build an interface for them to work with it. However, you should avoid putting much else there.
3. Rails maps controllers to views through naming conventions, unless your code specifies otherwise.
4. The h method and the sanitize method will remove most potentially dangerous markup.

## CHAPTER 3

Adding Web Style

The application presented in Chapter 2 is pretty appalling, visually. You're not likely to want to present pages that look like that to your visitors, unless they're fond of the early-1990s retro look. Rails provides a number of features that will help you make your views present results that look the way you think they should look, and do so consistently.

> This chapter will explore Rails features for supporting CSS and HTML, but it can't be an HTML or CSS tutorial. If you need one of those, try Jennifer Niederst Robbins' *Learning Web Design* (O'Reilly, 2007) or David Sawyer McFarland's *CSS: The Missing Manual* (O'Reilly, 2006).

I Want My CSS!

Figure 3-1, the result of the last chapter's coding, is not exactly attractive.

Figure 3-1. The hello page after the loop executes

Even this fairly hopeless page, however, can be improved with the bit of CSS shown in Example 3-1.

Example 3-1. A simple stylesheet for a simple page

```
body { font-family:sans-serif;
  }

h1 {font-family:serif;
  font-size: 24pt;
   font-weight: bold;
   color:#F00 ;
   }
```

Better CSS would of course be a good idea, but this will get things started. We could put this stylesheet right into the *index.html.erb* file as an internal `style` element, but it's usually easier to manage external stylesheets kept in separate files. As noted earlier, though, Rails has its own sense of where files should go. In this case, stylesheets should go into the *public/stylesheets* directory. We'll call Example 3-1 *hello.css*. To link it to the document, we'll need to add a link element in the document's head, as shown in Example 3-2. (You can find all of these files in ch03/hello004.)

Example 3-2. The Hello message with a hardcoded stylesheet link

```
<html>
<head><title><%=h @message %> </title>
    <link href="/stylesheets/hello.css" media="screen"
rel="Stylesheet" type="text/css" />
    </head>
```

```
<body>
<h1><%=h @message %></h1>
<p>This is a greeting from app/views/hello/index.html.erb</p>

<% for i in 1..@count %>
<p><%=h @bonus %></p>
<% end %>

</body>
</html>
```

Don't include the `public/` part in the `href` attribute, or Rails won't find the right thing to send. Rails does provide a more automatic way to do this: `style sheet_link_tag`. Instead of the `link` element shown in Example 3-2, you can just write:

```
<%= stylesheet_link_tag 'hello' %>
```

When Rails processes the document, it will convert that into:

```
<link href="/stylesheets/hello.css?1185389385" media="screen"
rel="Stylesheet" type="text/css" />
```

> The query string on the `href` is meant to change regularly in development mode, reducing the problem of your getting stuck with an old stylesheet in your web browser's cache and making it hard to see recent changes to the stylesheet.

If that isn't quite what you had in mind, you can pass `stylesheet_link_tag` more detailed parameters:

```
<%= stylesheet_link_tag 'hello', :media => "all", :type => "text/css",
:href => "/stylesheets/hello.css"  %>
```

This will produce:

```
<link href="/stylesheets/hello.css" media="all" rel="Stylesheet"
type="text/css" />
```

What happened there? What are all of those strange things with colons in front and => arrows behind? They're *named parameters* for the `style sheet_link_tag` method. The names with colons in front of them are called *symbols*, which is a bit confusing.

It's easiest to read the colon as meaning "the thing named" and the => as "has the value of." This means that the thing named `media` has the value of `all`, the thing named `type` has the value of `text/css`, and so on. The `style sheet_link_tag` method assembles all of these pieces to create the final `link` element. (And when you provide an `href` parameter, it overrides the name that was the first, unnamed parameter. This method is a bit messy that way.)

You can certainly create your own `link` elements if you prefer. The code approach may be useful for cases where you want to let Rails do the work, especially if, for example, your application is giving users a choice among a number of stylesheets.

The result, combining the HTML generated by the view with the newly linked stylesheet, is shown in Figure 3-2. It's not beautiful, but you now have control over styles.

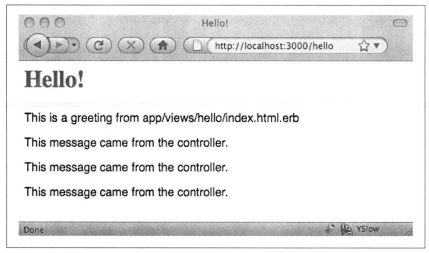

Figure 3-2. A very slightly prettier "Hello!" using CSS

Layouts

Back in Example 2-1, you saw that the view Rails originally generated only included an `h1` element and a `p` element—Rails didn't provide a full HTML document, with a `DOCTYPE`, `html` element, or `head` and `body` elements. Part of the reason for that is that Rails expects its views to work as part of a system, a system in which another document, a layout, provides all of that supporting infrastructure. Rails didn't automatically generate a layout, but creating one is easy.

 When Rails generates more complete scaffolding code (described in Chapter 5), it does produce a layout file. It just doesn't normally do it when generating a controller and view.

Splitting View from Layout

The final version of the Hello view, still using the simple controller from Example 2-4, looks like Example 3-3.

Example 3-3. The Hello view, containing markup that can move to a layout

```
<html>
<head><title><%=h @message %> </title>
<%= stylesheet_link_tag 'hello', :media => "all", :type => "text/css",
:href => "/stylesheets/hello.css"  %>
    </head>
<body>
<h1><%=h @message %></h1>
<p>This is a greeting from app/views/hello/index.html.erb</p>

<% for i in 1..@count %>
<p><%=h @bonus %></p>
<% end %>

</body>
</html>
```

To make this into a layout, break the view down into two files. The first, listed in Example 3-4, contains the logic specific to presenting that page, while the second, Example 3-5, contains the broader framing for the document. (Both are included in *ch03/hello005*.)

Example 3-4. The Hello view, reduced to its local logic

```
<h1><%= @message %></h1>
<p>This is a greeting from app/views/hello/index.html.erb</p>

<% for i in 1..@count %>
<p><%= @bonus %></p>
<% end %>
```

Example 3-5. A layout for the Hello view, in app/views/layouts/hello.html.erb

```
<html>
<head><title><%=h @message %> </title>
    <%= stylesheet_link_tag 'hello', :media => "all", :type => "text/css",
    :href => "/stylesheets/hello.css"  %>
</head>
<body>
(using layout)
<!--layout will incorporate view-->
<%= yield :layout %>

</body>
</html>
```

The (using layout) text just gives us a visible marker to see that content is coming from the layout. (It'll go away immediately after this example.) The <%= yield :layout%> tag tells Rails to shift its processing to the content that goes inside of the layout. (You can also use the simpler <%= yield %>.) When Rails encounters this, it will work on the Hello view, bring its content into the page, and then finish the layout, sending the combined results to the requesting browser.

For this to work, however, Rails needs to know where to find the layout. To work by default with the Hello controller and view, it should go in *app/views/layouts/* as *hello.html.erb*. Example 3-4 should replace the old *app/views/hello/index.html.erb*. When opened in the browser, the layout and view will combine to produce the HTML shown in Example 3-6 and Figure 3-3.

Example 3-6. Combining a layout and a view produces a complete result

```
<html>
<head><title>Hello! </title>
    <link href="/stylesheets/hello.css" media="all" rel="stylesheet" type="text/css"
/>
</head>
<body>
(using layout)
<!--layout will incorporate view-->
<h1>Hello!</h1>
<p>This is a greeting from app/views/hello/index.rhtml</p>

<p>This message came from the controller.</p>

<p>This message came from the controller.</p>

<p>This message came from the controller.</p>


</body>
</html>
```

There's another piece here worth noting, highlighted in Example 3-6. The title element contains the same content—coming from the @message variable —as the original view did. The layout has access to all of the same variables as the view. If you were creating a layout that was going to be used for many different controllers, you might want to choose a more specific variable name for that piece, say @page_title, and make certain that all of your controllers support it.

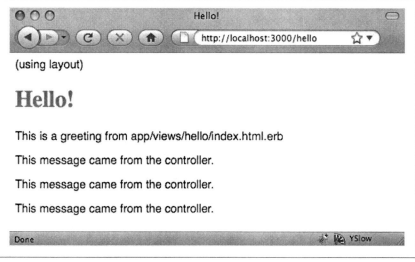

Figure 3-3. Applying a layout to a view

What's That Yield?

It kind of makes sense that a layout would yield control to a more specific template and then pick up again, but a `yield` has a more specific meaning in Ruby, one you'll doubtless see more often as you work with it.

Ruby programmers like to play with blocks. Blocks are nameless chunks of code, usually contained in curly braces ({}). Many Ruby methods can accept, in addition to the usual parameters, a block of code. When `yield` appears, that block of code gets executed. In this case, the block that gets called is the result of the controller and view template processing, and so the proper content gets inserted into the layout.

Creating a Default Layout

A lot of sites use the same general structure—headers, stylesheets, and often navigation—across many or all pages. While you certainly could create a copy of the layout file for every controller your application uses, that would violate a core principle of Rails: Don't Repeat Yourself, or DRY. Much of the time, it'll make much more sense to create a layout that acts as the default for your entire application, and only create different layouts for the cases where you actually need them.

Creating a default layout for your entire application is simple—just create a layout named *application.html.erb* in the *app/views/layouts* folder. So long as

Rails doesn't find a layout specific to your controller—and you don't tell it to do something different—Rails will use *application.html.erb* throughout your project, making it easy to create a consistent overall look. (This approach is demonstrated in *ch03/hello006*.) The naming conventions Rails follows to decide on a layout are shown in Figure 3-4.

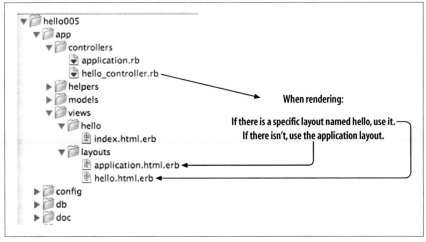

Figure 3-4. Deciding which layout to use, based on naming conventions

Choosing a Layout from a Controller

Left to its own devices, Rails assumes that each view has a layout file associated with it by the naming convention, or uses the default for the application. There are many cases, though, where groups of related views share a common layout, but that layout isn't necessarily the application default. It's much easier to manage that common layout from a single file rather than having to change a layout for every controller every time the design changes.

The simplest way to make this work is to have controllers specify what layout they would like to use. If standardization is your main purpose, adding a `layout` declaration like that shown in Example 3-7 will work.

Example 3-7. Specifying a layout choice in a controller

```
class HelloController < ApplicationController

  layout "standardLayout"

  def index
    @message="Hello!"

    @count=3
```

```
  @bonus="This message came from the controller."
  end
end
```

Instead of looking for *app/views/layouts/hello.html.erb* to be the layout, Rails will now look for *app/views/layouts/standardLayout.html.erb*.

The `layout` call can also take `nil` (for no layout) or a symbol as a method reference. If there is a method reference, that method will determine which layout is used. Example 3-8 shows what this might look like.

Example 3-8. Choosing a layout based on program calculations

```
class HelloController < ApplicationController

    layout :adminOrUser

    def index
      ...
    end

private
      def adminOrUser
        if adminAuthenticated
          "admin_screen"
        else
          "user_screen"
        end
      end
end
```

In this case, `layout` took a reference to the `adminOrUser` method, which returned either the `admin_screen` layout or the `user_screen` layout as its choice depending on the value of the `adminAuthenticated` variable (whose value is calculated somewhere else).

One other feature of `layout` is worth noting, though we're not ready to use it yet. If your application can return, say, XML or RSS instead of HTML, you may want to be able to turn off your HTML layout in cases where it won't be wanted. You might say:

```
layout "standardLayout", :except => :rss
layout "standardLayout", :except => [:rss, :xml, :text_only]
```

The first one uses the layout except when RSS has been requested, while the second uses the layout except for requests for RSS, XML, and text formats. You could also work the opposite way, saying to use the layout only for HTML:

```
layout "standardLayout", :only => :html
```

You can also select a layout (or no layout) using the render function. (You may want to do this if your controller includes multiple actions that need their own layouts.)

Sharing Template Data with the Layout

Layouts and view templates share the same information from the controller, but there may be times when a view template should include information that needs to be embedded in the layout. This might be navigation particular to different areas of a site, or personalization, or some kind of status bar, for instance, that shows the user how far they've gone through a particular task.

Example 3-9 shows a modified template that creates a numbered list HTML fragment that the layout in Example 3-10 will include separately—actually, *before*—it includes the main template output. The structure created by the `<% content_for(:list) do %>` code in Example 3-9 is called upon by the `<%= yield :name %>` tag in Example 3-10.

Example 3-9. index.html.erb with newly added HTML structure for separate inclusion

```
<h1><%=h @message %></h1>
<p>This is a greeting from app/views/hello/index.html.erb</p>

<% for i in 1..@count %>
<p><%=h @bonus %></p>
<% end %>

<% content_for(:list) do %>
<ol>
<% for i in 1..@count %>
<li><%=h @bonus %></li>
<% end %>
</ol>
<% end %>
```

Example 3-10. Layout template with added yield, exposing the list from Example 3-9

```
<html>
<head><title><%=h @message %> </title>
  <%= stylesheet_link_tag 'hello', :media => "all",
    :type => "text/css", :href => "/stylesheets/hello.css"  %>

</head>
<body>
<%= yield :list %>
<!--layout will incorporate view-->
<%= yield :layout %>

</body>
</html>
```

The result, shown in Figure 3-5, isn't exactly beautiful, but it demonstrates that a template can create content that a layout can include anywhere it likes.

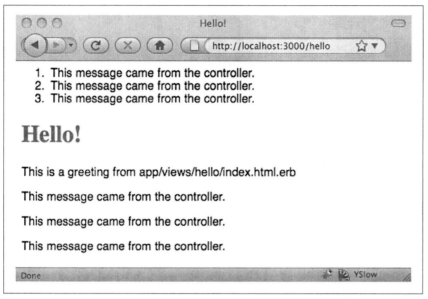

Figure 3-5. Layout including content created as a separate piece by a template

Always remember that this works because the template has executed before the layout adds its own ideas. You can communicate from the template to the layout, but not from the layout to the template.

Setting a Default Page

Before moving on to more "serious" concerns about developing applications, there's one question that web developers always seem to ask about 15 minutes into their first Rails experience:

How do I set a default page for the application?

The Rails welcome page, shown in Figure 1-2, is just plain ugly. There are two ways to change that:

- Edit the *public/index.html* file and put in something more to your liking
- Delete the *public/index.html* file and tweak the *config/routes.rb* file

The first one is pretty easy, but it doesn't integrate very tightly with your Rails application. The second approach lets you pick a controller that will run if the Rails application is run without specifying a controller—that is, in the test environment, by directly visiting *http://localhost:3000/*.

To make this work, you'll need to enter an extra line in the *config/routes.rb* file. Near the bottom of that, you'll see:

```
# You can have the root of your site routed with map.root --
# just remember to delete public/index.html.
# map.root :controller => "welcome"
```

Change the last line of that to:

```
map.root :controller => "hello", :action => "index"
```

Save the file, make sure you've deleted or renamed the *public/index.html* file, and restart your server. You should see something like Figure 3-6.

Figure 3-6. Accessing a controller by default, when the URL doesn't specify one

Don't worry if this edit seems mysterious. You'll learn more about how routing works starting in Chapter 4, with a lot more detail to come in Chapter 15.

Test Your Knowledge

Quiz

1. Where would you put your CSS stylesheet, and how should you connect it to your view?
2. How does Rails know which layout to apply to a particular view?
3. What does that `yield` thing do?
4. How do I send data from the view template to the layout?

Answers

1. Stylesheets go in the *public/stylesheets* directory, and you connect them to your views (or layouts) by putting a call to `stylesheet_link_tag` in the head element.
2. By default, Rails will apply the layout in *app/views/layout/application.html.erb* to all of your views. However, if there is a layout file in *app/views/layout/* that has the same name as a view, Rails will use that instead.
3. The `yield` method hands control to a different block of code, one that was passed with parameters. Rails often handles this quietly, making it easy to share data between, for example, layouts and views.
4. The layout has access to all of the same variables the view uses. You don't need to do anything special to pass variables to the layout, even if you want the layout to apply them early in your HTML document.

## CHAPTER 4

Controlling Data Flow: Controllers and Models

It's time to meet the key player in Rails applications. Controllers are the components that determine how to respond to user requests and coordinate responses. They're at the heart of what many people think of as "the program" in your Rails applications, though in many ways they're more of a switchboard. They connect the different pieces that do the heavy lifting, providing a focal point for application development. The model is the foundation of your application's data structures, which will let you get information into and out of your databases.

Getting Started, Greeting Guests

Controllers are Ruby objects. They're stored in the *app/controllers* directory of your application. Each controller has a name, and the object inside of the controller file is called *name*Controller.

Demonstrating controllers without getting tangled in all of Rails' other components is difficult, so for an initial tour, the application will be incredibly simple. (You can see the first version of it in *ch04/guestbook001*.) Guestbooks were a common (if kind of annoying) feature on early websites, letting visitors "sign in" so that the site could tell who'd been there. (The idea has since evolved into much more sophisticated messaging, like Facebook's "wall.")

 If you've left any Rails applications from earlier chapters running under script/server, it would be wise to turn them off before starting a new application.

To get started, create a new Rails application, as we did in Chapter 1. If you're working from the command line, type:

```
rails guestbook
```

Rails will create the usual pile of files and folders. Next, you'll want to change to the guestbook directory and create a controller:

```
cd guestbook
ruby script/generate controller entries
      exists  app/controllers/
      exists  app/helpers/
      create  app/views/entries
      exists  test/functional/
      create  app/controllers/entries_controller.rb
      create  test/functional/entries_controller_test.rb
      create  app/helpers/entries_helper.rb
```

If you then look at *app/controllers/entries_controller.rb*, which is the main file we'll work with here, you'll find:

```
class EntriesController < ApplicationController
end
```

This doesn't do very much. However, there's an important relationship in that first line. Your `EntriesController` inherits from `ApplicationController`. The `ApplicationController` object lives in *app/controllers/application.rb*, and it also doesn't do very much initially, but if you ever need to add functionality that is shared by all of the controllers in your application, you can put it into the `ApplicationController` object.

To make this controller actually do something, we'll add a method. For right now, we'll call it `sign_in`, creating the very simple object in Example 4-1.

Example 4-1. Adding an initial method to an empty controller

```
class EntriesController < ApplicationController

  def sign_in

  end

end
```

We'll also need a view, so that Rails has something it can present to visitors. You can create a *sign_in.html.erb* file in the *app/views/entries/* directory, and then edit it, as shown in Example 4-2.

You may remember from Chapter 2 that you could have had Rails create a method in the controller as well as a basic view at the same time that it created the controller, by typing:

```
ruby script/generate controller entries sign_in
```

You can work either way, letting Rails generate as much (or as little) code as you like.

Example 4-2. A view that lets users see a message and enter their name

```
<html>
<head><title>Hello <%=h @name %></title></head>

<body>
<h1>Hello <%=h @name %></h1>

<% form_tag :action => 'sign_in' do %>
   <p>Enter your name:
   <%= text_field_tag 'visitor_name', @name %></p>

   <%= submit_tag 'Sign in' %>

<% end %>
</body>
</html>
```

Example 4-2 has a lot of new pieces to it because it's using *helper methods* to create a basic form. Helper methods take arguments and return text, which in this case is HTML that helps build your form. The following particular helpers are built into Rails, but you can also create your own:

- The form_tag method takes the name of our controller method, sign_in, as its :action parameter.

- The text_field_tag method takes two parameters and uses them to create a form field on the page. The first, visitor_name, is the identifier that the form will use to describe the field data it sends back to the controller, while the second is default text that the field will contain. If the user has filled out this form previously, and our controller populates the @name variable, it will list the user's name. Otherwise, it will be blank.

- The last helper method, submit_tag, provides the button that will send the data from the form back to the controller when the user clicks it.

If you start up the server and visit *http://localhost:3000/entries/sign_in*, you'll see a simple form like Figure 4-1.

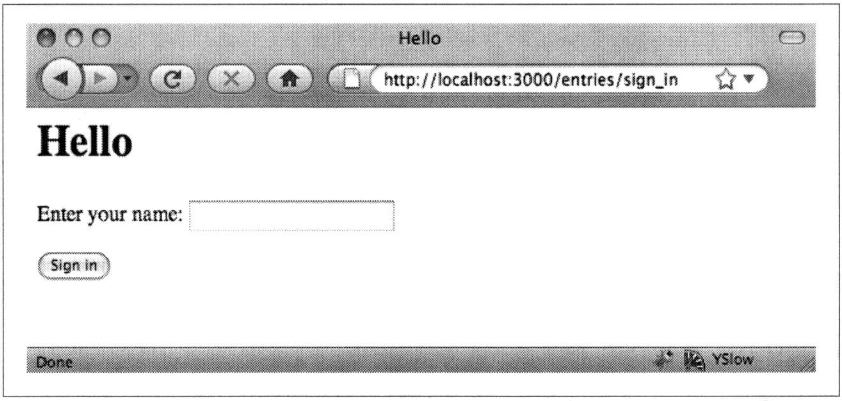

Figure 4-1. A simple form generated by a Rails view

> If you get an error message about a database not being found, you may want to explore the option described at the end of Chapter 1 in "Turning Off Databases, For Now." You'll need to turn them on again later in this chapter, though.

Now that we have a way to send data to our controller, it's time to update the controller so that it does something with that information. In this very simple case, it just means adding a line, as shown in Example 4-3.

Example 4-3. Making the sign_in method do something

```
class EntriesController < ApplicationController

  def sign_in
    @name = params[:visitor_name]
  end

end
```

The extra line gets the `visitor_name` parameter from the request header sent back by the client and puts it into `@name`. (If there wasn't a `visitor_name` parameter, as would be normal the first time this page is loaded, `@name` will just be blank.)

If you enter a name into the form, you'll now get a pretty basic hello message back as shown in Figure 4-2. The name will also be sitting in the form field for another round of greetings.

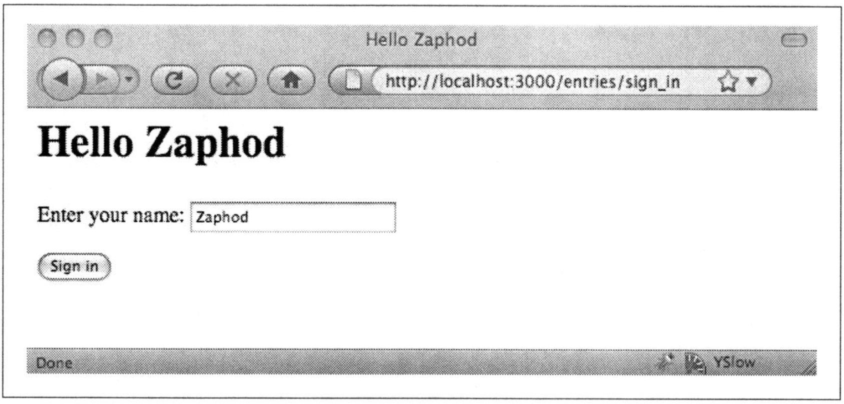

![Browser window titled "Hello Zaphod" showing URL http://localhost:3000/entries/sign_in. Page heading "Hello Zaphod" with a field labeled "Enter your name:" containing "Zaphod" and a "Sign in" button.]

Figure 4-2. A greeting that includes the name that was entered

If, instead of Figure 4-2, you get a strange error message about "wrong number of arguments (1 for 0)," check your code carefully. You've probably added a space between params and [, which produces a syntax error whose description isn't exactly clear.

This isn't incredibly exciting, admittedly, but it's a start. The controller is now receiving information from the user and passing it to a view, which can then pass more information.

There is one other minor point worth examining before we move on, though: how did Rails convert the *http://localhost:3000/entries/sign_in* URL into a call to the sign_in method of the entries controller? If you look in the *config* directory of your application, you'll find the *routes.rb* file, which contains two default rules for choosing what gets called when a request comes in:

```
map.connect ':controller/:action/:id'
map.connect ':controller/:action/:id.:format'
```

In this case, entries mapped to :controller, and sign_in mapped to :action. Rails used this simple mapping to decide what to call. We don't have an :id or a :format—yet. (And as Chapter 2 demonstrated, if there hadn't been an :action, Rails would have defaulted to an :action named index.) Figure 4-3 shows how Rails breaks down a URL to decide where to go.

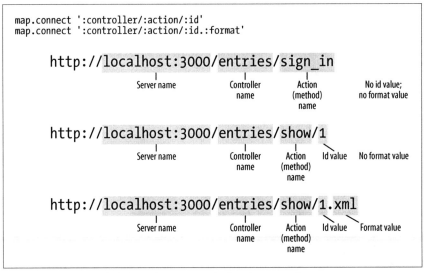

```
map.connect ':controller/:action/:id'
map.connect ':controller/:action/:id.:format'
```

Figure 4-3. How the default Rails routing rules break a URL down into component parts to decide which method to run

You can also see your routes by typing `rake routes` from the command line. This gives you a slightly more compact version and shows how Rails interpreted the *routes.rb* file.

Application Flow

The Rails approach to handling requests, shown in Figure 4-4, has a lot of moving parts between users and data.

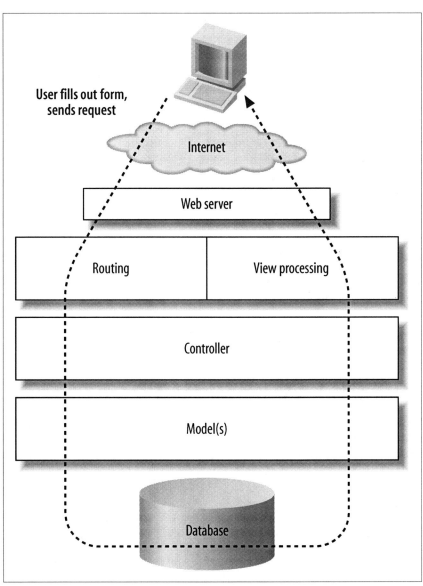

Figure 4-4. How Rails breaks down web applications

Rails handles URL processing instead of letting the web server pick which file to execute in response to the request. This allows Rails to use its own conventions for deciding how a request gets handled, called routing, and it allows developers to create their own routing conventions to meet their applications' needs.

The router sends the request information to a controller. The controller decides how to handle the request, centralizing the logic for responding to different kinds of requests. The controller may interact with a data model (or several), and those models will interact with the database if necessary. The person writing the controller never has to touch SQL, though, and even the person writing the model should be able to stay away from it.

Once the controller has gathered and processed the information it needs, it sends that data to a view for rendering. The controller can pick and choose among different views if it needs to, making it easy to throw an XML rendering on a controller that was originally expecting to be part of an HTML-generating process. You could offer a variety of different kinds of HTML—basic, Ajax, or meant for mobile—from your applications if necessary. Rails can even, at the developer's discretion, generate basic views automatically, a feature called *scaffolding*. Scaffolding makes it extremely easy to get started on the data management side of an application without getting too hung up on its presentation.

The final result comes from the view, and Rails sends it along to the user. The user, of course, doesn't need to know how all of this came to pass—the user just gets the final view of the information, which hopefully is what they wanted.

Now that you've seen how this works in the big picture, it's time to return to the details of making it happen.

Keeping Track: A Simple Guestbook

Most applications will need to do more with data—typically, at least, they'll store the data and present it back as appropriate. It's time to extend this simple application so that it keeps track of who has stopped by, as well as greeting them. This requires using models. (The complete application is available in *ch04/guestbook002*.)

 As the next chapter on scaffolding will make clear, in most application development you will likely want to create your models by letting Rails create a scaffold, since Rails won't let you create a scaffold after a model with the same name already exists. Nonetheless, understanding the more manual approach will make it much easier to work on your applications in the long run.

Connecting to a Database Through a Model

Keeping track of visitors will mean setting up and using a database. In Rails 2.0.2 and later, this should be easy when you're in development mode, as Rails now defaults to SQLite, which doesn't require explicit configuration. (Earlier versions of Rails required setting up MySQL, which does require configuration, which you'll still want to do for deployment as discussed in Chapter 18.) To test whether SQLite is installed on your system, try issuing the command `sqlite3 -help` from the command line. If it's there, you'll get a help message. If not, you'll get an error, and you'll need to install SQLite.

Once the database engine is functioning, it's time to create a model. Once again, it's easiest to use `script/generate` to lay a foundation, and then add details to that foundation. This time, we'll create a simple model instead of a controller and call the model `entry`:

```
ruby script/generate model entry
        exists  app/models/
        exists  test/unit/
        exists  test/fixtures/
        create  app/models/entry.rb
        create  test/unit/entry_test.rb
        create  test/fixtures/entries.yml
        create  db/migrate
        create  db/migrate/20080718193908_create_entries.rb
```

For our immediate purposes, two of these files are critical. The first is *app/models/entry.rb*, which is where all of the Ruby logic for handling a person will go. The second, which defines the database structures and thus needs to be modified first, is in the *db/migrate/* directory. It will have a name like *[timestamp]_create_entries.rb*, where [timestamp] is the date and time when it was created. It initially contains what's shown in Example 4-4.

Example 4-4. The default migration for the entry model

```
1  class CreateEntries < ActiveRecord::Migration
2    def self.up
3      create_table :entries do |t|
4
5        t.timestamps
6      end
7    end
8
9    def self.down
10      drop_table :entries
11    end
12 end
```

There's a lot to examine here before we start making changes. First, note on line 1 that the class is called `CreateEntries`. The model may be for a person, but the migration will create a table for more than one person. Rails names tables (and migrations) for the plural, and can handle most common English irregular pluralizations. (In cases where the singular and plural would be the same, you end up with an *s* added for the plural, so deer become deers and sheep become sheeps.) Many people find this natural, but other people hate it. For now, just go with it—fighting Rails won't make life any easier.

Also on line 1, you can see that this class inherits most of its functionality from the `Migration` class of `ActiveRecord`. ActiveRecord is the Rails library that handles all the database interactions. (You can even use it separately from Rails, if you want to.)

There are two methods defined here, on lines 2 (`self.up`) and 9 (`self.down`). The `self.up` method will be called when you order the migration run, and will create tables and columns your application needs. The `self.down` method will be called if you roll back the migration—effectively it provides you with "undo" functionality.

 This example takes the slow route through creating a model so you can see what happens. In the future, if you'd prefer to move more quickly, you can also add the names and types of data on the command line as you will do when generating scaffolding in the next chapter.

Both of these operate on a table called Entries—`self.up` creates it on line 3, while `self.down` destroys (drops) it on line 10. Note that the migration is not concerned with what kind of database it works on. That's all handled by the configuration information. You'll also see that migrations, despite working pretty close to the database, don't need to use SQL—though if you really want to use SQL, it's available.

Storing the names people enter into this very simple application requires adding a single column:

```
create_table :entries do |t|
  t.string :name
  t.timestamps
end
```

The new line refers to the table (t) and creates a column of type `string`, which will be accessible as `:name`.

 In older versions of Rails, that new line would have been written:

```
t.column :name, string
```

The old version still works, and you'll definitely see migrations written this way in older applications and documents. The new form is a lot easier to read at a glance, though.

The `t.timestamps` line is there for housekeeping, tracking "created at" and "updated at" information. Rails also will automatically create a primary key, `:id`, for the table. Once you've entered the new line (at line 4 of Example 4-4), you can run the migration with the Rake tool:

```
$ rake db:migrate
(in /Users/simonstl/rails/guestbook)
== 20080814190623 CreateEntries: migrating ====================
-- create_table(:entries)
   -> 0.0041s
== 20080814190623 CreateEntries: migrated (0.0044s) ============
```

Rake is Ruby's own version of the classic command-line Unix `make` tool, and Rails uses it for a wide variety of tasks. (For a full list, try `rake --tasks`.)

In this case, the `db:migrate` task runs all of the previously unapplied `self.up` migrations in your application's *db/migrate/* folder. (`db:rollback` runs the `self.down` migrations corresponding to the previous run, giving you an undo option.)

Now that the application has a table with a column for holding names, it's time to turn to the *app/models/entry.rb* file. Its initial contents are very simple:

```
class Entry < ActiveRecord::Base
end
```

The `Entry` class inherits from the ActiveRecord library's `Base` class, but has no functionality of its own. For right now, it can stay that way—Rails provides enough capability that nothing more is needed.

 Remember that the names in your models also need to stay away from the list of reserved words presented at *http://wiki .rubyonrails.org/rails/pages/ReservedWords*.

Connecting the Controller to the Model

As you may have guessed, the controller is going to be the key component transferring data that comes in from the form to the model, and then it will be the key component transferring that data back out to the view for presentation to the user.

Storing data using the model

To get started, the controller will just blindly save new names to the model, using the code highlighted in Example 4-5.

Example 4-5. Using ActiveRecord to save a name

```
class EntriesController < ApplicationController

  def sign_in
      @name = params[:visitor_name]
      @entry = Entry.create({:name => @name})

  end

end
```

The highlighted line combines three separate operations into a single line of code, which might look like:

```
@myEntry = Entry.new
@myEntry.name = @name
@myEntry.save
```

The first step creates a new variable, `@myEntry`, and declares it to be a new Entry object. The next line sets the name property of `@myEntry`—effectively setting the future value of the column named "name" in the Entries table—to the `@name` value that came in through the form. The third line saves the `@myEntry` object to the table.

The `Entry.create` approach assumes you're making a new object, takes the values to be stored as named parameters, and then saves the object to the database.

 Both the `create` and the `save` method return a boolean value indicating whether or not saving the value to the database was successful. For most applications, you'll want to test this, and return an error if there was a failure.

These are the basic methods you'll need to put information into your databases with ActiveRecord. (There are many shortcuts and more elegant syntax, as the next chapter will show.) This approach is also a bit too simple. If you visit *http://localhost:3000/entries/sign_in/*, you'll see the same empty form that was shown in Figure 4-1. However, because `@entry.create` was called, an empty name will have been written to the table. The log data that appears in the server's terminal window shows:

```
Entry Create (0.000522)   INSERT INTO "entries" ("name", "updated_at",
"created_at") VALUES(NULL, '2008-08-14 19:13:58', '2008-08-14 19:13:58')
```

The NULL is the problem here because it really doesn't make sense to add a blank name every time someone loads the form without sending a value. On the bright side, we have evidence that Rails is putting information into the

Entries table, and if we enter a name, say "Zaphod," we can see the name being entered into the table:

```
Entry Create (0.000409)   INSERT INTO "entries" ("name", "updated_at",
"created_at") VALUES('Zaphod', '2008-08-14 19:15:06', '2008-08-14 19:15:06')
```

It's easy to fix the controller so that NULLs aren't stored—though as we'll see in Chapter 7, this kind of validation code really belongs in the model. Two lines, highlighted in Example 4-6, will keep Rails from entering a lot of blank names.

Example 4-6. Keeping blanks from turning into permanent objects

```
class EntriesController < ApplicationController

  def sign_in
      @name = params[:visitor_name]
    if !@name.blank?
      @entry = Entry.create({:name => @name})
    end
  end

end
```

Now Rails will check the @name variable to make sure that it has a value before putting it into the database. !@name.blank? will test for both nil values and blank entries. (blank is a Rails method extending Ruby's String objects. The ! at the beginning means "not," which ensure that only values that are not blank will be accepted.)

If you want to get rid of the NULLs you put into the database, you can run rake db:rollback and rake db:migrate (or rake db:migrate:redo to combine them) to drop and rebuild the table with a clean copy.

```
== 1 CreateEntries: reverting ========================================
-- drop_table(:entries)
   -> 0.0029s
== 1 CreateEntries: reverted (0.0031s) ==============================

== 1 CreateEntries: migrating ========================================
-- create_table(:entries)
   -> 0.0039s
== 1 CreateEntries: migrated (0.0041s) ==============================
```

If you want to enter a few names to put some data into the new table, go ahead. The next example will show how to get them out.

Retrieving data from the model and showing it

Storing data is a good thing, but only if you can get it out again. Fortunately, it's not difficult for the controller to tell the model that it wants all the data, or for the view to render it. For a guestbook, it's especially simple, as we just want all of the data every time.

Getting the data out of the model requires one line of additional code in the controller, highlighted in Example 4-7.

Example 4-7. A controller that also retrieves data from a model

```
class EntriesController < ApplicationController

  def sign_in
      @name = params[:visitor_name]
    if !@name.blank? then
      @entry = Entry.create({:name => @name})
    end

    @entries = Entry.find(:all)

  end

end
```

The `Entry` object includes a `find` method—like `new` and `save`, inherited from its parent `ActiveRecord::Base` class without any additional programming. If you run this and look in the logs, you'll see that Rails is actually making a SQL call to populate the `@entry` array:

```
Entry Load (0.000633)   SELECT * FROM "entries"
```

Next, the view, still in *views/entries/sign_in.html.erb*, can show the contents of that array, letting visitors to the site see who's come by before, using the added lines shown in Example 4-8.

Example 4-8. Displaying existing users with a loop

```
<html>
<head><title>Hello <%=h @name %></title></head>

<body>
<h1>Hello <%=h @name %></h1>

<% form_tag :action => 'sign_in' do %>
    <p>Enter your name:
    <%= text_field_tag 'visitor_name', @name %></p>

    <%= submit_tag 'Sign in' %>

<% end %>
<p>Previous visitors:</p>
<ul>
<% @entries.each do |entry| %>
  <li><%=h entry.name %></li>
<% end %>
```

```
</ul>
</body>
</html>
```

The loop here iterates over the `@entries` array, running as many times as there are entries in `@entries`. `@entries`, of course, holds the list of names previously entered, pulled from the database by the model that was called by the controller in Example 4-7. For each entry, the view adds a list item containing the `name` value, referenced here as `entry.name`. The result, depending on exactly what names you entered, will look something like Figure 4-5.

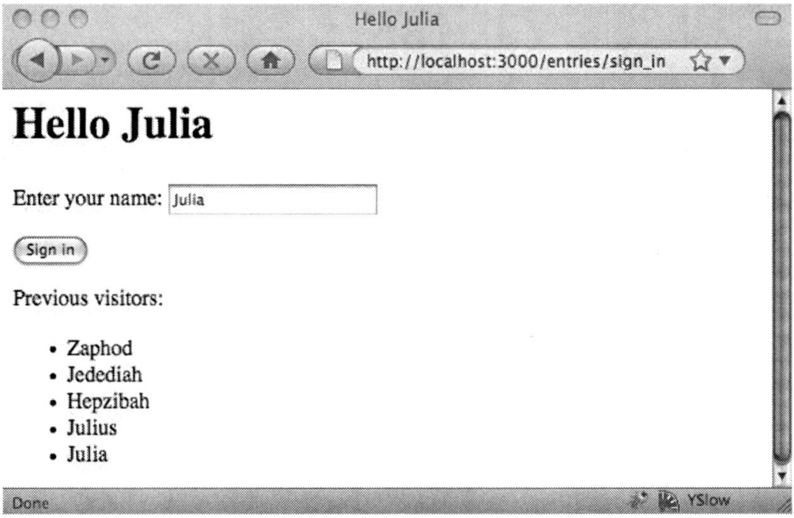

Figure 4-5. The guestbook application, now displaying the names of past visitors

It's a lot of steps, yes, but fortunately you'll be able to skip a lot of those steps as you move deeper into Rails. Building this guestbook didn't look very much like the "complex-application-in-five–minutes" demonstrations that Rails' promoters like to show off, but now you should understand what's going on underneath the magic. After the apprenticeship, the next chapter will get into some journeyman fun.

Looking Under the Hood

Every now and then you may find something missing, or need to see what exactly is coming into your view. Rails includes a number of useful pieces that, while you should never ever use them in production code, can help you see the data that Rails is providing to your view.

To see everything Rails is sending, add this to your view:

```
<%= debug(assigns) %>
```

The results of that are both overwhelming and kind of repetitive, but you can hunt through there for useful pieces. To see just the headers that came in with the request, you can use:

```
<%= debug(headers) %>
```

For just the parameters that came in from a request, use:

```
<%= debug(params) %>
```

Other arguments to debug that might be useful in certain situations are base_path, controller, flash, request, response, and session.

Finding Data with ActiveRecord

The find method is common in Rails, usually in controllers. It's constantly used as find(id) to retrieve a single record with a given id, and also used as find(:all) to retrieve an entire set of records. The find method is, however, capable of much more finesse, letting you control which records are returned and in what order. There are four basic ways to call find, and then a set of options that can apply to all of those uses:

find by id
> The find method is frequently called with a single id, as in find(id), but it can also be called with an array of ids, like find (id1, id2, id3, ...) in which case find will return an array of values. Finally, you can call find ([id1, id2]) and retrieve everything with id values between id1 and id2.

find all
> Calling find with an argument of :all will return all the matching values as an array. (You can also abbreviate find(:all) to just .all–User.all, for example.)

find first
> Calling find with an argument of :first will return the first matching value only. You'll probably want to specify :order to be certain which value you get. (You can also abbreviate find(:first) to just .first–User.first, for example.)

find last
> Calling find with an argument of :last will return the last matching value only. As with find(:first), you'll probably want to specify :order to be certain which value you get. (Again, you can abbreviate find(:last) to just .last–User.last, for example.)

The options give you much more control over what is queried and which values are returned. All of them actually modify the SQL statements used to query the database and can accept SQL syntax, but you don't need to know SQL to use most of them. This list of options is sorted by your likely order of needing them:

:conditions

The :conditions option lets you limit which records are returned. If, for example, you set:

```
find(:all, :conditions => "registered = true")
```

then you would only see records with a registered value of true. :conditions also has another form. You could instead write:

```
find(:all, :conditions => { :registered => true })
```

This will produce the same query and makes it a little more readable to list multiple conditions. Also, if conditions are coming in from a parameter or some other data source you don't entirely trust, you may want to use the array form of :conditions:

```
find(:all, :conditions => ["email = ?", email])
```

Rails will replace the ? with the value of email, after sanitizing it.

:order

The :order option lets you choose the order in which records are returned, though if you're using find(:first) or find(:last) it will also determine which record you'll see as first or last. The simplest way to use this is with a field name or comma-separated list of field names:

```
find(:all, :order => "family_name, given_name")
```

By default, the :order option will sort in ascending order, so the option just shown would sort family_name values in ascending order, using given_name as a second sort field when family_name values are the same. If you want to sort in descending order, just put DESC after the field name:

```
find(:all, :order => "family_name DESC, given_name DESC")
```

This will return the names sorted in descending order.

:limit

The :limit option lets you specify how many records are returned. If you wrote:

```
find(:all, :limit => 10)
```

you would receive only the first 10 records back. (You'll probably want to specify :order to ensure that they're the ones you want.)

:offset
> The :offset option lets you specify a starting point from which records should be returned. If, for instance, you wanted to retrieve the next 10 records after a set you'd retrieved with :limit, you could specify:
>
> ```
> find(:all, :limit => 10, :offset => 10)
> ```

:readonly
> Retrieves records so that you can read them, but cannot make any changes.

:group
> The :group option lets you specify a field that the results should group on, like the SQL GROUP BY clause.

:lock
> Lets you test for locked rows.

:joins, :include, :select, and :from
> These let you specify components of the SQL query more precisely. You may need them as you delve into complex data structures, but you can ignore them at first.

Rails also offers *dynamic finders*, which are methods it automatically supports based on the names of the fields in the database. If you have a given_name field, for example, you can call find_by_given_name*(name)* to get the first record with the specified *name*, or find_all_by_given_name*(name)* to get all records with the specified *name*. These are a little slower than the regular find method, but may be more readable.

Rails 2.1 and later versions also offer an elegant way to create more readable queries with the named_scope method for defining queries specific to particular models, which you should explore after you've found your way around find.

Test Your Knowledge

Quiz

1. Where would you put code to which you want all of your controllers to have access?
2. How do the default routes decide which requests to send to your controller?
3. What does the `self.up` method do in a migration?
4. What three steps does the `create` method combine?
5. How do you test to find out whether a submitted field is blank?
6. How can you retrieve all of the values for a given field?
7. How can you find a set of values that match a certain condition?
8. How can you retrieve just the first item of a set?

Answers

1. Code in the `ApplicationController` class, stored at *app/controllers/application.rb*, is available to all of the controllers in the project.
2. The default routes assume that the controller name follows the first slash within the URL, that the controller action follows the second slash, and that the ID value follows the third slash. If there's a dot (.) after the ID, then what follows the dot is considered the format requested.
3. The `self.up` method is called when Rake runs a migration forward. It usually creates tables and fields.
4. The `create` method creates a new object, sets its properties to those specified in the parameters, and saves it to the database.
5. You can test to see whether something is blank using an `if` statement and the `blank?` method, as in:
   ```
   if @name.blank? then
     something to do if blank
   end
   ```
6. To retrieve all values for a given object, use `find(:all)`.
7. To retrieve a set of values, use `find(:all, :conditions => conditions)`.

8. To get the first of a set, use `find(:first)`. You may need to set an `:order` parameter to make sure that your understanding of "first" and Rails' understanding of "first" are the same.

## CHAPTER 5

Accelerating Development with Scaffolding and REST

The example in the previous chapter contained the key components you need to work with Rails and began to demonstrate how they work together. Rails is more than just a set of components, however—it's a tightly knit package that includes tools to get you started more quickly. Rails can even teach you some best practices while making your work easier.

A First Look at Scaffolding

So, how do Rails developers build applications more quickly? One key piece of the puzzle is scaffolding. Instead of building a detailed controller and view, you can let Rails put up an interface to your data. In most cases, the scaffolding will be temporary, something you build on and replace, but in some cases the scaffolding may be enough to do what you need. The scaffolding also provides an excellent way to see what Rails' creators think is a good way to accomplish common tasks.

 If you're wondering what happened to the instant one-line dynamic scaffolding that used to be a constant part of the Rails sales pitch, it's gone. It disappeared in Rails 2.0, replaced by generated scaffolding that provides a much more solid foundation.

To get started, create a new application named people:

```
$ rails people
```

Then create a model and supporting scaffolding with a single command from the command line. (You can also find all of these files in *ch05/guestbook003*.)

```
$ ruby script/generate scaffold Person name:string
exists   app/models/
    exists   app/controllers/
    exists   app/helpers/
    create   app/views/people
    exists   app/views/layouts/
    exists   test/functional/
    exists   test/unit/
    create   app/views/people/index.html.erb
    create   app/views/people/show.html.erb
    create   app/views/people/new.html.erb
    create   app/views/people/edit.html.erb
    create   app/views/layouts/people.html.erb
    create   public/stylesheets/scaffold.css
dependency   model
    exists      app/models/
    exists      test/unit/
    exists      test/fixtures/
    create      app/models/person.rb
    create      test/unit/person_test.rb
    create      test/fixtures/people.yml
    create      db/migrate
    create      db/migrate/001_create_people.rb
    create   app/controllers/people_controller.rb
    create   test/functional/people_controller_test.rb
    create   app/helpers/people_helper.rb
     route   map.resources :people
```

This command makes Rails do a lot of different things. First, examine the initial line:

```
ruby script/generate scaffold Person name:string
```

It tells Rails to generate scaffolding, based around a model named `Person`, whose content is a `name` that is a `string`. If the model has more pieces to it—and most will—you can just keep listing the different data fields and their types.

Given this information, Rails goes on to create:

- Four views (index, show, new, and edit)
- A layout file for all of those views
- A stylesheet for all of those views
- A model (with accompanying tests and fixtures for the tests)
- A data migration to establish the tables needed for the model
- A controller to send data among the different components, and tests for it
- An empty file for helper methods
- A new route that will map user requests to the controller

You'll need to run the migration file with `rake db:migrate`, and then you can run `ruby script/server` to fire up the application. Visit *http://localhost:3000/people*, and you'll see something like Figure 5-1.

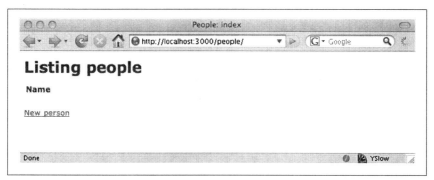

Figure 5-1. The index page of the newly generated application

While Figure 5-1 lacks the "Hello" of the application built in the previous chapter, and the form field to enter your name isn't right on the first page, it's still basically the same idea. You can see who visited, and you can enter new names. If you click on the "New person" link, you'll see the screen in Figure 5-2, which lets you enter a new name.

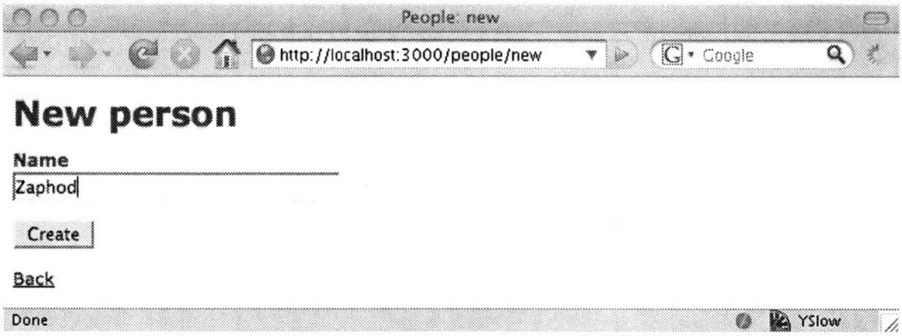

Figure 5-2. Entering a new name

When you enter a name and click the Create button, you'll see a page representing the newly created person, as shown in Figure 5-3. (The URL, though it points to a single person, still uses the plural form, "people," as the record is one of a set.)

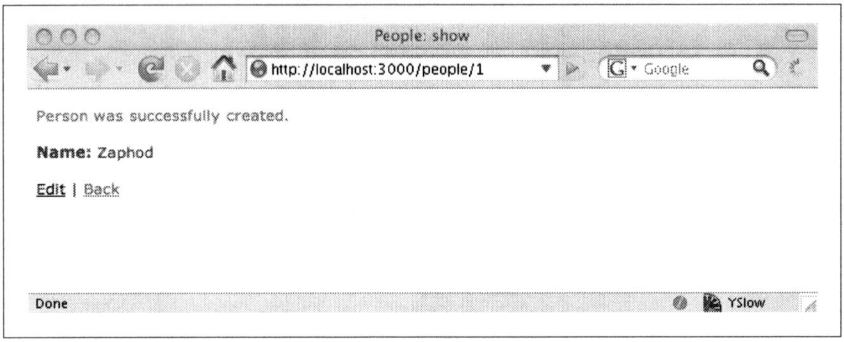

Figure 5-3. A newly created person

There are two options here. Edit will let you change the name (as shown in Figure 5-4), while clicking Back returns you to the original (index) page—only now you'll see the name in a table, as shown in Figure 5-5.

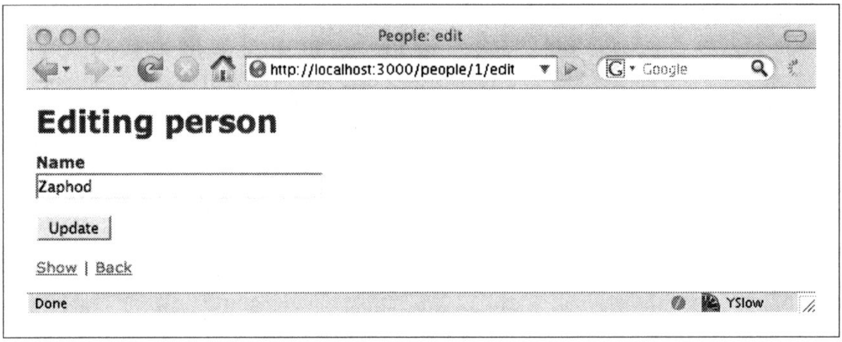

Figure 5-4. Updating an existing person

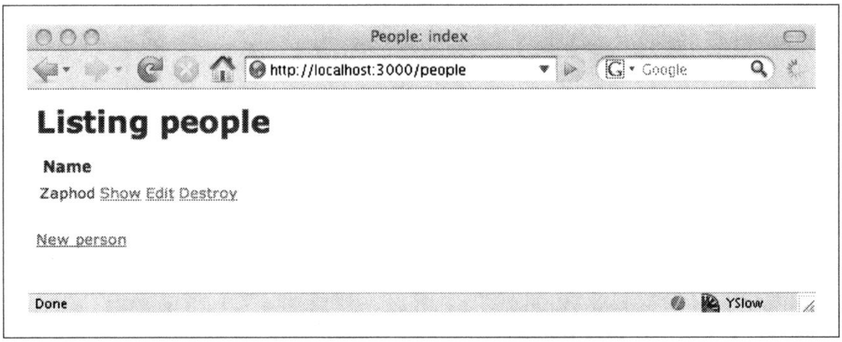

Figure 5-5. The new list of people, with options for modifying them

It's not quite as simple as the application built by hand in the previous chapter, but much of it is actually identical. The migration file looks just like the one created by hand (plus or minus some whitespace), and the model has exactly as much new code in it as the one built by hand: none at all.

The scaffolding's action takes place in the single line added to the routing file, in a controller that needs a careful explanation and in the views, which don't do very much that you haven't already seen before. To understand why this controller works the way it does, though, there's another story that needs to be told. Fortunately, it's a RESTful story.

REST and Controller Best Practices

REST is an approach to building web applications that takes as much advantage of the underlying structure of the web as possible. This makes a lot of things more comfortable:

- Users will find that the applications work as they'd like in their web browsers. They can bookmark pages and come back to them, and the URLs are actually meaningful.

- Network administrators can use all their preferred techniques for managing web traffic without worrying about disrupting an application.

- You, of course, get the greatest benefits. REST-based architecture is a very neat fit with Rails' MVC approach, and makes it easier to keep track of which code does what where. Rails 2.x is also set up to make it extremely easy for you to use REST, supporting a number of ways for you to say, "I'd like this to behave RESTfully."

REST doesn't create new techniques so much as dust off old techniques and encourage developers to use them as they were designed to be used. Of course, even early in the Web's development, developers hacked and slashed their way into a different style of programming, so there are some adjustments to make. Fortunately, Rails makes it easy to adjust and opens new horizons in doing so.

 REST stands for REpresentational State Transfer, which describes what happens but isn't the most immediately meaningful explanation.

Websites and Web Applications

Web developers have historically used two HTTP methods to get information into and out of sites: GET and POST. On the surface, GET used the "data-fits-into-the-query-string" approach, whereas POST used the "we-have-a-nice-clean-URL-with-data-elsewhere" approach. There's more to it than that, though.

Much of the Web is read-only, and for those applications GET worked very smoothly. Browser caches and proxy servers could check once in a while to see if a page had changed. For many applications, where POSTs were used to add new data and GETs were used to see that data, things weren't much more complicated. Unfortunately, though, the reliance on GET and POST overloaded those methods and created some problems.

For GET, the most obvious problem was that URLs became very large very quickly as more and more data was exchanged. Beyond that, though, were some other creative issues:

- Proxy servers generally treated a GET request as an opportunity to cache information and reduce the amount of traffic needed next time. This could lead to sensitive data stored on a not-necessarily-secure proxy server and could also create some strange problems around the proxy server checking whether the result had changed when another request came through with the same data.

- Some applications used links containing GET requests to ask for changes in data—even deletions. (Think *http://example.com/doIt/?action=delete*.) As the quest for speed became more important, developers came up with browser extensions that pre-fetched information from links in the document... and activated these actions without the user expecting it. Oops.

The general rule with GET has become "make sure that none of your GET requests do anything dangerous." GET requests are supposed to be *idempotent*, yielding the same result even when issued multiple times. No GET request changes the results of the next GET request to the same resource, for example.

 PUT and DELETE requests are also supposed to be idempotent—PUTting the same thing repeatedly yields the same data that was PUT, while DELETE-ing the same thing repeatedly yields the same nothingness. HEAD requests, which are basically a GET returning headers only, are also idempotent.

POST had a simpler problem that could be avoided through careful programming, and a harder problem that was largely political:

- Pretty much nothing created with POST was bookmarkable, unless the receiving application immediately created a redirect to something reflecting the result of the POST. Entire applications were often written so that users could bookmark only the front page. For internal applications this might be tolerable, but all these POST requests also blocked search engines, which pretty much only used GET.

- Once it became clear that using GET for heavy lifting created problems, POST wound up carrying nearly all of the data transfers from users to the server, and then pretty much all purely computer-to-computer transfers. XML-RPC, SOAP, and most discussions of "web services" really meant "HTTP POST to a given URL" when they said Web.

The old way of working with the Web mostly worked, but it clearly had some dark corners and plenty of room for improvement. As it turned out, all the pieces needed for that improvement already existed.

Toward a Cleaner Approach

Although developers had become accustomed to using just these two methods, and browsers had given them the greatest support, HTTP had more pieces to offer than just GET and POST. The two most important of these are PUT and DELETE, which combine with GET and POST to give HTTP a complete set of verbs for manipulating data.

 HTTP also has a HEAD method, which is kind of a GET-lite frequently used to check on the freshness of cached data, and OPTIONS and TRACE. These aren't used explicitly in REST models.

How can you manage data with just POST, GET, PUT, and DELETE?

As it turns out, it's a familiar question for many programmers, who often work with the cheerfully named CRUD model, which stands for Create, Read, Update, and Destroy. If you've worked with SQL, you're already familiar with INSERT, SELECT, UPDATE, and DELETE. That basic set of verbs manages practically everything we do with databases, and the art of using SQL is about skillfully combining those generic verbs with specific data to accomplish the tasks you need to accomplish.

In Rails, this is typically described as show, create, update, and destroy, as you saw in the links in Figure 5-5. You'll also see that pattern in the controller Rails creates as part of the scaffolding. *Working this way requires a shift in the way developers think about controllers*, and about writing web applications generally.

The example created in the previous chapter treated the controller as a container for actions, for verbs. You could, if you wanted, write an entire Rails application in a single controller, with a method for every action it offers the user, and views to match. Those methods would then work with a variety of different models, getting information into and out of the application. If that became too large a mess, you could use a number of controllers to group different methods, though there would be lots of different ways to group them.

The example built with scaffolding takes a very different approach. The publicly available verbs are standardized—each controller implements the same verbs. Instead of being a container for a wide variety of actions, the controller becomes a standardized piece connecting a data model to the Web: a noun.

This maps perfectly to the way that REST expects the Web to work. Our familiar URLs (or Uniform Resource Identifiers, URIs, as REST prefers to call them) connect the client to a *resource* on the server. These resources are the nouns that the HTTP verbs work on, and the controller makes sure that those standardized verbs work in predictable ways on the data models underneath.

REST offers one last bonus. "Resources" are information, not necessarily information frozen into a particular representation. If a user wants the same information in XML instead of HTML, the resource should (if you're being nice, and Rails is nice by default) be able to provide the information as XML. By using Rails' RESTful features, you're not just creating a website, but a resource that other applications can interact with. This also makes it much easier to create Ajax applications on top of Rails, and to build mashups. Effectively, it's what a rich interpretation of "Web Services" should have meant in the first place.

 Thinking too hard about resources can lead to some complicated philosophical irritations. The authors have learned through painful experience that trying to sort out the proper relationship of XML namespaces to the resources that identify them is infinitely complicated, as is interpreting the meaning of a fragment identifier (*#id*) in any situation where the same resource can produce multiple data representations.

The answer to these irritations is simple: don't think about them. If you find yourself going down the resource philosophy rathole, step back and focus on something more practical. These issues can create the occasional practical problem, but generally they sit quietly unless stirred up.

Examining a RESTful Controller

Rails scaffolding is a very conscious implementation of REST, an example generally worth emulating and extending. Even in cases where browser limitations keep REST from working as simply as it should, Rails fills the gaps so that you can focus on building your application, not on corner cases. The simple one-field application shown earlier is enough to demonstrate the principles that Rails has used to generate the scaffolding.

Opening the *app/controllers/people_controller.rb* file reveals Example 5-1. It defines seven methods, each prefaced with a sample of the HTTP request that should call it. This chapter will explore each method individually, but take a moment to explore the whole thing and get a feel for what's going on, and how these methods are similar and different.

Example 5-1. A RESTful controller created as part of Rails scaffolding

```
class PeopleController < ApplicationController
  # GET /people
  # GET /people.xml
  def index
    @people = Person.find(:all)

    respond_to do |format|
      format.html # index.html.erb
      format.xml  { render :xml => @people }
    end
  end

  # GET /people/1
  # GET /people/1.xml
  def show
    @person = Person.find(params[:id])

    respond_to do |format|
      format.html # show.html.erb
      format.xml  { render :xml => @person }
    end
  end

  # GET /people/new
  # GET /people/new.xml
  def new
    @person = Person.new

    respond_to do |format|
      format.html # new.html.erb
      format.xml  { render :xml => @person }
    end
  end

  # GET /people/1/edit
  def edit
    @person = Person.find(params[:id])
  end

  # POST /people
  # POST /people.xml
```

```
  def create
    @person = Person.new(params[:person])

    respond_to do |format|
      if @person.save
        flash[:notice] = 'Person was successfully created.'
        format.html { redirect_to(@person) }
        format.xml  { render :xml => @person, :status => :created, :location =>
@person }
      else
        format.html { render :action => "new" }
        format.xml  { render :xml => @person.errors, :status =>
:unprocessable_entity }
      end
    end
  end

  # PUT /people/1
  # PUT /people/1.xml
  def update
    @person = Person.find(params[:id])

    respond_to do |format|
      if @person.update_attributes(params[:person])
        flash[:notice] = 'Person was successfully updated.'
        format.html { redirect_to(@person) }
        format.xml  { head :ok }
      else
        format.html { render :action => "edit" }
        format.xml  { render :xml => @person.errors, :status =>
:unprocessable_entity }
      end
    end
  end

  # DELETE /people/1
  # DELETE /people/1.xml
  def destroy
    @person = Person.find(params[:id])
    @person.destroy

    respond_to do |format|
      format.html { redirect_to(people_url) }
      format.xml  { head :ok }
    end
  end
end
```

How can this scaffold support seven methods when REST only has four verbs?
If you look closely, the first four methods are all based on GET requests for
slightly different things:

- The index method answers GET requests for a listing of all the available data.
- The show method answers GET requests to display a single record from the dataset.
- The new method answers GET requests for a form to create a new record. (It doesn't actually create a record directly—note the use inside the method of new but not save.)
- The edit method answers GET requests for an editable version of a single record from the dataset, gathering its components and sending them out as a form.

The other three methods are the other three REST verbs:

- The create method responds to POSTs that send new data to create a new record. If it can create it, the method then redirects to a page showing the new record.
- The update method responds to PUTs that send data modifying an already existing record. Like create, it tests whether the change was successful, and redirects.
- The destroy method responds to DELETEs, obliterating the requested record.

Figure 5-6 illustrates the processing paths these seven methods support and how they're reached.

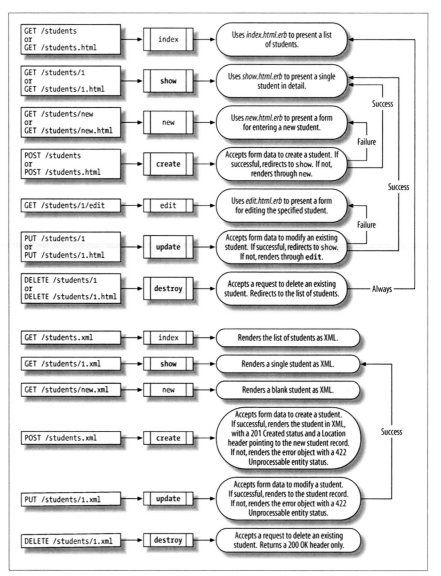

Figure 5-6. The many paths through a REST-based resource

All of these methods reach the controller thanks to the line the generator added to *routes.rb*:

```
map.resources :people
```

Unlike `map.connect`, which defined a simple routing by fragmenting the URL, `map.resources` expects a particular set of routes reflecting RESTful expectations. If you want to see the full set of routes it created, run `rake routes`. You'll see something like:

```
rake routes
(in /Users/simonstl/rails/guestbook)
             people GET    /people                      {:action=>"index",
:controller=>"people"}
   formatted_people GET    /people.:format              {:action=>"index",
:controller=>"people"}
                    POST   /people                      {:action=>"create",
:controller=>"people"}
                    POST   /people.:format              {:action=>"create",
:controller=>"people"}
         new_person GET    /people/new                  {:action=>"new",
:controller=>"people"}
 formatted_new_person GET  /people/new.:format          {:action=>"new",
:controller=>"people"}
        edit_person GET    /people/:id/edit             {:action=>"edit",
:controller=>"people"}
formatted_edit_person GET  /people/:id/edit.:format     {:action=>"edit",
:controller=>"people"}
             person GET    /people/:id                  {:action=>"show",
:controller=>"people"}
   formatted_person GET    /people/:id.:format          {:action=>"show",
:controller=>"people"}
                    PUT    /people/:id                  {:action=>"update",
:controller=>"people"}
                    PUT    /people/:id.:format          {:action=>"update",
:controller=>"people"}
                    DELETE /people/:id                  {:action=>"destroy",
:controller=>"people"}
                    DELETE /people/:id.:format          {:action=>"destroy",
:controller=>"people"}
                           /:controller/:action/:id
                           /:controller/:action/:id.:format
```

That's a huge collection of new pieces, but don't worry—the basic handling for all of those pieces has already been created for you.

If your applications stay simple enough, these methods will take care of most of your needs for getting information from views to models and back again. You're welcome to skip the next section and jump to the end of the chapter if you'd prefer to work on getting things built immediately, but there's much more to learn from these simple bits of code if you're interested. They are an excellent guide to the basics of getting things done in Rails.

Index: An Overview of Data

Example 5-2 contains the `index` method, the most likely starting point for a visitor exploring the data.

Example 5-2. The index method shows all the records in HTML or XML

```
# GET /people
# GET /people.xml
def index
  @people = Person.find(:all)

  respond_to do |format|
    format.html # index.html.erb
    format.xml  { render :xml => @people }
  end
end
```

As the comments indicate, this responds to requests for *people* or for *people.xml*. Just as Example 4-7 did, it makes a call to the `Person` model's `find` method, passing it the parameter `:all` to indicate that it should return everything. The big change here from the previous example is that this method can return the information as XML, not just as HTML, because of the `respond_to do |format|` block.

The `respond_to` method is a feature of `ActionController`, a wrapper that lets you create responses in various formats while building on the same data. The `format` object comes to the controller through Rails routing, typically identifying that a particular request wants a response in HTML, XML, or maybe JSON format. How does Rails know what the client wants? Through the HTTP Accept header and through the file extension on the URL. (In the routing files, you'll frequently see `:format` to pick up the file extension.)

 If you want to return JSON, you'll want to explore the `to_json` method.

Calls to `format` are testing whether this particular request wants that format as a response. If it does, Rails runs the block of code that follows `for mat.type`. The reference to the *index.html.erb* file is just a comment, set off by #. That comment (and others like it through the generated controller) is there to make it easier for humans to see what Rails will do, not to tell Rails what to do.

 If it's easier, you can think of `respond_to` as being like a `switch...case` statement, though the underlying mechanism is a little different. Figuring out exactly how it works is a project better reserved for when you're feeling very comfortable with Ruby—but you don't need a deep understanding of the details to use it.

The default scaffold tests for HTML and XML, though other formats, like JSON and RJS are available. This controller will, depending on what the client wants, either use the standard HTML-generating view for a response or generate an XML file from the @people object. Figure 5-7 shows how an XML response might look in the browser.

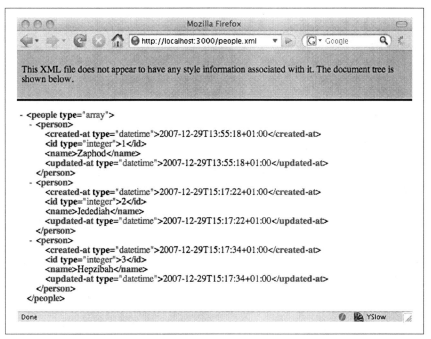

```
- <people type="array">
  - <person>
      <created-at type="datetime">2007-12-29T13:55:18+01:00</created-at>
      <id type="integer">1</id>
      <name>Zaphod</name>
      <updated-at type="datetime">2007-12-29T13:55:18+01:00</updated-at>
    </person>
  - <person>
      <created-at type="datetime">2007-12-29T15:17:22+01:00</created-at>
      <id type="integer">2</id>
      <name>Jedediah</name>
      <updated-at type="datetime">2007-12-29T15:17:22+01:00</updated-at>
    </person>
  - <person>
      <created-at type="datetime">2007-12-29T15:17:34+01:00</created-at>
      <id type="integer">3</id>
      <name>Hepzibah</name>
      <updated-at type="datetime">2007-12-29T15:17:34+01:00</updated-at>
    </person>
  </people>
```

Figure 5-7. An XML response listing people

 The render method isn't very picky about how it generates the XML. If you need to create XML that reliably maps to a particular schema, you'll probably want to use Builder templates to create specific XML views. However, even this default makes it easy to get started.

Show: Just One Row of Data

Example 5-3 contains the show method, the most likely starting point for a visitor exploring the data.

Example 5-3. The show method extracts one row of data to display

```
# GET /people/1
# GET /people/1.xml
```

```
def show
  @person = Person.find(params[:id])

  respond_to do |format|
    format.html # show.html.erb
    format.xml  { render :xml => @person }
  end
end
```

The only new feature here is the use of `find` with the `:id` value taken from the parameters. Rails' routing will populate the `:id` value based on the number following the controller name in the URL, whether or not a format is specified. The `:id` value is central to Rails' RESTful processing approach, as resources have controller names that identify their source and `:id` values that let users and developers focus more tightly on specific records.

New: A Blank Set of Data Fields

Example 5-4 contains the `new` method, which gives data to be added to the database its form.

Example 5-4. The new method collects data structure information and sends it to a form

```
# GET /people/new
# GET /people/new.xml
def new
  @person = Person.new

  respond_to do |format|
    format.html # new.html.erb
    format.xml  { render :xml => @person }
  end
end
```

The `new` method highlights Rails' strength in working flexibly with data structures. The call to `Person.new` creates a new blank data structure based on the `Person` model, but Rails uses that data structure in an unusual way. This controller will simply pass it to the view in *new.html.erb*, without ever having to consider questions like, "What is the schema for this data?" The controller is spared the problem of worrying about the structures that come through the model and can simply pass them on to the next level of Rails components.

Remember, the `new` method creates a blank data structure, but it doesn't actually do anything to the database. The blank structure created here will be used as a template for the view to do its work, and then thrown away. The actual changes to the database will come when the `create` method receives data for a new record, and it will populate and save a new record.

Edit: Hand Me That Data, Please

The edit method, shown in Example 5-5, is the last of the GET-based methods, and the simplest.

Example 5-5. The edit method collects a record to send it out for user editing.

```
# GET /people/1/edit
  def edit
    @person = Person.find(params[:id])
  end
```

edit retrieves a single Person record and passes it on to the view, which will populate a form with the data and let the user make changes. Like new, edit itself doesn't make any changes. The actual changes to the data will come in through the update method.

Create: Save Something New

The create method, shown in Example 5-6, is extremely busy relative to its peers, doing a lot of things other methods haven't done before.

Example 5-6. The create method saves an incoming record to the database

```
# POST /people
  # POST /people.xml
  def create
    @person = Person.new(params[:person])

    respond_to do |format|
      if @person.save
        flash[:notice] = 'Person was successfully created.'
        format.html { redirect_to(@person) }
        format.xml  { render :xml => @person, :status => :created,
:location => @person }
      else
        format.html { render :action => "new" }
        format.xml  { render :xml => @person.errors,
:status => :unprocessable_entity }
      end
    end
  end
```

The first thing that the create method does is create a new Person object based on the :person parameters from the form. The scaffolding forms, as the next chapter will demonstrate, return the data neatly packaged so that Rails doesn't have to inspect every field. It can move through as a unit.

The respond_to do |format| block also does much more here. It opens with:

```
    if @person.save
```

This does two things. First, it attempts to save the record to the database through the Person model. Second, @person.save returns a true or false value that the if statement will process to determine what it should send back to the user.

If it's true—i.e., the save was successful—the application uses the flash functionality (described in the next chapter, where you can see what it connects to) to let the user know the operation was a success.

Then, if the request wanted HTML back, it redirects the user to the show method for the new @person object, using the redirect_to helper method. (redirect_to understands the routing table and can reliably send the visitor to the right place.) If the request wanted XML back, it executes a more complicated rendering:

```
render :xml => @person, :status => :created, :location => @person
```

As it was for index and the other methods, the XML will be generated based on the @person object. The HTTP response will also include a 201 Created status header and identify its location as where the @person object can be shown. (200 OK is the normal header, though 404 Not Found is probably the header most people recognize.)

The response if there's an error—@person.save returned false—is to report back to the user, sending the incoming data to another copy of the form for creating people:

```
       else
          format.html { render :action => "new" }
          format.xml  { render :xml => @person.errors,
   :status => :unprocessable_entity }
       end
```

If an HTML response has been requested, the user will just get a blank field for a new entry attempt. If an XML response was requested, the sender will get a little more information back—a 422 Unprocessable Entity message and the errors from the @person object.

Put This Updated Record In

The update method, shown in Example 5-7, is much like the create method except that it responds to a PUT instead of a POST and updates a record instead of creating one. Otherwise, it's very similar.

Example 5-7. The update method changes a record and saves the result

```
# PUT /people/1
# PUT /people/1.xml
def update
```

```
  @person = Person.find(params[:id])

  respond_to do |format|
    if @person.update_attributes(params[:person])
      flash[:notice] = 'Person was successfully updated.'
      format.html { redirect_to(@person) }
      format.xml  { head :ok }
    else
      format.html { render :action => "edit" }
      format.xml  { render :xml => @person.errors,
:status => :unprocessable_entity }
    end
  end
end
```

The request will include an ID value in the URL that the Rails router will send as :id to the controller. Like a POST request, it will also come with parameters, which in this case will represent the updated data.

The key lines here are:

```
@person = Person.find(params[:id])
...
if @person.update_attributes(params[:person])
```

While the create method used new to create a fresh record from the parameters that arrived with the form, the update method uses find to get the record that is to be changed based on :id, and then it uses the update_attributes method to try changing those values to the parameters from the form. The value returned by update_attributes determines whether it sends back successful responses or an error message.

The successful response to an XML update is notably different from the successful response to an XML create—instead of sending the new XML document, all that the updater gets is HTTP headers, created with the head method, indicating a 200 OK response.

Destroy It

The final method is destroy, shown in Example 5-8, which responds to HTTP DELETE requests.

Example 5-8. The destroy method removes a Person record

```
# DELETE /people/1
  # DELETE /people/1.xml
  def destroy
    @person = Person.find(params[:id])
    @person.destroy

    respond_to do |format|
```

```
      format.html { redirect_to(people_url) }
      format.xml  { head :ok }
    end
  end
```

One notable aspect of this code is that it contains absolutely nothing that will ask the sender to reconsider. Make certain that your view code asks users if they really truly mean it *before* you call this method. (The views generated by the scaffolding do ask, fortunately.)

Destroying a record is a two-step process. First, Rails locates the object to destroy by its :id with the find method, and then it issues a call to that object's destroy method. Unlike save or update_attributes, the destroy method is just assumed to have happened. Since there isn't actually a record to show, the response uses a redirect to the main list of entries as its HTML response and a blank OK as its XML response.

 If you'd like to experiment with some much more powerful scaffolding, you might want to explore ActiveScaffold, which is available from *http://activescaffold.com/*. It goes far beyond the basics Rails provides, into Ajax and a higher level of automation.

Now that you've seen how all of these pieces work, it's time to do more creative things with the pieces. The next chapter will examine how to do a lot more with forms and data models and how to use the controller to connect them.

Micro-Applications

While much of the excitement around Rails lies in its ability to create large-scale Web 2.0 applications quickly, it has another powerful side that's less frequently discussed. Thanks to scaffolding and Rails' transparent use of SQLite, you can quickly and easily build smaller applications with Rails, keeping track of whatever information you'd like.

Even with a single table, it's easy to build things like address lists, infinitely expandable glossaries, expense trackers, and so on. With the multimodel approaches you'll learn in Chapter 9, you'll be able to build more sophisticated applications that manage a lot more data but still don't require huge amounts of effort to build or run. Add the authentication features in Chapter 12, and you can even share your applications with some friends.

Most people think of applications scaling up, but the ability to scale down comfortably makes it a lot easier to experiment with Rails development and to solve some of the minor data-handling problems life presents.

Escaping the REST Prison

While REST is extremely powerful, developers used to working in other environments may be cursing at this point, wondering whether they really need to build every part of their application according to this weird new paradigm.

Don't worry: you don't have to. You could, if you wanted, stick with the GET/POST approach shown in earlier chapters. Rails doesn't enforce RESTfulness.

However, you may want to explore a combination of approaches. If a page is only ever going to be reached with GET, use a simple controller and view or even a static page where appropriate. If a page needs to manage more sophisticated data input and output, then use REST to simplify that process. In a more complex application, it might make sense to use REST for cases where data is coming in or being edited, and to use simpler controllers for situations where the application is just presenting information.

The remainder of this book is going to use the combination approach. REST is just too convenient for getting structured data in and out of a website to ignore, but when REST isn't necessary, there's no need to let it dominate.

Test Your Knowledge

Quiz

1. How many files does Rails create in response to a single `script/generate scaffold` request?
2. In REST, how do HTTP GET, PUT, POST, and DELETE map to the "CRUD" of create, read, update, and destroy?
3. What does "idempotent" mean?
4. How do you make sure a result can be bookmarked?
5. Why do four basic REST functions end up making seven different methods in the controller?
6. What does `map.resources :people` mean?
7. How do you specify responses in different formats?
8. How does an ID value connect to a specific resource?
9. What happens if you send a Rails application a chunk of XML?

Answers

1. Rails creates a lot of files in response to a `script/generate scaffold` request, though some of them may exist already. It will create index, show, new, and edit view files, as well as one with the name of the object specified. It will also create a model, test, test fixture, migration, controller, test controller, and helper class, and add a route to the routing table. So, the answer is usually 12.

2. GET maps to read. POST maps to create. PUT maps to update. DELETE maps to destroy.

3. Idempotent means that you can call the same method as many times as you want and still get the same result. A GET request should be idempotent, and no matter how many GET requests you make, none of those GET requests will change what is returned on the next call.

4. The easiest way to make sure that something can be bookmarked is to make it consistently accessible through a GET request to a particular URL. (Making this work with other request methods often means presenting their results as a redirect to a GET. That way the results are bookmarkable, and the transaction only happens once.)

5. The four REST methods map neatly to CREATE, READ, UPDATE, and DELETE for a single resource, but there are a few other operations needed to make the application more usable to humans. All of them use GET. `index` shows a listing of all the resources available. The `new` method provides a form you can use to create a new resource. The `edit` method provides a form you can edit to modify an existing resource. Those forms then call the `create` and `update` methods, respectively.

6. `map.resources :people` creates a huge collection of routes that connect specific URLs to the REST methods for working with `:people` objects.

7. You can provide replies in different formats using the `respond to do | format|` call inside of a controller.

8. By default, the Rails uses REST-based routing to connect to resources whose primary key matches the ID value provided in the URI.

9. If you send the XML as part of a POST or PUT, Rails will check the XML to see if it matches Rails' expectations for the data structure that should go there. If it doesn't match, it will reply with an error. If it does match, it will create a new record based on the data (POST) or modify an existing record (PUT).

## CHAPTER 6

Presenting Models with Forms

The previous chapter showed how Rails makes it easy to create simple applications using scaffolding, but a key aspect of Rails scaffolding is that it isn't meant to be permanent. This doesn't necessarily mean that you'll tear it down completely and start over, but it usually means that you'll at least make substantial improvements to make it more attractive. This is especially important where information is coming in from users. While Rails scaffolding provides basic functionality, you're very likely going to want to improve on the forms it creates.

More Than a Name on a Form

To demonstrate a reasonably complete set of HTML form features, the application needs to support more than one data field and needs to support fields in a variety of different types. Rails, because it works with a wide variety of databases, supports a narrower set of types than each of those databases. The types of fields that Rails supports through ActiveRecord include:

```
:string
:text
:integer
:float
:decimal
:datetime
:timestamp
:time
:date
:binary
:boolean
```

The :string type is generally limited to 255 characters, whereas :text can hold longer data. The :integer, :float, and :decimal types all hold numbers, although integers may not have a fractional part to the right of the decimal point.

The :datetime, :timestamp, :time, and :date types hold the classically complicated combination values used to represent dates and times. The :binary type can hold unstructured binary data, often called BLOBs for Binary Large Objects. (You'll need to decide how you want to handle binary data—just stuffing it into a database isn't always the right answer.) Finally, the :boolean is the simplest type, accepting only the values of 1 and 0, equal to true and false.

HTML forms offer a variety of ways to enter data that doesn't map one-to-one to the data types Rails uses:

- Text fields (normal, hidden, and password)
- Text areas
- Checkboxes
- Radio buttons
- Selection lists (including multiple selections and grouped selections)
- File uploads
- Other buttons (submit, reset)

To demonstrate how these pieces work with ActiveRecord data types, we'll create an application with the following data fields:

Ordinary strings
    Name, secret, country, email

Long strings
    Description

Boolean
    "Can we send you email?"

Numbers
    An integer for specifying graduation year, a floating-point number for body temperature, and a decimal for price

Dates and Times
    The user's birthday and a favorite time of day

 File uploads deserve separate coverage, so we will explore them in Chapter 8 in the section "Adding a Picture by Uploading a File" on page 129."

Yes, these choices are somewhat whimsical, but they'll provide a framework in which to explore how Rails supports data types and how you can build on that support.

Generating HTML Forms with Scaffolding

Although this application is approaching the point beyond which much generated code becomes more of a hassle than a help, it makes sense to create one last round of scaffolding, replacing the application from the previous chapter. After this, we'll work within the same application for a while, as this kind of tearing down and rebuilding is only a good idea at the very, very beginning of a project.

To get started, create a new application. Move or rename the old guestbook application to get it out of the way, and then run `rails guestbook`. Then, run the following clunky mess from the command line at the top level of the newly created application:

```
script/generate scaffold Person name:string secret:string country:string
email:string description:text can_send_email:boolean graduation_year:integer
body_temperature:float price:decimal birthday:date favorite_time:datetime
```

This kind of long list of data structures in the scaffolding is annoying. It's hard to type, and what's worse, if you find that you made a mistake after you've already modified the generated code, you have a painful choice.

You can either rerun the scaffolding generation and lose all your changes to the logic, or you can modify the migration, the model, and the views by hand. Rails scaffolding generators just overwrite the old code—there's no support for more subtle fixes.

Neither of these is a fun way to fix a typo, so remember: when you first generate scaffolding, it's easier to get things right the first time. This doesn't mean you need to get everything right all at once—no one ever does—but adding new features to code is generally much more fun than fixing a typo. It may be easiest to set up the command in a text editor and then paste it in after checking it carefully. (You can also find the resulting files for this particular command in *ch06/guestbook004*.)

Before going further, examine the `self.up` method in the migration this created in *db/migrate/001_create_people.rb*, shown in Example 6-1. (It won't actually be *001_create_people.rb*—the *001* will be replaced by a timestamp in newer versions of Rails.)

Example 6-1. Creating a richer table with many data types from a migration

```
def self.up
    create_table :people do |t|
        t.string :name
        t.string :secret
        t.string :country
        t.string :email
        t.text :description
```

```
      t.boolean :can_send_email
      t.integer :graduation_year
      t.float :body_temperature
      t.decimal :price
      t.date :birthday
      t.time :favorite_time

      t.timestamps
    end
  end
```

As requested, Rails created a structure containing many fields of various types. For now, this will do for a demonstration, though eventually there will be change in the data model that requires change to the migration. Run `rake db:migrate`, and the migration will build the database table for the application.

Next, it's time to look at the form that Rails created for making new people, *app/views/people/new.html.erb*, shown in Example 6-2 with key features highlighted.

Example 6-2. The new.html.erb file contains basic form functionality

```erb
<h1>New person</h1>

<%= error_messages_for :person %>

<% form_for(@person) do |f| %>
  <p>
    <b>Name</b><br />
    <%= f.text_field :name %>
  </p>

  <p>
    <b>Secret</b><br />
    <%= f.text_field :secret %>
  </p>

  <p>
    <b>Country</b><br />
    <%= f.text_field :country %>
  </p>

  <p>
    <b>Email</b><br />
    <%= f.text_field :email %>
  </p>

  <p>
    <b>Description</b><br />
    <%= f.text_area :description %>
  </p>

  <p>
```

```
  <b>Can send email</b><br />
  <%= f.check_box :can_send_email %>
</p>

<p>
  <b>Graduation year</b><br />
  <%= f.text_field :graduation_year %>
</p>

<p></para>
  <b>Body temperature</b><br />
  <%= f.text_field :body_temperature %>
</p>

<p>
  <b>Price</b><br />
  <%= f.text_field :price %>
</p>

<p>
  <b>Birthday</b><br />
  <%= f.date_select :birthday %>
</p>

<p>
  <b>Favorite time</b><br />
  <%= f.datetime_select :favorite_time %>
</p>

<p>
  <%= f.submit "Create" %>
</p>
<% end %>

<%= link_to 'Back', people_path %>
```

There are some useful new features in the highlighted parts. First, at the top of the form, is:

```
<%= error_messages_for :person %>
```

This displays any validation errors in the data fields, an interface component you'll want to consider carefully as you develop richer data. (Do you want to present error messages at the top? Mixed in with the form? Both?)

The form_for method sets up an f variable that the other methods here will rely on for context. Because it is so central to form building with Rails, it is described in depth in the next section.

The :description, which is intended to be a longer piece of text, gets a textarea to contain it:

```
<%= f.text_area :description %>
```

Similarly, the boolean :can_send_email gets a checkbox:

```
<%= f.check_box :can_send_email %>
```

All of the numbers get plain text_fields, but the date and time are handled differently:

```
<%= f.date_select :birthday %>
...
<%= f.datetime_select :favoriteTime %>
```

Rails has its own set of controls for handling the always-thorny problem of entering dates and times. They might not be exactly the approach you prefer, but for now, they're the default. As you can see in Figure 6-1, they're easily the most intricate form control Rails generates by default, but using a series of drop-down boxes to specify a date and time isn't most people's idea of fun. Replacing them isn't simple, though.

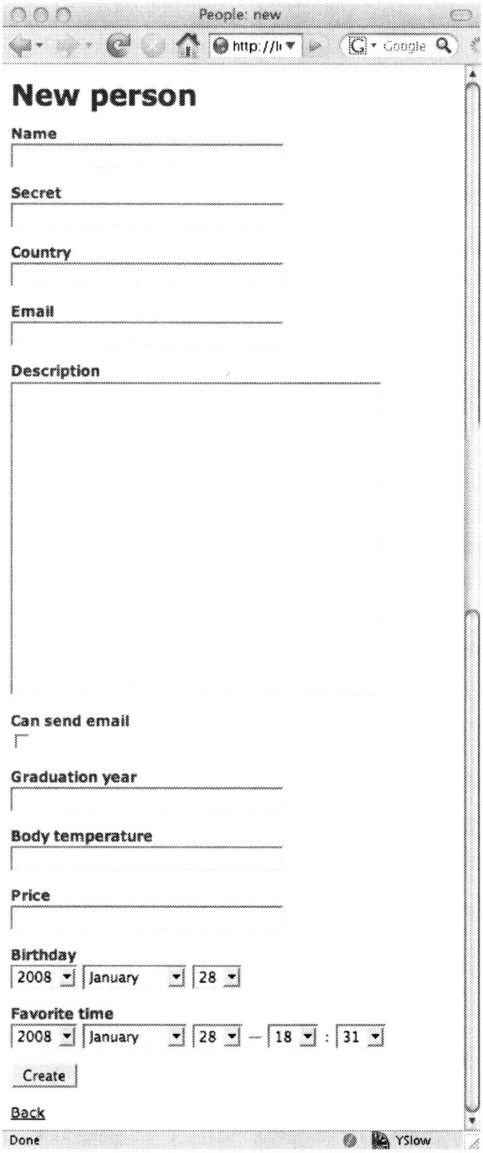

Figure 6-1. Basic form generated by Rails scaffolding

Figure 6-1 is a foundation for a form, but it's also a challenge. Users generally want something that is more exciting that this, and more helpful.

To create especially helpful forms, you'll likely want to use Ajax, as explored in Chapter 16. However, even without Ajax, there are lots of opportunities for improvement beyond what's shown here.

Form As a Wrapper

The form_for helper method sets up the entire form, creating the HTML form element but also providing context for all of the fields in the form. The form_for method is a bit sneaky, too. Both the *new.html.erb* view and the *edit.html.erb* view use form_for the same way:

```
<% form_for(@person) do |f| %>
...
<% end %>
```

However, the generated form element looks very different, depending on what exactly is in @person. If @person is just an empty object structure, form_for will work on the assumption that this is to create a new object. If @person actually contains data, however, form_for will assume that its form is editing that object and create a different-looking form element, plus a hidden field to enable Rails' REST capabilities.

When given an empty @person object, form_for prepares for a new person:

```
<form action="/people" class="new_person" id="new_person" method="post"><div
style="margin:0;padding:0"><input name="authenticity_token" type="hidden"
value="f80a01b9f14d38e0816877e832637e3cc9e668a1" /></div>
```

Note that the action goes to people, generically. The class and id reflect a new person, and the method is simply post.

When given an @person object with content, however, form_for switches to editing a person:

```
<form action="/people/1" class="edit_person" id="edit_person_1" method="post">
<div style="margin:0;padding:0"><input name="_method" type="hidden"
value="put" /><input name="authenticity_token" type="hidden"
value="f80a01b9f14d38e0816877e832637e3cc9e668a1" /></div>
```

The action now goes to a URL that includes the ID of the object being edited, and the class and id attributes change values. The method stays at post—but the hidden input with the name _method almost immediately after the form is there to indicate that it should really be treated as a put. (As Chapter 5 noted, browsers don't all support the HTTP verbs PUT and DELETE, so this input element is designed to help Rails get around that, using POST but indicating that it should be treated differently.)

Rails' REST capabilities make form_for seem extra smart, but if you're not creating forms explicitly for a RESTful environment, you need to know a few more things about this method. form_for understands Rails' routing and will choose its attributes based on that routing.

The form_for method is part of ActionView's FormHelper module, and the way that Rails' RESTful scaffolding uses it relies quite completely on its default behavior. Rails takes @person as its one clue to what you want and treats it as a much more complex call to form_for. The form_for object can take more arguments:

A type
> Instead of just listing @person and letting form_for guess at the structure we intended, this could have specified :person as the type, followed by the @person object.

A URL
> The :url named parameter lets you specify a URL for the action attribute. It's unlikely that you'll just point directly to a URL, unless it's one outside of your Rails application. More typically you'll ask Rails to create a URL that points to a controller in your application, something like :url => { :action => "celebrate" }.

HTML attributes
> The scaffolding populated the form element's method, class, and id attributes automatically, but if you wanted to specify an id of spe cial_form, a class of my_form, and a method of put, you could specify:

```
:html => { :id => 'special_form', :class => 'my_form', method => 'put' }
```

Combined into one, somewhat strange call, this could look like:

```
<% form_for :person, @person, :url => { :action => "celebrate" },
:html => { :id => 'special_form', :class => 'my_form',
method => 'put' } do |f| %>
```

The form_for method also sets up the variable f, which provides the context all of the other fields will need to do their work, letting you use a shorter form to call their helper methods. (You don't have to call this variable f, but it's a conveniently short while still memorable-enough name.)

Also, Rails has created an input element named authenticity_token, which is based on the session ID. Rails uses this internally to minimize cross-site request forgery (CSRF) attacks, as discussed in Chapter 18. This only gets used for PUT, POST, and DELETE requests—GET requests should all be safe by design. (If, of course, you designed your application so that GET requests just return information, not change it.)

If other developers want to script your Rails application from the outside, they certainly can—that's what the XML side of REST is for.

Finally, you should know that you can create forms in Rails applications without using form_for. You can, of course, create HTML forms by hand. Rails also offers the form_tag method for creating forms as well as a set of form field helper methods (also ending in _tag) if you want to create forms programmatically, but aren't binding them directly to a model.

Creating Text Fields and Text Areas

Rails' scaffolding included only two kinds of text fields in the body of the form:

```
<%= f.text_field :name %>
...
<%= f.text_area :description %>
```

Creating a field using text_field results in a single-line form field, generating HTML like:

```
<input id="person_name" name="person[name]" size="30" type="text" />
```

The text_area results aren't much more complicated, though they support rows and columns rather than just a size in characters:

```
<textarea cols="40" id="person_description" name="person[description]"
rows="20"></textarea>
```

Both of these use a convention to come up with an id attribute, one that could be handy if you need to apply stylesheets. Both also use a convention to create the name attribute, *type[property]*, which you'll need to know if you want to create HTML forms by hand that feed into Rails controllers. The rest is fairly generic—a size of 30 characters for the text_field and 40 columns by 20 rows for the text_area.

If you want to add more attribute values to your text_area or text_field, or change the default values, you can just add named parameters. For example, to change the size of the description to 30 columns by 10 rows, you could write:

```
<%= f.text_area :description, :cols => 30, :rows => 10 %>
```

This will generate:

```
<textarea cols="30" id="person_description" name="person[description]"
rows="10"></textarea>
```

That same approach works for any attribute you want to add or modify, though you should definitely be cautious about modifying the name attribute, which the Rails controller will use to figure out which data maps to which object property.

There are two other options for text fields that Rails supports. You've already seen Rails use the first, hidden fields, for things like the `authenticity_token` field and the `_method` hack, but both of those just kind of happened. If you want to create an explicit hidden field, use the `hidden_field` method, like:

```
<%= f.hidden_field :graduation_year %>
```

The graduation year value will be included in the page, but not visibly:

```
<input id="person_graduation_year" name="person[graduation_year]"
type="hidden" />
```

(Hidden fields are probably not what you want in forms creating new objects, but you may find other uses for them elsewhere in your applications.)

The other type of text field is useful mostly for passwords and related tasks. You can create a password field using the `password_field` method. In this example, it would be good for hiding the `secret` field, as in:

```
<%= f.password_field :secret %>
```

which generates:

```
<input id="person_secret" name="person[secret]" size="30"
type="password" />
```

That input field will put up asterisks for each character entered, hiding the value of the field from shoulder-surfing wrong-doers.

> You can use `text_area`, `text_field`, and the other form-field-generator methods without the `f` context object at the start of them. If you want to do that, you need to specify an object directly in the call, though, as the first argument. That would look like:
>
> ```
> <%= text_area :person, :description %>
> ```
>
> instead of:
>
> ```
> <%= f.text_area :description %>
> ```
>
> You can use either version within a `form_for` tag, which is very helpful when you need to mix code from multiple sources.
>
> If you're looking through the Rails API documentation and wondering why what they describe looks a bit different from what you're writing, this may be the cause of the disconnect.

Creating Checkboxes

Checkboxes are mostly simple. They can be checked or not checked, and Rails maps their contents to a boolean value transparently. This simple request for a checkbox:

```
<%= f.check_box :can_send_email %>
```

yields this bit of HTML:

```
<input id="person_can_send_email" name="person[can_send_email]" type="checkbox"
value="1" /><input name="person[can_send_email]" type="hidden" value="0" />
```

That's a little more complicated than expected, though. Why is there a second input element of type hidden? It's another Rails workaround, providing a default value in case the checkbox isn't checked:

> Since HTTP standards say that unchecked checkboxes don't post anything, we add a hidden value with the same name as the checkbox as a workaround.[*]

If the checkbox is checked, that value will go through. If not, the value of the hidden input with the same name will go through.

The check_box method has a few more tricks to offer. As was possible with the text fields, you can specify additional attributes—perhaps class for CSS styling?—with named parameters:

```
<%= f.check_box :can_send_email, :class => 'email' %>
```

This will produce a checkbox with a class attribute:

```
<input class="email" id="person_can_send_email" name="person[can_send_email]"
type="checkbox" value="1" /><input name="person[can_send_email]" type="hidden"
value="0" />
```

You can also specify that the box should be checked if you want, which will override the value that comes into the form from the underlying object. Use this with caution:

```
<%= f.check_box :can_send_email, {:class => 'email', :checked=>"checked"} %>
```

Notice that there are now curly braces around the arguments that specify attributes. They aren't strictly necessary, but checkboxes allow for some additional arguments where they will be necessary, even if there is only one attribute given a value. More precisely, you can also specify return values in place of 1 and 0 if you'd like, if your code is set up to support them:

```
<%= f.check_box :can_send_email, {:class => 'email'}, "yes", "no" %>
```

This will generate:

[*] From the API docs (*http://api.rubyonrails.com/classes/ActionView/Helpers/FormHelper .html*).

```
<input class="email" id="person_can_send_email" name="person[can_send_email]"
type="checkbox" value="yes" /><input name="person[can_send_email]" type="hidden"
value="no" />
```

For most of the helper functions that create form components, the options
hash is the last argument, and you can just list the named parameters for the
attribute values at the end, without the braces around them. However, because
checkboxes have the arguments for checked and unchecked values *after* the
options hash, you need to specify the attributes in the middle, in curly braces,
if you specify values for checked and unchecked. Ruby will give you strange
errors if the braces are missing and the values appear at the end. (If you don't
specify values for checked and unchecked, you can just include named parameters without the braces as usual.)

 If you're using Rails' built-in boolean type to store data from
your checkboxes, don't specify values for checked and unchecked. The default 1 and 0 are correct for this situation, and
Rails won't know what to do with other values (unless, of
course, you provide code for processing them).

Creating Radio Buttons

Creating radio buttons is a little more complicated and not something that the
scaffolding will do for you. Just as when you create radio buttons in HTML,
radio buttons in Rails are created as independent objects, united only by a
naming convention. Radio buttons are often effectively used for small selection
lists, so this example will focus on the country field, offering just a few options.

For the first round, we'll just create some linked buttons by brute force, as
shown in Example 6-3.

Example 6-3. Asking Rails to create a specific list of linked radio buttons

```
<p>
    <b>Country</b><br />
    <%= f.radio_button :country, 'USA' %> USA<br />
    <%= f.radio_button :country, 'Canada' %> Canada<br />
    <%= f.radio_button :country, 'Mexico' %> Mexico<br />
</p>
```

This will generate the result shown in Figure 6-2.

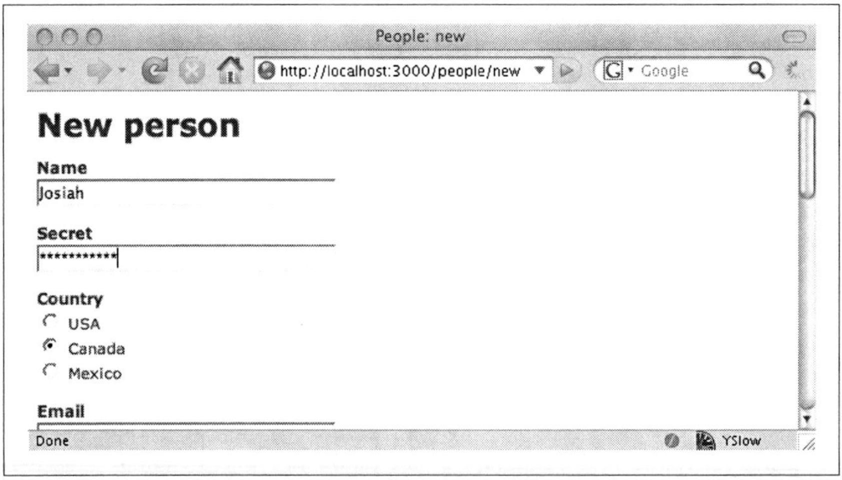

Figure 6-2. Simple radio buttons added to a Rails-based form

The HTML this created is pretty simple:

```
<p>
    <b>Country</b><br />
    <input id="person_country_usa" name="person[country]" type="radio"
value="USA" /> USA<br />
    <input id="person_country_canada" name="person[country]" type="radio"
value="Canada" /> Canada<br />
    <input id="person_country_mexico" name="person[country]" type="radio"
value="Mexico" /> Mexico<br />
</p>
```

If the underlying :country object had had a value that matched any of these, Rails would have added a checked="checked" attribute to the input element. Since it's a new object, none of these is checked by default and the user has to check one themselves.

You probably won't always want to specify each of the buttons and its label by hand in the view template. Creating a set of radio buttons from a hash isn't difficult and makes it easier for a controller to specify what should appear in a view. Example 6-4 creates a hash (this should normally come from the controller), sorts it, and then uses it to create a set of four radio buttons.

Example 6-4. Creating a sorted set of linked radio buttons from a hash

```
<% nations = { 'United States of America' => 'USA', 'Canada' => 'Canada', 'Mexico'
=> 'Mexico', 'United Kingdom' => 'UK' }%>

  <p>
    <b>Country</b><br />
    <% list = nations.sort
```

```
list.each {|x| %>
  <%= f.radio_button :country, x[1] %> <%= h(x[0]) %><br />
<% } %>
</p>
```

The first line creates a `nations` hash. The long names act as keys to shortened country names as values. Why? Well, if you think about how radio buttons work, human users are selecting the keys (the long names) that lead to the values (the short names) that we actually send to the computer. (This will also make it much easier to change the radio buttons into a selection list later.)

Within the area that previously listed radio buttons explicitly, there is Ruby code that sorts the hash into an array, using `sort`. Then `list.each` loops over the array, running once for each object in the array. In this case, because the hash had two values, the x array that comes out of the loop contains the key, indexed at 0, and the value, indexed at 1. The next line puts the key, `x[0]`, into the value of the radio button and uses the longer name, `x[1]`, for the label, using the `f.radio_button` method to create the actual markup.

Figure 6-3 shows the resulting radio buttons. The generated HTML underneath them looks like:

```
<p>
    <b>Country</b><br />

        <input id="person_country_canada" name="person[country]" type="radio"
value="Canada" /> Canada<br />

        <input id="person_country_mexico" name="person[country]" type="radio"
value="Mexico" /> Mexico<br />

        <input id="person_country_uk" name="person[country]" type="radio"
value="UK" /> United Kingdom<br />

        <input id="person_country_usa" name="person[country]" type="radio"
value="USA" /> United States of America<br />

    </p>
```

Figure 6-3. Radio buttons generated from a sorted hash

Of course, you won't usually generate radio buttons by declaring a hash explicitly. Radio buttons and selection lists are both typically used in Rails to connect one data model to another. Chapter 9 will get into greater detail about how multiple models work.

Creating Selection Lists

Selections lists are, in many ways, like radio buttons on a larger scale. Rather than filling a screen with radio buttons, a list lets you hide the options except during that critical time when you're actually making a selection. Showing radio buttons for over 190 countries would take up a huge amount of screen real estate. Selection lists offer a much more compact but still convenient way for users to make choices.

Rails has a number of helper methods for creating selection lists, but the simplest place to start is the `select` method. In its most basic form, `select` takes two arguments: the attribute that populates it and a set of choices. Choices can be represented in a number of different ways, from a simple array of strings to a hash or other more complex set of values.

At the time this was written, this simplest form of select wasn't actually documented in the Rails API docs. If you look at the documentation for a function and it seems like it's more complex than you need, it's sometimes worth experimenting to see whether a simpler form will work. The docs often seem to give priority to more complex use cases. (As you become a guru, you'll likely be able to look at the Rails source code and figure it out, but Ruby's many options make it tricky at first.)

Using an array of strings, the call to create a selection list might look like:

```
<p>
    <b>Country</b><br />
    <%= f.select (:country, ['Canada', 'Mexico', 'United Kingdom', 'United States of
America'])%>
</p>
```

This generates:

```
<p>
    <b>Country</b><br />
    <select id="person_country" name="person[country]"><option
value="Canada">Canada</option>
<option value="Mexico">Mexico</option>

<option value="United Kingdom">United Kingdom</option>
<option value="United States of America">United States of America</option></select>
    </p>
```

When working from a simple list of strings, Rails creates option elements whose value attributes—the values sent back to the server—are the same as the content displayed to the user, as shown in Figure 6-4.

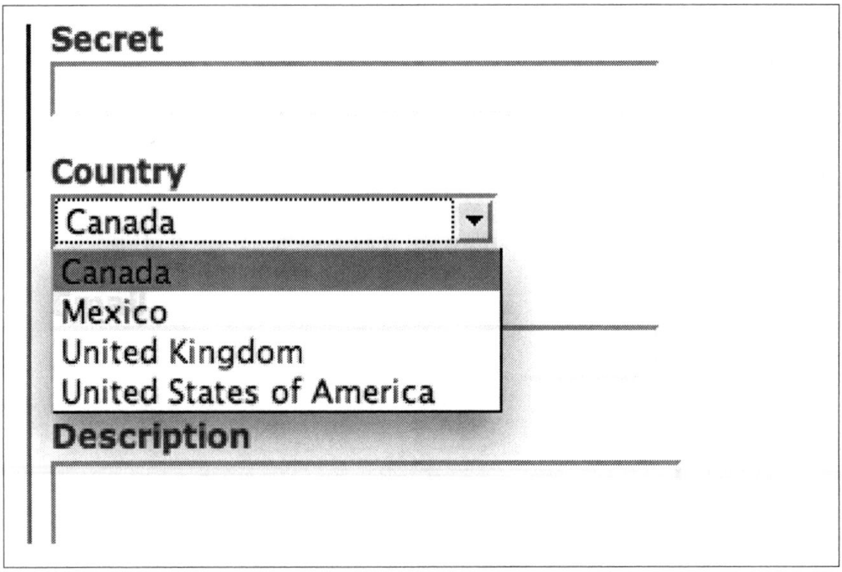

Figure 6-4. A selection list created from an array of strings

You can be a little more specific about what you want by using a two-dimensional array. The display values come first, and the values that go to the server come second:

```
<p>
    <b>Country</b><br />
    <%= f.select (:country, [ ['Canada', 'Canada'],
                              ['Mexico', 'Mexico'],
                              ['United Kingdom', 'UK'],
                              ['United States of America', 'USA'] ])%>
</p>
```

This still looks the same as the result in Figure 6-4, but the underlying HTML has changed a bit:

```
<p>
    <b>Country</b><br />
    <select id="person_country" name="person[country]"><option
value="Canada">Canada</option>
<option value="Mexico">Mexico</option>

<option value="UK">United Kingdom</option>
<option value="USA">United States of America</option></select>
</p>
```

The new value attributes for the United Kingdom and United States of America reflect the explicit choices made in the underlying array.

You can also set a default choice for your selections by adding a `selected` named parameter:

```
<%= f.select (:country, [ ['Canada', 'Canada'],
                          ['Mexico', 'Mexico'],
                          ['United Kingdom', 'UK'],
                          ['United States of America', 'USA'] ],
                :selected => 'USA')%>
```

This generates the same markup, except that the `option` element for USA now looks like:

```
<option value="USA" selected="selected">United States of America</option>
```

You can also use `select` with a hash, instead of specifying the array. Example 6-5 shows how this looks much like it did for the radio buttons in Example 6-4.

Example 6-5. Creating a sorted selection list from a hash

```
<% nations = { 'United States of America' => 'USA', 'Canada' => 'Canada', 'Mexico'
=> 'Mexico', 'United Kingdom' => 'UK' }%>

  <p>
    <b>Country</b><br />
        <% list = nations.sort %>
        <%= f.select :country, list %>
  </p>
```

Rails also offers a number of specific selection fields, including one for countries (`country_select`) and one for time zones (`time_zone_select`). Additionally, if you decide that you want to get really fancy, you can create multilevel selection lists with `option_groups_from_collection_for_select`. You can also create selection lists that let users choose multiple values by setting the `:multiple` option to `true`.

The `country_select` method has proven a bit controversial, mostly because of the base list of countries it uses. Future versions of Rails may be moving it out of the main framework and into a plug-in.

Dates and Times

Rails also provides support for basic date and time entry, as was shown in the form generated by the scaffolding. The scaffolding started out with:

```
  <p>
    <b>Birthday</b><br />
    <%= f.date_select :birthday %>
  </p>

  <p>
```

```
<b>Favorite time</b><br />
<%= f.datetime_select :favorite_time %>
</p>
```

And these generated the neat-looking but very inconvenient selection lists shown in Figure 6-5.

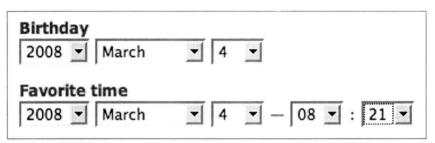

Figure 6-5. Rails default approach of using selection lists for dates and times

Besides the `date_select` and `datetime_select` methods, Rails also offers `time_select` and has a variety of helper methods for individual pieces of dates and times. Rails offers some options that can make these interfaces more customizable, but picking days off a 31-item selection list or minutes off a 60-item list is pretty much always going to be a less-than-fun user experience. You'll probably want to turn to more attractive date and time interfaces from Ajax libraries or revert to simple text boxes, but in case you have an application where you want to use these methods, the options for them include:

`:start_year`
> By default, Rails sets the start year to five years before the current date. You can specify an earlier (or later) date if you need to, by specifying `:start_year => `*value*.

`:end_year`
> Rails also sets the end year to five years after the current date. Again, you can specify a later (or earlier) date by specifying `:end_year => `*value*.

`:use_month_numbers`
> If you'd prefer to have the months listed by number rather than by name, set `:use_month_numbers => true`.

`:discard_day`
> Some date applications don't need days. You can set `:discard_day => true` to simply not include the day field. You can also do the same with `:discard_month` or `:discard_year`, and for times and datetimes, you can do the same with `:discard_hour`, `:discard_minute`, and `:discard_sec onds`.

`:disabled`

> Setting `:disabled => true` tells Rails to show the date, but doesn't allow change. The values will appear in gray.

`:include_blank`

> Setting `:include_blank => true` tells Rails to include a blank choice at the top of each selection list, so users don't have to specify every single component of a date.

`:include_seconds`

> Specifying `:include_seconds => true` adds a field for seconds to times and datetimes.

`:order`

> Using the `order` option lets you specify the sequence for the different components of the date or time. You list the components as an array, such as `:order => [:month, :day, :year]`.

Labels

Rails supports a common feature of HTML that makes forms feel much more professional: labels. When labels are explicitly connected to the fields, clicking on the label shifts focus to the field. It gives users a bigger target to hit and simplifies accessibility as well.

Labels are easy. To make the headline "Name" associate with the field right below it, the scaffolding code uses:

```
<p>
    <%= f.label :name %><br />
    <%= f.text_field :name %>
</p>
```

The generated HTML contains a bit of extra information the browser uses to make the association:

```
<p>
    <b><label for="person_name">Name</label></b><br />
    <input id="person_name" name="person[name]" size="30" type="text" />
</p>
```

If you click on the word "Name," focus will shift to the field for entering a name just below it.

If you want the label to say something other than the name of the field, just add a string as the second argument, as in:

```
<%= f.label :name, 'Your name' %>
```

This will generate:

```
<b><label for="person_name">Your name</label></b><br />
```

The label method is a nice feature, but at the same time it seems as if there's a good deal of repetition going on in this code.

Creating Helper Methods

So far, this chapter has shown you how to use a number of the helper methods that come with Rails. You can also create your own helper methods. There are lots of good reasons to do so:

Less repetition
> You can come closer to Rails' DRY (Don't Repeat Yourself) ideal if you can combine multiple pieces into a single invocation.

More readable code
> You can see more obviously which pieces of your code are actually doing the same work when they call the same method, instead of perpetually reinventing the wheel.

More consistency
> The same code used in multiple places will rarely stay identical.

Sharing across views
> Multiple views within an application can reference the same helper methods.

Creating helper methods might not be your very first priority in creating an application, but once you have a basic idea of what you want to create in your views, it's a good idea to start assembling common tasks into helper methods.

Within the application directory structure, helper methods go into the *app/helpers* directory. At this point, the guestbook application will have two files there: *application_helper.rb* and *people_helper.rb*. Helper methods that are defined in *application_helper.rb* are available to views throughout the entire Rails application, whereas methods defined in *people_helper.rb* are only available to views that pertain to operations on the **person** model. For now, the helper methods built in this section can go in *people_helper.rb* and graduate to *application_helper.rb* if you think they're worth sharing across the application.

If you have helper methods with the same names in *people_helper.rb* and in *application_helper.rb*, the method in *people_helper.rb* will take precedence.

The first helper method will take the Example 6-4 code for generating radio buttons from a hash. Example 6-6 shows what's left when this is reduced to a call to the buttons helper method.

Example 6-6. Creating a sorted set of linked radio buttons from a hash

```
<% nations = { 'United States of America' => 'USA', 'Canada' => 'Canada', 'Mexico'
=> 'Mexico', 'United Kingdom' => 'UK' }%>

<p>
  <b>Country</b><br />
  <%= buttons(:person, :country, nations) %>
</p>
```

The buttons method is in the *people_helper.rb* file, the contents of which are shown in Example 6-7.

Example 6-7. Creating a sorted set of linked radio buttons from a hash

```
1   module PeopleHelper
2
3   def buttons(model_name, target_property, button_source)
4       html=''
5       list = button_source.sort
6       list.each do|x|
7         html << radio_button(model_name, target_property, x[1])
8         html << h(x[0])
9         html << '<br />'
10      end
11      return html
12  end
13
14  end
```

There's a lot going on in the buttons method. It's contained by the People Helper module, which was originally empty in the version created by the scaffolding. Lines 2 through 13 are all new additions. This version of buttons, defined starting on line 3, looks more like the older version of the helper functions, taking a model name as its first argument, then the targeted property, and then the source from which the radio buttons will be created.

Because the helper function isn't in the view, there isn't any ERb markup here. Instead, the helper function builds a string, starting in line 4. Often, the first declaration of the string includes the first tag, but as the radio buttons don't have a containing element, this starts with the empty string. Lines 5 and 6 are the same logic for sorting the hash as was used in the original code from Example 6-3, but the contents of the loop, in lines 7 to 9, are very different.

Lines 7 through 9 all append something to the html variable, using the << operator. Line 7 appends radio button markup created through Rails' radio_but ton helper. Line 8 appends the text the user will see, and line 9 appends a <br / > tag, putting a line break between the buttons. Rails developers often avoid mixing explicit markup with code, preferring to use content_tag or other helper methods—but you can use markup here if you think it's appropriate.

Line 10 just closes the loop over the hash, but line 11 is a bit unusual. Explicit return statements aren't necessary in Ruby methods unless you're returning multiple results or want to break at an unexpected time. Ruby will assume that the last variable you touched is the return value. However, using return is a good way to avoid surprises, and if you feel like writing briefer code, you can leave off return and just write html there.

If you leave off line 11 completely, however, you'll have an unpleasant surprise, shown in Figure 6-6. It looks like html was the last variable touched in line 9, but the each loop block, which closes in line 10, is actually considered the last thing touched. The value of the block is the underlying array, which gets mashed together to yield this unfortunate result.

Country
CanadaCanadaMexicoMexicoUnited KingdomUKUnited States of AmericaUSA

Figure 6-6. Instead of radio buttons, an unpleasant squashed list

Letting Helper Methods Make Choices

A more sophisticated helper method, shown in Example 6-8, could check the list of items to select from, and decide whether to represent it as a radio buttons or a list, depending on length. It adds an extra if statement, highlighted in the code. This may or may not be a level of smarts you want to build into your helper methods, but it certainly demonstrates how custom helper methods can assemble just a little more logic for your views.

Example 6-8. A helper method that chooses between radio buttons and selection lists

```
def button_select(model_name, target_property, button_source)
    html=''
    list = button_source.sort
    if list.length <4
      list.each {|x|
        html << radio_button(model_name, target_property, x[1])
        html << h(x[0])
```

```
      html << '<br />'
      }
    else
      html << select(model_name, target_property, list)
    end

    return html
    end
end
```

There are a lot more things you could do in a helper method, from adding labels to your form components (addressing a complaint from the previous section) to handling calculations.

A More Elegant Helper Method

While the helper method in Example 6-8 works, its foundation is a loop that builds a long string of HTML, using the << operator to concatenate additional content. Example 6-9 is a slightly more idiomatic Ruby version, skipping the creation of an explicit html variable and letting Ruby's default handling of return values handle what gets sent back to the page.

Example 6-9. A more elegant version of the helper method

```
def button_select(model_name, target_property, button_source)
    list = button_source.sort
    if list.length < 4
      list.collect do |item|
          radio_button(model_name, target_property, item[1]) +
h(item[0])
      end.join('<br />')
    else
      select(model_name, target_property, list)
    end
end
```

Putting the Form Body in a Partial

All the changes to the *new.html.erb* form are great, but there's still one annoying problem: the *edit.html.erb* form needs to be consistent with *new.html.erb*. For some reason, the Rails scaffolding ignores the "Don't Repeat Yourself" mantra, and puts duplicate code into both pages.

Fortunately, Rails also provides a mechanism that lets you avoid this duplication. Example 6-10 shows the new version of the *new.html.erb* form, and Example 6-11 shows the new version of the *edit.html.erb* form.

Example 6-10. new.html.erb, using a partial

```
<h1>New person</h1>

<%= render :partial => 'form' %>

<%= link_to 'Back', people_path %>
```

Example 6-11. edit.html.erb, using a partial

```
<h1>Editing person</h1>

<%= render :partial => 'form' %>

<%= link_to 'Show', @person %> |
<%= link_to 'Back', people_path %>
```

Where'd all the actual content go? Into another file in the same *app/views/ people* directory, called *_form.html.erb*, shown in Example 6-12. The underscore at the start of the name tells Rails that this is a file containing a partial, and when Rails goes looking for a partial referenced from either of these *.html.erb* files, it will seek *_form.html.erb*. Example 6-12 skips any reference to either new or edited material—which is fine, since the original code worked either way.

Example 6-12. The _form.html.erb file's contents

```
<%= error_messages_for :person %>

<% form_for(@person) do |f| %>
  <p>
    <b>Name</b><br />
    <%= f.text_field :name %>
  </p>

  <p>
    <b>Secret</b><br />
    <%= f.text_field :secret %>
  </p>

  <p>
    <b>Country</b><br />
    <%= f.select (:country, [ ['Canada', 'Canada'],
                              ['Mexico', 'Mexico'],
                              ['United Kingdom', 'UK'],
                              ['United States of America', 'USA'] ]) %>
  </p>

  <p>
    <b>Email</b><br />
    <%= f.text_field :email %>
  </p>
```

```
<p>
  <b>Description</b><br />
  <%= f.text_area :description, :rows => 10, :cols => 30 %>
</p>

<p>
  <b>Can send email</b><br />
  <%= f.check_box :can_send_email %>
</p>

<p>
  <b>Graduation year</b><br />
  <%= f.text_field :graduation_year %>
</p>

<p>
  <b>Body temperature</b><br />
  <%= f.text_field :body_temperature %>
</p>

<p>
  <b>Price</b><br />
  <%= f.text_field :price %>
</p>

<p>
  <b>Birthday</b><br />
  <%= f.date_select :birthday %>
</p>

<p>
  <b>Favorite time</b><br />
  <%= f.datetime_select :favorite_time %>
</p>

<p>
  <%= f.submit "Submit" %>
</p>
<% end %>
```

Partials are great for avoiding some kinds of repetition, offering a flexible means of sharing consistent pieces of pages across your application. Chapter 8 will cover a few additional options that might help you do even better at avoiding repetition.

Test Your Knowledge

Quiz

1. How many properties and data types can you specify in a call to `script/generate scaffold`?
2. Where does Rails actually specify the data types for properties?
3. What is the difference between the `form_for` method and the `form_tag` method explored earlier?
4. How do you add HTML attributes to the HTML generated by Rails' helper methods?
5. Why does Rails' `check_box` helper create an extra hidden form field?
6. How do you specify which option in a selection box is the default?
7. Where should you put helper methods you create?
8. Why would you use a partial?

Answers

1. As many as your operating system will let you put on a single command line. They get inconvenient quickly—if you want to add a huge number, you may want to edit that command line in a text editor and make sure it's right before putting it in.
2. The only place that the data types are specified *in Rails* is in the migrations. Once the migrations build the database, Rails gets its understanding of the data types from the database. (This is very different from Java development, for example.)
3. The `form_for` method creates an entire environment with context based on an `ActiveRecord` class that other helper methods can use to create their own fields within the form. The `form_tag` method is mostly about wrapping the form in an appropriate form tag. The helpers called inside of `form_tag` are on their own.
4. You can generate HTML attributes using named parameters put inside of a parameter named :html, such as :html => { :id => 'per son_form', :class => 'generic_form' }, or you can just pass the parameters directly, without wrapping them in the :html => { ... }.
5. The `input` element with a `hidden` type is there to ensure that a value is returned to the Rails application if the checkbox isn't checked.
6. You specify a default value with the :selected named parameter.

7. Helper methods go in the *app/helpers* directory. Helpers that should be available across the entire application go into *application_helper.rb*, while helpers that apply to a specific view go into files named `viewname_helper.rb`.

8. Partials let you put code that would otherwise repeat across your application into a single convenient location. They're a perfect example of Rails' support for its "Don't Repeat Yourself" mantra.

## CHAPTER 7

Strengthening Models with Validation

At this point, you have most of the ingredients needed to create simple web applications in Rails, provided you're willing to stick to a single database table. There's one large problem remaining: users (and programs connecting through web services) don't always put in the data you want them to put in. Making your application work reliably requires checking information as it comes in and interacting with users so that they know how to get it right.

 As you'll see throughout this chapter, Rails expects all data validation to happen in the model layer and provides tools that make it easy to do there. If you find yourself putting data-checking code into the views or the controllers, pause for a moment—you're quite likely doing something wrong.

The one probable exception is if you're adding warnings for users working in your forms, avoiding a round trip to the server, but you should never rely on those to limit your data to the correct types. All that work should do is give users more information more rapidly.

Without Validation

You might think, since the examples in Chapter 6 defined data types, that Rails will be doing some basic content checking—ensuring that numeric data actually includes numbers, for example.

Nope. Rails and the Rails scaffolding give you places where you can add validation code, but absolutely none of it is built-in. The easiest way to see what happens is to try putting in bad data, as shown in Figure 7-1.

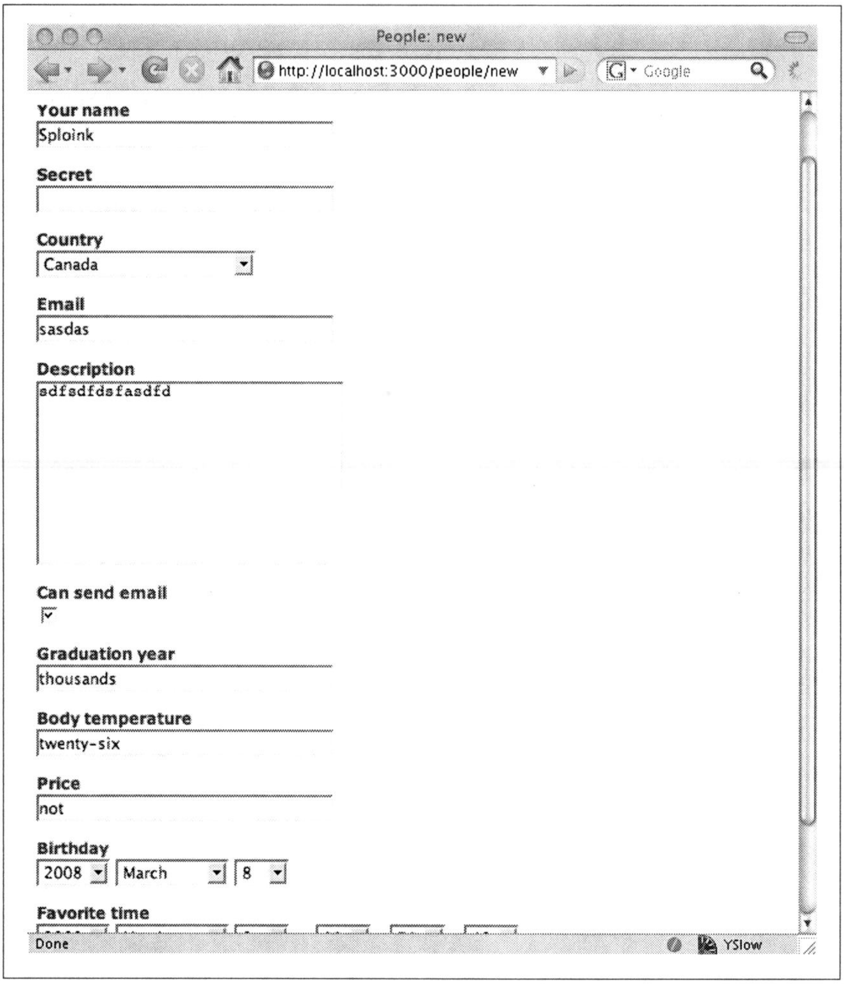

Figure 7-1. Entering bad data into a form

The text fields might not be the data you want, but at least they're text. The boolean value and the dates are constrained to a few choices by the interface design already—you can't choose bad data. However, "thousands," "twenty-six," and "not" aren't numbers. But Rails doesn't care—it accepts those strings and converts them to a number: 0 (zero), as shown in Figure 7-2.

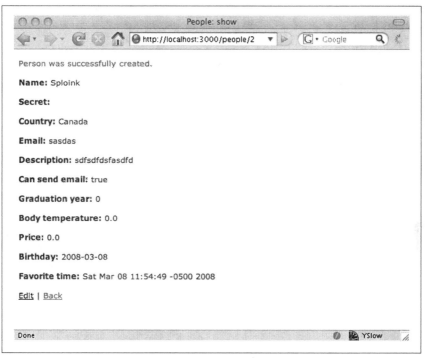

Figure 7-2. Nonnumeric data converted to zeros in a "successful" creation

You can see what happened by looking at the data that scrolled by in the script/server window when the request went in. You don't need a detailed understanding of SQL to find the problem—looking at the data going in will show it. Example 7-1 lists the data going into the Rails app and then shows the SQL INSERT with the data moving out from the Rails app to the database.

Example 7-1. Behind the scenes for bad data flowing to the application

```
Processing PeopleController#create (for 127.0.0.1 at 2008-03-08 18:42:04) [POST]
  Session ID:
BAh7ByIKZmxhc2hJQzonQWNOaW9uQ29udHJvbGxlcjo6Rmxhc2g60kZsYXNo%0ASGFzaHsABjoKQHVzZWR7
ADoMY3NyZl9pZCI1NmMxZGE3NDdiMmY3NDQzZWIz%0AZWM1NmQzNDFkZjBhYjM%3D--
ca58de858eb31bb2b1c88e0f1939fe085641c576
  Parameters: {"commit"=>"Create",
"authenticity_token"=>"8a2e7ade080a91f5c872cd8c783d2282576d6117",
"action"=>"create", "controller"=>"people", "person"=>{"name"=>"Sploink",
"birthday(2i)"=>"3", "favorite_time(5i)"=>"54", "birthday(3i)"=>"8",
"favorite_time(6i)"=>"49", "price"=>"not", "country"=>"Canada",
"body_temperature"=>"twenty-six", "description"=>"sdfsdfdsfasdfd",
"graduation_year"=>"thousands", "favorite_time(1i)"=>"2008",
"favorite_time(2i)"=>"3", "secret"=>"", "can_send_email"=>"1",
"favorite_time(3i)"=>"8", "email"=>"sasdas", "birthday(1i)"=>"2008",
"favorite_time(4i)"=>"11"}}
```

```
Person Create (0.000524)   INSERT INTO people ("name", "updated_at", "price",
"country", "body_temperature", "description", "birthday", "graduation_year",
"can_send_email", "favorite_time", "secret", "created_at", "email")
VALUES('Sploink', '2008-03-08 18:42:04', 0.0, 'Canada', 0.0, 'sdfsdfdsfasdfd',
'2008-03-08', 0, 't', '2008-03-08 11:54:49', '', '2008-03-08 18:42:04', 'sasdas')
Redirected to http://localhost:3000/people/2
Completed in 0.01586 (63 reqs/sec) | DB: 0.00052 (3%) | 302 Found
[http://localhost/people]
```

The parameters are complicated by the many pieces of incoming dates that use a naming convention to identify their parts, but it's clear that "thousands," "twenty-six," and "not" went into the Rails application. In the SQL command going to the database, price and body_temperature went in as 0.0, while grad uation_year went in as 0.

Between receiving the data and sending it to the database, Rails converted those values to numbers. The strings became zero (0.0), since they weren't actually numeric. Fixing this problem will require spending some time in the model, developing barriers that check incoming data and stop it if they don't match your application's requirements.

The Original Model

The *person.rb* file has been lurking in the *models* directory since the application was created. You might expect it to contain a list of fields for each person, defining data types and such. Instead, it looks like Example 7-2.

Example 7-2. The foundation of all Rails models

```
class Person < ActiveRecord::Base
end
```

That's pretty quiet, because the connections between Rails and the database are running purely on naming conventions. The Rake migration set up the database, as Example 6-1 demonstrated, and that's where all the data type information went. Perhaps it's even disturbingly quiet, as most object-oriented programming includes some specific information about object properties in the class definition that creates them.

Rails' minimalist approach to model classes, however, lets you focus on the pieces you need to contribute to the model. Having the definitions elsewhere may mean that you sometimes have to look around to figure out what you're working on—especially if you're modifying code someone else wrote—but it also makes a clean slate truly clean.

If the emptiness really bothers you, you could put the info from the migration or even the script/generate call into a comment here for quick reference. Of course, if you write another migration later, your quick reference might rapidly prove out of date.

The Power of Declarative Validation

You could write code that tests each property's value as it arrives, and there may be times when you need to do that, but Rails offers a simpler approach that works for the vast majority of cases: *declarative validation*. (You can find the complete example shown here in *ch07/guestbook005*.)

Instead of checking to see if a value is present, for instance, you can just write:

```
# the name is mandatory
validates_presence_of :name
```

The validates_presence_of declaration activates Rails' internal validation tools, which can automatically block the addition of a record that's missing a name and report an error to the user, as shown in Figure 7-3.

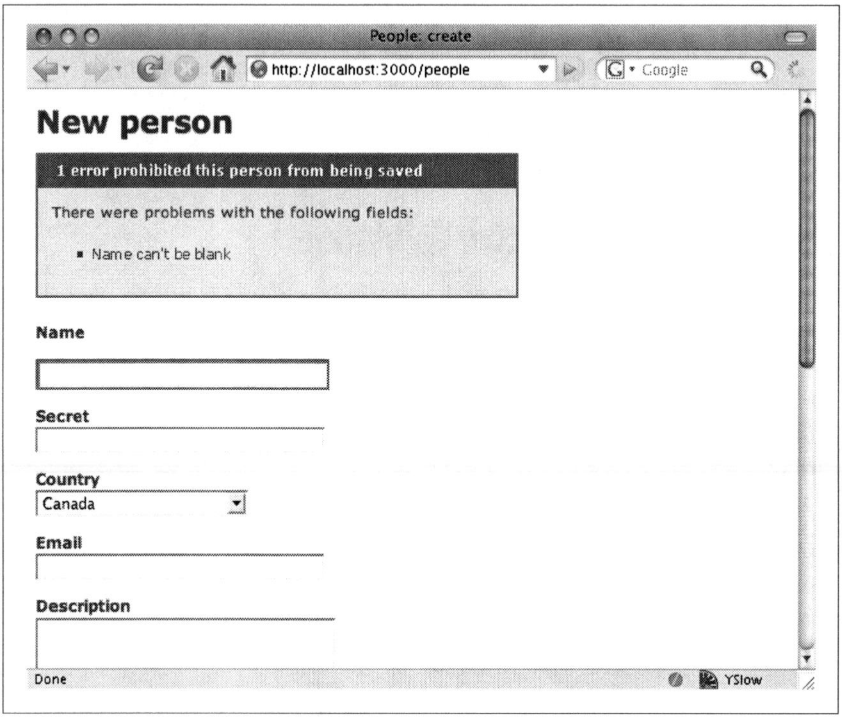

Figure 7-3. Failing a simple validation

How did the model reach through the controller, all the way into the view, and make that happen? It's worth walking back through once to trace the path Rails took. Example 7-3 shows the HTML that generated those messages.

Example 7-3. Model errors reported in HTML from the view

```
<div class="errorExplanation" id="errorExplanation"><h2>1 error prohibited this
person from being saved</h2><p>There were problems with the following
fields:</p><ul><li>Name can't be blank</li></ul></div>

<form action="/people" class="new_person" id="new_person" method="post"><div
style="margin:0;padding:0"><input name="authenticity_token" type="hidden"
value="b23eb784af45413f54bf73d49ea6eccd8115f3ee" /></div>
  <p>
    <b>Name</b><br />
    <div class="fieldWithErrors"><input id="person_name" name="person[name]"
size="30" type="text" value="" /></div>
  </p>
```

The first piece, the errorExplanation div, came from this line of code in the view (or partial):

```
<%= error_messages_for :person %>
```

Rails inserted the `fieldWithErrors` div around the name field through the usual field creation method in the view (or partial):

```
<%= f.text_field :name %>
```

This kind of automatic error presentation is another reason it's a good idea to use Rails' built-in methods for creating fields, rather than handcoding your own HTML in them.

The controller also took part in the action. If you look back at the `PeopleCon troller`'s `create` method, you'll see:

```
# POST /people
# POST /people.xml
def create
  @person = Person.new(params[:person])

  respond_to do |format|
    if @person.save
      flash[:notice] = 'Person was successfully created.'
      format.html { redirect_to(@person) }
      format.xml  { render :xml => @person, :status => :created, :location => @person }
    else
      format.html { render :action => "new" }
      format.xml  { render :xml => @person.errors, :status =>
:unprocessable_entity }
    end
  end
end
```

If the controller has an error, `@person.save` will fail, returning `false`. If the request is for HTML, the controller will render a new copy of the form for creating a new person entry. All of the error information will pass through to that view automatically. If it is an XML request, it will also report back the errors.

One major benefit of putting validation in the model is that your validation will apply to any effort to change your data—whether it came from users over the Web, from programs accessing your application through REST-based web services, or from something you built into the program yourself.

Now that we've seen how the errors flow out from the model to the view, it's time to examine how to set up the validation declarations that make it all happen.

Managing Secrets

While we'd like visitors to enter their names, it's usually best not to be too picky about names, because they come in so many varieties. On the other hand, the :secret field is ripe with opportunities for demanding expectations. Along the way, this example will demonstrate how you can use multiple validations on the same field in sequence.

Customizing the Message

The :secret field needs to be present. Sometimes, though, it's worth telling a user why a particular mistake matters rather than just insisting, "*field_name* can't be blank." Rails makes that easy to do by letting you specify a :message to go with your validation. If the validation fails, the user sees the :message. The code below adds a message to the test for :secret's presence:

```
# secret is also mandatory, but let's alter the default Rails message to be
# more friendly
validates_presence_of :secret,
  :message => "must be provided so we can recognize you in the future"
```

If the user leaves the :secret field blank, they'll see a custom error message as shown in Figure 7-4.

Even if the user provides a :secret, though, not all :secrets are created equal. Another set of validations will test the actual content of :secret, as shown here:

```
# ensure secret has enough letters, but not too many
validates_length_of :secret, :in => 6..24

# ensure secret contains at least one number
validates_format_of :secret, :with => /[0-9]/,
  :message => "must contain at least one number"

# ensure secret contains at least one upper case
validates_format_of :secret, :with => /[A-Z]/,
  :message => "must contain at least one upper case character"

# ensure secret contains at least one lower case
validates_format_of :secret, :with => /[a-z]/,
  :message => "must contain at least one lower case character"
```

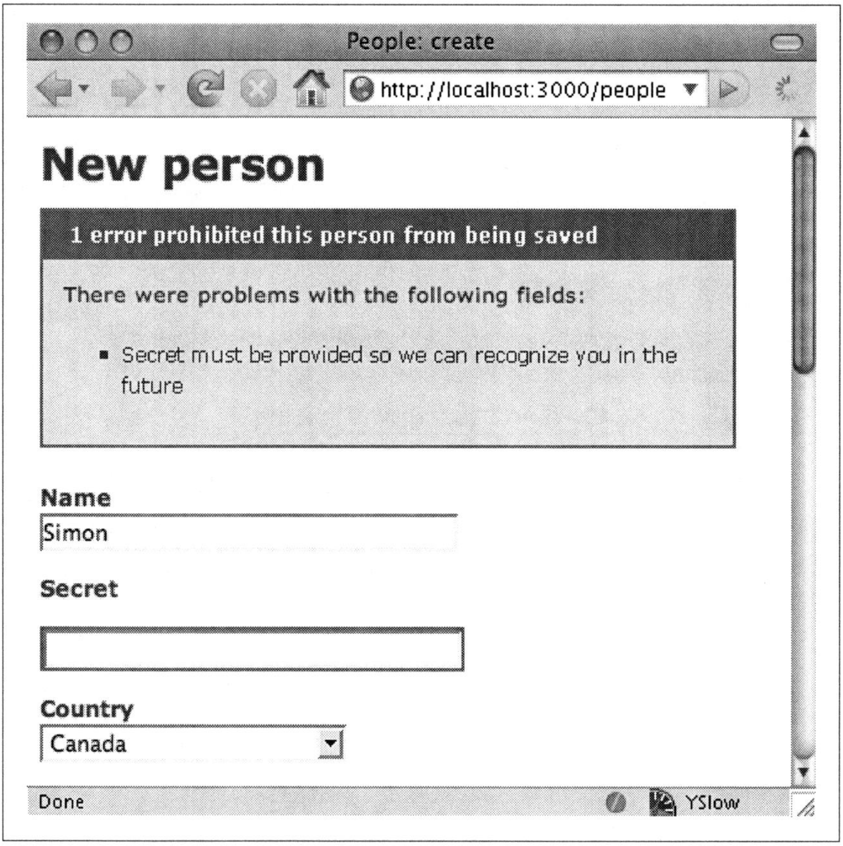

Figure 7-4. A custom error message sent to the user

The first of these validations tests the length of :secret, making sure that it lies between a 6-character minimum and a 24-character maximum:

```
validates_length_of :secret, :in => 6..24
```

Rails is smart enough that if a user enters a secret that's too short, it will report back that:

```
Secret is too short (minimum is 6 characters)
```

And it will do the same for the maximum. There probably isn't any need to customize the :message. However, the next three validations use the power of regular expressions. Regular expressions, or *regexes*, are compact but powerful patterns that Rails will test against the value of :secret. If the testing of :secret against the regular expression specified in :with returns true, then the validation passes and all is well. If it flunks the test, then the specified message will go out to the user.

All of these tests will be performed in sequence, and the user will see an error message reflecting all the tests that flunked. For example, a blank :secret will yield the full set shown in Figure 7-5.

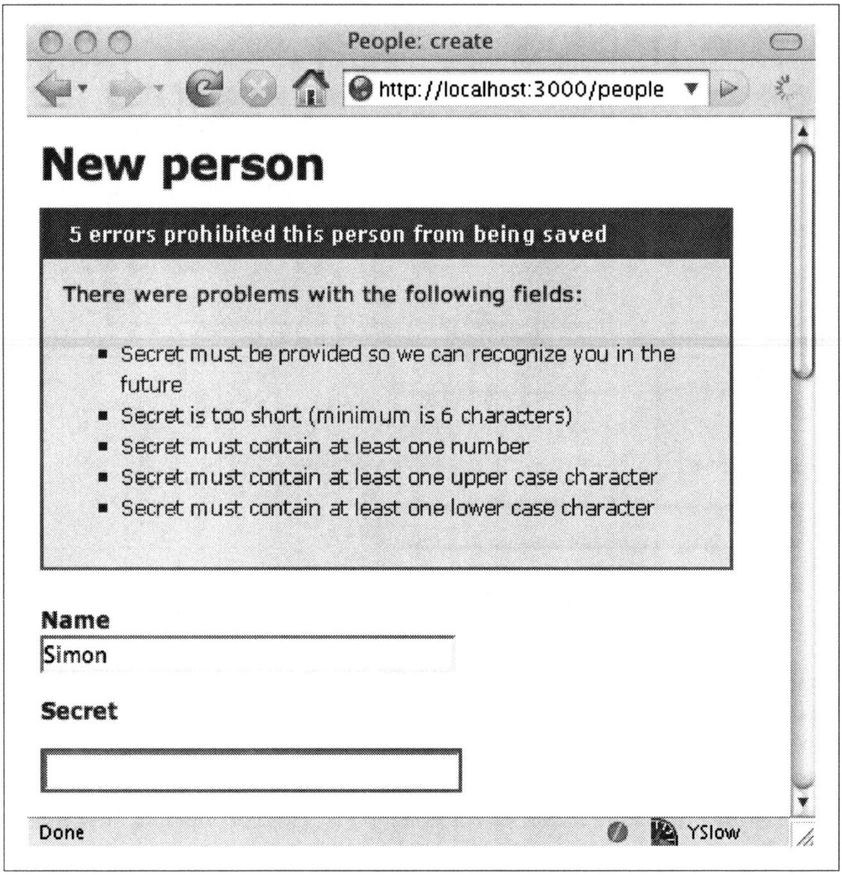

New person

5 errors prohibited this person from being saved

There were problems with the following fields:

- Secret must be provided so we can recognize you in the future
- Secret is too short (minimum is 6 characters)
- Secret must contain at least one number
- Secret must contain at least one upper case character
- Secret must contain at least one lower case character

Name

Simon

Secret

Figure 7-5. A multiply validated (and multiply flunked) secret

 Regular expressions are a complex subject you can study to nearly infinite depth. Appendix C offers "An Incredibly Brief Guide to Regular Expressions," which can get you started. Jeffrey Friedl's *Mastering Regular Expressions* (O'Reilly, 2006) is pretty much the classic overview of the field, but Tony Stubblebine's *Regular Expression Pocket Reference* (O'Reilly, 2007) is a concise guide to the capabilities and syntax in different environments.

Limiting Choices

The form created in the previous chapter only supported four values for the :country field. Limiting the values in the form, however, isn't very limiting. Other values could come in from other forms or, more simply, from an XML request using the REST interface. If we want to limit the values it can have, the data model is the place to do that:

```
# the country field is a controlled vocabulary: we must check that
# its value is within our allowed options
  validates_inclusion_of :country, :in => ['Canada', 'Mexico', 'UK', 'USA'],
    :message => "must be one of Canada, Mexico, UK or USA"
```

The validates_inclusion_of method requires an :in parameter that lists the possible choices as an array, and in this case :message specifies what the user will see if it fails. There's also a validates_exclusion_of method that's very similar, but flunks if the value provided matches one of the specified values.

Testing Format with Regular Expressions

Regular expressions are useful for ensuring that :secret contained certain patterns, but sometimes you want make sure that a field actually matches a pattern. The :email field is a good candidate for this, even though the simple regular expressions used to check email addresses are hard to read if you haven't spent a whole lot of time with regular expressions:

```
# email should read like an email address; this check isn't exhaustive,
# but it's a good start
  validates_format_of :email,
    :with => /\A([^@\s]+)@((?:[-a-z0-9]+\.)+[a-z]{2,})\Z/i,
    :message => "doesn't look like a proper email address"
```

The validates_format_of method takes a field to check and a regular expression for the :with parameter. You'll want to provide a :message parameter, since Rails isn't going to know how to turn the regular expression into meaningful explanations for ordinary web application users.

Seen It All Before

Validation isn't always about the specific content of a field coming in. Sometimes it's about how incoming data compares to existing data. The simplest and probably most common comparison is that for uniqueness. You don't want multiple users to have the same username, or you don't want multiple objects to have the same supposedly unique identifier, and so on.

You could write some code that checks all of the entries in your existing database to make sure that the new entry is unique, but Rails is happy to do that for you:

```
# how do we recognize the same person coming back? by their email address
# so we want to ensure the same person only signs in once
validates_uniqueness_of :email, :case_sensitive => false,
    :message => "has already been entered, you can't sign in twice"
```

The :case_sensitive property lets you specify whether textual values should be compared so that differences in case matter. The default value is true, but as email addresses are not case-sensitive, false is a better option here. The :message is useful for explaining just what happened.

By default, validates_uniqueness_of checks :email only against the other values in the same database column. If you wanted to ensure that data was unique across multiple columns, the :scope property would let you do that. For instance, to check :email against :email plus :name against :name and :secret against :secret, you could write:

```
validates_uniqueness_of :email, :case_sensitive => false,
    :scope => [:name, :secret],
    :message => "has already been entered, you can't sign in twice"
```

Using :scope makes more sense in more complicated applications with multiple unique identifiers.

Numbers Only

While many fields accept any text the user wants to provide, applications tend to prefer 4.1 to "four and one-tenth" for numeric fields. By default, as Figure 7-2 showed, Rails doesn't check that only numeric data goes into numeric fields. When it puts text data into the database, the type conversion will yield a zero—probably not what's appropriate most of the time. Of course, though, Rails lets you check this easily, along with a lot of details that you may need to support your particular use of numbers. The :graduation_year field, for example, comes with a lot of constraints as well as some openness. That's easy to check using validates_numericality_of:

```
# Graduation year must be numeric, and within sensible bounds.
# However, the person may not have graduated, so we allow a
# nil value too. Finally, it must be a whole number (integer).
validates_numericality_of :graduation_year, :allow_nil => true,
    :greater_than => 1920, :less_than_or_equal_to => Time.now.year,
    :only_integer => true
```

The first parameter here actually relaxes constraints. Specifying :allow_nil => true allows the value to stay blank. Only nonblank values will have their value checked.

:allow_nil is available for all of the validates methods. You'll want to use it wherever you don't mean to place demands on users.

The next two parameters are a verbose way of saying > and <=. The validates_numericality_of methods offers a set of parameters for testing numbers:

equal_to
: Tests that the value being validated is equal to the value provided in the parameter.

even
: Tests that the value is an even number (dividing by 2 yields no remainder).

greater_than
: Tests that the value being validated is greater than the value provided in the parameter.

greater_than_or_equal_to
: Tests that the value being validated is greater than or equal to the value provided in the parameter.

less_than
: Tests that the value being validated is less than the value provided in the parameter.

less_than_or_equal_to
: Tests that the value being validated is less than or equal to the value provided in the parameter.

odd
: Tests that the value is an odd number (dividing by 2 yields a remainder of one).

only_integer
: Tests that the value being validated is an integer, with no fractional part.

The named parameters have values. For the methods that make comparisons, the value is the argument against which the incoming value will be compared. These can be simple values or method calls, such as :less_than_or_equal_to => Time.now.year. For the boolean tests (even, odd, only_integer), the value specifies whether or not the test counts for validation, and the default value for all of them is false.

The next two fields, :body_temperature and :price, are also numbers, with relatively simple validations:

```
# Body temperature doesn't have to be a whole number, but we ought to
# constrain possible values. We assume our users aren't in cryostasis.
```

```
validates_numericality_of :body_temperature, :allow_nil => true,
    :greater_than_or_equal_to => 60,
    :less_than_or_equal_to => 130, :only_integer => false

validates_numericality_of :price, :allow_nil => true,
    :only_integer => false
```

A Place on the Calendar

You could test date components individually, but more typically you'll want to test whether or not the date falls within a given range. Rails makes this easy with the validates_inclusion_of method, already examined previously, and its inverse, validates_exclusion_of:

```
# Restrict birthday to reasonable values, i.e., not in the future and not
# before 1900
validates_inclusion_of :birthday,
    :in => Date.civil(1900, 1, 1) .. Date.today,
    :message => "must be between January 1st, 1900 and today"
```

The :in parameter actually takes a list of possible values (an enumerable object, technically), and in this case the definition creates a list of values between January 1, 1900 (thanks to the Date.civil method) and today's date (thanks to the Date.today method).

Testing for Presence

The :allow_nil parameter noted earlier lets you say that things don't need to be present, but there are also times when the *only* validation you want to perform is to make certain that a given field contains a value. In this case, validates_presence_of is extremely convenient:

```
# Finally, we just say that favorite time is mandatory.
# While the view only allows you to post valid times, remember
# that models can be created in other ways, such as from code
# or web service calls. So it's not safe to make assumptions
# based on the form.
validates_presence_of :favorite_time
```

As the comment reminds, while an HTML form can make some explicit demands of users, you should avoid writing code that assumes that all data will be coming in through the form. Using REST-based approaches, a lot of your objects may arrive or be changed through XML or JSON sent over HTTP.

Beyond Simple Declarations

The tests shown above are valuable, but also limited. They test a single value against a limited set of possibilities and don't allow interactions among different values. While Rails makes it easy to do easy things, it fortunately also make it fairly easy to do more complicated things. (You can find these more complicated examples in *ch07/guestbook006*.)

Test It Only If

One of the simplest tests is to require a validation if, and only if, another condition is met. The `:if` parameter, available on every test, lets you define those conditions. (There's a corresponding `:unless` parameter that works similarly but in the opposite direction.) The easiest way to use `:if` is to point it at a method that returns a boolean value. That way your code can stay readable, and you can put whatever complications are involved in the test into a more maintainable and testable separate method.

This example uses the value of the `:can_send_email` field to determine whether the `:description` field must have a value. Neither is a field that would typically need much validation, but they can easily be treated as connected:

```
# if person says 'can send email', then we'd like them to fill their
# description in, so we understand who it is we're sending mail to
validates_presence_of :description, :if => :require_description_presence?

# we define the supporting condition here
def require_description_presence?
  self.can_send_email
end
```

The `validates_presence_of` method will only perform its test if the condition specified by the `:if` parameter returns `true`. The `:if` parameter's value comes from the `require_description_presence?` method, which in this case simply returns the value of `can_send_mail`.

> There are two small things to note about the `require_descrip tion_presence?` method. First, its name ends in a question mark, which is an easy way to flag that a method returns a boolean value. Second, it doesn't seem to do anything—but Ruby returns the value of the last thing touched, so the value of `self.can_send_email` becomes the return value. (And `self` here and throughout is optional, more a verbal tic for reminding the programmer of what's being called than a necessary part of the program.)

Do It Yourself

While Rails' built-in validation is very helpful for a broad range of data check-ing, there are always going to be times when it's just not enough. For example, while Rails can check the length of a string in characters, it didn't have a method that checks the length of a string in words until Rails 2.2 added `vali dates_length_of`.

Performing such checks requires two steps. First, you need to create a method called `validate`. ActiveRecord will always call the validate method if one is present. It's best, however, not to perform your validations directly in that method. Instead, put calls to readily identifiable methods that contain your custom logic. To indicate that validation failed, use `self.errors.add`, as shown in Example 7-4. This will tell Rails that there is an error and which field it applies to, as well as give you a chance to add a message to the user.

Example 7-4. Custom validation with validate and self.errors

```
def validate
    validate_description
end

def validate_description
  # only do this validation if description is provided
  unless self.description.blank? then
    # simple way of calculating words: split the text on whitespace
    num_words = self.description.split.length
    if num_words < 5 then
      self.errors.add(:description, "must be at least 5 words long")
    elsif num_words > 50 then
      self.errors.add(:description, "must be at most 50 words long")
    end
  end
end
```

When you perform validation this way, Rails does less work for you. The `unless self.description.blank?` line is necessary because you can't just spec-ify `allow_nil => true`. Similarly, there aren't any automatically generated messages. You have to provide them. And finally, of course, you're responsible for all of the validation logic itself.

 Rails also offers a `validates_each` method that can help you create more descriptively named validations. For more, see *http://apidock.com/rails/ActiveModel/Validations/ClassMe thods/validates_each*.

Test Your Knowledge

Quiz

1. How much type-checking does Rails do against the types you specified in your migrations?
2. What happens when a validation error is reported?
3. How do you customize the error notifications users see when their data doesn't match up to your validator's expectations?
4. How do you test the detailed syntax of user-entered data to make sure it matches a particular pattern?
5. If there's more than one error reported by the validator methods, what does Rails do?
6. How do you specify if something may be either valid or blank?
7. How do you specify that a value has to be outside of a particular range?
8. How can you specify that a validation applies only if another value in the form has a particular value?

Answers

1. Rails does no type-checking by default. It just coerces the data that came in to the matching type, and if it doesn't match, too bad. You have to provide explicit validation code for every field you create.
2. Validation errors block the saving of records. The model sends the data back through the controller to the view, adding messages about what is wrong with the data so the view can display them.
3. The `:message` named parameter lets you provide a specific notification. Rails will do some notifying by default, in basic cases, but you're generally wise to add your own messages.
4. The `validates_format_of` method lets you test against regular expressions, or you can write your own more complicated tests by extending validation through the `validate` method.
5. Rails will report all of the messages from all of the validating methods to the user and highlight all of the fields with errors. It won't save the data to the database until it is submitted again and passes validation.
6. You can allow blank entries by specifying `:allow_nil => true` on your validation. That permits the field to either have a correct value or no value at all.

7. The `validates_exclusion_of` method lets you make sure a value is outside of a given range.

8. The `:if` parameter lets you define conditions where validation applies.

## CHAPTER 8

Improving Forms

Now that you can safely get information between your users and your applications, it's time to examine some ways to do it better. Here are a few more features to explore:

- Supporting file uploads, a common website feature that steps outside of the simple form field to database column mapping
- Designing form builders, which make it easier to create forms that look the way you think they should, not the way Rails does it by default

Once you've figured out these pieces, you'll have a reasonably complete understanding of the options Rails offers for creating classic web applications. Ajax still lies ahead, but the basics are still useful for a wide variety of situations.

Adding a Picture by Uploading a File

Since we're building a collection of people, it might be nice to know what they look like. Adding file uploads to Rails applications requires making changes in several different places:

- The form for creating and editing a person needs a file upload field.
- The model representing person data needs to handle the file data.
- A new migration needs to add a field for the file extension, because pictures come in different formats.
- The view that shows a person should display the picture, too!

One key piece of a Rails application is missing here: the controller. The controller doesn't actually need to do anything more than it is already doing: passing data between the view and the model. One more piece of data, even a big chunk like a photo file, isn't going to make a difference to that default handling. (You can find the complete files for this example in *ch08/guest-book007*.)

 This chapter will show how to handle uploaded files directly. There are some plug-ins, notably `attachment_fu`, `file_col umn`, and `paperclip`, that can handle uploaded files for you. Unfortunately, they have their own challenges, particularly in installation, and won't be covered in this book.

File Upload Forms

The simplest step seems to be adding the file upload field to the form:

```
<p>
  <b>Photo</b><br />
  <%= f.file_field :photo %>
</p>
```

Well, almost. Including a file upload changes the way an HTML form is submitted, changing it to a multipart form. For creating a new person, this means shifting from an HTML result that looks like:

```
<form action="/people" method="post">
```

to a result that looks like:

```
<form action="/people/" enctype="multipart/form-data" method="post">
```

Adding the enclosure type means that Rails will know to look for an attachment after the main body of form field data has arrived.

Addressing that means that there's some additional work required on the form tag, created by the `form_for` method in our partial, *_form.html.erb*. In the old form, before the upload was added, it looked like:

```
<% form_for(@person) do |f| %>
```

In the new form, it has a lot more pieces:

```
<% form_for(:person, @person,
  :url => { :action => ( @person.new_record? ? "create" : "update" ) },,
  :html => { :multipart => true,
    :method => (@person.new_record? ? :post : :put)}) do |f| %>
```

Why the sudden climb in complexity?

The shorter original version relies on Rails to do *record identification*, examining the object in `@person` and applying a whole set of defaults based on what it finds. When there's a file upload involved, however, `:multipart` changes to `true`. Making that change means explicitly specifying a lot of the pieces Rails had taken care of for you previously, most notably the path for the URL and the method choice for submission. Rails does a lot of great things automatically, hiding complexity, but when its automatic choices aren't the right ones, that complexity has to emerge.

The `:url => { :action => ( @person.new_record? ? "create" : "update" ) }` call will check the routing tables to generate a URL, while `@person.new_record? ? :post : :put` checks to see if the `@person` object is empty. If it is, the form will use POST; if not, it will use PUT.

 Recent versions of Rails will let you avoid some of this complexity, shifting to the simpler `form_for(@post, :html => {:multipart => true })`. Still, it's useful to understand what lurks underneath.

Model and Migration Changes

Adding a photo requires somewhat more effort than adding another ordinary field to the application, mostly because it (usually) doesn't make sense to store potentially large chunks of media data like photos directly in a database. For this demonstration, it makes much better sense to store the photo in the filesystem, renamed to match the ID of the person it goes with.

There's still one catch that requires accessing the database, though: photo files come in lots of different formats, and there's little reason to restrict users to a single format. That will require keeping track of which file extension is used for the uploaded file by storing that in the database. Doing that will require creating a migration, in addition to adding a lot of logic to the model. The combination of filesystem and database use is shown in Figure 8-1.

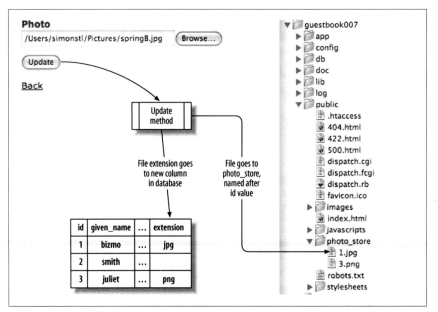

Figure 8-1. Uploading a file into the public directory, with metadata stored in the database

A migration for an extension

Chapter 10 will explore migrations in much greater depth, but this migration is relatively simple. Rails will apply migrations in the sequence of their filenames, with the opening number being the critical piece. The *db/migrate* folder already contains a migration whose name ends in *_create_people.rb*, defining a CreatePeople class. To make it easy for us to figure out what's going on, the next migration will contain an AddPhotoExtensionToPerson class. Following the same naming convention, this will be a timestamp followed by *_add_photo_extension_to_person.rb*. To create the migration file, enter:

```
script/generate migration add_photo_extension_to_person
```

For more detail on creating migrations by hand, see Chapter 10. This one is simple enough that you can probably follow along without the full tutorial, though.

The newly generated migration won't have much in it, but you need to add details. There doesn't need to be very much inside this migration, as it only creates (and destroys, if necessary) one field, :extension, of type :string:

```
class AddPhotoExtensionToPerson < ActiveRecord::Migration
  def self.up
```

```
    add_column :people, :extension, :string
  end

  def self.down
    remove_column :people, :extension
  end
end
```

When this migration is run, it will add a new column to the :people table that will be used to store :extension data. If rolled back, it deletes that column.

To run the migration, just run `rake db:migrate` as usual. The Rake tool will find the new migration file, know that it hasn't run it yet, and add the column to the existing :people table, as requested.

Extending a model beyond the database

Data storage issues should all be handled in the model. Normally, Rails will save any properties that come into the model that have names corresponding to columns in the corresponding database table.

 Behind the scenes, ActiveRecord keeps track of which tables contain which columns and uses that information to generate a lot of code automatically. In development mode, it checks tables and generates code constantly, which is part of why development mode is slow but extremely flexible.

However, the migration just shown didn't create a column that would map to :photo; just one for :extension. This is deliberate. Because these photos will be stored as files outside of the database, Rails *shouldn't* handle them automatically. Explicit model code, in *app/models/person.rb*, will have to do that. Fortunately, Rails has an easy (and declarative) way to make sure the code for storing the photo runs after the rest of validation has happened, with its `after_save` callback method;

```
# after the person has been written to the database, deal with
# writing any image data to the filesystem
  after_save :store_photo
```

Unfortunately, Rails doesn't have a built-in `store_photo` method. That requires coding.

The `after_save` method is one of several callback methods supported by ActiveRecord. Note that there are after and before methods for `create`, `destroy`, `save`, `update`, `validation`, `validation_on_create`, and `validation_on_update`. If you need to tweak ActiveRecord's data-handling, these can be valuable tools.

`store_photo`, the last method in the `Person` class, will call on some other methods that also need to be written, but it's probably still easiest to look at `store_photo` first before examining the methods on which it depends:

```
private

# called after saving, to write the uploaded image to the filesystem
def store_photo
  if @file_data
    # make the photo_store directory if it doesn't exist already
    FileUtils.mkdir_p PHOTO_STORE
    # write out the image data to the file
    File.open(photo_filename, 'wb') do |f|
      f.write(@file_data.read)
    end
    # ensure file saved only when it newly arrives at model being saved
    @file_data = nil
  end
end
```

First, note that this method comes after the `private` keyword, making it invisible outside of the model class to which it belongs. Controllers and views shouldn't be calling `store_photo` directly. Only other methods within the same model should be able to call it. (It's not required that you make this method private, but it makes for cleaner code overall.)

Within the method itself, the first line, `if @file_data`, is simple—if there is actually data to be stored, then it's worth proceeding. Otherwise, this isn't necessary. Then there's a call to Ruby's file-handling classes, creating a directory for the photos. (This causes no harm if the directory already exists.) The next few lines open a file whose name is specified by *photo_filename*, write the data to it, and close it. At the end, `store_photo` sets `@file_data` to nil to make sure the file doesn't get stored again elsewhere in the application.

This takes care of saving the file, which is the last thing done as the model finishes up its work on a form submission, but more details get attended to earlier, paving the way for saving the file. The `photo=` method takes care of a few details when a submission arrives:

```
# when photo data is assigned via the upload, store the file data
# for later and assign the file extension, e.g., ".jpg"
def photo=(file_data)
```

```
unless file_data.blank?
  # store the uploaded data into a private instance variable
  @file_data = file_data
  # figure out the last part of the filename and use this as
  # the file extension. e.g., from "me.jpg" will return "jpg"
  self.extension = file_data.original_filename.split('.').last.downcase
end
end
```

The def for this method looks a bit unusual because it takes advantage of a Rails convention for writing to model attributes. Writing def photo=(file_data) creates a method that grabs the file_data content for :photo, which Rails creates based on the contents of the file_field from the HTML form. It defines what happens when person.photo is assigned a value. That file_data content gets moved to an @file_data instance variable that is private to the model but is accessible to any of the methods within it. (@file_data is what store_photo referenced, for instance.)

The photo= method also handles the one piece of the filename that will get stored in the database—the file extension. It gets the original name, splits off the piece after the last ., and lowercases it. (You don't have to be this draconian, but it does make for simpler maintenance.) Note that photo= just assigns a value to the extension variable of the current Person object. ActiveRecord will save that value automatically, as it maps to the :extension column created by the migration.

The next few pieces are filename housekeeping:

```
# File.join is a cross-platform way of joining directories;
# we could have written "#{RAILS_ROOT}/public/photo_store"
PHOTO_STORE = File.join RAILS_ROOT, 'public', 'photo_store'

# where to write the image file to
def photo_filename
  File.join PHOTO_STORE, "#{id}.#{extension}"
end

# return a path we can use in HTML for the image
def photo_path
  "/photo_store/#{id}.#{extension}"
end
```

PHOTO_STORE provides the application with a path to this Rails application's *public* directory, where static files can go. The photo_filename method gets called by store_photo when it needs to know where the photo file should actually go on its host machine's filesystem. You can see that instead of preserving the original filename, it uses the id—the primary key number for this Person—when it creates a name for the photo. This may seem like overkill, but it has the convenient virtue of avoiding filename conflicts. Otherwise, if multiple people had uploaded *me.jpg*, some of them would be surprised by the results.

The photo_path method handles filename housekeeping for views that need to display the image. It's unconcerned with where the file exists in the server's file system and focuses instead on where it will appear as a URL in the Rails application. Again, photo_path uses the id to create the name. Its one line, a string, actually *is* the return value.

There's another housekeeping function that supports the view. Not everyone will necessarily have a photo, and broken image icons aren't particularly attractive. To simplify dealing with this, the model includes a has_photo method that checks to see if there's a file corresponding to the id and extension of the current record:

```
# if a photo file exists, then we have a photo
def has_photo?
  File.exists? photo_filename
end
```

Remember, Ruby will treat the last value created by a method as its return value—in this case, the response to File.exists?. This returns true if there is a file corresponding to the id and extension, and false if there isn't.

Showing it off

The last piece that the application needs is a way to show off the picture. That's a simple addition in the *show.html.erb* view:

```
<p>
  <b>Photo:</b>
    <% if @person.has_photo? %>
      <%= image_tag @person.photo_path %>
    <% else %>
      No photo.
    <% end %>
</p>
```

The has_photo? method from the model lets the view code decide whether or not to create an img element for the photo. If there is one, it uses the model's photo_path method for the src attribute, pointing to the file in the *public* directory's *photo_store* directory. If not, there's plain text with the message "No photo" rather than a broken image icon.

Results

It's time to try this code. Running rake db:migrate updates the database:

```
== 2 AddPhotoExtensionToPerson: migrating ========================
-- add_column(:people, :extension, :string)
   -> 0.0757s
== 2 AddPhotoExtensionToPerson: migrated (0.0759s) ===============
```

Running `ruby script/server` fires up the application, which at first glance looks very similar to earlier versions, as shown in Figure 8-2. (And yes, displaying everyone's "secret" isn't very secret, but we'll get to a much better solution in Chapter 12.)

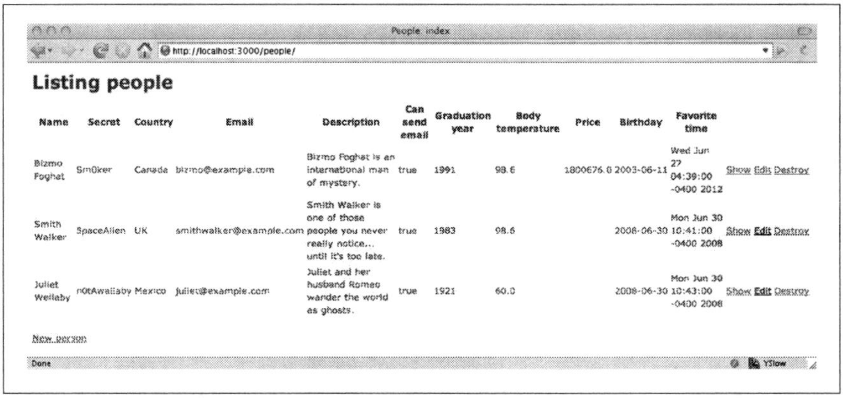

Figure 8-2. A list of users who might have photos

If you click the "New Person" link or go to edit an existing record, you'll see a new field for the photo, highlighted in Figure 8-3.

When a photo is uploaded, it is stored in the application's *public* directory, in a *photo_store* directory, as shown in Figure 8-4. Note that there is a skipped number—only records which actually have photos leave any trace here.

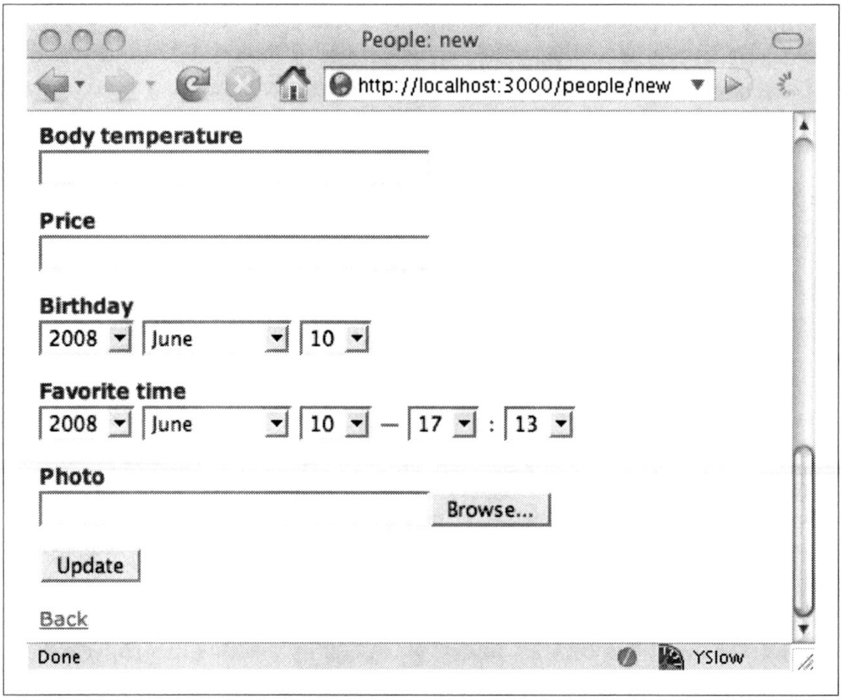

Figure 8-3. A file field in the person form

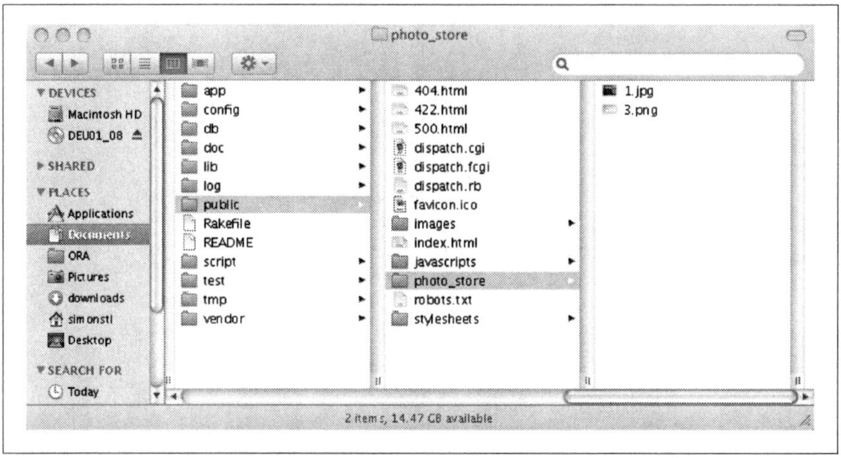

Figure 8-4. Stored photos in the public/photo_store directory

Showing a page for a record that includes a photo yields the photo embedded in the page, as shown in Figure 8-5. (Note that at present there aren't any constraints on photo size. You could constrain it, but you'll have to install a graphics library, configure it, and connect it to Ruby and Rails.)

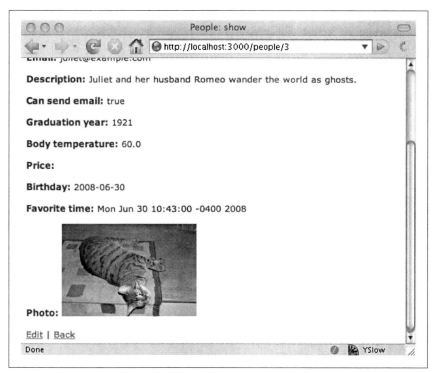

Figure 8-5. A record displaying an uploaded photo

Records that don't have an associated photo just get the "No photo" message shown in Figure 8-6.

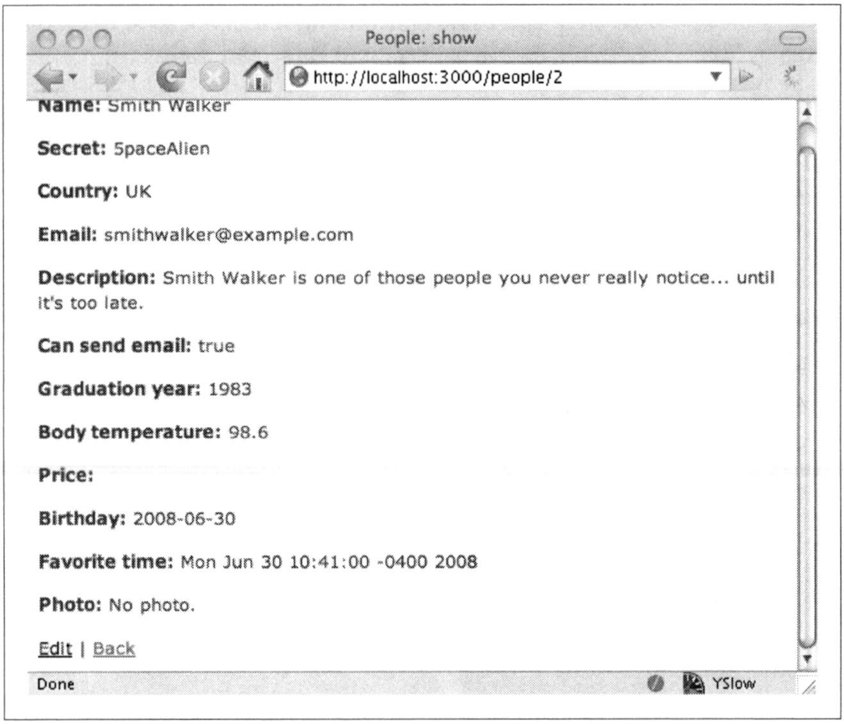

![Browser window showing People: show page at http://localhost:3000/people/2]

Name: Smith Walker

Secret: 5paceAlien

Country: UK

Email: smithwalker@example.com

Description: Smith Walker is one of those people you never really notice... until it's too late.

Can send email: true

Graduation year: 1983

Body temperature: 98.6

Price:

Birthday: 2008-06-30

Favorite time: Mon Jun 30 10:41:00 -0400 2008

Photo: No photo.

<u>Edit</u> | <u>Back</u>

Figure 8-6. A record unadorned with a photo—but spared a broken image icon

This isn't quite a simple process, but multimedia usually stretches frameworks built around databases. Rails is flexible enough to let you choose how to handle incoming information and work with the file system to develop a solution that fits. (And if this isn't quite the right solution for you, don't worry—many people are working out their own solutions to these issues and sharing them.)

 It is possible for programs treating your application as a REST-based web service to send photos as multipart/form-data. However, Rails' default approach to generating XML responses won't give them an easy way to retrieve the photos unless the programs understand the photo_store/*id.extension* convention.

Standardizing Your Look with Form Builders

While Rails scaffolding is a convenient way to get started, you may have noticed that it's pretty repetitive and not especially attractive. Some of this can be fixed with judicious use of CSS, but Rails supports more permanent fixes through the use of *form builders*. Creating form builders is an opportunity to define how your data will be presented to users and how they'll interact with that data. Form builders also let you create abstractions that keep programmers out of the visual details of your application while still giving them full access to views.

The basic concepts behind form builders are simple, though you can use them to create complex and intricate components. You can use form builders in multiple ways, starting from simple wrapping of your own special types and developing through more complex ways to change the ways forms are written.

 You can also combine form builders with Ruby metaprogramming to create your own terse yet descriptive syntaxes for creating forms, but metaprogramming is *way* beyond the scope of this book. If you encounter an application with view code that looks nothing like you expected, though, that may be what's going on.

Supporting Your Own Field Types

Chapter 6 showed how Rails supported a variety of data types by default, including a more complicated (if not very user-friendly) set of controls for entering dates. While the built-in set of widgets is helpful, you're definitely not limited to it. You can build reusable form components that match your needs more precisely.

This can be very useful when you have components that take the same limited set of values. Chapter 6 showed a helper method for creating drop-down lists or radio buttons depending on the number of choices, culminating in Example 6-10, which is repeated here as Example 8-1.

Example 8-1. A helper method for creating select lists

```
def button_select(model_name, target_property, button_source)
    list = button_source.sort
    if list.length < 4
      list.collect do |item|
         radio_button(model_name, target_property, item[1]) +
h(item[0])
      end.join('<br />')
    else
      select(model_name, target_property, list)
    end
end
```

Rather than create a generic helper method whose focus is on the kind of HTML it generates, it can be more appealing to create a form builder method whose focus is on data that's appropriate for a given model. Linking the HTML specifically to a given model makes it vastly easier to keep interfaces consistent. Example 8-2, included in *ch08/guestbook008*, shows a form builder method, country_select, that is designed specifically for use with the :country field.

Example 8-2. A form builder, stored in app/helpers/tidy_form_builder.rb, providing a method more tightly bound to the expectations of the country field

```
class TidyFormBuilder < ActionView::Helpers::FormBuilder

# our country_select calls the default select helper with the
# choices already filled in
  def country_select(method, options={}, html_options={})
    select(method, [['Canada', 'Canada'],
                    ['Mexico', 'Mexico'],
                    ['United Kingdom', 'UK'],
                    ['United States of America', 'USA']],
                  options, html_options)
  end
end
```

Note that form builders, which go in the *app/helpers* directory, all inherit from the ActionView::Helpers::FormBuilder class. (Prior to version 2.2, Rails had its own country_select method with a much larger selection of countries, but this demonstration overrides it.) The methods inside the class will then be made available to views that specify that they want to use this helper.

The country_select method is built using the select helper method already explored in Chapter 6. It takes a method parameter and options and html_options, like the select method does. What does the method parameter do? You probably think of the method as the field—:name, for example. You can see how much more tightly bound country_select is to :country—it wouldn't be of much use for any other field, unless you have, say, different kinds of fields expecting the same list of countries. The result is a select field seeded with the choices you've deemed acceptable for country.

 Note that the options and html_options arguments are simply passed through. Preserving them offers developers more flexibility when they go to apply your form builder in different situations.

Calling the form builder requires two things. First, the view has to reference the TidyFormBuilder, and then it has to actually call country_select. Unlike helper classes, where a naming convention is enough to connect supporting code with the view, form builders require an explicit call. (You will likely use the same builder for multiple views in any case, as :country might turn up in a lot of different contexts.)

As was the case for the multipart form, calling the builder means using an expanded declaration on form_for, this time adding a :builder parameter:

```
<% form_for(:person, @person,
  :url => person_path(@person),
  :html => { :multipart => true,
    :method => (@person.new_record? ? :post : :put)},
  :builder => TidyFormBuilder) do |f| %>
```

Rails will know to look for TidyFormBuilder in /app/helpers/ tidy_form_builder.rb. Actually, calling the method is pretty simple. Just replace:

```
<p>
    <%= f.label :country %><br />
    <%= f.select (:country, [ ['Canada', 'Canada'],
                      ['Mexico', 'Mexico'],
                      ['United Kingdom', 'UK'],
                      ['United States of America', 'USA'] ]) %>
</p>
```

with:

```
<p>
  <%= f.label :country %><br />
  <%= f.country_select :country %>
</p>
```

The results will be identical, but the logic around the country object is much better encapsulated, and just plain easier to use, in the builder version.

Adding Automation

The Rails helper methods are certainly useful, but they tend to map directly to HTML markup. When you have multiple related markup components for a single field, code can start to feel messy very quickly. That's true even when they're as simple as an input field with a label, like this from the scaffolding:

```
<p>
    <%= f.label :name %><br />
    <%= f.text_field :name %>
</p>
```

Multiply that by a hundred fields, and there's a lot of repetitive code around. Remember, the Rails mantra is "Don't Repeat Yourself" (DRY), and there's a huge opportunity to avoid repetition here.

Although it's kind of a separate task from the country selector, this can also happen easily inside of the TidyFormBuilder, as shown in *ch08/guestbook008*.

In fact, it's easy for it to take place there because methods in the builder can use the same names as the helper methods and subclass them, adding the extra functionality needed to simplify the view code. About the only tricky part is making sure that your subclassed methods use the same signature—list of parameters—as the originals, which just means checking the Rails API documentation:

```
def text_field(method, options={})
  ...
end
```

The `text_field` method takes a `method` parameter. The `options` array is the usual set of options. Once the signature is set up, the single line of code inside combines a label with a call to the original method to create a return value:

```
def text_field(method, options={})
  label_for(method, options) + super(method, options)
end
```

Calling `super`, in the second half of this line, means to call the original `text_field` method, which gets passed the `method` and `options` objects. The first half of the line calls another method, however, adding the label. The `label_for` method is declared at the end of the `TidyFormBuilder` class and is `private`, as it is for internal use only:

```
private

def label_for(method, options={})
  label(options.delete(:label) || method) + "<br />"
end
```

The `label` method is the same as usual and is concatenated to a `<br />` tag, but there's something tricky going on in the arguments:

```
(:label || method)
```

This looks for an option named `:label`, letting you specify label text for the field through a `:label` parameter. Accessing the `:label` value through `delete` seems strange, but `delete` does two things: it removes the `:label` parameter from the `options` array, which will keep it from passing through to the `super` call, and it also returns the `:label` parameter's value, if there is one. (This was optional in Rails 2.1, but appears to be mandatory in Rails 2.2 and later.) If there isn't a `:label`, the `||` will fall through to `method`, which will create a label with the default—the internal name of the field.

The call to create a field is now much simpler:

```
<%= f.text_field :name %>
```

The other methods, with more complex signatures, need a bit more code, but it's the same basic logic, as these two demonstrate:

```
def datetime_select(method, options = {}, html_options = {})
  label_for(method, options) + super(method, options, html_options)
end

def select(method, choices, options = {}, html_options = {})
  label_for(method, options) + super(method, choices, options, html_options)
end

def check_box(method, options = {}, checked_value = "1", unchecked_value = "0")
  label_for(method, options) + super(method, options, checked_value,
unchecked_value)
end
```

And again, the calls to create a select list and a checkbox become simpler:

```
<%= f.check_box :can_send_email %>

<%= f.datetime_select :favorite_time %>
```

There's one last bit to notice. Remember how `country_select` calls the `select` method? It now calls the method that provides the label. That means that you can simplify:

```
<p>
  <%= f.label :country %><br />
  <%= f.country_select :country %>
</p>
```

to:

```
<p>
<%= f.country_select :country %>
</p>
```

The next step will reduce this even further, while making it easier to style and manipulate the resulting HTML.

Integrating Form Builders and Styles

All of those `<p>` and `</p>` tags are calling out for simplification, but there's another opportunity here: to add additional information to the form that will help users fill it out properly. The `WrappingTidyBuilder`, included in *ch08/ guestbook010*, builds on the prior `TidyBuilder`, supporting its `coun try_select` method and its methods for providing labels. It also, however, takes advantage of the work it's putting into wrapping to add some extra information to fields that are required. This requires a few extra components:

- A `:required` option specified in calls from the view
- A `wrap_field` method that puts the opening and closing tags around the label and form fields
- Calls to `wrap_field` from the other methods

- A bit of extra code in the label method that adds a textual indicator that a field is required
- Support for the new wrapper in a CSS stylesheet used for pages built with these methods
- Linking that CSS stylesheet to your application through an addition to the layout file

The :required option is specified in calls to the form builder's methods, if desired:

```
<%= f.text_field :name, :required => true %>

<%= f.password_field :secret, :required => true %>

<%= f.country_select :country, :required => true %>
```

:required, in this code, is only about how the field should be presented. Specifying whether a field should genuinely be required is better done in the model validation described in Chapter 7.

The wrap_field method, like the label_for method, comes after private in the code, making it callable only within the class or subclasses. It's not very complicated, choosing what value to use for the class attribute based on the contents of the :required option:

```
def wrap_field(text, options={})
    field_class = "field"
    if options[:required]
      field_class = "field required"
    end
    "<div class='#{field_class}'>" + text + "</div>"
  end
```

By default, class, which gives CSS stylesheets a hook for formatting the div, will just contain "field." It's a form field. If :required is true, however, it will have the value "field required." The class attribute can contain multiple values separated by spaces, so this means that the stylesheet can format this div as both a form field and as required.

The other methods need to call wrap_field, which makes them slightly more complicated. Therefore, the following:

```
def text_field(method, options={})
    label_for(method, options) + super(method, options)
  end
```

grows to become this:

```
def text_field(method, options={})
   wrap_field(label_for(method, options) + super(method, options), options)
  end
```

Looking through the parentheses, this means that `wrap_field` gets called with the text generated by the older methods, along with the options that it also needs to explore.

This wrapping happens for all of the public methods in `WrappingTidyBuilder`, with one important exception: `country_select`. Why? Because `country_select` already calls `select`, which will do the wrapping for it.

Connecting a field option to CSS styling is a good idea, but there's one problem: not every browser uses CSS. Remember Lynx, the text-only web browser? It's still out there, and so are a lot of different browsers that don't use CSS. Some are screen readers, others are simplified browsers for cell phones and other devices. To address that possibility, modifying `label_for` will add an asterisk to required fields, using the same logic that `wrap_field` had used:

```
def label_for(method, options={})
  extra = ""
  if options[:required]
    extra = " <span class='required_mark'>*</span>"
  end
  label(options.delete(:label) || method) + extra + "<br />"
end
```

If the `:required` option is set to `true`, this means that the label will have an extra `<span class='required_mark'>*</span>` appended after the label and before the `<br />` break between the label and the field.

The last piece needed is a stylesheet. The stylesheet itself will go into the *public/stylesheets/* directory, and here is called *public.css*. From there, it will be accessible to your application through the web server at */stylesheets/public.css*.

As you can see, though this isn't a book on CSS, four styles are defined. One is for the field, another for the label inside the field, another for the asterisk in the `required_mark`-classed span, and a last one is for the fields marked `required`:

```
/* styles for our forms */

div.field {
  margin-top: 0.5em;
  margin-bottom: 0.5em;
  padding-left: 10px;
}

div.field label {
  font-weight: bold;
}

div.field span.required_mark {
  font-weight: bold;
  color: red;
}
```

```
/* draw attention to required fields */

div.required {
  padding-left: 6px;
  border-left: 4px solid #dd0;
}
```

One last piece is needed—the application needs to reference this new style-sheet. The easiest way to do this is to add a line to the */app/views/layouts/people.html.erb* file, using the `stylesheet_link_tag` helper method:

```
<!DOCTYPE html PUBLIC "-//W3C//DTD XHTML 1.0 Transitional//EN"
        "http://www.w3.org/TR/xhtml1/DTD/xhtml1-transitional.dtd">

<html xmlns="http://www.w3.org/1999/xhtml" xml:lang="en" lang="en">
<head>
  <meta http-equiv="content-type" content="text/html;charset=UTF-8" />
  <title>People: <%= controller.action_name %></title>
  <%= stylesheet_link_tag 'scaffold' %>
  <%= stylesheet_link_tag 'public' %>
</head>
<body>

<p style="color: green"><%= flash[:notice] %></p>

<%= yield  %>

</body>
</html>
```

So, what does all this look like? Figure 8-7 gives you a sense of what's happened. Note the bars along the left edge of the required fields (yellow on the screen) and the red asterisks after their labels.

The first time through, this seems like a lot of work. And the first time through, it is. The good news, however, is that once you've done this, all that work is easy to reuse. You can change the stylesheet without having to go back to the layout. You can change the `wrap_field` method to do whatever you like. Once the infrastructure is built, it's much easier to change the details or to assign different details to different people working on a project, without fear of collision.

Figure 8-7. Extra formatting created through a form builder and CSS

Test Your Knowledge

Quiz

1. How much change did the controller need to handle file uploads?
2. Why did the form_for method suddenly explode in complexity when the MIME type of the returned data changed?
3. What goes into a migration when you add a field to a table?
4. How do you make methods invisible (and uncallable) outside of their class?

5. Are form builders for binding presentation to a specific piece of your model, or for supporting more general form construction?

6. Do builders map to controllers automatically?

7. Why (and when) are form builders worth the extra trouble of creating them?

Answers

1. The controller needed no change at all. All of the changes were in the views, to give users the ability to upload and display the file, and in the model, to handle the file when it arrived and when it was needed.

2. The form_for method looks much more complex because we'd been using a simplified form of it that assumes a lot of defaults. Change those defaults, and you need to specify much, much more.

3. A migration that adds a field needs an add_column call defining the field in the self.up method and a remove_column call in the self.down method.

4. Placing method definitions after the private keyword makes them usable only within the class.

5. They can be used for both general form construction and the creation of reusable components tightly bound to a particular model. You can even mix the two approaches in the same class.

6. No. Helper methods can bind to controllers through naming conventions, but using form builders requires adding a :builder argument to your form_for call.

7. Form builders are a great idea when they let you avoid repeating yourself. Used properly, they can make it easy for an application to look consistent, even if many different developers are working on different parts of the project.

## CHAPTER 9

Developing Model Relationships

Everything you've done so far has been in the context of an application with one and only one table. That's actually enough power to run a lot of different projects, from contact managers to time-series data collection. However, you'll quickly find that most of the projects for which it's worth creating a web application require more than just one table. Fortunately, Rails makes that easy, giving you the tools you need to create multiple tables and manage even complex relationships between them.

> If you don't know much about databases, now is a good time to visit Appendix B, *An Incredibly Brief Introduction to Relational Databases*. Up to this point, it's been possible to largely forget that there was a relational database underneath the application, except for some mechanics. From this point on, you'll need to understand how tables work in order to understand how Rails models work. (You still don't need to understand SQL, however.)

Working with multiple tables is, on the surface, pretty simple. Every Rails model maps to a table, so working with multiple tables just means working with multiple models. The hard part is managing the relationships between the tables—which in Rails demands managing the relationships between models.

Most of the steps for working with multiple models are the same as for working with single models, just done once for each table. Once the models are created, though, the real work begins. Some of it can be done easily and declaratively, while other parts require thinking ahead and writing your own code. This chapter marks the point where Rails itself can't directly support the operations suggested by your data models, and so there's a lot of coding to do. While the scaffolding still provides a helpful supporting framework, there's a lot of editing to do on models, migrations, routes, controllers, and views.

 Once again, it's important to emphasize how much easier it is to create a Rails application from scratch rather than trying to build it on top of an existing database. If you're trying to retrofit an old database with a shiny new Rails interface, odds are good that you need a much more advanced book than this one. You'll need to learn what goes on behind the scenes, not just how they work when all is well.

Connecting Awards to Students

The guestbook example of the previous few chapters isn't the best foundation on which to demonstrate a multi-table application, so it's time to change course. If you'd like to get an overview of the structures this chapter will create, these structures will be the same as those introduced in Appendix B, using students, awards, and courses. (The first version of them can be found in *ch09/students001*.)

Start by creating a new application:

```
rails students
```

If necessary, cd students, and then create a student model and the usual related scaffolding:

```
script/generate scaffold student given_name:string middle_name:string
family_name:string date_of_birth:date grade_point_average:decimal
start_date:date
```

Then create a second model, award, and its scaffolding:

```
script/generate scaffold award name:string year:integer student_id:integer
```

The students application now contains two models, one for students and one for awards. Students will receive awards, and awards will be connected to students, but Rails doesn't know that yet. The script/generate command gives a hint of this because it includes a student_id field, an integer that will connect to the (unspecified but automatic) id field of the students model.

Establishing the Relationship

To tell Rails about the connections between the two models, you need to modify the models. In *app/models/student.rb*, add the following between the class line and the end:

```
# a student can have many awards
has_many :awards
```

And in *app/models/award.rb*, add:

```
# every award is linked to a student, through student_id
belongs_to :student
```

These two declarations establish a relationship between the two models. Student records have awards—students don't have to have awards, but they can have many of them. Awards, however, for purposes of this example, are always linked to students.

 Technically, has_many and belongs_to are method names. They just happen to look like declarations, and it's a lot easier to think of them that way.

Now Rails knows about the connections between the models. What is it going to do to support that relationship, and what's still up to you?

Rails doesn't add automatic checking or validation to ensure that the relationships between objects work. It doesn't require, for example, that every award have a valid student_id. It doesn't change the scaffolding that was already built. Establishing the connection in the model is just the first step toward building the connection into your application.

Rails does provide some help in doing that, though. With these declarations, Rails adds methods to your classes, making it much easier for a student object to work with its award objects and for an award object to work with its student objects. You can find a complete listing of the methods added in the API documentation for has_many and belongs_to. For now, it probably makes sense to show how the association can help.

Supporting the Relationship

There is only one reference to a possible connection in the original forms created by the scaffolding: a student field, meant to hold the student_id, on the forms for entering and editing awards, shown in Figure 9-1. (You'll need to run rake db:migrate and ruby script/server to make the form appear.)

Figure 9-1. A basic awards form, where you can guess student numbers

As it turns out, while you can enter numbers corresponding to students in the student field (if you know them, figuring them out from the URLs for student records), there isn't any constraint on the numbers that go there. Awards can go to nonexistent students. It's easy to improve the situation, though, by adding a select field to the *app/views/awards/new.html.erb* view:

```
<p>
    <%= f.label :student_id %><br />
    <%= f.select :student_id, Student.find(:all , :order => "family_name,
given_name").collect {|s|
        [(s.given_name + " " + s.family_name), s.id]} %>
    </p>
```

The highlighted piece there might seem indigestible, but it's a fairly common way to create select lists based on related collections. The select method needs a field to bind to—:student_id—as its first parameter. The second parameter is a collection for the list to display. Student gets an object referring to the students model. The find method, which you've encountered before in *show.html.erb* templates, retrieves the list of all (:all) student records, sorted by family name and then given names (thanks to the :order parameter).

 Although calling Student.find(:all) works, it's better practice for views to reference only the instance variables—i.e., the variables with names prefixed by @—rather than connecting directly to a model.

The find method doesn't quite finish the work, though. You could stop here, if you were content to list object reference information in the select field. To show something a little more meaningful, however—both to the human user and to the program interpreting what comes back from the form—you need to specify both what gets displayed in the select field and the value that will get sent back.

That's where the collect method is useful. It takes a block as an argument ({}). The |s| is a very brief way of saying that Ruby should loop through the collection of students and put each row into a variable named s. On each iteration of the loop, the block will return an array, contained in [and]. Each of those arrays, which will become lines in the select list, will have two values. The first is the name of the student, generated by concatenating its given_name to a space and its family_name. That value will be displayed to the user. The second is the id value for the student, and that value will be what comes back from the form to the server.

All of that work creates the simple form shown in Figure 9-2, with its drop-down box for students.

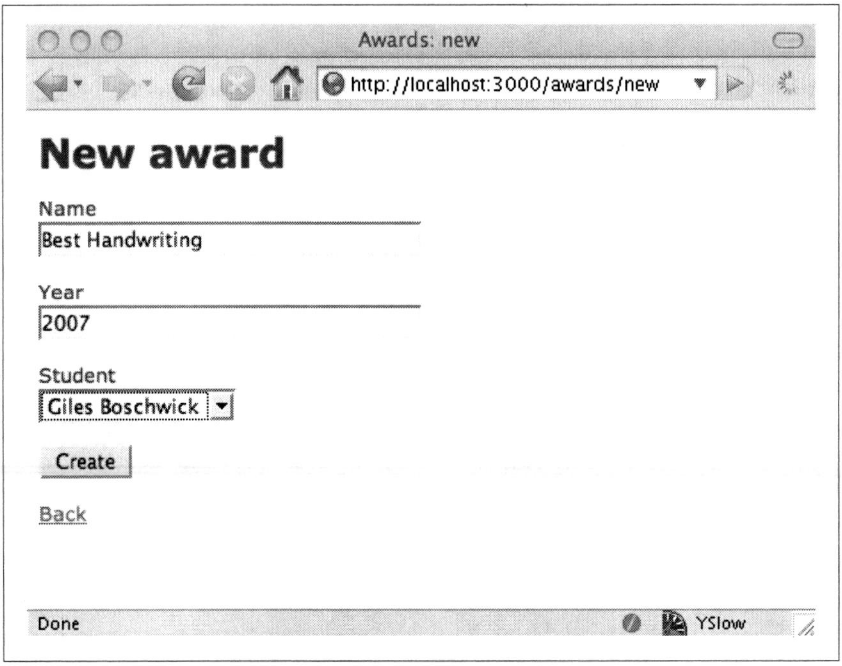

Figure 9-2. An awards form that minimizes guesswork about students

When the user submits this form, Rails gets back a "1" identifying the student's id. (At least it will if the students table looks like Figure B-1 in Appendix B.) That will go in the student_id field in the table. A "1" will be puzzling for humans, though. To fix that, in *app/views/awards/*, in *show.html.erb*, and *index.html.erb*, you might want to replace:

```
<%=h @award.student_id %>
```

with:

```
<%=h @award.student.given_name %> <%=h @award.student.family_name %>
```

Note that the @award variable (just award in *index.html.erb*) suddenly has a new method. Of course it understood student_id—that's a field defined by the original script/generate command. But the student method, and its methods given_name and family_name, are new. Those features are the result of Rails recognizing the belongs_to declaration and providing a more convenient notation for getting to the specific student that this particular award belongs_to.

While using student is great, there's one problem with the code just shown— it keeps repeating itself to combine given_name and family_name. There's a way to avoid that and to simplify most of this code. In the model for student (in *app/models/student.rb*), add a method called name that returns a simpler form:

```
def name
  given_name + " " + family_name
end
```

Like the methods representing database fields, the name method will be available from awards, as in:

```
<%=h @award.student.name %>
```

or:

```
<%= f.select :student_id, Student.find(:all).collect {|s|
    [s.name, s.id]} %>
```

You'll now get the cleaner-looking result shown in Figure 9-3 for a little less work.

 The name method creates what is often called an attribute on the model, acting as a method for retrieving its value. If you want to create attributes which can be assigned values, the convention would suggest a name like name=, along the lines of the photo= method described in "Extending a model beyond the database" on page 133.

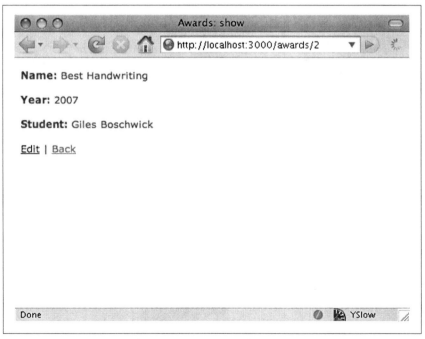

Figure 9-3. Showing a record with a name instead of a student ID number

Awards are now connected to students, but there still isn't any enforcement of that connection, just a form field that makes it difficult to enter anything else. Even with the form, though, there are corner cases—someone could, for example, delete a student after the form had been sent to a user. Or, more likely, a REST request could send XML with a bad student_id—fixing up the view hasn't changed anything in the model.

Guaranteeing a Relationship

Rails itself doesn't provide a simple mechanism for validating that the stu dent_id matches a student. You could, if you're handy with the underlying database, add such constraints through migrations. If you'd rather do something that feels like it's Rails, however, and operates within the model instead of the database, you can install the validates_existence_of plug-in. From your application's top directory, issue the command:

```
ruby script/plugin install
http://svn.hasmanythrough.com/public/plugins/validates_existence/
```

and add this line underneath the belongs_to declaration of *app/models/ award.rb*:

```
validates_existence_of :student
```

Now, if you restart the server and try to save an award record with a student that doesn't exist, you'll get a message like that shown in Figure 9-4. (Note that because the student was deleted, his or her name isn't available in the select list, and Giles Boschwick comes up again.)

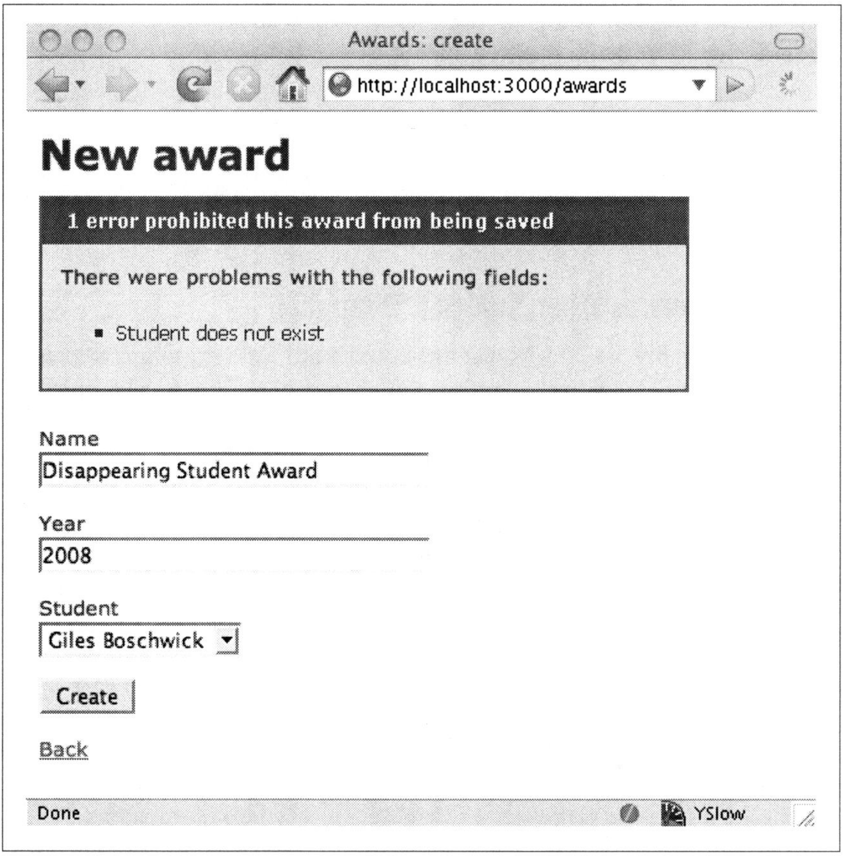

Awards: create
http://localhost:3000/awards
New award
1 error prohibited this award from being saved
There were problems with the following fields:
Student does not exist
Name
Disappearing Student Award
Year
2008
Student
Giles Boschwick
Create
Back
Done
YSlow

Figure 9-4. Enforcing the existence of students for every award

If you don't check for the existence of the student, then users will see a strange and incomprehensible message about a nil object when the view tries to process `award.student.name`, so this is most likely an improvement. For more information on `validates_existence_of`, including discussion on whether it's a good idea in the first place, see *http://blog.hasmanythrough.com/2007/7/14/validate-your-existence*.

> As that blog entry notes, you could decide to use Rails' built-in `validates_associated` method for this purpose, but it goes beyond checking whether there *is* an associated record all the way into checking whether there is a *valid* associated record. Depending on your needs, that could be more appropriate, but `validates_existence_of` is lighter-weight.

Later in this chapter, you'll see another approach to connecting awards to students that helps avoid these problems: nested resources.

Connecting Students to Awards

So, awards now have a basic understanding of the student records to which they connect. What can student records do with awards?

Removing Awards When Students Disappear

Although in reality, you might want to keep award listings around when students leave, for demonstration purposes it's worth considering the problem of orphaned records. The `validates_existence_of` plug-in described earlier can check that a corresponding student record exists at the time the award record is created, but once the record has been created, validation doesn't notice, for example, if the student is deleted. Keeping award records in sync with student records requires something more active.

Rails makes it very easy to make sure that when student records are deleted, the corresponding awards records are also deleted. You just need to add an option to the `has_many` declaration in *app/models/student.rb*:

```
has_many :awards, :dependent => :destroy
```

This is powerful and easy, but beware: those deletions will take place without any further confirmation. Once the user agrees to delete a student record, all of the awards records connected to that student will also disappear.

Counting Awards for Students

While adding the awards list to the main list of students could get really verbose, it does make sense to add a count of awards received to the list of students. If you add the set of awards listed in Figure B-3 of Appendix B, you'll have an awards list like that shown in Figure 9-5.

Adding a count of these awards to the students list that's in *app/views/students/index.html.erb* is simple. There needs to be a new column for awards, so at the end of the first row (in the first `tr` element), add:

```
<th>Awards</th>
```

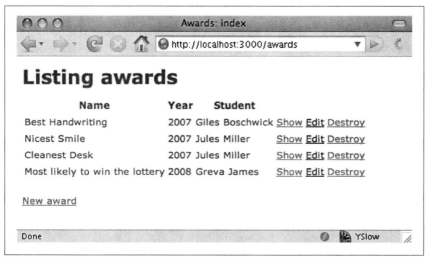

Figure 9-5. A brief students list

And then, after:

```
<td><%=h student.start_date %></td>
```

add:

```
<td><%=h student.awards.count %></td>
```

Just as every award object now has a student object because of belongs_to, every student object has an awards object, thanks to the has_many declaration. Getting a count of awards for that student is as simple as specifying count. Figure 9-6 shows the results of these additions.

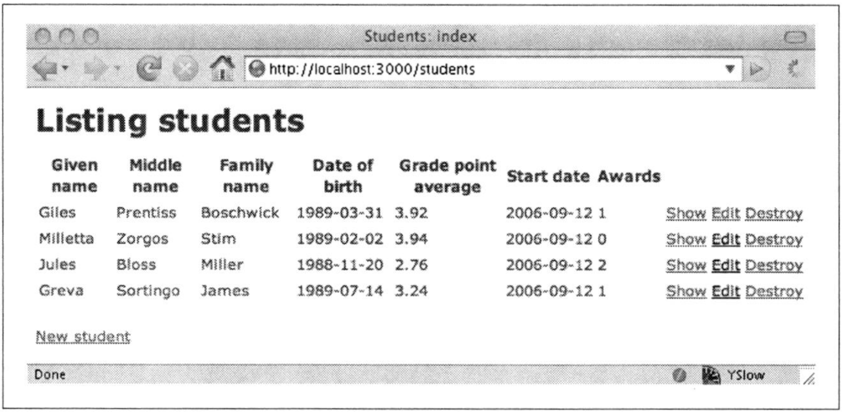

Figure 9-6. A students list complete with count of awards

You'll probably want to format them more beautifully, but the basic data is there. It also makes sense to add a list of awards to each of the individual student views, so that users can see what students have won as they review the records. Thanks to the **awards** method, it isn't difficult to add an awards table to *app/views/students/show.html.erb*:

```
<h3>Awards</h3>
<table>
  <tr>
    <th>Name</th>
    <th>Year</th>
    <th>Student</th>
  </tr>

<% for award in @student.awards %>
  <tr>
    <td><%=h award.name %></td>
    <td><%=h award.year %></td>
    <td><%=h award.student.name %></td>
  </tr>
<% end %>
</table>
```

In the view, the **@student** variable contains the current student. Running a for loop over the collection returned by **@student.awards**, which contains only the awards for the current student, lets you put the information about the awards into a table. You'll get a result like that shown in Figure 9-7.

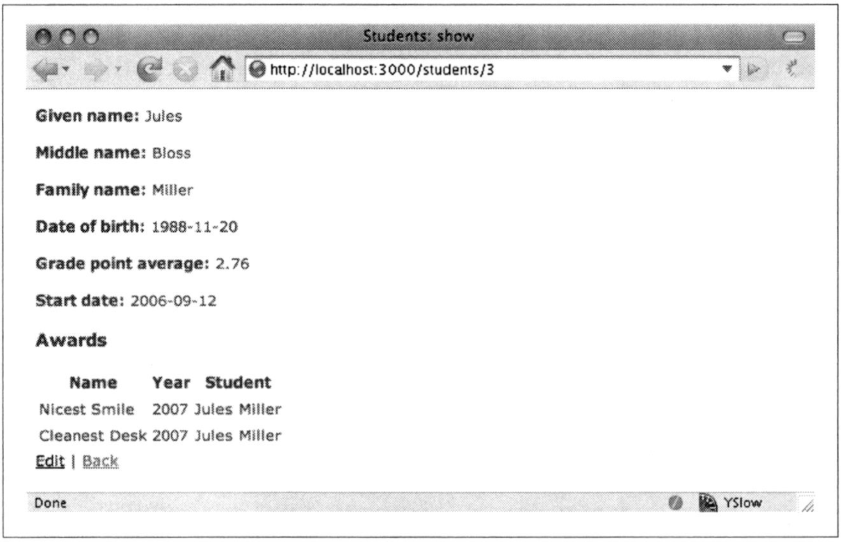

Figure 9-7. A student record with awards listed

Nesting Awards in Students

The connections between students and awards are workable, but the way that the two models are handled by the web application doesn't reflect their actual roles in the data models. Depending on your application and your preferences, this may be perfectly acceptable. There is, however, a better way to represent the awards model that more clearly reflects its relationship to students, implemented in *ch09/students002*.

The models will stay the same, and the views will stay almost the same. The main things that will change are the routing and the controller logic. Chapter 13 will explain routing in much greater depth, but for now it's worth exploring the ways that routing can reflect the relationships of your data models.

 If the work involved in creating a nested resource seems overwhelming, don't worry. It's not mandatory Rails practice, though it is certainly a best practice. Unfortunately, it's just complicated enough that it's hard to automate—but maybe someday this will all disappear into a friendlier `script/generate` command.

Changing the Routing

Near the top of the *config/routes.rb* file are the lines:

```
map.resources :awards
```

```
map.resources :students
```

Delete them, and replace them with:

```
map.resources :students, :has_many => [ :awards ]
```

It's another has_many relationship, which is this time expressed as a parameter to map.resources. You don't need to specify the belongs_to relationship. Yes, this is kind of a violation of "Don't Repeat Yourself," but at the same time it expresses a resource relationship, not simply a data model relationship.

You'll still be able to visit *http://localhost:3000/students/*, but *http://localhost:3000/awards/* will return an error. The routing support that the link_to methods expected when the original scaffolding was built has been demolished. The views in the *app/views/awards* directory are now visible only by going through students, and this change of position requires some changes to the views.

Instead of the old URLs, which looked like:

```
http://localhost:3000/awards/2
```

the URLs to awards now follow a more complicated route:

```
http://localhost:3000/students/3/awards/2
```

That added students/3 reflects that the award with the id of 2 belongs to the student with the id of 3.

Changing the Controller

While changing the routing is a one-line exercise, the impact on the controller is much more complicated. Most of it reflects the need to limit the awards to the specified student. Example 9-1 shows the new controller, with all changes bolded and commented. Most of the changes simply add the student object as context.

Example 9-1. Updating a controller to represent a nested resource

```ruby
class AwardsController < ApplicationController

  before_filter :get_student
  # :get_student is defined at the bottom of the file,
  # and takes the student_id given by the routing and
  # converts it to an @student object.

  def index
    @awards = @student.awards
    # was @awards = Award.find(:all)

    respond_to do |format|
      format.html # index.html.erb
      format.xml  { render :xml => @awards }
    end
  end

  def show
    @award = @student.awards.find(params[:id])
    # was Award.find(params[:id])

    respond_to do |format|
      format.html # show.html.erb
      format.xml  { render :xml => @award }
    end
  end

  def new
    @award = @student.awards.build
    # was @award = Award.new

    respond_to do |format|
      format.html # new.html.erb
      format.xml  { render :xml => @award }
    end
```

```ruby
    end

  # GET /awards/1/edit
  def edit
    @award = @student.awards.find(params[:id])
    # was @award = Award.find(params[:id])
  end

  # POST /awards
  # POST /awards.xml
  def create
    @award = @student.awards.build(params[:award])
    # was @award = Award.new(params[:award])

    respond_to do |format|
      if @award.save
        flash[:notice] = 'Award was successfully created.'
        format.html { redirect_to([@student, @award]) }
                    # was redirect_to(@award)
        format.xml  { render :xml => @award, :status => :created, :location =>
@award }
      else
        format.html { render :action => "new" }
        format.xml  { render :xml => @award.errors, :status =>
:unprocessable_entity }
      end
    end
  end

  def update
    @award = @student.awards.find(params[:id])
    # was @award = Award.find(params[:id])

    respond_to do |format|
      if @award.update_attributes(params[:award])
        flash[:notice] = 'Award was successfully updated.'
        format.html { redirect_to([@student, @award]) }
                    # was redirect_to(@award)
        format.xml  { head :ok }
      else
        format.html { render :action => "edit" }
        format.xml  { render :xml => @award.errors, :status =>
:unprocessable_entity }
      end
    end
  end

  def destroy
    @award = @student.awards.find(params[:id])
    # was @award = Award.find(params[:id])
    @award.destroy

    respond_to do |format|
      format.html { redirect_to(student_awards_path(@student)) }
```

```
                            # was redirect_to(awards_url)
        format.xml  { head :ok }
    end
  end

  private
  # get_student converts the student_id given by the routing
  # into  an @student object, for use here and in the view.
  def get_student
    @student = Student.find(params[:student_id])
  end
end
```

Most of these changes, in some form or another, convert a reference to awards generally to a reference to an award that applies to a particular student. You'll see some naming inconsistencies as that context forces different syntax: find(:all) simply disappears, new becomes build, and awards_url becomes student_awards_path. These new, different methods are created automatically by Rails thanks to the routing changes made earlier. Eventually these shifts will feel normal to you.

The new AwardsController uses one new technique. It starts with a before_fil ter, a call to code that will get executed before everything else does. In this case, the before_filter calls the get_student method, which helps reduce the amount of repetition in the controller. The controller will receive the stu dent_id value from routing, taking from the URL. Practically all of the time, though, it makes more sense to work with the corresponding Student object. The get_student method takes the student_id and uses it to retrieve the matching object and place it in the @student variable. That simplifies the methods in the controller and will also be used in the views.

 It's not hard to imagine a circumstance in which users want a complete list of awards and students. You can still provide one —it's just an extra step beyond the nested resource, requiring its own routing, controller method, and view.

Changing the Award Views

If users visit the new URLs at this point, they'll get some strange results. Rails routing originally defined one set of methods to support the old approach, and not only the results but also the method names and parameters need to change.

In the old version of *app/views/awards/index.html.erb*, the Show/Edit/Destroy links looked like Example 9-2, while the updated version looks like Example 9-3. Updates are marked in bold.

Example 9-2. Code for displaying awards before nesting by student

```erb
<h1>Listing awards</h1>

<table>
  <tr>
    <th>Name</th>
    <th>Year</th>
    <th>Student</th>
  </tr>

<% for award in @awards %>
  <tr>
    <td><%=h award.name %></td>
    <td><%=h award.year %></td>
    <td><%=h award.student.name %></td>
    <td><%= link_to 'Show', award %></td>
    <td><%= link_to 'Edit', edit_award_path(award) %></td>
    <td><%= link_to 'Destroy', award, :confirm => 'Are you sure?', :method =>
:delete %></td>
  </tr>
<% end %>
</table>

<br />

<%= link_to 'New award', new_award_path %>
```

Example 9-3. Displaying the awards on a student-by-student basis

```erb
<h1>Awards for <%=h @student.name %></h1>

<% if @student.awards.count > 0 %>
  <table>
    <tr>
      <th>Name</th>
      <th>Year</th>
    </tr>

  <% for award in @awards %>
    <tr>
      <td><%=h award.name %></td>
      <td><%=h award.year %></td>
      <td><%= link_to 'Show', [@student, award] %></td>
      <td><%= link_to 'Edit', edit_student_award_path(@student, award) %></td>
      <td><%= link_to 'Destroy', [@student, award], :confirm => 'Are you sure?',
:method => :delete %></td>
    </tr>
  <% end %>
  </table>

  <br />
<% else %>
  <p><%=h @student.given_name %> hasn't won any awards yet.</p>
<% end %>
```

```
<p>
  <%= link_to 'New award', new_student_award_path(@student) %> |
  <%= link_to 'Back', @student %>
</p>
```

In the new version, Example 9-3, the additional information about the student informs nearly every interaction. The headline (h1) has acquired the name of a specific student, rather than just being "Awards" generally. There's extra logic—the if and else statements—to make sure that awards are only displayed for students who have awards, presenting a polite message for students without award.

The largest changes, however, are in the logic that creates links. The Show and Destroy links change arguments, from just award to [@student, award], reflecting the additional information link_to will need to create a proper link. The links for Edit and New Award call a different method, new_stu dent_award_path, which will work through the nested resource routing to generate a link pointing to the right place. Given an argument for both a student and an award, it will generate a link to edit that award; given just a student argument, it will generate a link to create a new award for that student.

There's also a new Back link that goes back to the student's page. That's completely new navigation, necessary because of the extra context this page now has. Figure 9-8 shows what all of this looks like for Jules Miller, with his two awards, while Figure 9-9 shows the result for Milletta Stim, who hasn't won any yet.

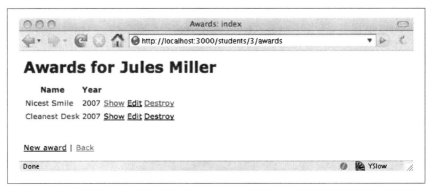

Figure 9-8. The awards list, scoped to a particular student

Figure 9-9. The awards list, when the student doesn't have any awards yet

The changes to *show.html.erb* are smaller, turning the links from:

```
<%= link_to 'Edit', edit_award_path(@award) %> |
<%= link_to 'Back', awards_path %>
```

to:

```
<%= link_to 'Edit', edit_student_award_path(@student, @award) %> |
<%= link_to 'Back', student_awards_path(@student) %>
```

The information displayed is the same, and context has little effect except on the links. Everything still looks like Example 9-3, except that the URL is different and you'd see a different link in the status bar if you rolled over Edit or Back.

There are also some minor changes to *new.html.erb* and *edit.html.erb*. Both of them get new headlines:

```
<h1>New award for <%=h @student.name %></h1>
```

and:

```
<h1>Editing award for <%=h @student.name %></h1>
```

Both of them change their `form_for` call from:

```
<% form_for(@award) do |f| %>
```

to:

```
<% form_for([@student, @award]) do |f| %>
```

Given an array of arguments instead of a single argument, `form_for` can automatically adjust to get the routing right for its data. The rest of the form fields look the same, except that the `select` call to create the picklist for students disappears completely, as that information comes from context.

And yet again, the links at the bottom change (though only the second line applies to *new.html.erb*):

```
<%= link_to 'Show', [@student, @award] %> |
<%= link_to 'Back', student_awards_path(@student) %>
```

Figure 9-10 shows the form for entering a new award in use, and Figure 9-11 shows the form for editing an existing award.

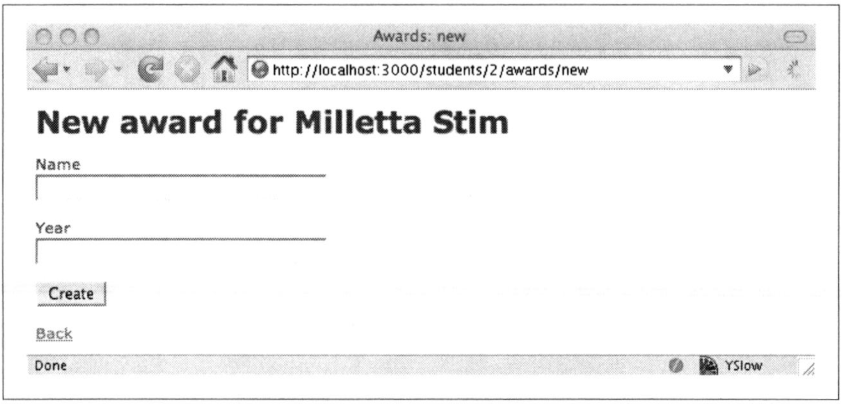

Figure 9-10. Entering a new award for a particular student

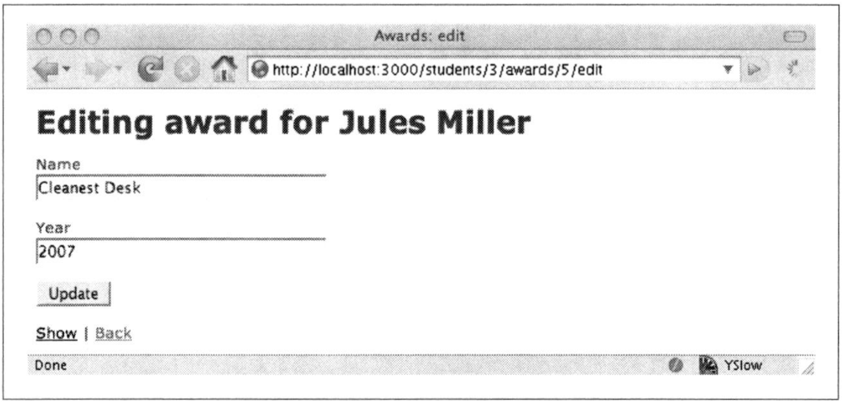

Figure 9-11. Editing an award—note the disappearance of the select box

Connecting the Student Views

There's one last set of things to address: adding links from the student views to the awards views. Awards used to have their own independent interface, but now they're deeply dependent on students. There are only two places where adding links makes clear sense, though: in the index listing and in the view that shows each student.

In *show.html.erb*, add a link to the awards for the student between Edit and Back with:

```
<%= link_to 'Awards', student_awards_path(@student) %> |
```

As shown in Figure 9-12, that'll give you a path to the awards for a student. (You might drop the existing list of awards there, too.)

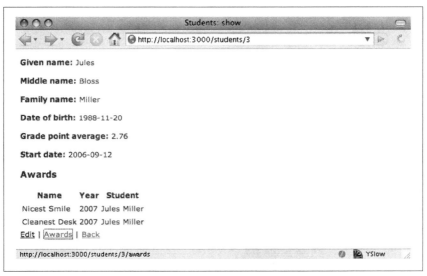

Figure 9-12. Adding a link from a student to a student's awards

That may actually be all the interface you want, but sometimes it's easier to look at a list of students and click on an Awards button for them. To add that, you need to add a column to the table displayed in *index.html.erb*. Between the links for Edit and Destroy, add:

```
<td><%= link_to 'Awards', student_awards_path(student) %></td>
```

The result will look like Figure 9-13. If users click on the Awards links, that will bring them to pages like Figures 9-8 and 9-9.

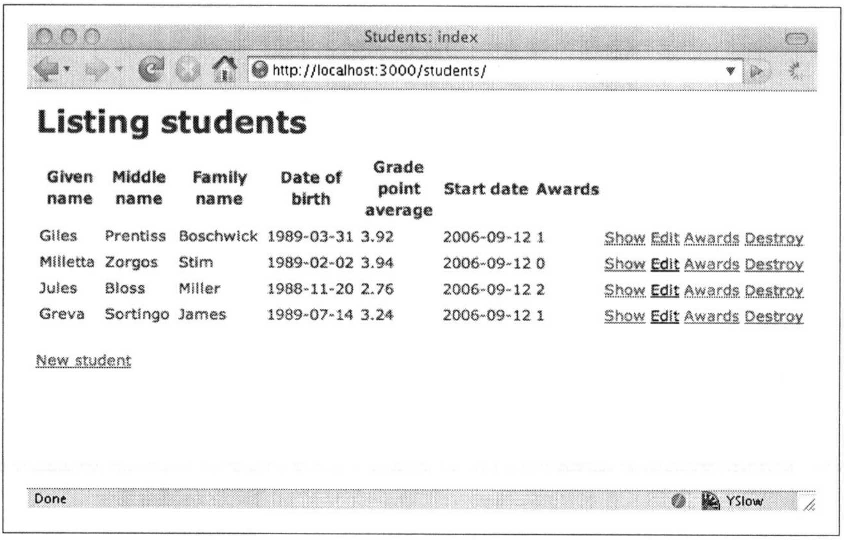

Figure 9-13. Students listing with connection to awards for each

Is Nesting Worth It?

Shifting awards from having their own interface to an interface subordinate to students was a lot of work. It's fairly clear why nesting resources is the "right" approach in Rails—it makes the has_many/belongs_to relationship explicit on every level, not just in the model. The work in the routing and the controller establishes the changes necessary for both the regular web user interface and the RESTful web services interface to work this way. The views, unfortunately, take some additional effort to bring in line, and you may have had a few ideas of your own while reading this about how you'd like them to work.

In the abstract, nesting is a great idea, but at the same time, it requires a lot of careful work to implement correctly in the views layer. That work may or may not be your first priority, though if you're going to nest resources, it's easier done earlier in the implementation process rather than later.

If you've built nested resources, you may find situations where you need to build additional interfaces. Sometimes the supposedly subordinate model is the main one people want to work with. In the awards example, most of the time people might want to know what awards a student has received, or add an occasional award, and the nested interface will work just fine. However, if lots of awards are given out across an entire school at the end of the year, and one person has the task of entering every award into the system, that person might want a more direct interface rather than walking through the nesting.

This situation could be addressed with an extra view that looked more like the ones earlier in the chapter.

Whether or not you decide to nest your own resources, you now have the information you need to do so, and you'll know what you're working with should you encounter Rails applications built using nested resources.

Many-to-Many: Connecting Students to Courses

The other frequent relationship between tables or models is many-to-many. A student, for example, can be taking zero or more courses, while a course can have zero or more students. (Students with zero courses might not yet have registered for anything, while courses with zero students might be awaiting registration or just unpopular.)

The relationship between the two is, from a modeling standpoint, even, so there won't be any need for nested resources, just a lot of connections. As usual, it makes sense to move up from the database through models to controllers and views to produce the code in *ch09/students003*. And also as usual, while Rails provides you with a foundation, you're still going to need to add a lot to that foundation.

 Remember, don't name a table "classes," or you will have all kinds of strange Rails disasters because of name conflicts. "Courses" is a safer option.

Creating Tables

Building a many-to-many relationship requires creating tables—not just a single table, but a many-to-many relationship that will require adding two tables beyond the student table already in the application. One will be the actual course list, and the other the table that joins courses to students, as shown in Figure B-5 of Appendix B. Creating the course list—which will need a full set of scaffolding—is simple:

```
script/generate scaffold course name:string
```

Creating the join table requires an extra few steps. Start by creating a migration:

```
script/generate migration CreateCoursesStudents
```

Doing this will create a migration file in *db/migrate* with a name that ends in *create_courses_students.rb*. Unfortunately, when you open it, all you'll see is:

```
class CreateCoursesStudents < ActiveRecord::Migration
  def self.up
  end
```

```
      def self.down
      end
    end
```

Once again, you've reached the boundaries of what autogenerated code will do for you, for the present. Creating the connecting table will require coding the migration directly. A simple approach, building just on what you've seen in previous generated migrations, looks like:

```
class CreateCoursesStudents < ActiveRecord::Migration
  def self.up
    create_table :courses_students, :id => false do |t|
      t.integer :course_id, :null => false
      t.integer :student_id, :null => false
    end
  end

  def self.down
    drop_table :courses_students
  end
end
```

All of this depends on meeting Rails' expectations for naming conventions. The table name is the combination of the two models being joined in alphabetical order, and the fields within the table are id values for each of the other models. Like all good migrations, it has a self.up method for creating the table and a self.down that removes it.

There is one performance-related issue to consider here. Rails has used the id value for tables as its main approach for getting data into and out of them rapidly. The id value, which you don't have to specify, is automatically indexed. If you want your application to be able to move through the many course_id and student_id values in this table, however, you'll need to add an index, as in:

```
class CreateCoursesStudents < ActiveRecord::Migration
  def self.up
    create_table :courses_students, :id => false do |t|
      t.integer :course_id, :null => false
      t.integer :student_id, :null => false
    end

    # Add index to speed up looking up the connection, and ensure
    # we only enrol a student into each course once
    add_index :courses_students, [:course_id, :student_id], :unique => true
  end

  def self.down
    remove_index :courses_students, :column => [:course_id, :student_id]
    drop_table :courses_students
```

```
    end
end
```

Indexes will be explained in greater detail in Chapter 13. Before moving on to the next steps, run `rake db:migrate` to build your tables.

Connecting the Models

Like `has_many` and `belongs_to`, `has_and_belongs_to_many` is a declaration that goes in the model. In *app/models/student.rb*, add:

```
# a student can be on many courses, a course can have many students
has_and_belongs_to_many :courses
```

And in *app/models/course.rb*, add:

```
# a student can be on many courses, a course can have many students
has_and_belongs_to_many :students
```

That's all you need to do to establish the connection. Rails will automatically —thanks to naming conventions—use the `courses_students` table you built to keep track of the connections between students and courses.

You may find it useful to add some convenience methods to the model, depending on what you need in your interfaces. In the `students` model, it makes sense to add some logic that answers basic questions and returns some information that Rails won't provide automatically. These build, of course, on the `courses` object that Rails did add to the model. First, a convenience method checks to see whether a given student is enrolled in a specified course:

```
def enrolled_in?(course)
    self.courses.include?(course)
end
```

The `enrolled_in?` method uses the `include?` method of `courses` to check whether a particular course is included in the list. If it is, then the student is enrolled, and `include?` and `enrolled_in?` will both return `true`. Otherwise, they return `false`.

The `enrolled_in?` convenience method will get called many times as the number of courses grows, executing the same query repeatedly. For now, its clarity is probably more important than its performance, but as you get more familiar with how Rails interacts with databases, you will want to optimize this method for better performance.

A similarly useful convenience method returns the list of courses that a student is not yet enrolled in, making it easy to create logic and forms that will let them enroll:

```
def unenrolled_courses
    Course.find(:all) - self.courses
end
```

This one-liner does some tricky set arithmetic. First, it calls `Course.find(:all)` to get a full list of all the courses available. Then it calls `self.courses` to get a list of the courses that already apply to this particular student. Finally, it does subtraction—set subtraction—removing the courses in `self.courses` from the full list. The - doesn't just have to mean subtracting one number from another.

 The `has_and_belongs_to_many` relationship is somewhat controversial, and some developers may prefer to use a `has_many :through` relationship, creating the intermediate table by hand.

Adding to the Controllers

Many-to-many relationships don't demand the kinds of controller change that nested resources did. You don't need to change method calls inside of the generated code, but you may want to add some additional methods to support functionality for both courses and students. While the added methods in the models focused on data manipulation, the methods in the controllers will add logic supporting interfaces to that data. The basic RESTful interfaces will remain, and the new interfaces will supplement them with some extra functionality specific to the combination of the two models.

In *app/controllers/courses_controller.rb*, the currently simple application only needs one extra method:

```
# GET /courses/1/roll
def roll
  @course = Course.find(params[:id])
end
```

The `roll` method, which will need a *roll.html.erb* view, will just provide a list of which students are in a given course, for roll call. The `:id` parameter will identify which course needs a list.

There's more to add in *app/controllers/students_controller.rb*, as we need a way to add students to and remove them from courses. First, though, it makes sense to create a means of listing which courses a student is in:

```
# GET /students/1/courses
def courses
  @student = Student.find(params[:id])
  @courses = @student.courses
end
```

As the :get_student method did for awards, the courses method takes an id value given it by the routing and turns it into an object—in this case a pair of objects, representing a given student and the courses he or she is taking.

The next two methods are pretty different from the controller methods the book has shown so far. Instead of passing data to a view, they collect information from the routing and use it to manipulate the models, and then redirect the user to a more ordinary page with the result. The first, course_add, takes a student_id and a single course_id and adds the student to that course:

```
# POST /students/1/course_add?course_id=2
# (note no real query string, just
# convenient notation for parameters)

def course_add

  #Convert ids from routing to objects
  @student = Student.find(params[:id])
  @course = Course.find(params[:course])

  unless @student.enrolled_in?(@course)
    #add course to list using << operator
    @student.courses << @course
    flash[:notice] = 'Course was successfully added'
  else
    flash[:error] = 'Student was already enrolled'
  end
  redirect_to :action => :courses, :id => @student
end
```

The course_add method uses the enrolled_in? method defined earlier in the model to check if the student is already in the course. If not, it adds the appropriate course object to the list of courses for that student and reports that all went well using flash[:notice]. If the student was already enrolled, it blocks the enrollment and reports the problem using flash[:error]. Then it redirects to a list of courses for the student, which will show the flash message as well as the list.

The remove method, for demonstration purposes, is a little bit different. It accepts a list of courses to remove the student from. It then tests the list to see if the student was actually enrolled and deletes the record connecting the student to the course if so. It also logs the removal to the info log of the application, and then redirects to the same page as course_add, listing the courses for a student:

```
# POST /students/1/course_remove?courses[]=
def course_remove

    #Convert ids from routing to object
    @student = Student.find(params[:id])

    #get list of courses to remove from query string
    course_ids = params[:courses]

    unless course_ids.blank?
      course_ids.each do |course_id|
        course = Course.find(course_id)
        if @student.enrolled_in?(course)
          logger.info "Removing student from course #{course.id}"
          @student.courses.delete(course)
          flash[:notice] = 'Course was successfully deleted'
        end
      end
    end
    redirect_to :action => :courses, :id => @student
end
```

Adding Routing

Making those controllers work requires telling Rails that they exist and how they should be called. Again, Chapter 13 will explain routing in greater depth, but you can add extra methods to an existing REST resource through its :member named parameter. To add the roll method to the routing the scaffolding created, add a :member parameter to the line in *config/routes.rb*:

```
map.resources :courses, :member => { :roll => :get }
```

For students, there are more methods, so the arguments are a bit more complicated, though generally similar:

```
map.resources :students, :has_many => [ :awards ],
    :member => { :courses => :get, :course_add => :post,
      :course_remove => :post}
```

At this point, Rails knows how to find the extra methods. All that's left is adding support for them to the views.

Supporting the Relationship Through Views

Cementing the relationship between students and courses requires giving users access to the functionality provided by the controllers and models. This can happen on several levels—application-wide navigation, showing counts in related views, and view support for the newly created controllers.

Establishing navigation

The views created by the scaffolding give basic access to both the students and the courses, but there's no user-interface connection, or even a navigation connection, between them. A first step might add links to both the student pages and the course pages, letting users move between them. As this is moving toward navigation for the application and as it will get used across a lot of different pages, it makes sense to create a navigation partial for easy reuse.

To do that, create a new file, *app/views/_navigation.html.erb*. Its contents are simple, creating links to the main lists of students and courses:

```erb
<p>
  <%= link_to "Students", students_url %> |
  <%= link_to "Courses", courses_url %>
</p>

<hr />
```

You could reference this partial from every view, but that's an inconvenient way to reference a partial that was meant to reduce the amount of repetition needed in the first place. Instead, add it to the layouts for each model in *app/views/layouts*. In each file, insert the boldfaced code below the body tag and above the paragraph for flash notices:

```erb
<body>

<%= render :partial => '/navigation' %>

<p style="color: green"><%= flash[:notice] %></p>
```

Every page in the application will now have links to the Students and Courses main index page, as shown in Figure 9-14.

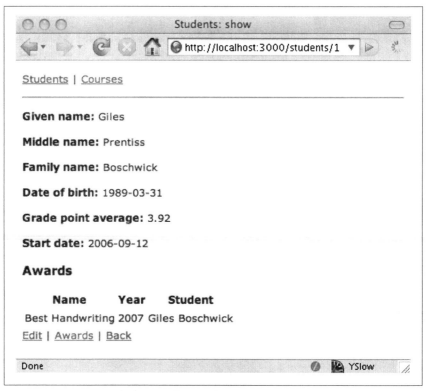

Figure 9-14. Navigation links to Students and Courses

 It may be neater to create a folder inside *app/views/* to hold your partials, instead of just leaving them in *app/views/*.

Showing counts

The index page for students, *app/views/students/index.html.erb*, currently lists a count for awards, and you can add a count for courses the same way. You need to insert a heading, `<th>Courses</th>`, in the first tr element, just before `<th>Awards</th>`, and then insert:

```
<td><%=h student.courses.count %></td>
```

just before the count of awards. Figure 9-15 shows what this looks like, though the header names are abbreviated a bit to make the table fit better. Note that there aren't any students in courses yet—the interface for adding them hasn't yet been built.

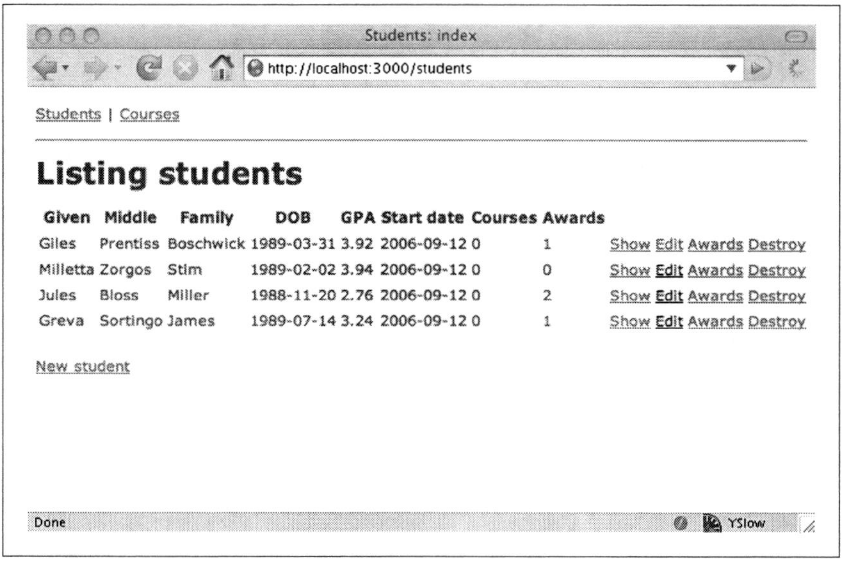

Figure 9-15. Students list showing course counts

Although the *app/views/courses/index.html.erb* file has less in it, you can add
`<th>Enrolled</th>` in the first `tr` element and insert:

```
<td><%=h course.students.count %></td>
```

Figure 9-16 shows the courses list, which hasn't been shown previously, though the RESTful interface made it easy to add the courses used in Appendix B.

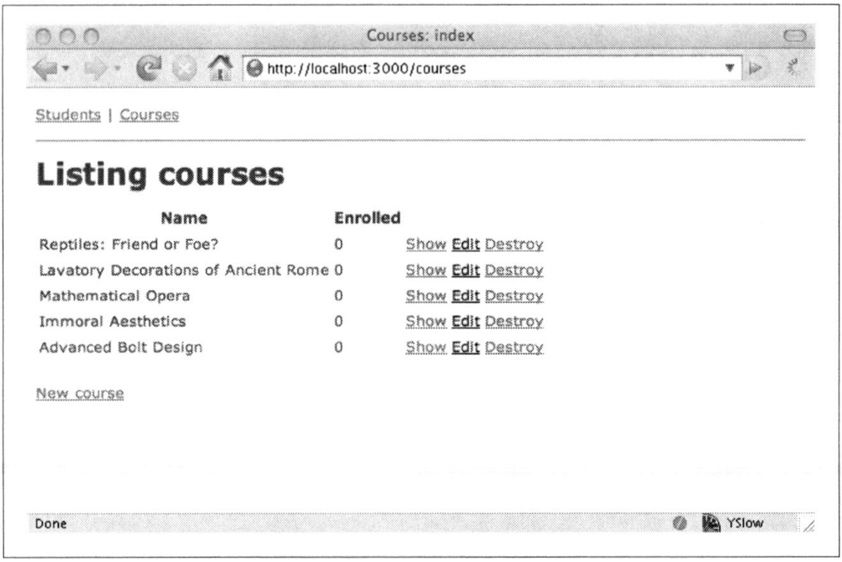

Figure 9-16. Course list showing enrollment counts

Again, no one is registered for any courses yet, so adding that functionality is a natural next step.

Enrolling students in courses

The critical piece for connecting students to courses is, of course, the form for adding courses to students. That form could be linked from the main list if you wanted, but for now we'll update the *app/views/students/show.html.erb* form so that it acts as the gateway to a student's awards and courses. There are two pieces to this. First, add a list of courses, perhaps in place of the awards list:

```
<p>
  <b>Courses:</b>
  <% if @student.courses.count > 0 %>
    <%= @student.courses.collect {|c| link_to(c.name, c)}.join(", ")%>
  <% else %>
    Not enrolled on any courses yet.
  <% end %>
</p>
```

This is much more compact than the table of awards. The `if` checks to see whether the student is registered for any courses. If so, it builds a compact list of courses using the `collect` method. If not, it just says so.

Second, add a link in the cluster of `link_to` calls at the bottom of the file:

```
<%= link_to 'Edit', edit_student_path(@student) %> |
<%= link_to 'Courses', courses_student_path(@student) %> |
```

```
<%= link_to 'Awards', student_awards_path(@student) %> |
<%= link_to 'Back', students_path %>
```

Bear in mind that where the navigation partial called courses_url, this calls courses_student_path with a specific student. That will take the user to a page such as *http://localhost:3000/students/1/courses*—which hasn't been created yet. To create that page, create a *courses.html.erb* file in the *app/views/students* directory. Example 9-4 shows one possible approach to creating a form for registering and unregistering students from courses.

Example 9-4. A courses.html.erb view for registering and removing students from courses

```
<h1><%= @student.name %>'s courses</h1>

<% if @courses.length > 0 %>
  <% form_tag(course_remove_student_path(@student)) do %>
  <table>
    <tr>
      <th>Course</th>
      <th>Remove?</th>
    </tr>
  <% for course in @courses do %>
    <tr>
      <td><%=h course.name %></td>
      <td><%= check_box_tag "courses[]", course.id %></td>
    </tr>
  <% end %>
  </table>
  <br />

  <%= submit_tag 'Remove checked courses' %>
  <% end %>
<% else %>
<p>Not enrolled in any courses yet.</p>
<% end %>

<h2>Enroll in new course</h2>

<% if @student.courses.count < Course.count then %>
  <% form_tag(course_add_student_path(@student)) do %>
    <%= select_tag(:course,
      options_from_collection_for_select(@student.unenrolled_courses,
        :id, :name)) %>
    <%= submit_tag 'Enroll' %>
  <% end %>
<% else %>
  <p><%=h @student.name %> is enrolled in every course.</p>
<% end %>

<p><%=link_to "Back", @student %></p>
```

This view contains two forms. Unlike most of the previous forms, these are created with the `form_tag` rather than the `form_for` method because they aren't bound to a particular model. The first form appears if the student is already enrolled in any courses, allowing the user to remove them from those courses. The second form appears if there are courses that the student hasn't yet enrolled in. (More sophisticated program logic might set a different kind of limit.) Each of the forms connects to a controller method on students—`course_remove` for the first one and `course_add` for the second.

The form for removing courses uses a list of checkboxes generated from the list of courses, while the form for adding them uses the somewhat more opaque but very powerful `options_from_collection_for_select` method. This helper method takes a collection—here, the list of courses returned by `@student.unen rolled_courses`, and two values. The first, `:id`, is the value to return if a line in the select form is chosen, and the second, `:name`, is the value the user should see in the form.

For information on the many more helper methods available for creating select lists, see `FormHelper`, `FormTagHelper`, and `FormOptionsHelper` in Appendix D.

Figure 9-17 shows the page before a student has registered for any courses, while Figure 9-18 shows the confirmation and removal options available once the student has signed up for their first course.

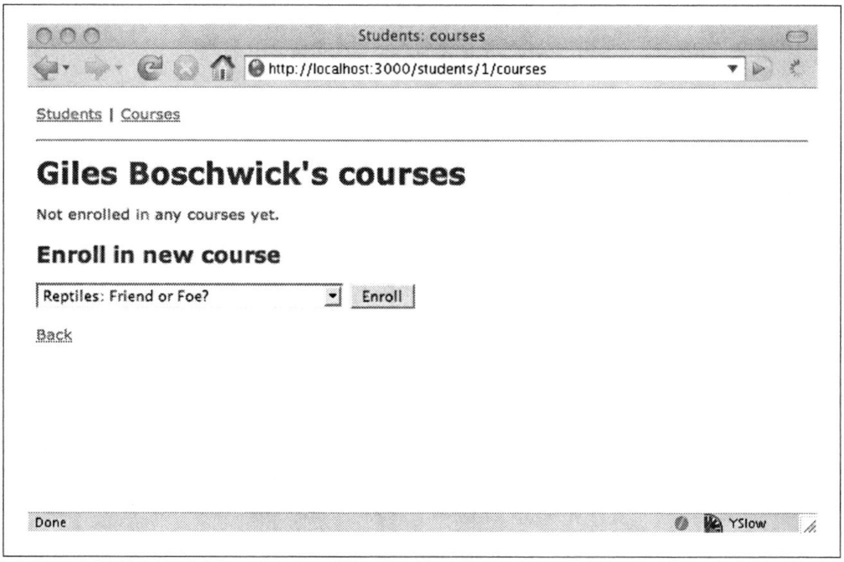

Figure 9-17. Adding courses, the first time around

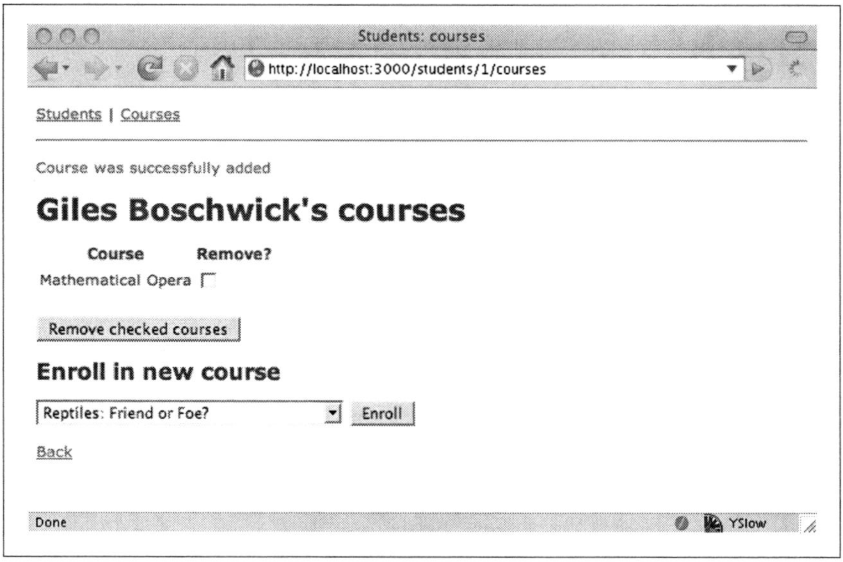

Figure 9-18. Adding or removing courses after a student has signed up

The checkboxes will create the parameters for course_remove and are a good choice when you want to operate on multiple objects at once. The select box is much slower and produces the results needed for the single-parameter course_add. You will, of course, want to choose interface components that match your users' needs.

There's one last component in need of finishing: the view that corresponds to the roll method on the courses controller. In *app/views/courses/show.html.erb*, add this link between the scaffolding's link_to calls for Edit and Back:

```
<%= link_to 'Roll', roll_course_path(@course) %> |
```

That will add the link shown in Figure 9-19, which will let users get to the list of students.

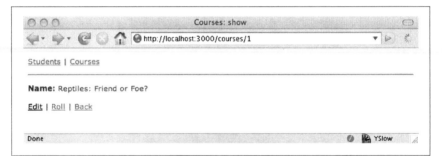

Figure 9-19. A (very brief) course description with a link to the roll call list

The actual roll call list code, shown in Example 9-5, is another simple table.

Example 9-5. Generating a roll call list through the connections from courses to students

```
<h1>Roll for <%=h @course.name %></h1>

<% if @course.students.count > 0 %>
  <table>
    <tr>
      <th>Student</th>
      <th>GPA</th>
    </tr>
    <% for student in @course.students do %>
    <tr>
      <td><%=link_to student.name, student %></td>
      <td><%=h student.grade_point_average %></td>
    </tr>
    <% end %>
  </table>
<% else %>
  <p>No students are enrolled.</p>
<% end %>

<p><%= link_to "Back", @course %></p>
```

The list of students is accessible from the @course object that the roll method in the controller exposed. That method didn't have anything specific to do with students, but because the students for the course are included in the course object, all of their information is available for display in the table, as shown in Figure 9-20. The links that link_to generated let you go directly to the student's record, making it easy to modify students who are in a particular course.

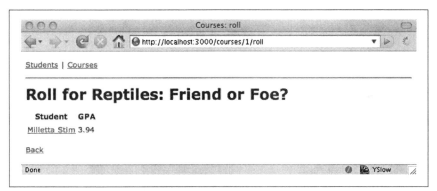

Figure 9-20. A roll call that connects to records for students in the class

What's Missing?

At this point, you should be starting to get a sense of what's involved in building a real Rails application. These examples really just scratch the surface, both of what's necessary and of what's possible.

While the students and courses application has gone much further into Rails than previous applications, it's still largely built on the scaffolding. The connections between course and student interfaces could be deepened. The new methods, while certainly functional, don't follow the same clean architectural lines that their RESTful predecessors had, taking a more direct path to getting things done. And finally, they don't offer the same XML-in/XML-out functionality of their RESTful predecessors.

There are also a few more relationships you can explore as you get further into Rails development. The has_and_belongs_to_many relationship can be used, for example, to connect a table to foreign keys in the same table, creating a *self-referential* join. There's also has_many :through, which lets you connect one table to another through an intermediate table, rather than directly with a foreign key. And finally, there's has_one, which is much like has_many, but limits itself to one connection.

Which of those opportunities are priorities for you depends on the needs of your own application. You may have related tables that need only occasional connections, or tables whose connections aren't modified directly by users. An XML-based API may be central for you, or it may be a pointless luxury that the RESTful scaffolding already overindulges in. Your allegiance to REST may not yet be that firm, in any event.

There's always more you could do, but at this point you have the basics you need to build real applications. The next few chapters will give you additional tools and techniques, and there's always more to learn, but congratulations! You now know most of what needs to be done to build an application.

Test Your Knowledge

Quiz

1. Where do you specify data relationships?
2. How much effort does Rails put into enforcing relationships between models?
3. What does the `collect` method do?
4. How can you check to see whether a related record exists?
5. Why would you want to go to the trouble of creating a nested resource?
6. When would you use a `before_filter`?
7. What does `form_for` do when it is passed an array for its first argument?
8. What two columns are needed in a join table?
9. Why would you want to index the columns of a join table?
10. Where do you tell Rails about new methods you've added to the scaffolding?

Answers

1. Relationships are specified in models. The models on both sides of any given relationship must identify how they relate to the other model. For example, a `has_many` relationship in one model should be matched by a `belongs_to` relationship in another model.
2. Rails doesn't put any effort into enforcing relationships between models. If you have constraints to impose, you need to create code that checks and enforces them.

3. The `collect` method iterates over a collection and gathers the results from a block. It's an easy way to turn a list of data into a `select` list, for instance.

4. You could check for a related record with `find`, but in most validation contexts it's easier to use the `validates_existence_of` plug-in. (If you want to check for a related *valid* record, then Rails' built-in `validates_associated` will work.)

5. Nested resources have some programming aesthetic appeal, but they're also useful for making relationships explicit and easily enforceable.

6. `before_filters` are useful anytime you have code that should run in advance of all of the any other methods being called. It might be initialization code, or code that tests that certain conditions have been met.

7. The `form_for` method uses the first argument to establish the target for the form's results. If the first argument is a single object, it will create a URL pointing to that object. If the first argument is an array containing more than one object, it assumes that the first object contains the second, and generates a URL reflecting a nested resource relationship.

8. A join table needs a column to store `id` values for each of the two models it connects. By Rails conventions, these columns are named *model*_id. A column linking to students, for example, should be `student_id`.

9. Indexing both of the columns in a join table will give you much better response times than leaving them unindexed.

10. You'll need to add information about new methods in the *routes.rb* file, and create views for them as well.

## CHAPTER 10

Managing Databases with Migrations

Migrations might seem strange at first, but over time they'll become a very ordinary part of your work, whether you generate them automatically or customize them by hand. Rails' approach to managing data structures is very different from the traditional separation of database design from programming. While Rails still maintains a separate toolkit for defining data structures, that toolkit attempts to improve on the traditional SQL Data Definition Language (DDL) by wrapping DDL in Ruby code.

Migrations are something of a world of their own in the Rails environment, but they are still recognizably Rails, built into the same development process. Migrations are all written in Ruby code, using a fairly small set of conventions. This book has used migrations throughout—you can write much of a Rails application without them—but until the last chapter (and then only once), those migrations were generated using Rails' inventive scripts. Once you move past those scripts, migrations are a little more difficult, but still not that complicated.

 The details of migrations may not be your first priority. You can safely skip this chapter and come back to it if database and data structure management seem like good reading for a really rainy day.

What Migrations Offer You

Migrations are part of Rails' general effort to separate developers from direct contact with databases. From a Rails perspective, databases are kind of a "giant hash in the sky," a conveniently persistent storage system for data that shouldn't need much direct attention. While it's good to have a general idea of the database structures underneath your application and to know what tables and rows are so you can communicate with people outside of Rails development, in many ways Rails itself represents a revolt against database culture in web programming.

Migrations reflect the approach Rails takes to databases. Rails expects database structures to grow and change as the application itself grows and changes. There won't be a large planning meeting at the start of a project to lay out database structures and responsibility for maintaining them—responsibility for the database lies with the same programmers who are writing the rest of the code. Those programmers will make changes as and when they see fit.

As a result, migrations are effectively lists of changes. Each migration is a set of instructions that applies to the results of the previous migration. The first migration creates the first table and probably some rows and columns, and later migrations can create their own tables or modify existing tables.

Also, understanding that programmers can (and do) make mistakes, each migration contains both a path forward (in self.up) and a path backward (in self.down). As long as both paths work, migrations offer an incredibly flexible approach that lets you make changes to your database whenever and wherever necessary.

Because Rails works hard at staying independent of any given database implementation, migrations also offer you a convenient technique for creating your application using one database for development or testing and yet another for deployment. They also offer a means of moving improvements created by developers after an application has been released to the live release of that application—though, of course, patching live databases supporting real users who might complain remains a scary project.

It's generally a good idea to stick to migrations when managing databases for use with Rails. You may know a lot about MySQL, SQLite, PostgreSQL, Oracle, or whatever database engine you've chosen, and be able to tweak your application's database for better performance. Everything will go along fine —until Rails discovers that its migrations' opinion of what your database contains is different from what is actually there.

You may especially have a hard time rolling back migrations as a result, and it'll require careful work to transfer the work you did in the database to the live production environment as well.

You certainly *can* work on your databases directly. It's probably wise, however, to be very cautious about doing that until you're completely confident in how these interactions work.

Migration Basics

Migrations are maintained in files stored in the *db/migrate* folder. Each file contains one more-or-less discrete set of changes to the underlying database. Unlike most of the code you write, migrations are not automatically run when you start up Rails, instead waiting for an explicit command from the rake tool.

Migration Files

Prior to Rails 2.1, migration files had relatively comprehensible names, such as *001_create_people.rb*. Rails 2.1 brought a new naming convention, in which the first part of the name changed from being a sequential number to being a much longer timestamp, like *20080701211008_create_students.rb*. The new wider names are incredibly annoying if you're just one developer creating applications on a laptop with a narrow screen, but help avoid name collisions if you're a developer working on a team where multiple people can check in their own migrations. (Perhaps the team developers have larger monitors as well?)

While you can create migration files by hand, if you're going to work with migrations in the new world of timestamps, you should probably stick to using script/generate, which will handle all of that for you. Many script/gener ate calls will create migrations as part of their work toward creating a model and supporting infrastructure, but if you just want to create a blank migration, enter the command script/generate migration NameOfMigration, where Name OfMigration is a reasonably human-comprehensible description of what the migration is going to do. (For the name, you can use CamelCase or under scores_between_words.) Your result, depending on the name you give it, will look something like Example 10-1.

Example 10-1. An empty migration file, fresh from script/generate

```
class EmptyMigration < ActiveRecord::Migration
  def self.up
  end

  def self.down
  end
end
```

All migrations are descended from `ActiveRecord::Migration`. The `self.up` and `self.down` methods are the heart of the migration. In theory, at least, they should be strictly symmetrical. Everything created in `self.up` should vanish when `self.down` is called, leaving the database structure in the same state it had before the migration was run. If you let these two methods get out of sync, you'll have a very hard time recovering.

> As always, the `script/generate` command has smarts and surprises. If you name a migration along the lines of `AddAgeToPeo ple` and specify `age:integer`, Rails will create a migration which adds a field named `age` to the `people` table, sparing you some typing.

Most of the rest of the chapter will examine what you can put inside of those two methods.

> While you'll obviously be paying attention when writing your applications, and the generators shouldn't create problems, there's one situation that might still bite you: an unsaved file you're editing. If you think you've made changes and run the migration forward, but didn't save the file, and then save the file and roll the migration back....
>
> Unfortunately, fixing it really depends on what exactly you did. Just be careful to make sure that you've saved all of your files when editing migrations before running them.

Running Migrations Forward and Backward

You apply migrations to the database using the Rake tool. You can run `rake --tasks` to see the ever-growing list of tasks it supports, and most of the database-related tasks are prefixed with `db:`. While you're learning Rails, there are only three tasks that you really need to know, and a fourth you should know about:

db:migrate

> You'll run rake db:migrate frequently to update your database to support the latest tables and columns you've added to your application. If you run your application and get lots of strange missing or nil object errors, odds are good that you forgot to run rake db:migrate. It also updates the *db/schema.rb* file, which is a one-stop description of your database.

db:rollback

> If you made changes but they didn't quite work out, rake db:rollback will let you remove the last migration applied. If you want to remove multiple migrations, you can specify rake db:rollback STEP=*n*, where *n* is the number of migrations you want to go back. Be careful—when Rails deletes a column or table, it discards the data. It also updates the *db/schema.rb* file, which is a one-stop description of your database.

db:drop

> If things have gone really wrong with your migrations, rake db:drop offers you a "throw it all away and start over" option, obliterating the database you've built—and all its data.

db:reset

> Using rake db:reset is a little different from using rake db:drop—it obliterates the database and then builds a new one using the *db/schema.rb* file, reflecting the last structure you'd created.

db:create

> The rake db:create command tells the database to create a new database for your application, without requiring you to learn the internal details of whatever database system you're using. (You must, of course, have the right permissions to create that database.)

Most of the time, rake db:migrate will be your primary interaction with rake. When you run it, it will show information on each migration it runs, as shown in Example 10-2, using the migrations from the previous chapter. (The start of each migration is bolded to make it easier to review the output.)

Example 10-2. Output from Rake, for a set of four migrations

```
S:students001c simonstl$ rake db:rollback
(in /Users/simonstl/Documents/RailsOutIn/current/code/ch09/students001c)
S:students001c simonstl$ rake db:migrate
(in /Users/simonstl/Documents/RailsOutIn/current/code/ch09/students001c)
== 20080701211008 CreateStudents: migrating ============================
-- create_table(:students)
   -> 0.0046s
== 20080701211008 CreateStudents: migrated (0.0048s) ===================

== 20080701211027 CreateAwards: migrating ==============================
-- create_table(:awards)
```

```
        -> 0.0054s
== 20080701211027 CreateAwards: migrated (0.0056s) =====================

== 20080705141325 CreateCourses: migrating ============================
-- create_table(:courses)
        -> 0.0031s
== 20080705141325 CreateCourses: migrated (0.0034s) ====================

== 20080705141333 CreateCoursesStudents: migrating ====================
-- create_table(:courses_students, {:id=>false})
        -> 0.0026s
-- add_index(:courses_students, [:course_id, :student_id], {:unique=>true})
        -> 0.0039s
== 20080705141333 CreateCoursesStudents: migrated (0.0071s) ============
```

The timing information may be more than you need to know, but you can see
what got called in what migration. If something goes wrong, it will definitely
let you know.

Rails will happily let you perform operations on multiple tables from within a single migration. Eventually, that may be
an attractive option, but when you're first starting out, it's
usually easier to figure out what's going on, especially what's
going wrong, when each migration operates only on a single
table.

Inside Migrations

The easiest way to familiarize yourself with migrations is (as is often the case
with Rails) to examine what Rails puts in them with script/generate. In
Chapter 9 we created a students model with:

```
script/generate scaffold student given_name:string middle_name:string
family_name:string date_of_birth:date grade_point_average:decimal
start_date:date
```

That code generated many files, but the migration it created went into *db/
20080701211008_create_students.rb* and contained the code shown in Example 10-3.

Example 10-3. Code for setting up a table, generated by a scaffolding call

```
class CreateStudents < ActiveRecord::Migration
  def self.up
    create_table :students do |t|
      t.string :given_name
      t.string :middle_name
      t.string :family_name
      t.date :date_of_birth
      t.decimal :grade_point_average
```

```
      t.date :start_date

      t.timestamps
    end
  end

  def self.down
    drop_table :students
  end
end
```

You can also generate migrations with `script/generate migration migration_name`. Normally, migrations that create new tables start their names with `create`, while migrations that add to existing tables start their names with `add`.

Working with Tables

Most of the activity in the migration generated by the scaffolding, shown in Example 10-1, is in the `self.up` method. `self.down` drops the whole students table, which also disposes of any contents it had, so it can skimp on details, just ordering `drop_table :students`. As you might suspect, `drop_table` just removes the table and all of its columns and data completely.

The `self.up` method uses `create_table` for two purposes. First, it creates the `:students` table. Second, it establishes a context. Much like `form_for` with its block and its f variable for establishing context, `create_table` creates a block and conventionally uses a t variable for context.

The rest of the calls inside the `create_table` block begin with that t. While they look like declarations, making migrations nearly as easy to read as database schemas, they are actually method calls, using the name of the data type as the method.

 There isn't any listing here for an `id` value, even though Rails uses ids for practically everything. Rails will automatically add an id to tables you create with `create_table`, unless you specify the `:id => false` option.

Data Types

As noted earlier, Rails supports 11 data types directly:

```
:string
:text
:integer
:float
```

```
:decimal
:datetime
:timestamp
:time
:date
:binary
:boolean
```

Each of these types can be created by calling its name after t.. For example, t.string :given_name creates a column in the :students table of type string that's named given_name. And t.date :date_of_birth creates a column in the :students table of type date that's named date_of_birth.

In older versions of Rails (prior to 2.0), those two declarations would have been written:

```
t.column :given_name, string
t.column :date_of_birth, string
```

You may still encounter this older form in old documentation and in code. It still works, but it's less convenient, so use the newer form.

t.timestamps is not the same as t.timestamp. It is unique, a convenience method Rails uses to manage creation and modification times as created_at and updated_at columns. (You can remove timestamps with t.remove_time stamps.)

Each of the data types can accept named parameters as well:

- All of them accept :default => *value*, though the results may not be what you expect since this doesn't pass through to the model. New models won't have the default value, users won't see them, and they'll be overwritten by whatever the users enter, even if it's nothing.

- All types also accept :null => true|false, where the boolean value identifies whether or not a null value is acceptable. Set this to false to limit the column to nonnull values.

- :string, :text, :binary, and :integer types accept :limit => *size*. The *size* is the permitted length of the value in characters or bytes.

- The :decimal data type also accepts :precision and :scale parameters. The :precision parameter specifies how many digits the number can have, while the :scale parameter specifies how many of those digits appear after the decimal point.

Always specify `:precision` and `:scale` if your application might move across different databases, like the common case of SQLite in development and MySQL in production. Different databases treat `:decimal` slightly differently, but specifying these parameters will minimize surprises.

You may find it useful to express these constraints in the migration for implementation in the database layer, but in most cases you'll probably find it easier to establish these in the model layer, with the validations discussed in Chapter 7. (Sometimes specifying `:precision` and `:scale` is recommended for `:dec imal` types because of database incompatibilities, however.)

You can, if necessary, create custom types specific to a given database. If you really, truly are certain you want to do that, study the `config.active_record.schema_format` setting that's in the *config/environment.rb* file. In general, though, while it's nice to know that you *can* do this, you usually *shouldn't*.

Working with Columns

When you're first starting out, most of your data structure creation will be whole tables at a time. Once you've established your application, however, new ideas are bound to flow. You'll probably create some new tables, but you'll also create or remove columns within your existing tables. Conveniently, migrations support `add_column` and `remove_column` methods.

Chapter 8 used a migration to add a column for file extensions:

```
class AddPhotoExtensionToPerson < ActiveRecord::Migration
  def self.up
    add_column :people, :extension, :string
  end

  def self.down
    remove_column :people, :extension
  end
end
```

The first argument for `add_column` is the table to add the column to. The second argument is the name of the column, and the third column is the type. You can add extra options as discussed earlier in the "Data Types" on page 197" section if you want, as named parameters following the type.

The `remove_column` method is simpler, taking just the table and the column to remove. There's also a `remove_columns` method that lets you specify multiple column names.

Indexes

Indexes (or indices if you prefer) speed up information retrieval, but slow down writes because the index also has to be updated. By default, the only column Rails tells the database to index is the `id` column, which it references constantly. If you have other columns that you'll be searching regularly, notably columns in join tables, you'll definitely want to learn about `add_index` and `remove_index`. The many-to-many example in Chapter 8 used them in a migration for building the join table between courses and students:

```
class CreateCoursesStudents < ActiveRecord::Migration
  def self.up
    create_table :courses_students, :id => false do |t|
      t.integer :course_id, :null => false
      t.integer :student_id, :null => false
    end

    # Add index to speed up looking up the connection, and ensure
    # we only enrol a student into each course once
    add_index :courses_students, [:course_id, :student_id], :unique => true
  end

  def self.down
    remove_index :courses_students, :column => [:course_id, :student_id]
    drop_table :courses_students
  end
end
```

After this migration's `self.up` method has created the `courses_students` table, it calls the `add_index` method. The first argument is always the table to receive the index. The second argument can either be the column to be indexed or an array listing columns. You could have indexed each of the columns in the above `add_index` method with two calls:

```
add_index :courses_students, :course_id, :unique => true
add_index :courses_students,:student_id, :unique => true
```

However, calling the `add_index` method with a two-component array created a different kind of index, indexing the values of each column to the other. For a join table, that's the most efficient approach.

You can also specify two options. The first, `:unique`, indicates whether all values in the column have to be unique. The examples just shown set it to `true`, but if you're indexing content other than `id` values, the default of `false` may be more appropriate. (More typically these kinds of constraints are applied in Rails rather than the database, at the model level.) You can also name the index through the `:name` parameter.

In `self.down`, the `remove_index` method gets called *before* the `drop_table` method. It doesn't need any options, and it simply removes the index.

Other Opportunities

Migrations offer many other possibilities for creative database manipulation, advanced development, and general trouble-causing. The `ActiveRecord::Con nectionAdapters::SchemaStatements` class, which contains the most of the methods useful for creating migrations, offers a wide variety of other options you may want to explore. Some, like `add_order_by_for_association_limit ing!`, are simply obscure, though they may be the right thing for a certain situation. Others, like `rename_column` and `rename_table`, have fairly obvious functionality. Here's the list of what's out there:

```
add_order_by_for_association_limiting!
add_timestamps
assume_migrated_upto_version
change_column
change_column_default
change_table
columns
distinct
initialize_schema_migrations_table
native_database_types
options_include_default?
remove_timestamps
rename_column
rename_table
structure_dump
table_alias_for
table_alias_length
table_exists?
```

The Rails documentation describes all of these in much greater depth.

One final method, not listed here, is worth noting: `execute`. The `execute` method lets you issue SQL commands to the database. If you're really fond of SQL, that may be something you want to explore, though it's probably not the best option for your first few outings with Rails.

Test Your Knowledge

Quiz

1. How do you run migrations forward?
2. How do you create a new migration?
3. What should the `self.down` method do in a migration?
4. What Rails data type should you use to represent currency values?
5. How do you add a new field to a record?

Answers

1. With the `rake db:migrate` command.
2. To keep in line with Rails' timestamp-based naming convention, it's best to use `script/generate migration NameOfMigration`, and then edit the resulting file in the *db/migrate* directory.
3. The `self.down` method defines what should happen if the migration is rolled back using `rake db:rollback`. The tables, column, and indexes created in `self.up` need a corresponding removal process in `self.down`.
4. The `:decimal` type is the most precise way to keep track of money. It can keep track of cents to the right of the decimal point and will contain values with a fixed number of decimal places much more accurately than `:float`.
5. New fields get created with `add_column`, as "fields" are represented as columns and the records that contain them as rows.

## CHAPTER 11

Debugging

When you're first starting out in Rails, it's easy to wonder what exactly is going on at any given moment. Web applications by their very nature are tricky to debug, as so much happens before you see an answer. Fortunately, Rails includes tools to figure out what's going wrong while applications are running. Debugging tools keep evolving, but there's a basic set you should understand from the beginning.

Creating Your Own Debugging Messages

I'm sure it was facetious, but an old programmer once told me that "the real reason the PRINT statement was invented was for debugging." While it may not be aesthetically pleasing to dump variable values into result screens, it's often the easiest thing to do in early development. All controller instance variables are available to the view, so if you want to see what they contain, you can just write something like:

```
<%= @student %>
```

to display the contents of @student. However, if the object has much complexity and isn't just a string, it will insert something like:

```
#<Student:0x21824f8>
```

into the HTML for the page. All you'll see is the #.

Rails does, however, offer a way to make this more useful. The DebugHelper class offers a helper method named debug. While it won't magically debug your programs, it will present these kinds of messages in a slightly prettier form, as YAML (Yet Another Markup Language). Instead of <%= @student %>, for example, you could write <%= debug(@student) %>. The debug method would give you:

```
--- !ruby/object:Student
attributes:
  start_date: "2006-09-12"
  updated_at: 2008-07-17 23:04:03
  id: "2"
  family_name: Stim
  given_name: Milletta
  date_of_birth: "1989-02-02"
  created_at: 2008-07-03 18:34:59
  grade_point_average: "3.94"
  middle_name: Zorgas
attributes_cache: {}
```

If you need to take a quick look at what's happening and see it on the page where it's happening, this can be a useful technique.

Logging

You may not have thought of it this way, but you've been working with Rails logs since the first time you entered **script/server**. All of that information flowing by is the development log. You can find all of it in the *log* directory of your application, stored in the *development.log* file. (There are also *test.log* and *production.log* files there for use when your application runs in test or development mode, as described in the next chapter.)

While Rails is certainly generous with the information that it sends to the log in development mode, that sheer volume can make it hard to find things. It may also not be sending what you want to see. If you want to send something specific to the log, use the **logger** object in your model, controller, or view. In a model or controller, this would look like:

```
logger.info 'This is a message to send to the log'
```

while in the view it would look like:

```
<% logger.info 'This is a message to send to the log' %>
```

You can use **<%=** rather than **<%** to send the message to both the screen and the logger if you want to combine a visible message with a permanent record:

```
<%= logger.info 'This is a message for the view and the log' %>
```

The user would then see "This is a message for the view and the log" on her screen, and it would also be stored in the log file.

One piece of information that is logged and is worth pointing out is timing information. You'll find lines in the log like:

```
Completed in 0.01451 (68 reqs/sec) | Rendering: 0.00775 (53%) |
DB: 0.00093 (6%) | 200 OK
```

That tells you how fast the whole thing was completed, how long the view processing took (rendering), and how long the database processing (DB) took. The last entry on the line is the HTTP response. You should note that Rails can probably execute the code much faster when in production; during development, it's loading, reloading, and logging a lot of extra information.

There may also be times you want to make certain that certain information isn't logged. This is most important for sensitive information and is easily accomplished with the `filter_parameter_logging` method:

```
filter_parameter_logging :password
```

You can put these calls in the controllers that receive the affected parameters. However, if you want to filter parameters that apply to many controllers (like password data), it's safest to put these calls in *app/controllers/application.rb*, where they will apply to all controllers.

Working with Rails from the Console

Rails is so thoroughly web-facing that it can be difficult to imagine working with it from the command line, but it does indeed offer `script/console`. When you run `script/console` rather than `script/server`, Rails starts up a special environment using the Interactive Ruby Shell (irb) instead of firing up a web server. This shell has the full context of your application, so you can load data from your databases, play with models, and generally take a look around.

 You can, if you want, have `script/console` and `script/server` running at the same time in different windows.

The console shell lets you interact with your application from the command line with the full powers of Ruby at your disposal. Most Ruby books include a lot more detail about irb, some even running all of their examples there, but in Rails it's good mostly for playing with models and testing methods.

To get started, try running `script/console --sandbox` in one of your applications, say the final students/courses application from Chapter 9. You'll see something like:

```
SimonMacBook:students001c simonst1$ script/console --sandbox
Loading development environment in sandbox (Rails 2.1.0)
Any modifications you make will be rolled back on exit
>>
```

If you actually want to make changes to your database, you can leave off the --sandbox option (which can be abbreviated -s). For the first few visits, it feels safer to know that none of the changes made from the console will last beyond the console session. Everything gets rolled back once the session ends.

To start actually working with some data, load an object into a variable. Rails will not only load the object, it will show all the details of the underlying fields. (It always shows the return value.)

```
>> s=Student.find(2)
=> #<Student id: 2, given_name: "Milletta", middle_name: "Zorgos",
family_name: "Stim", date_of_birth: "1989-02-02", grade_point_average:
#<BigDecimal:1e8104c,'0.394E1',8(8)>, start_date: "2006-09-12",
created_at: "2008-07-03 18:34:59", updated_at: "2008-07-03 18:34:59">
```

The model included something that isn't shown here, though: a simpler name method. You can call that from the console, too:

```
>> s.name
=> "Milletta Stim"
```

All of the methods on the model are available to you here. In fact, if you're going to be working with one object for a long time, you can create a new irb console session that's in the context of that object. This lets you call methods and explore without constantly prefacing method names with the variable you used:

```
>> irb s
>> name
=> "Milletta Stim"
>> cList=courses
=> [#<Course id: 1, name: "Reptiles: Friend or Foe?", created_at:
"2008-07-05 18:05:04", updated_at: "2008-07-05 18:05:04">,
#<Course id: 5, name: "Advanced Bolt Design", created_at: "2008-07-05
18:06:35", updated_at: "2008-07-05 18:06:35">]
>>
```

When you're done working inside of this object, you can just type quit or exit, and you'll be back at a >> prompt, but no longer in the object.

You can, of course, change the values in your objects as well:

```
>> s.middle_name='Zorgas'
=> "Zorgas"
```

If you want to see what values have changed—before you save them—you can use the y method (for YAML, a convenient data exchange format):

```
>> y s
--- !ruby/object:Student
attributes:
  start_date: "2006-09-12"
  updated_at: 2008-07-03 18:34:59
  id: "2"
```

```
    given_name: Milletta
    family_name: Stim
    date_of_birth: "1989-02-02"
    middle_name: Zorgas
    grade_point_average: "3.94"
    created_at: 2008-07-03 18:34:59
  attributes_cache: {}

changed_attributes:
  middle_name: Zorgos
=> nil
>>
```

You can also call the save method:

```
>> s.save
=> true
```

The reported return value is true, so the save succeeded. (When the sandboxed session ends, this will be rolled back.)

The console provides two convenience objects you may want to use on their own. The first, helper, gives you instant access to all of the helper methods in your application. If you want to test out a method with a set of arguments, just call the method from helper, as in this call to number_to_human_size:

```
>> helper.number_to_human_size 1092582135
=> "1 GB"
```

The other convenience object, app, gives you access to your full application context, including the routing table. This lets you do things like test your routing with:

```
>> app.url_for :action=>"index", :controller=>"courses"
=> "http://www.example.com/courses"
>> app.url_for :action=>"new", :controller=>"courses"
=> "http://www.example.com/courses/new"
```

You can also test named routes, which are ubiquitous in RESTful development, but first you need to activate access to the methods which present them with:

```
>> include ActionController::UrlWriter
```

Then you can do things like:

```
>> new_course_path
=> "/courses/new"
```

You can also call your controllers using the app object, using the app.get, app.post, app.put, and app.delete methods from ActionController::Integra tion::Session. The results of these may not be exactly what you expect. For example:

```
>> app.get "/students/2"
=> 200
```

The 200 just means that the request was processed successfully and some kind of response produced. A 404 would be the classic "Not Found" error, meaning that Rails couldn't find an action matching that path. You can take a closer look at what happened by asking the app object for the parameters:

```
>> app.controller.params
=> {"action"=>"show", "id"=>"2", "controller"=>"students"}
```

This breakdown makes it clear how the routing interpreted the request and called the controller. You can also get to the response itself, though the presentation isn't quite beautiful:

```
>> app.response.body
=> "<!DOCTYPE html PUBLIC \"-//W3C//DTD XHTML 1.0 Transitional//EN\"\n
\"http://www.w3.org/TR/xhtml1/DTD/xhtml1-transitional.dtd\">\n\n<html
xmlns=\"http://www.w3.org/1999/xhtml\" xml:lang=\"en\" lang=\"en\">\n<head>\n
<meta http-equiv=\"content-type\" content=\"text/html;charset=UTF-8\" />\n
<title>Students: show</title>\n  <link
href=\"/stylesheets/scaffold.css?1215267158\" media=\"screen\" rel=\"stylesheet\"
type=\"text/css\" />\n</head>\n<body>\n<p>\n\t<a
href=\"http://www.example.com/students\">Students</a> |\n\t<a
href=\"http://www.example.com/courses\">Courses</a>\n</p>\n\n<hr />\n<p
style=\"color: green\"></p>\n\n<p>\n  <b>Given name:</b>\n  Milletta\n</p>\n\n<p>\n
<b>Middle name:</b>\n  Zorgas\n</p>\n\n<p>\n  <b>Family name:</b>\n
Stim\n</p>\n\n<p>\n  <b>Date of birth:</b>\n  1989-02-02\n</p>\n\n<p>\n  <b>Grade
point average:</b>\n  3.94\n</p>\n\n<p>\n  <b>Start date:</b>\n  2006-09-
12\n</p>\n\n<p>\n  <b>Courses:</b>\n  \n\t<a href=\"/courses/1\">Reptiles: Friend
or Foe?</a>, <a href=\"/courses/5\">Advanced Bolt Design</a>\n  \n</p>\n\n<a
href=\"/students/2/edit\">Edit</a> |\n<a href=\"/students/2/courses\">Courses</a>
|\n<a href=\"/students/2/awards\">Awards</a> |\n<a
href=\"/students\">Back</a>\n\n\n</body>\n</html>\n"
```

You can also see all of the header information, doubtlessly more than you explicitly set:

```
>> app.headers
=> {"cache-control"=>["private, max-age=0, must-revalidate"], "status"=>["200 OK"],
"etag"=>["\"34cbf61016b9bd898bb3df9eec96dc79\""], "content-type"=>["text/html;
charset=utf-8"], "x-runtime"=>["0.16691"], "set-cookie"=>[], "content-
length"=>["1148"]}
```

If you're working from the console and making changes to the code at the same time, there's one more key command you'll want to know: reload!. Rails' console isn't as instantly adapting, even in development mode, as its web interfaces. When you issue the reload! command, the console will reload your updated application code and use it. There's just one thing to watch out for, though: if you've created objects already, they'll still be using the old code. You'll need to tear them down and replace them if you want to test them out with the new code.

The console is a great place to "get your hands dirty" and play with code directly. It lets you tinker with your application much more directly than is easily possible through the web interface. However, it definitely has some limitations. It'll probably take a while to grow comfortable using it—the error messages are often cryptic. It's obviously not a great place to experiment with interfaces. It's very easy to enter a typo and not figure it out before something important has changed or broken.

Most importantly, though, the console is outside of your main application flow. Testing in the console is not usually testing the way the application really works. Not only that, it's not a structured set of tests so much as poking around to see what happens. While the console is useful, it's definitely not your only or best choice for making sure your application behaves correctly.

The Ruby Debugger

The console is fun for tinkering and can be extremely useful for trying things out, but it's a completely separate process from the way you (and your users) normally run Rails applications.

If you do a search on Rails debugging, you'll find lots of information on the Rails breakpointer. Unfortunately, the breakpointer depended on a bug in Ruby itself, one that was fixed in Ruby 1.8.5, so the breakpointer is now defunct. Instead, the most common current approach uses the Ruby debugger. It's installed as a gem called *ruby-debug*. From the command line, you can install it with:

```
$ sudo gem install ruby-debug
Password:
Building native extensions.  This could take a while...
Building native extensions.  This could take a while...
Successfully installed linecache-0.43
Successfully installed ruby-debug-base-0.10.1
Successfully installed ruby-debug-0.10.1
3 gems installed
Installing ri documentation for linecache-0.43...
Installing ri documentation for ruby-debug-base-0.10.1...
Installing ri documentation for ruby-debug-0.10.1...
Installing RDoc documentation for linecache-0.43...
Installing RDoc documentation for ruby-debug-base-0.10.1...
Installing RDoc documentation for ruby-debug-0.10.1...
```

If you're on Windows or certain Linux installs, the sudo part may be unnecessary.

If you get a "Can't find header files for ruby" error message, your Ruby install has left off some of the developer-only components. Header files are not installed automatically with Mac OS X, for example. You'll need to install Xcode tools from the *Optional Installs/Xcode Tools.mpkg* directory on the Leopard DVD. (This is a large and long install!) On other platforms, you may need to install a *ruby-devel* package.

Once the gem is installed, you can use Ruby debugger with any Rails application on your computer, but you have to tell the Rails app to make the debugger available. To do this, open the *config/environments/development.rb* file and add the line:

```
require "ruby-debug"
```

This will make the debugger available in development mode (where you are now). You should probably only add it so that it applies in development mode, and leave `test.rb` and `production.rb` alone.

The next step is to add the debugger call in one of the controller methods. For a test, modify the `create` method in *app/controllers/students_controller.rb* (as is done in *ch11/students005*) so that it looks like:

```
def create
    @student = Student.new(params[:student])
    debugger
    respond_to do |format|
      if @student.save
        flash[:notice] = 'Student was successfully created.'
        format.html { redirect_to(@student) }
        format.xml  { render :xml => @student, :status => :created, :location =>
@student }
      else
        format.html { render :action => "new" }
        format.xml  { render :xml => @student.errors, :status =>
:unprocessable_entity }
      end
    end
  end
```

Now, when you start the application with **script/server**, visit *http://localhost: 3000/students/new*, and enter a new student, you'll see something like Figure 11-1.

The most important part of Figure 11-1 is the status bar at the lower left: Waiting for localhost.... That's unusual, unless you've accidentally put an infinite loop into your application. If you check the logs in the window where you ran **script/server**, you'll see that it's waiting for your input at an (**rdb: 1**) prompt:

```
Processing StudentsController#new (for 127.0.0.1 at 2008-07-18 17:36:08) [GET]
  Session ID: BAh7BzoMY3NyZl9pZCIlODAyYjI1YTBiM2VhZGRiNzQxOGFiNjdmMmUzMDIx
NjUiCmZsYXNoSUM6JOFjdGlvbkNvbnRyb2xsZXI6OkZsYXNoOjpGbGFzaEhh
c2h7AAY6CkB1c2VkewA=--bc9174a5ce9b68d09c31910b2052c35034350eee
  Parameters: {"action"=>"new", "controller"=>"students"}
Rendering template within layouts/students
Rendering students/new
Rendered _navigation (0.00010)
Completed in 0.14174 (7 reqs/sec) | Rendering: 0.13218 (93%) | DB: 0.00000 (0%) |
200 OK [http://localhost/students/new]
/Users/simonstl/Documents/RailsOutIn/current/code/ch11/students001d/app/controllers
/students_controller.rb:45
respond_to do |format|
(rdb:1)
```

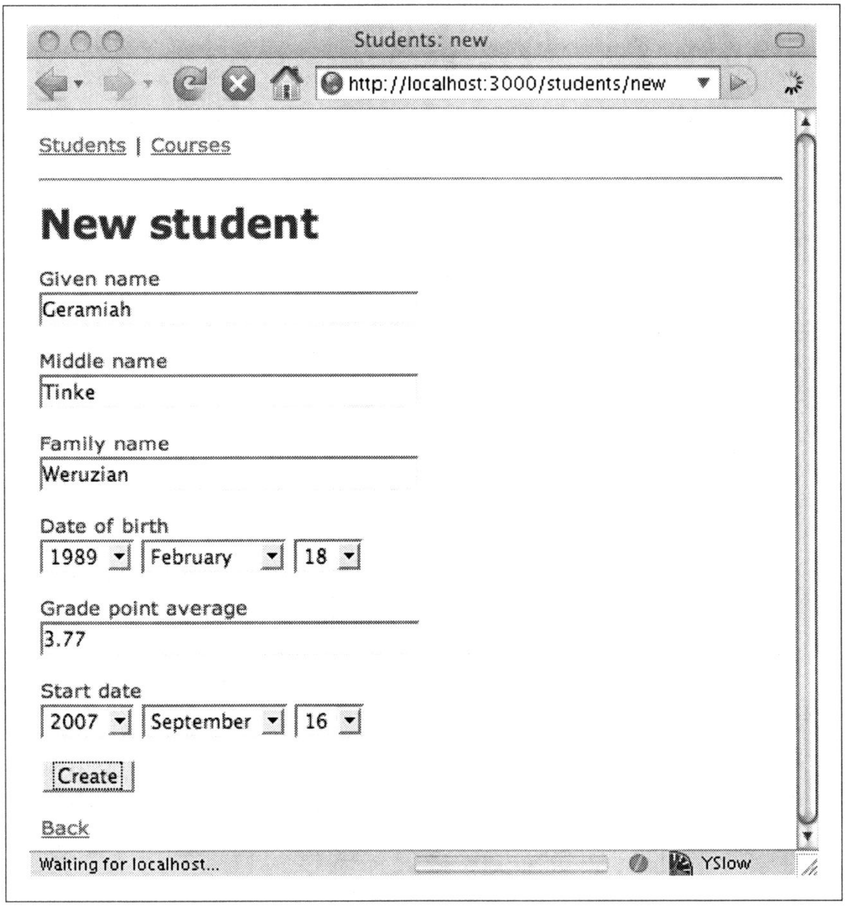

Figure 11-1. Waiting for a response because the debugger kicked in

The line above the prompt is the next statement to be executed, if you type next. Unsurprisingly, it's the line right after debugger. If you type list, you can see where you are, marked by =>:

```
(rdb:1) list
[40, 49] in
/Users/simonstl/Documents/RailsOutIn/current/code/ch11/students001d/app/controllers
/students_controller.rb
   40  # POST /students
   41  # POST /students.xml
   42    def create
   43      @student = Student.find(params[:id])
   44
=> 45      respond_to do |format|
   46        if @student.save
   47          flash[:notice] = 'Student was successfully created.'
   48          format.html { redirect_to(@student) }
   49          format.xml  { render :xml => @student, :status => :created,
:location => @student }
```

To see a list of the available commands, type help. The main ones you'll need at first to move through code are:

- next (or step) to move forward to the next line
- cont to leave the debugger and let the program continue
- quit to leave the debugger *and* shut down Rails

Following code for any extended period will likely drop you into the Rails framework code, which may be confusing at first. You'll want to enter your debugger commands and other breakpoints close to where you think problems exist, or patiently wait for Rails to get out of your way.

While you're in the debugger, you will probably want to inspect variables, which you can do with the p (or pp) command:

```
(rdb:1) p @student
#<Student id: 6, given_name: "Geramiah", middle_name: "Tinke", family_name:
"Weruzian", date_of_birth: "1989-02-18", grade_point_average:
#<BigDecimal:20de0d8,'0.377E1',8(8)>, start_date: "2007-09-16",
created_at: "2008-07-18 21:39:05", updated_at: "2008-07-18 21:39:05">
```

If you want prettier view of the data or if you're just more comfortable in irb, you can jump into irb and tinker as you like. When you're done working in irb, type exit or quit and you'll be returned to the debugger shell. (When you enter irb, the prompt changes to >>, and when you exit, it returns to (rdb:#), where # is a number.) For example, the following session goes into irb to print the @student object as YAML, using the y command explored earlier:

```
(rdb:1) irb
>> y @student
--- !ruby/object:Student
```

```
attributes:
  start_date: "2007-09-16"
  updated_at: 2008-07-18 21:39:05
  id: "6"
  family_name: Weruzian
  given_name: Geramiah
  date_of_birth: "1989-02-18"
  created_at: 2008-07-18 21:39:05
  grade_point_average: "3.77"
  middle_name: Tinke
attributes_cache: {}

=> nil
>> exit
/Users/simonstl/Documents/RailsOutIn/current/code/ch11/students001d/app/
controllers/students_controller.rb:62
respond_to do |format|
(rdb:1)
```

In development mode, Rails will reload your files for every request before you get into the debugger, but if you want the debugger to reload your files for every step, you can issue the command set autoreload. It will go much more slowly, but sometimes that's OK for delicate surgery.

For much more detail on using the Ruby debugger with Rails, including features like setting breakpoints from within the debugger and TextMate integration, check out Patrick Lenz's excellent tutorial at *http://www.sitepoint.com/article/debug-rails-app-ruby-debug*.

Test Your Knowledge

Quiz

1. What's the easiest way to present debugging information in a Rails view?
2. Where can you find information about how quickly different aspects of a request were handled?
3. How can you test routing from the console?
4. How do you tell your program to support the Ruby debugger?
5. How do you let your program continue when you exit the Ruby debugger?

Answers

1. The debug method makes it easy to present the complete contents of an object in a mostly readable YAML representation..

2. Rails includes a lot of timing information in its development log, which is available both in the terminal window for `script/server` and in the *log/development.log* file.

3. You can test simple routes by calling `app.url_for`. If you need to test named routes, `include ActionController:UrlWriter` and then try calling the path methods.

4. By adding `require "ruby-debug"` to the *config/environments/development.rb* file.

5. When you use the `cont` command, rather than the `quit` command, the debugger lets Rails get back to what it was doing. The `quit` command exits the debugger and shuts down the application.

## CHAPTER 12

Testing

Testing can spare you much of the work you learned to do in the previous chapter, replacing spot-check debugging with more structured and thorough repetitive testing. Ruby culture places a high value on testing, and Ruby and Rails have grown up with agile development methods where testing is assumed to be a normal part of development. While testing is a complicated subject worthy of a book or several, it's definitely worthwhile to start including tests early in your project development, even while you're still learning the Rails landscape.

Rails provides a number of facilities for creating and managing tests. This chapter will explore Rails' basic testing setup and note some options for building more advanced test platforms. (Examples for this chapter are in *ch12/students006*.)

 Many developers use RSpec, an additional framework for testing noted at the end of this chapter, but it's worth understanding the foundations provided in Rails itself.

Test Mode

Up to this point, all the code in this book has been run in development mode. Rails supports three different environments for running applications. Each of them has its own database, as well as its own settings:

Development
    Development is the default mode. In development mode, Rails loads and reloads code every time a request is made, making it easy for you to see changes without a cache getting in the way. It's also typical to use SQLite as the database, as Rails isn't going to be working at high speed anyway.

Test

Test mode runs like production mode, without reloading code, and has its own database so that tests can run against a consistent database. You could use a fancier database for test mode (and might want to if you suspect strange database interactions), but for getting started, the default of SQLite is fine.

Production

Production mode maximizes Rails' efficiency. It doesn't reload code, enabling it to cache the program and run much faster. Logging is much briefer and error messages are shortened, as giving users a complete stack trace probably isn't helpful. It also does more automatic and directed caching of results, sparing users a wait for the same code to run again.

You can switch among the three modes by using the -e option of `script/server`:

```
script/server -e production
```

The settings for all three modes are in the *config* directory. The *environment.rb* file contains default configuration settings used by all three modes, but the *environments* directory contains *development.rb*, *production.rb*, and *test.rb* files whose settings override those in *environment.rb*.

The *database.yml* file contains the database connection settings for all three modes. By default, it specifies SQLite databases named *db/development.sqlite3*, *db/test.sqlite3*, and *db/production.sqlite3*. Chapter 18 will explore other possible database installations, particularly for production, but for now, these defaults are fine. It's time, though, to set up a database for testing.

Setting Up a Test Database with Fixtures

Automated testing needs a stable database environment in which to do its work. The contents of the development database will—and should—change on a regular basis as you tinker, try things out, and experiment to see just how well everything works. This is wonderful for a human development process, but that level of change is dreadful when a computer is testing an application. Once the testing framework is told which value to check for, it can't choose another value because it knows someone else was playing with the data. In fact, if previous tests change the data, the order in which tests are conducted could itself become an issue, masking some bugs and falsely reporting others.

Rails provides this stable environment two ways. First, as noted earlier, it maintains a separate test environment, complete with its own database. Second, the testing environment expects that developers will define stable data, called *fixtures*, for use in that database. Every time a new test is run, the database is reset to that stable set of data. It's a slow way to do things, but it's extremely reliable.

Fixtures are written in YAML. You don't need to know much about YAML to use and create them, however. Rails, in fact, has been creating fixtures along with scaffolding all along. If you check the *test/fixtures* directory of the courses and students application, you'll see files named *awards.yml, courses.yml,* and *students.yml*. Their contents aren't particularly exciting, though, as Example 12-1 demonstrates.

Example 12-1. The students.yml fixture file created by Rails

```
# Read about fixtures at http://ar.rubyonrails.org/classes/Fixtures.html

one:
  given_name: MyString
  middle_name: MyString
  family_name: MyString
  age: 1
  grade_point_average: 9.99
  start_date: 2008-06-27

two:
  given_name: MyString
  middle_name: MyString
  family_name: MyString
  age: 1
  grade_point_average: 9.99
  start_date: 2008-06-27
```

Each field has a value, set by the Rails generator to reflect its type, and there are two records, but you may want something more reflective of the data your application is likely to contain, like Example 12-2.

Example 12-2. A more realistic, though still brief, students.yml fixture

```
giles:
  given_name: Giles
  middle_name: Prentiss
  family_name: Boschwick
  date_of_birth: 1989-02-15
  grade_point_average: 3.92
  start_date: 2006-09-12

milletta:
  given_name: Milletta
  middle_name: Zorgos
  family_name: Stim
  date_of_birth: 1989-04-17
  grade_point_average: 3.94
  start_date: 2006-09-12
```

```
jules:
  given_name: Jules
  middle_name: Bloss
  family_name: Miller
  date_of_birth: 1988-11-12
  grade_point_average: 2.76
  start_date: 2006-09-12
```

It's up to you whether you'd like the data to echo the development database, but somewhat meaningful data can be useful when you're trying to find your way through results, especially failures.

 If you try to run tests based on the generated fixtures and your migrations set constraints on which fields can be null, you'll get a lot of mysterious errors. In SQLite, they suggest that your database and all of its tables are missing—even though they're not. When using MySQL, the error message at least narrows things down to fields, but that still doesn't explain why there's a problem.

The scaffold fixtures may work for testing incredibly simple applications, but most of the time you'll be much better off defining your own fixtures carefully.

There's more you can do in upgrading fixtures than improving readability, however. The fixtures Rails created don't know very much about relationships between models because the fixtures were generated before you told Rails about the relationship. So, for example, the generated fixture for awards looks like Example 12-3.

Example 12-3. The generated awards.yml fixture, without much real data

```
one:
  name: MyString
  year: 1
  student_id: 1

two:
  name: MyString
  year: 1
  student_id: 1
```

Rails knows that student_id is a number and gives it a value of 1, which should connect to a student, although as you might have noticed in Example 12-1, the *students.yml* fixture didn't include id values. The database might start its id count at 1, or it might not.

Fixture data isn't validated before it's loaded into the database. While this might conceivably offer more testing flexibility, you should never assume that fixture data will validate against the model until you've made certain that it does.

Example 12-4 shows a better way to create this fixture, taking advantage of the names in the *student.yml* file that was shown in Example 12-2.

Example 12-4. The awards.yml fixture, populated with semi-real data and links to students

```
# instead of computing student_id for each award and giving students
# explicit id fields, we reference the student by the name of their
# fixture

skydiving:
  name: Sky Diving Prowess
  year: 2007
  student: giles

frogman:
  name: Frogman Award for Underwater Poise
  year: 2008
  student: jules
```

It's important to note that the names of students used to make the connections aren't coming from the given_name field. They're the names that were assigned to each student object in the fixture. The same thing applies to the fixture, only it can actually refer to multiple students, not just one. The original fixture, shown in Example 12-5, doesn't even specify any students for courses. Example 12-6, by contrast, establishes relationships, using the names of the fixtures.

Example 12-5. The generated courses.yml fixture, with very little content

```
one:
  name: MyString

two:
  name: MyString
```

Example 12-6. The courses.yml fixture, populated with sort of real data

```
# instead of making us write elaborate and fragile data structures,
# the fixtures engine knows how to turn the 'students' list into a
# collection of records to insert into the courses_students table.

opera:
  name: Mathematical Opera
  students: giles, milletta

# it's safest to quote strings, especially if they contain colons
reptiles:
```

```
name: "Reptiles: Friend or Foe?"
students: giles, jules

immoral:
  name: "Immoral Aesthetics"
  students: milletta
```

The fixtures setup is smart enough to establish the many-to-many connection between courses and students and build the necessary table, when given data like Example 12-6.

 You can edit these files by hand, or you can generate fixtures from the development database with the `ar_fixtures` plug-in. You can find out more about `ar_fixtures` at *http://railsify .com/plugins/8-ar_fixtures*. You can even create dynamic fixtures if you want, though that's well beyond the scope of this book.

Once you have your fixtures set up, you can try running `rake test`. You'll probably get a lot of errors, because the tests themselves aren't well set up. A lot of errors is a normal place to start in testing, however—it just means there's a lot to fix!

When you run `rake test`, Rails will clone the structure (but not the content) of your development database into the test database. It doesn't run the migrations against the test database directly, but it does check to make sure your database is up-to-date with its migrations. If it isn't, you'll get a warning like:

```
You have 4 pending migrations:
  20080627135838 CreateStudents
  20080627140324 CreateCourses
  20080627144242 CreateCoursesStudents
  20080627150307 CreateAwards
Run "rake db:migrate" to update your database then try again.
```

If you get major error messages that sound like your database can't be found, as noted in the warning earlier, check your fixtures to ensure that every field your migrations said had to be there has an actual value.

Once you have the fixtures set up, it's time to move on to the tests.

Unit Testing

Unit testing lets you work with your data on a pretty atomic level—checking validations, data storage, and similarly tightly focused issues. Rails scaffolding gives you only a very simple placeholder file, shown in Example 12-7. That file

---

is definitely not sufficient for any real testing, and you should add unit tests that test validations for each field in your model.

 Unit testing, in Rails' unique way of performing it, is only about testing models. If you have previous experience with testing in other environments, this can be confusing. If Rails is your first testing experience, don't worry about it, but remember that unit testing in Rails is different from unit testing elsewhere.

Example 12-7. The mostly useless generated unit test file, test/unit/award_test.rb

```
require 'test_helper'

class AwardTest < ActiveSupport::TestCase
  # Replace this with your real tests.
  def test_truth
    assert true
  end
end
```

Example 12-7 does show one feature of testing—the **assert** statement, which expects its argument to return **true** and reports a test failure if it doesn't. (You can also use deny to report failure on **true**.)

Unit tests are pretty straightforward to write, though are rarely exciting code. In general, they should reflect the validations performed by the model. Example 12-8 shows a definition for the award model that highlights some easily tested constraints.

Example 12-8. An award model with constraints defined

```
class Award < ActiveRecord::Base
  # every award is linked to a student, through student_id
  belongs_to :student

  validates_presence_of :name, :year

  # particular award can only be given once in every year
  validates_uniqueness_of :name, :scope => :year,
    :message => "already been given for that year"

  # we started the award scheme in 1980
  validates_inclusion_of :year, :in => (1980 .. Date.today.year)
end
```

Unit tests work on a single instance of a model, so the uniqueness constraint isn't an appropriate test, but the presence of names and years as well as the year being 1980 or later is easily tested. Example 12-9 shows a set of tests, stored in *test/unit/award_test.rb*, that check to make sure that the year constraint is obeyed.

Example 12-9. Testing to ensure that the year constraint behaves as expected

```
class AwardTest < ActiveSupport::TestCase
  def test_validity_of_year

    # test for rejection of missing year
    award = Award.new({:name => "Test award"})
    assert !award.valid?

    # test under lower boundary
    award.year = 1979
    assert !award.valid?

    # lower boundary
    award.year = 1980
    assert award.valid?

    # top boundary
    award.year = Date.today.year
    assert award.valid?

    # top boundary case, award isn't valid for next year
    award.year = Date.today.year + 1
    assert !award.valid?
  end
end
```

All of the tests in the `test_validity_of_year` method call the `valid?` method of the `award` object created in the first line. The `valid?` method checks an object with a set of values against the validations specified in the model definition. In this case, each assertion pushes against a rule about the value for `year`.

> Unit test purists prefer to have only one assertion per test. In normal unit testing, they're completely correct—this ensures that tests are isolated from each other, reducing the odds of missing an error or reporting false errors. However, Rails "unit" tests are really model tests, which are something a little different, and it may or may not be appropriate to limit tests to a single assertion.

First, the newly created award has a `:name` argument specified, but no `:year`. That award object should fail validation because the model checks for the presence of `year`. Then the method assigns a value that is too low to be acceptable and again looks for a failure. Then it tests right on the minimum value, looking this time for a positive result. The next two assertions test on the top

---

boundary and then just beyond that boundary. The first should work, and the second should not.

 If you ever feel like simply having a test fail, the flunk method lets you fail with a message.

Awards are relatively simple, however. The many-to-many courses-students relationship is a lot more complicated. It's easier to test from one side, though, rather than trying to test from both, so courses will get the simple test file shown in Example 12-10, just checking that the course has a name, while students get the much more complicated tests shown in Example 12-11.

Example 12-10. Simple tests for the courses model, just examining basic functionality

```
require 'test_helper'

class CourseTest < ActiveSupport::TestCase
  def test_validity
    course = Course.new
    assert !course.valid?
    course.name = "New course"

    assert course.valid?
  end
end
```

Example 12-11. More complicated tests for students, testing validity and whether they can be enrolled in courses

```
require 'test_helper'

class StudentTest < ActiveSupport::TestCase

  fixtures :students, :courses

def test_validity
    elvis = Student.new({:given_name => "Elvis",
        :family_name => "Prendergast"})
    assert !elvis.valid?
    elvis.date_of_birth = "1989-02-03"
    elvis.start_date = Date.today
    assert elvis.valid?
  end
end

  def test_name
    elvis = Student.new({:given_name => "Elvis",
        :family_name => "Prendergast"})
    assert_equal elvis.name, "Elvis Prendergast"
```

```
    end

def test_enrolled_in
   giles = students(:giles)
   assert giles.enrolled_in?(courses(:reptiles))
   assert !giles.enrolled_in?(courses(:immoral))
end

  def test_unenrolled_courses
    giles = students(:giles)
    milletta = students(:milletta)
    assert_equal [courses(:reptiles)], milletta.unenrolled_courses
    assert_equal [courses(:immoral)], giles.unenrolled_courses
    elvis = Student.new({:given_name => "Elvis",
      :family_name => "Prendergast"})
    assert_equal Course.find(:all), elvis.unenrolled_courses
  end
```

The first line of the class specifies the fixtures that need to be loaded for these tests:

```
    fixtures :students, :courses
```

The first two test methods in the class, test_validity and test_name, are much like the tests used on awards, simply ensuring that the student model behaves as described. The test_validity method creates a new object and first makes sure that it fails when missing required information, then adds the information and makes sure that it passes. (You could, of course, add extra assertions to test each additional field.)

The test_name method creates a student with a given and family name, then tests the name method to see if it returns the expected value. It uses a new method, assert_equal, that expects the values of its two arguments to be equal. If they aren't, it reports a failure. (There's also assert_not_equal for the opposite situation.)

The next two methods, test_enrolled_in and test_unenrolled_courses, are more complicated and rely on the fixtures heavily. The test_enrolled_in method doesn't actually set any values, it just checks to see whether a given student—the one identified as :giles—is enrolled in the courses specified:

```
    def test_enrolled_in
       giles = students(:giles)
       assert giles.enrolled_in?(courses(:reptiles))
       assert !giles.enrolled_in?(courses(:immoral))
    end
```

According to the courses fixture, which was shown in Example 12-6, Giles (:giles in the fixtures) should be enrolled in Reptiles, Friend or Foe (:reptiles), but not enrolled in Immoral Aesthetics (:immoral). This test makes sure that the enrolled_in? method reflects that.

The last test method here, test_unenrolled_courses, relies on the fixtures and also creates a new record for comparison:

```
def test_unenrolled_courses
    giles = students(:giles)
    milletta = students(:milletta)
    assert_equal [courses(:reptiles)], milletta.unenrolled_courses
    assert_equal [courses(:immoral)], giles.unenrolled_courses
    elvis = Student.new({:given_name => "Elvis",
        :family_name => "Prendergast"})
    assert_equal Course.find(:all), elvis.unenrolled_courses
end
```

The first two lines create student objects from the fixture identifiers. The first assert_equal call checks to make sure that the list of classes in which milletta is not enrolled is an array containing the Reptiles, Friend or Foe (:reptiles) class, which corresponds to the fixture. Then, the next call checks that giles is not enrolled in Immoral Aesthetics (:immoral). Finally, the method creates a new elvis student, and checks to make sure that his list of unenrolled courses is the same as the list of all courses. He hasn't enrolled in anything yet, after all!

If you run these tests, you'll get a brief report. (rake test:units lets you run only the unit tests, or you can use rake test or just rake to run all of the tests.)

```
$ rake test:units
(in /Users/simonstl/Documents/RailsOutIn/current/code/ch12/students005)
/System/Library/Frameworks/Ruby.framework/Versions/1.8/usr/bin/ruby -Ilib:test
"/Library/Ruby/Gems/1.8/gems/rake-0.8.1/lib/rake/rake_test_loader.rb"
"test/unit/award_test.rb" "test/unit/course_test.rb" "test/unit/student_test.rb"
Loaded suite /Library/Ruby/Gems/1.8/gems/rake-0.8.1/lib/rake/rake_test_loader
Started
......
Finished in 0.190025 seconds.

6 tests, 15 assertions, 0 failures, 0 errors
- [functional and integration tests] -
```

The periods under Started each represent a successful test, while an F would represent a failure and E an error, something that interfered with running the test.

If a test fails, you'll see something like:

```
$ rake test:units
(in /Users/simonstl/Documents/RailsOutIn/current/code/ch12/students005)
/System/Library/Frameworks/Ruby.framework/Versions/1.8/usr/bin/ruby -Ilib:test
"/Library/Ruby/Gems/1.8/gems/rake-0.8.1/lib/rake/rake_test_loader.rb"
"test/unit/award_test.rb" "test/unit/course_test.rb" "test/unit/student_test.rb"
Loaded suite /Library/Ruby/Gems/1.8/gems/rake-0.8.1/lib/rake/rake_test_loader
Started
F.....
Finished in 0.155343 seconds.
```

```
   1) Failure:
test_validity_of_year(AwardTest)
    [./test/unit/award_test.rb:10:in `test_validity_of_year'
     /Library/Ruby/Gems/1.8/gems/activesupport-
2.1.0/lib/active_support/testing/setup_and_teardown.rb:33:in `__send__'
     /Library/Ruby/Gems/1.8/gems/activesupport-
2.1.0/lib/active_support/testing/setup_and_teardown.rb:33:in `run']:
<false> is not true.

6 tests, 12 assertions, 1 failures, 0 errors
```

That's the result you'd get by removing the ! from line 10 of *award_test.rb*. The rest of that error message isn't particularly useful, but knowing which test failed and on which line is certainly helpful.

After finishing this section, unit tests may seem to test things that are perhaps too simple. These were just little pokes and prods, checking to see whether something fairly obvious would happen or not. There are a few reasons these (and other kinds of tests) are valuable, however:

- Unit tests accumulate over time, and as a project grows, especially when multiple developers work on it, they serve as a warning that something has changed, probably not for the better.

- Most programmers think about creating code and then testing it afterward. A different, perhaps more effective approach, is to write tests first and then write code that answers the tests. There may be more back and forth to it than that, as development often inspires more functionality and more tests, but defining tests first creates a clear target to aim for. This is known as Test-Driven Development (TDD).

- Once you've written a test, it'll run every time you tell Rails to perform testing. You don't need to go back through your application by hand to make sure that things that once worked still worked—the test suite will tell you.

These simple tests of models may seem too simple, but they build a critical foundation that other work can build on.

Functional Testing

Unit testing checks on data validation and simple connections, but there's a lot more happening in the typical Rails application. Controllers are the key piece connecting data to users, supporting a number of complex interactions that need more sophisticated testing than checking validation or data. Controllers need functional tests that can examine the actions they were supposed to perform. In Rails, these tests are defined in files in the *tests/functional* directory.

 Functional testing, in Rails' unique way of performing it, is only about testing controllers. Again, if you have previous experience with testing in other environments or move on later to other environments, this can be confusing.

Unlike the unit tests generated by Rails, which did nothing, the functional tests created by the REST scaffolding at least provide a basic structure that's useful. (The functional tests created for ordinary controllers are a placeholder like the unit test one.) The *courses_controller_test.rb* file shown in Example 12-12 is capable of calling the REST methods and making sure they work—except, of course, the fixtures generated by the scaffolding will create problems.

Example 12-12. An almost-functional functional test set generated by Rails for the courses controller

```
require 'test_helper'

class CoursesControllerTest < ActionController::TestCase
  def test_should_get_index
    get :index
    assert_response :success
    assert_not_nil assigns(:courses)
  end

  def test_should_get_new
    get :new
    assert_response :success
  end

  def test_should_create_course
    assert_difference('Course.count') do
      post :create, :course => { }
    end

    assert_redirected_to course_path(assigns(:course))
  end

  def test_should_show_course
    get :show, :id => courses(:one).id
    assert_response :success
  end

  def test_should_get_edit
    get :edit, :id => courses(:one).id
    assert_response :success
  end
```

```
def test_should_update_course
  put :update, :id => courses(:one).id, :course => { }
  assert_redirected_to course_path(assigns(:course))
end

def test_should_destroy_course
  assert_difference('Course.count', -1) do
    delete :destroy, :id => courses(:one).id
  end

  assert_redirected_to courses_path
end
end
```

The only fundamental problem with these tests is that the reference to :one points to the broken fixtures created by the scaffolding, the ones shown back in Example 12-5. You could use it with the new fixtures by making a few changes, highlighted in Example 12-13, which also adds a bit more specific detail to the test.

Example 12-13. An improved functional test for the courses controller

```
require 'test_helper'

class CoursesControllerTest < ActionController::TestCase
  def test_should_get_index
    get :index
    assert_response :success
    assert_not_nil assigns(:courses)
  end

  def test_should_get_new
    get :new
    assert_response :success
  end

  def test_should_create_course
    assert_difference('Course.count') do
      post :create, :course => { :name => "Cattle Rustling" }
    end

    assert_redirected_to course_path(assigns(:course))
  end

  def test_should_show_course
    get :show, :id => courses(:opera).id
    assert_response :success
  end

  def test_should_get_edit
    get :edit, :id => courses(:opera).id
    assert_response :success
  end
```

```
def test_should_update_course
  put :update, :id => courses(:opera).id, :course => { :name => "Singing" }
  assert_redirected_to course_path(assigns(:course))
end

def test_should_destroy_course
  assert_difference('Course.count', -1) do
    delete :destroy, :id => courses(:opera).id
  end

  assert_redirected_to courses_path
end
end
```

The changes are relatively minor, shifting from the generic :one to its replacement in the courses fixture, :opera, and supporting names for courses when they're created instead of using blank names, which the model forbids. However, creating functional tests, or modifying them as will be necessary to support the nested resource approach awards use, requires understanding a new set of assertions and methods for calling controllers. Both let you test what the controller would have done in response to an HTTP call.

Calling Controllers

Controllers are called using the get, put, post, and delete methods, with the actual method to be called listed as the first argument and any necessary parameters listed as named parameters after that. Functional testing does not actually create an HTTP request and answer it. Instead, it skips over the issues of routing and goes to the controller directly.

 If you want to make HTTP requests in your tests, you can— but in the integration testing.

For RESTful calls, you'll want to test all seven of the methods Rails generates, four with get and one each with put, post, and delete. For other controllers, you'll want to write calls for each method and address them appropriately. The get method as shown here only passes an id value, but you can set other parameters as desired. The put and post methods both need additional parameters to work, however, taking a :course that itself contains a :name. Think of these as form fields rather than objects. For example, the post looks like:

```
post :create, :course => { :name => "Cattle Rustling" }
```

The post method will call the controller's create method, giving it parameters for a :course. The only parameter here is :name, set to Cattle Rustling. It works the same as entering Cattle Rustling into a form that was fed to this method.

 Instead of specifying the method name with a symbol, you can pass these methods a URL fragment as a string. However, you should leave that usage to integration testing, covered later in this chapter.

Testing Responses

The new assertion methods relate to specific controller actions and their effects:

assert_not_nil_assigns
> Allows the test to check on whether the controller set values for the view to use, though the test doesn't actually call the view. This just makes sure that a given variable is not left as nil.

assert_response
> Compares the HTTP response code that the controller sends to its argument. :success is the most common argument (for 200 OK), while :redirect (for 300–399 responses), :missing (404), and :error (500–599) are also common. (If you have a specific response in mind, you can just give the HTTP response code number as the argument.)

assert_redirected_to
> Lets you check not just the response code, but the location to which the controller redirected the request.

assert_difference
> Makes it easy to check on the number of records in the database, taking a method to call and an integer reflecting the difference. An added record would just be +1, the default, while a deleted record would be −1. assert_difference takes a block as its argument and must wrap around the call to the controller with do and end statements. (There's also an assert_no_difference for when you don't want there to be any difference.)

Most of these are fairly readable, but it's worth examining the most complicated test in detail:

```
def test_should_create_course
  assert_difference('Course.count') do
    post :create, :course => { :name => "Cattle Rustling" }
  end
```

```
      assert_redirected_to course_path(assigns(:course))
    end
```

This method tests the creation of a course. It opens with an `assert_differ ence` method, which will check the count of courses at the beginning and check again when it encounters the end statement. Between those checks, the `post` method calls the course controller's `create` method. As an argument, `post` sends `create` what looks like a form for a course, specifying a `:name` of `Cattle Rustling`. After that, `assert_difference` reaches the end and checks to see if the `count` indeed increased by 1, the default. If the `count` didn't increase, the assertion reports a failure, but otherwise, it reports success.

The second assertion checks to where the method redirected the visitor. It uses the `assigns` method to reach into the variables the controller created and get the `course` object, and checks that the path specified by the redirection is the same as the path to that `course` object created using `course_path`.

Dealing with Nested Resources

Making awards a nested resource under students took some work in Chapter 9, and similar considerations apply in the testing process as well. Example 12-14 shows the functional tests for awards, from *tests/functional/ awards_controller_test.rb*, highlighting areas that needed additional information to support the nesting.

Example 12-14. Adding support for a nested resource to functional testing

```
require 'test_helper'

class AwardsControllerTest < ActionController::TestCase
  def test_should_get_index
    get :index, :student_id => students(:giles).id
    assert_response :success
    assert_not_nil assigns(:awards)
  end

  def test_should_get_new
    get :new, :student_id => students(:giles).id
    assert_response :success
  end

  def test_should_create_award
    assert_difference('Award.count') do
      post :create, :award => { :year => 2008, :name => 'Test award' },
:student_id => students(:giles).id
    end

    assert_redirected_to student_award_path(students(:giles), assigns(:award))
  end
```

```
def test_should_show_award
  get :show, :id => awards(:skydiving).id, :student_id => students(:giles).id
  assert_response :success
end

def test_should_get_edit
  get :edit, :id => awards(:skydiving).id, :student_id => students(:giles).id
  assert_response :success
end

def test_should_update_award
  put :update, :id => awards(:skydiving).id, :award => { }, :student_id =>
students(:giles).id
  assert_redirected_to student_award_path(students(:giles), assigns(:award))
end

def test_should_destroy_award
  assert_difference('Award.count', -1) do
    delete :destroy, :id => awards(:skydiving).id, :student_id =>
students(:giles).id
  end

  assert_redirected_to student_awards_path(students(:giles))
end
end
```

All of these echo the changes in Chapter 9 and are necessary to making the tests work with a nested resource that needs a student context for its controller to operate. The method names for paths change, gaining a student_ prefix, and all of the calls to get, put, post, and delete also need a :student_id parameter.

Running these functional tests should produce results such as:

```
$ rake test:functionals
(in /Users/simonstl/Documents/RailsOutIn/current/code/ch12/students005)
/System/Library/Frameworks/Ruby.framework/Versions/1.8/usr/bin/ruby -Ilib:test
"/Library/Ruby/Gems/1.8/gems/rake-0.8.1/lib/rake/rake_test_loader.rb"
"test/functional/awards_controller_test.rb"
"test/functional/courses_controller_test.rb"
"test/functional/students_controller_test.rb"
Loaded suite /Library/Ruby/Gems/1.8/gems/rake-0.8.1/lib/rake/rake_test_loader
Started
.........................
Finished in 0.608977 seconds.

25 tests, 53 assertions, 0 failures, 0 errors
```

Integration Testing

Integration testing is the most complicated testing Rails supports directly. It tests complete requests coming in from the outside, running through routing, controllers, models, the database, and even views. Rails does not generate any integration tests by default, as creating them requires detailed knowledge of the complete application and what it is supposed to do. Integration tests are stored in *tests/integration* and look much like the classes for other kinds of tests. They call similar methods and also make assertions, but the assertions are different and the flow can cover multiple interactions, as Example 12-15 demonstrates.

Example 12-15. An integration test that tries adding a student

```
require 'test_helper'

# Integration tests covering the manipulation of student objects

class StudentsTest < ActionController::IntegrationTest

  def test_adding_a_student
    # get the new student form
    get '/students/new' # could be new_students_path

    # check there are boxes to put the name in
    # trivial in our case, but illustrates how to check output HTML
    assert_select "input[type=text][name='student[given_name]']"
    assert_select "input[type=text][name='student[family_name]']"

    assert_difference('Student.count') do
      post '/students/create', :student => {
        :given_name => "Fred",
        :family_name => "Smith",
        :date_of_birth => "1999-09-01",
        :grade_point_average => 2.0,
        :start_date => "2008-09-01"
      }
    end

    assert_redirected_to "/students/#{assigns(:student).id}"
    follow_redirect!

    # for completeness, check it's showing some of our data
    assert_select "p", /Fred/
    assert_select "p", /2008\-09\-01/
  end

end
```

Instead of calling the create method directly, as the functional tests would do, test_adding_a_student starts by using the get method—with a URI fragment rather than a function name—to retrieve the form needed for adding a student.

Next, the method examines that form with assert_select, one of Rails' methods for testing HTML documents to see if they contain what you expect them to contain. In the first of those two statements, assert_select tries to match the pattern:

```
input[type=text][name='student[given_name]']
```

That would be an input element with a type attribute set to text and a name attribute set to student[given_name]. (The single quotes are necessary to keep the [and] from causing trouble with the match pattern syntax.) The form should match that, as it contains:

```
<input id="student_given_name" name="student[given_name]" size="30"
  type="text" />
```

Once Rails has performed those assertions, it moves to actually submitting a new student. There's no way (yet) for Rails to actually fill in the form and press the submit button, but the test does the next best thing, issuing a POST request that reflects what the form would have done, from inside of an assert_differ ence call that looks for an added student:

```
assert_difference('Student.count') do
    post '/students/create', :student => {
      :given_name => "Fred",
      :family_name => "Smith",
      :date_of_birth => "1999-09-01",
      :grade_point_average => 2.0,
      :start_date => "2008-09-01"
    }
  end
```

Again, the call is to a URL, not to a method name, though this post call includes parameters designed to reflect the structure that would be returned by the form Rails generated. The page showing this student, Fred Smith, should come back from Rails for display through a redirect, so the next assertion watches for that:

```
assert_redirected_to "/students/#{assigns(:student).id}"
```

The assertion can grab the id value for the new student, whatever it is, from the controller, using the all-powerful assigns method. If it gets sent somewhere other than it expects, it will report failure.

The next call is fairly self-explanatory:

```
follow_redirect!
```

There's one last step needed here: checking that response to see if it reflects expectations. Following the redirect lets the test continue to the final part of

---

the interaction, in which Rails shows off the newly created student. Here, the test uses more `assert_select` statements in a slightly different syntax:

```
assert_select "p", /Fred/
assert_select "p", /2008\-09\-01/
```

When given a string and a regular expression as arguments, `assert_select` will look for elements of the type given in the string (here, p) that contain values matching the expression. Appendix C has more details on regular expressions, but the first of these is just the string Fred, while the other is an escaped version of 2008-09-01. These are, of course, the values that the test set earlier, and they should appear in the document. Will they?

```
$ rake test:integration
(in /Users/simonstl/Documents/RailsOutIn/current/code/ch12/students005)
/System/Library/Frameworks/Ruby.framework/Versions/1.8/usr/bin/ruby -Ilib:test
"/Library/Ruby/Gems/1.8/gems/rake-0.8.1/lib/rake/rake_test_loader.rb"
"test/integration/students_test.rb"
Loaded suite /Library/Ruby/Gems/1.8/gems/rake-0.8.1/lib/rake/rake_test_loader
Started
.
Finished in 0.368834 seconds.

1 tests, 7 assertions, 0 failures, 0 errors
```

It all worked.

Creating useful integration tests is difficult. It requires plotting a path through your application, deciding which pieces are relevant, and which are not. As your application grows in complexity and interdependence, they may become critical, though smaller applications can often do without them for a long while.

 If `assert_select` isn't enough for your view-testing experiments, Rails offers many more options, including `assert_tag`, `assert_no_tag`, `assert_dom_equal`, `assert_dom_not_equal`, `assert_select_encoded`, and `assert_select_rjs`.

Beyond the Basics

Testing is central to Rails development, but virtually everyone has a different perspective on what they want from testing. While the tools demonstrated in this chapter provide a common core of functionality, many developers supplement or replace the testing approach built into Rails with other alternatives. If you want to explore further, these might be worth checking out:

autotest

The autotest plug-in (or zentest) runs tests for you in the background. It waits for you to make changes to code, then runs tests addressing the files that changed. For an introduction, see *http://ph7spot.com/articles/getting _started_with_autotest.*

mocha

The mocha plug-in provides an extensive toolkit for letting your tests call methods that you've overridden, guaranteeing that your tests will operate against a consistent set of interactions—even if you haven't really implemented those parts of your application yet. For more information, see *http://mocha.rubyforge.org/.*

rcov

Testing is great, but what if your tests only cover part of your code and don't actually try out the broken parts? rcov lets you see which parts of your code are actually covered by your tests. To learn more about code coverage and rcov, see *http://eigenclass.org/hiki.rb?rcov.*

RSpec

RSpec takes testing to a totally different level, letting you create stories with your code, testing the results of those stories in a way that lets you see what was supposed to happen and what did or didn't happen as well. It makes it much easier in particular to create tests first and then write code to fill them in. For a lot more on RSpec, visit *http://rspec.info/.*

Even if you stick with the basic Rails testing functionality, your applications should prove much more reliable and your need for debugging much less.

Test Your Knowledge

Quiz

1. What three modes can Rails run applications under?
2. How much data do you need to put into fixtures?
3. Can the results of one test mess up the results of a test that comes later?
4. How do you check to see whether a variable was assigned a value?
5. How do you check to make sure a variable contains an acceptable value?
6. What kind of component gets tested with Rails functional tests?
7. How do you send a controller a fake HTTP POST request?
8. How do you know whether a controller redirected a request?

9. How can you tell whether a response includes a **td** element containing a particular value?

Answers

1. Rails can run in development mode, test mode, and production mode.
2. Your fixtures should include all the kinds of data you want to run tests against.
3. Each test should be completely independent, as Rails will reload all of the fixtures between tests. No test should have an effect on any other test.
4. **validates_presence_of** lets you check whether a variable has a value.
5. The **valid?** method lets you ask a model if its value would pass validation.
6. In Rails, functional tests are tests of controllers.
7. The **post** method lets you see how a controller would respond to a POST request.
8. The **assert_redirected** method lets you test whether the controller sent a simple response or a redirect.
9. The **assert_select** method lets you specify an element name and a match pattern it should contain, and tells you whether an element whose content matches that pattern exists.

## CHAPTER 13

Sessions and Cookies

The Web was built to do one thing at a time. Each request is, from the point of view of the client and server, completely independent of every other. A group of requests might all operate on the same database, and there can be clear paths from one part of an application to another, but for the most part, HTTP and scalable web application design both try to keep requests as independent as possible. It makes the underlying infrastructure easier.

Rails balances that simplicity of infrastructure with application developers' need for a coherent way to maintain context. Rails supports several mechanisms keeping track of information about users. If you want to keep track of users manually, you can work with cookies. If you want to keep track of users for a brief series of interactions, Rails' built-in session support should meet your needs.

 If you want to keep track of users on a long-term basis, you'll want to use the authentication tools covered in Chapter 14.

Getting Into and Out of Cookies

Like nearly every web framework, Rails provides support for cookies. Cookies are small pieces of text, usually less than 4 KB long, that servers can set on browsers and browsers will pass back with requests to servers. Browsers keep track of where cookies came from and only report cookies' values to the server where they came from originally. JavaScript code can reach into a cookie from a web page, but Rails itself is more interested in setting and receiving cookies through the HTTP headers for each request and response.

When cookies first appeared, they were loved by developers who saw them as a way to keep track of which user was visiting their site, and hated by privacy advocates. Much of that uproar has calmed, because cookies have become a key part of functionality that users like, but there's still potential for abuse.

To stay on the good side of potentially cranky users, it's best to set cookie lifetimes to relatively brief periods and use longer cookies only when users request them (as in the classic "remember me" checkboxes for logins). Never store sensitive information directly in cookies, either!

In most cases, your application probably doesn't need to access cookies directly. Rails' built-in support for sessions and the tools for user authentication can both manage all of the overhead of keeping track of users for you. However, if you want to use cookies directly, either because you have specific needs for them or because you're interacting with other code (say, a JavaScript library) that expects a particular cookie to provide it with a key value, then the demonstration below should give you a clear idea how it works. Figure 13-1 provides an overall picture of how cookies flow through an application.

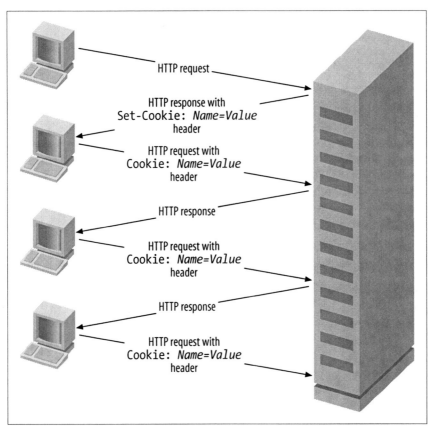

Figure 13-1. The flow of cookies between Rails, the browser, and code in the browser

Because cookies are about storing data on the client, not the server, a really simple example will do. To get started, this example will build on one of the simplest examples in this book so far, the first version of the entry controller with its sign_in method from Chapter 4. (Code for this example is in *ch13/ guestbook011.*)

 If you'd rather create a new blank copy of this application, run rails guestbook, then cd guestbook if necessary, and then finally ruby script/generate controller entry.

Example 13-1 shows the new *app/controllers/entry_controller.rb* file, with changes from the Chapter 4 version in bold.

Example 13-1. Keeping track of names entered with a cookie

```
class EntryController < ApplicationController
  def sign_in
    @previous_name = cookies[:name]
    @name = params[:visitor_name]
    cookies[:name] = @name
  end
end
```

The new first line collects the previous name entered from the cookie and stores it as `@previous_name` so the view can display it. (The cookie data comes to the server through the HTTP request headers.) The second line, as before, gathers the new name from the `:visitor_name` field of the form, and the third line stores that name (even if it's empty) as a cookie that will be transmitted to the browser through the HTTP response headers.

The view in *app/views/entry/sign_in.html.erb* just needs three extra lines to show the previous name if there was one, as shown in Example 13-2.

Example 13-2. Reporting a previous name to the user

```
<html>
<head><title>Hello <%=h @name %></title></head>

<body>
<h1>Hello <%=h @name %></h1>
<% form_tag :action => 'sign_in' do %>
   <p>Enter your name:
   <%= text_field_tag 'visitor_name', @name %></p>

   <%= submit_tag 'Sign in' %>
<% end %>
<% unless @previous_name.blank? %>
<p>Hmmm... the last time you were here, you said you were <%=h @previous_name
%>.</p>
<% end %>
</body>
</html>
```

This tests to see whether a previous name was set and, if so, presents the user with what they'd entered. All this really does is demonstrate that the cookie is keeping track of something entered in a past request, making it available to the current request.

The HTTP headers that carry the cookie back and forth are normally invisible, though not that interesting. You can see cookie information in most browsers through a preferences or info setting. At the beginning, this application looks much like its predecessor, as shown in Figure 13-2.

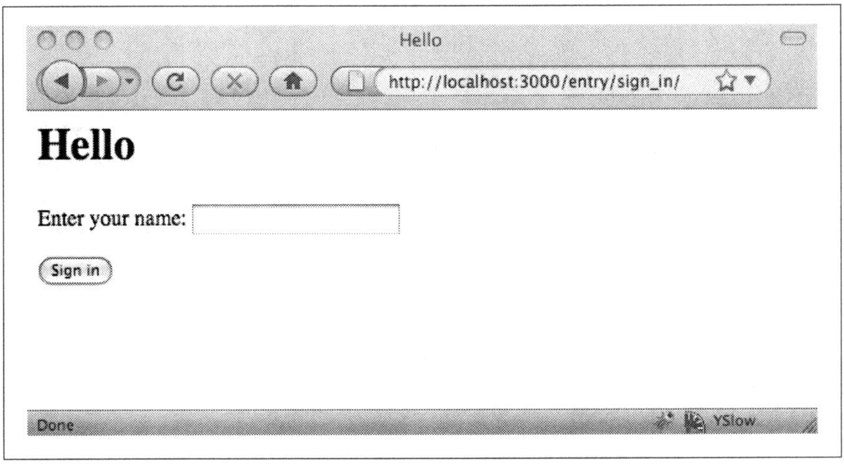

Figure 13-2. A simple name form, though now one with a cookie behind it

In Firefox 3.0, you call up the cookie inspection window at Tools/Page Info, then the Security tab, and then the View Cookies button halfway down the screen on the righthand side. You'll see something like Figure 13-3.

For now, the :name cookie is the one that matters, and as you can see, its content is blank. It came from localhost, because this is a test session on the local machine. The path is set to /, the Rails default, making it accessible to any page that comes from the localhost server. It gets sent with all HTTP connections and will expire "at end of session"—as soon as the user quits the browser. Users can, of course, delete the cookie immediately with the Remove Cookie button.

If you enter a name, say, "Zimton," and click the "Sign-in" button, you'll see something like Figure 13-4.

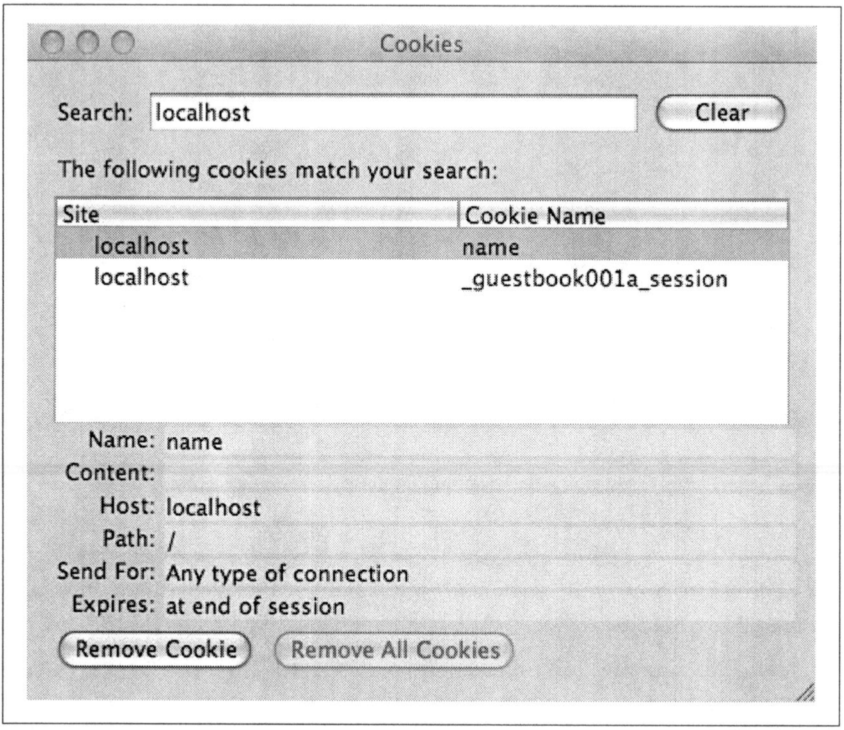

Figure 13-3. A cookie named "name" with a blank value

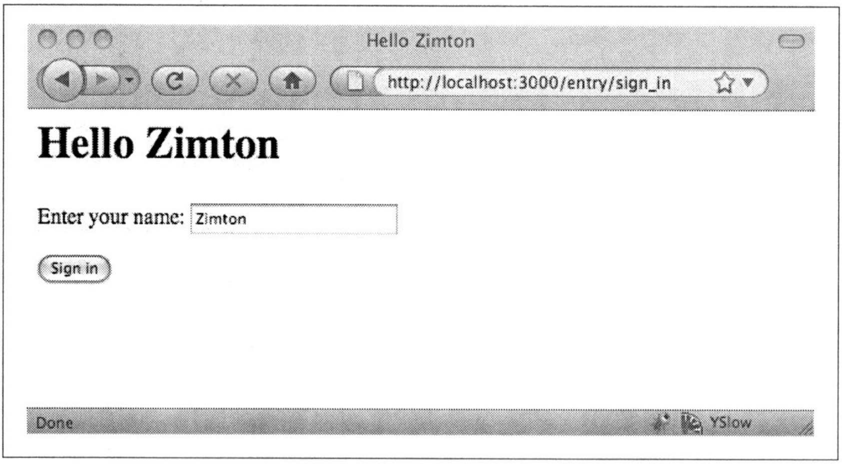

Figure 13-4. The form, with a new name set

Because the :name cookie was previously set to an empty string, the query message still isn't shown, but this time the trigger is set. If you inspect the cookie, you'll see that the :name cookie's value is now "Zimton," as shown in Figure 13-5.

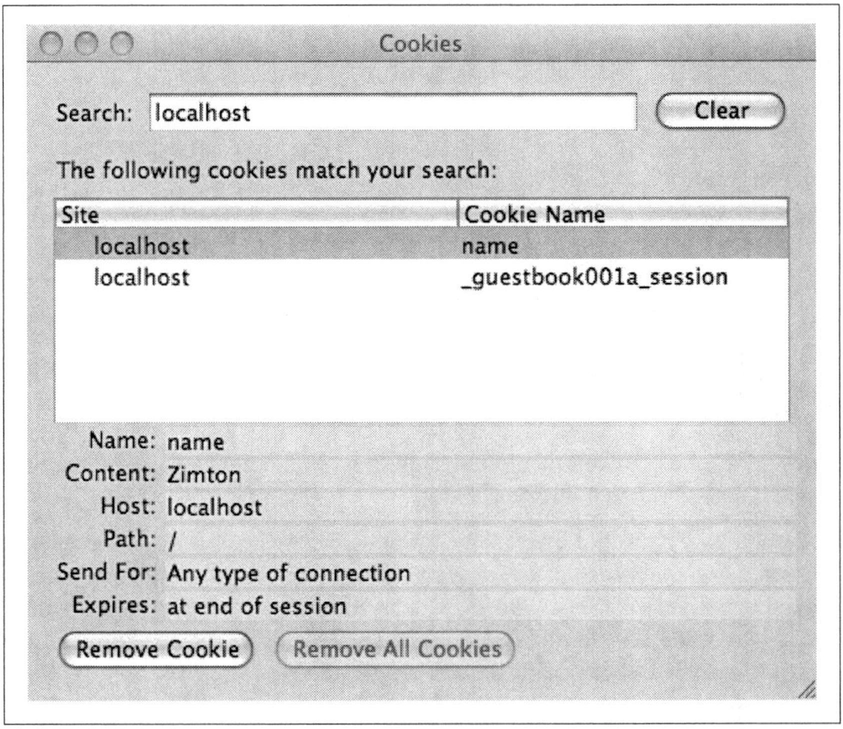

Figure 13-5. The name cookie, now set with a value of "Zimton"

If you enter a new name, say "Zimtonito," and click the "Sign-in" button, the Rails application will get "Zimtonito" through the form, while still getting "Zimton" from the cookie. This time, it will ask why the name has changed, as shown in Figure 13-6.

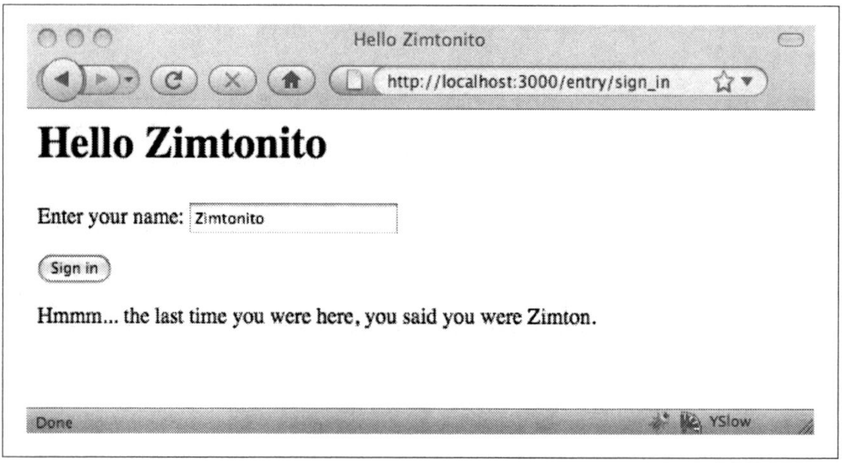

Figure 13-6. Changing names over the session produces a response

Storing the name information in the cookie gives Rails a memory of what happened before and lets it notice a change.

If you choose to use cookies directly, rather than relying on Rails' other mechanisms for keeping track of interactions across requests, there are a few more parameters you should know about when setting cookies. If you set more than just a value for a cookie, the syntax changes. To set both a value and a path for the :name cookie, for example, you would change:

```
cookies[:name] = @name
```

to:

```
cookies[:name] = { :value => @name, :path => '/entry' }
```

The available parameters include:

:value

The value for the cookie, usually a short string. (Typically this is a database key, but make sure not to store anything genuinely secret.)

:domain

The domain to which the cookie applies. This has to be a domain that matches with the domain the application runs at. For example, if an application was hosted at *http://myapp.example.com*, :domain could be set to *http://myapp.example.com* or *http://example.com*. If it was set to *http://ex ample.com*, the cookie could be read from *http://myapp.example.com*, *http://yourapp.example.com*, or *http://anything.example.com*.

`:path`

> The path to which the cookie applies. Like `:domain`, the `:path` must be all or part of the path from which the call is being made. From */entry/ sign_in*, it could be set to */*, to */entry*, or to */entry/sign_in*. The cookie can only be read from URLs that could have set that path. (By default, this is */*, making the cookie available to everything at your domain.)

`:expires`

> The time at which the cookie will expire. The easiest way to set this is with Ruby's time methods, such as `5.minutes` or `12.hours.from_now`.

`:secure`

> If set to `true`, the cookie is only reported or sent over secure HTTP (HTTPS) connections.

`:http_only`

> If `true`, the cookie is transmitted over HTTP or HTTPS connections, but is not available to JavaScript code on those pages.

Anytime you find yourself using cookies, especially if you're doing complicated things with cookies, you should consider using sessions or authentication instead.

Storing Data Between Sessions

Cookies are useful for keeping track of a piece of information between page changes, but as you may have noticed in Figures 13-3 and 13-5, Rails was already setting a cookie, a session cookie, with each request. Rather than manage cookies yourself, you can let Rails do all of that work and move one step further back from the details. (This example is available in *ch13/guestbook012*.)

Sessions are a means of keeping track of which user is making a given request. Rails doesn't know anything specific about the user, except that he has a cookie with a given value. Rails uses that cookie to keep track of users and lets you store a bit of information that survives between page requests.

You can set and retrieve information about the current session from the `ses sion` object, which is available to your controller and view. Because it's a better idea in general to put logic into the controller, Example 13-3, which is a new version of the *app/controllers/entry_controller.rb* file, shows what's involved in storing an array in the `session` object, retrieving it, and modifying it to add names to the list. Virtually all of it replaces code that was in Example 13-1, with only the retrieval of the name from the form staying the same.

Example 13-3. Working with an array stored in the session object

```
class EntryController < ApplicationController
    def sign_in
    #get names array from session
    @names=session[:names]

    #if the array doesn't exist, make one
    unless @names
      @names=[]
    end

    #get the latest name from the form
    @name = params[:visitorName]

    if @name
      # add the new name to the names array
      @names << @name
    end

    # store the new names array in the session
    session[:names]=@names
  end
end
```

Most of the new code is about working with an array rather than a simple field.
It's not a big problem if a string is empty, whereas trying to add new entries
to a nonexistent array is a bigger problem. The `sign_in` method gets the
names array from the `session` object and puts it in `@names`. If the `session` object
doesn't have a names object, it will return nil, so the `unless` creates a `names`
array if necessary. Then the method retrieves the latest `visitorName` from the
form and adds it to the `@names` array. The very last line puts the updated version
of the `@names` array back into the `session` object so that the next call will have
access to it.

> Example 13-3 is more verbose than it needs to be, as you could
> work on session[:names] directly. However, it's a bit clearer
> to work with the @names instance variable, and this approach
> lets the view work strictly with instance variables.

The view requires fewer changes—just a test that the list of names exists and
a loop to display the names if it does. The changes to *app/views/entry/
sign_in.html.erb* are highlighted in Example 13-4.

Example 13-4. Reporting a set of previous names to the user

```
<html>
<head><title>Hello <%=h @name %></title></head>
```

```
<body>
<h1>Hello <%=h @name %></h1>

<% form_tag :action => 'sign_in' do %>
  <p>Enter your name:
  <%= text_field_tag 'visitorName', @name %></p>

  <%= submit_tag 'Sign in' %>
<% end %>

<% if @names %>
<ul>
  <% @names.each do |name| %>
    <li><%=h name %></li>
  <% end %>
</ul>
<% end %>

</body>
</html>
```

As Figures 13-7 through 13-9 demonstrate, the application now remembers what names have been entered before.

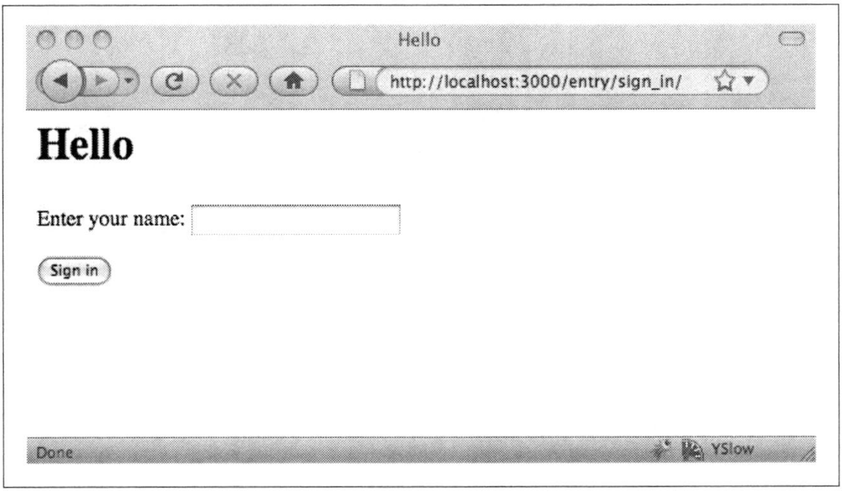

Figure 13-7. The first iteration, where no previous names are recorded in the session object

Figure 13-8. The second iteration, where one previous name has been recorded in the session object

Figure 13-9. The third iteration, where two previous names have been recorded in the session object

If you quit your browser and return, or try a different browser, you'll get the empty result shown in Figure 13-8 again, as the session changes. This application is very different from the application at the end of Chapter 4, which stored names from everyone in the same database. Because this application relies on the session object, only the names entered in this browser at this time will appear. That session identifier will vanish when the user quits their browser because the session cookie will be deleted, and those names will no longer be accessible.

The `session` object builds on the cookie functionality described in the previous section, but Rails takes care of all the cookie handling. For simple applications, where you're just going to store something small in the session, you now know everything you need to know and can skip ahead if you'd like.

There are, of course, more details, more things you can tweak. First of all, you can turn sessions off if you have an application that doesn't need them and want a little speed boost. Just add `session :off` at the top of controller classes or, for the whole application, in *app/controllers/application.rb*. (You can turn individual controllers back on with `session :on`, and the documentation for `ActionController::SessionManagement` shows many more options for controlling when sessions are used.)

Just as with cookies, you can limit the use of sessions to secure HTTPS connections. To do so, just start off with session `:session_secure => true`. Sessions will stop working over regular HTTP connections and only work when HTTPS is in use.

The hard question about sessions is where the data is actually stored. A key reason that HTTP is stateless is that it takes a lot of computing time to look up the state for every single transaction. Those queries can become a bottleneck, especially when you want to do things like distribute an application across multiple servers. Rails offers a number of options for solving those problems. There are only two you should consider when getting started, however. Both are illustrated in Figure 13-10.

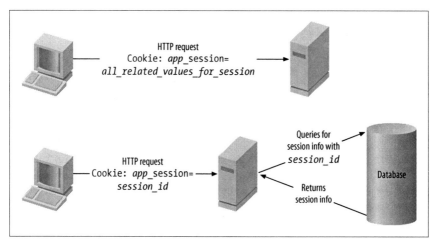

Figure 13-10. Two models for storing data in sessions

The first, the CookieStore, is what Rails uses by default. All of the data that goes into the session object for a given session is stored directly in the cookie Rails uses to track the session. In some ways, this is extremely convenient— all the session information comes with the request, and the users' browsers become a gigantic distributed data storage system for the Rails application. On the other hand, this limits the overall storage to 4K, the limit of cookie size, and it means that all of the session information is constantly transferred back and forth in a simple and easily decrypted hash. If you can accept the size limit and the openness, though, it's easy.

The second approach, the ActiveRecord SessionStore, stores only an identifier token in the session cookie, and stores the actual session data in the database. To make this work, you need to make a change in the *config/environment.rb* file. First, find:

```
# Use the database for sessions instead of the cookie-based default,
# which shouldn't be used to store highly confidential information
# (create the session table with "rake db:sessions:create")
# config.action_controller.session_store = :active_record_store
```

and then delete the # marked in bold. You'll also have to, as the comment notes, run rake db:sessions:create to create the necessary database support for session storage, and should then also run db:migrate. You'll also need to edit the *app/controllers/application.rb* file to uncomment the :secret. You won't have to change anything about the way you actually use the session object in your controllers. Rails will automatically switch over to the database approach. The only change you might notice is the removal of that 4K limit.

Even without the 4K limit, you'll find that it's much more efficient to store only minimal information in the session, preferably an identifier that can link to the necessary information in your application. It reduces the overhead for every request substantially.

Flashing in Rails

The Rails flash mechanism doesn't support state across separate user requests like the other mechanisms in this chapter. (Nor does it have anything to do with Adobe's Flash technology.) It does, however, provide an easy way to maintain state within a user request that gets answered with a redirect.

When a controller calls redirect_to, which is common in RESTful PUT and POST handling, the method that gets the redirect starts off with a fresh set of variables. You can't work in one controller method and then pass the rest of the work to another controller method while retaining the variable context.

There's one exception to this context reset—the flash mechanism. Most of the time, flash just gets used for sending messages from a controller to a view generated by another controller, as in this scaffolding excerpt:

```
flash[:notice] = 'Course was successfully updated.'
format.html { redirect_to(@course) }
```

In the layout for the course views, this line reveals the contents of that `flash`:

```
<p style="color: green"><%= flash[:notice] %></p>
```

Although `:notice` is the most common key used with flash, you could also use `:warning`, `:error`—or any other key that seems appropriate to your task. (`:notice`, `:warning`, and `:error` work automatically with the templates Rails generates, which is convenient.)

There are only a few catches. First, you should always keep the contents of the `flash` simple and small. It's stored in the session and, like everything else in the session, should be as lightweight as possible. Second, the contents only survive one redirect. If you want to keep the contents across multiple redirects, you'll need to call `flash.keep` before each additional redirect. Similarly, you can call `flash.discard` to get rid of the flash.

Also, you should note that you don't have to have a redirect to use flash—it's perfectly good for sending messages immediately, too, though it might be good form to specify `flash.now`, which discards the flash value after its first use.

Test Your Knowledge

Quiz

1. How much information should you store in cookies?
2. How do you specify how long a cookie will last?
3. Where does Rails normally store the information you put in the cookie object?
4. What does calling `flash.now` do?

Answers

1. You should store as little information in cookies as your application can manage.
2. Cookie lifespans default to expiring when the user quits the browser, but can be set to more specific lengths of time with the `:expires` parameter.
3. By default, Rails stores the cookie objects information directly in the cookie, on the user's browser, but note that you can change this by modifying your *config/environment.rb* file.

4. The `flash.now` method lets you set a value to be sent to the user, but ensures that the value will be cleared before any reloads or redirects.

## CHAPTER 14

Users and Authentication

While sessions expand your application-building possibilities, almost any interactive application that will be around for a while needs to be able to keep track of users. You might be a little startled to hear that Rails itself doesn't include any mechanisms for tracking users, unlike most current web frameworks. That isn't so much a failure as an opportunity for developers to create their own authentication approaches. When getting started, however, it's probably wisest to work with the commonly used `restful_authentication` plug-in. (The code for this example is available in *ch14/students007*.)

 Note that the `restful_authentication` plug-in is based on the older `acts_as_authenticated` plug-in. Many applications use, and much documentation describes, `acts_as_authenticated`, which has similar data structures but doesn't operate in a RESTful way.

Installation

Authentication is a complicated enough project that it's worth fitting into a more sophisticated application, like the students and courses example. The first step toward adding authentication to it is to install the `restful_authenti cation` plug-in. From the application directory, enter:

```
$ script/plugin install http://svn.techno-
weenie.net/projects/plugins/restful_authentication
```

 More recent versions of `restful_authentication` have moved to a different location, *git://github.com/technoweenie/restful-authentication.git*. Using that version, which has changed slightly from the one described here, will require you to install Git on your computer. For more on Git, see *http://git.or.cz/*.

The next step is using the plug-in to generate the many classes needed to actually implement authentication. While the generator can take many arguments, the two most important at the outset are what you want to call your user model and what you want to call your session model. For now, `user` and `session` make sense:

```
$ script/generate authenticated user session
```

 The documentation suggests `sessions` instead of `session`. It's not entirely clear why, but we find `session` makes for more readable code, if a tiny bit more work. Others seem to do the same as well.

Running this `script/generate` also brings up some documentation beyond the usual list of files, including suggestions for routes that would use some of the initially generated methods. Integrating it into an existing application will take this work down a slightly different path, but the general idea—having users sign up, log in, and log out—remains the same.

Storing User Data

Before users can do any of that, though, Rails needs a table for storing their data. The generator created a migration file in *db/migrate*, with a name ending in *create_users*, shown in Example 14-1.

Example 14-1. The migration for creating users in the database

```
class CreateUsers < ActiveRecord::Migration
  def self.up
    create_table "users", :force => true do |t|
      t.column :login,                      :string
      t.column :email,                      :string
      t.column :crypted_password,           :string, :limit => 40
      t.column :salt,                       :string, :limit => 40
      t.column :created_at,                 :datetime
      t.column :updated_at,                 :datetime
      t.column :remember_token,             :string
      t.column :remember_token_expires_at,  :datetime

    end
  end

  def self.down
    drop_table "users"
  end
end
```

There's no pressing need to change this, but if you know you have plans for additional fields about your users, you could add additional columns. (This migration uses the older t.column syntax rather than the newer t.*datatype* syntax, but it should still be clear what's being created here.) To create the table, run rake db:migrate.

Sessions don't have a model or migrations—they're just a controller that operates on users, so there isn't anything more to do with them yet.

Controlling Sessions

At this point, you can actually create a new user by running script/server and visiting *http://localhost:3000/users/new*, as shown in Figure 14-1.

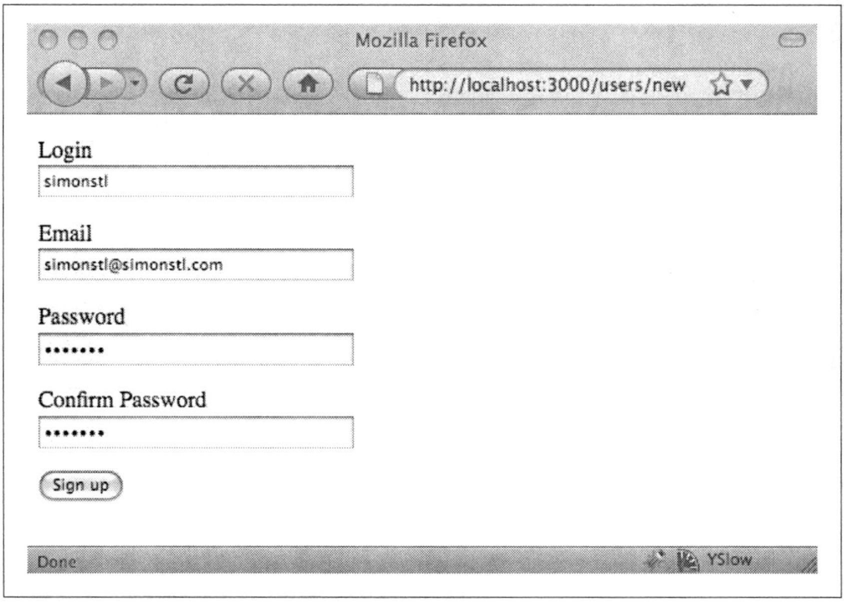

Figure 14-1. Creating a new user in the default form

While the sign-up will actually work—you can tell if you check the logs—the submission just gets redirected to the top-level page, which in this case is still the Rails welcome page. That's not very helpful. (On the bright side, if the passwords don't match, that warning will come through and the form reloads.)

Keep track of this first account—it will make things much simpler when it's time later in the chapter to create an administrator.

Similarly you can log in. Well, you can almost log in. One side effect of using session rather than sessions is that a route in *config/routes.rb* needs to change from:

```
map.resource :session
```

to:

```
map.resource :session, :controller => 'session'
```

Otherwise, you'll get a NameError.

While you're in the *routes.rb* file, just below the line for :session, add:

```
map.signup '/signup', :controller => 'users', :action => 'new'
map.login '/login', :controller => 'session', :action => 'new'
map.logout '/logout', :controller => 'session', :action => 'destroy'
```

Once this is set up, you can connect to *http://localhost:3000/login* and find the login page shown in Figure 14-2.

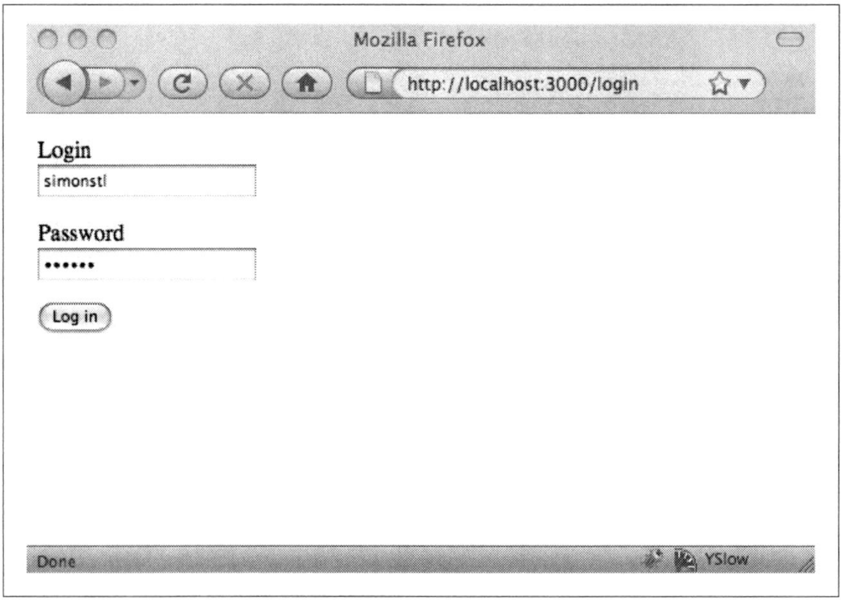

Figure 14-2. Logging in for the first time

A successful login, once again, returns the user to the Rails welcome page. A failed login just brings up the login page, with no explanation of what happened. A call to /logout isn't much better—the user is logged out, but only sees the welcome page as a result. Things are working, but not in ways that are yet very helpful.

There are lots of ways to tackle this problem, but starting at the top, with a welcome page, might be a good place to start. The welcome page should offer users a chance to log in and might someday contain additional information about the site. There isn't much to it, though—it doesn't actually do anything except display, so while it needs a controller (like the Hello World example in Chapter 2), most of its content is in the view and layout.

To get started, delete or rename the *public/index.html* file. In the *config/routes.rb* file, find the line near the bottom that says:

```
# map.root :controller => "welcome"
```

and delete the #, turning on that route. As Chapter 15 will explain, this will tell Rails to route requests for *http://localhost:3000/* (or whatever the top-level domain is for your Rails application) to the welcome controller and, by default, to its index method.

Next, generate that welcome controller:

```
$ script/generate controller welcome
```

Replace the contents of the mostly blank *app/controllers/welcome_controller.rb* with:

```
class WelcomeController < ApplicationController
  layout 'general'

  def index
  end

end
```

The blank index method will give routing something to point to, and specifying a layout makes it easy to provide some surrounding context for the results. The next steps are to create that general layout and a view to display when index is called. The general layout, stored in *views/layouts/general.html.erb*, looks like Example 14-2.

Example 14-2. A layout for the welcome page and any other pages that don't fit some other layout

```
<!DOCTYPE html PUBLIC "-//W3C//DTD XHTML 1.0 Transitional//EN"
    "http://www.w3.org/TR/xhtml1/DTD/xhtml1-transitional.dtd">

<html xmlns="http://www.w3.org/1999/xhtml" xml:lang="en" lang="en">
```

```
<head>
  <meta http-equiv="content-type" content="text/html;charset=UTF-8" />
  <title><%= controller.action_name %></title>
  <%= stylesheet_link_tag 'scaffold' %>
</head>
<body>

<%= render :partial => '/navigation' %>

<% if flash[:notice]%>
  <p style="color: green"><%= flash[:notice] %></p>
<% end %>
<% if flash[:error] %>
  <p style="color: red"><%= flash[:error] %></p>
<% end %>

<%= yield  %>

</body>
</html>
```

This is similar to the layouts created for earlier versions of the application. One key feature is support for flash messages, which should replace the eerie silence of the previous iteration of logging in. The call to the navigation partial gives the welcome page a connection to the rest of the application.

Next, the *views/welcome/index.html.erb* file needs to provide the content of that welcome page, as shown in Example 14-3.

Example 14-3. The welcome page, in HTML with a few helpers

```
<h1>Welcome</h1>
<% if current_user %>
<p>Hi, <%=h current_user.login %>.</p>
<% else %>
<p>Please <%= link_to "log in", login_path %> to use the system,
 or <%= link_to "sign up", signup_path %> for a new account.</p>
<% end %>
```

Editing the *public/index.html* file might have been a shorter path to a welcome page, but this approach lets the welcome page vary by whether a user is already signed in or not. If the user is already logged in, the page welcomes the user back with the login name. If not, the user is offered the choice of logging in or creating a new account, thanks to link_to calls referencing the named paths added to *routes.rb* earlier. The current_user method tests whether the user has logged in previously.

However, if you try to run this now, you'll just get a NameError—Rails doesn't know what current_user means. Since practically every controller in the application should have access to authentication functionality, the easiest way to make the current_user method available is to modify the *controllers/appli-*

cation.rb file instead of individual controller files. All of the controllers inherit from the `ApplicationController` class it defines, and a change here will echo to them as well.

Just change:

```
class ApplicationController < ActionController::Base
```

to:

```
class ApplicationController < ActionController::Base
  include AuthenticatedSystem
```

Once this is saved, you can open *http://localhost:3000/* and see the welcome shown in Figure 14-3.

Figure 14-3. A welcome screen when no one is actually logged in

Now you can log in, and when the login redirects you to the welcome screen, you can tell something happened, as shown in Figure 14-4. Similarly, the page for creating accounts will also report success, as shown in Figure 14-5. (The default behavior logs users in automatically when they create accounts.)

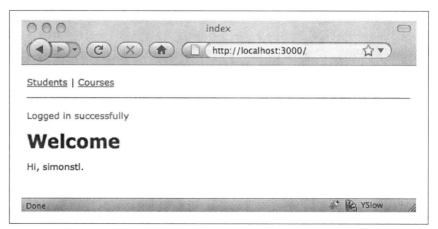

Figure 14-4. The welcome screen after a successful login

Figure 14-5. The welcome screen after creating an account

It would, of course, be nice to have a way to log out. The existing navigation partial, in *views/_navigation.html.erb*, can be easily modified to support that across the entire application with a few extra lines:

```
<p>
<%= link_to "Welcome", root_path %> |
<%= link_to "Students", students_url %> |
<%= link_to "Courses", courses_url %>
<% if current_user %>
  | <%= link_to "Logout", logout_path %>
<% end %>
</p>

<hr />
```

Now, if a user is logged in, they'll see welcome and logout options no matter where in the application they're working, as shown in Figure 14-6. As Figure 14-7 shows, logging out takes users back to the welcome page, which no longer shows the Logout option.

All of the login and logout functionality works well. There's just one kind of major problem: it doesn't actually do anything yet. Users can still view, create, edit, and delete courses, students, and awards, whether or not they log into the application. Fortunately, that's easily done by adding one line to each of the controller classes, *except* welcome, session, and user, which should stay open.

Below the class declaration but before any of the methods, just add:

```
before_filter :login_required
```

For example, in the *app/controllers/courses_controller.rb* file, change:

```
class CoursesController < ApplicationController

  # GET /courses
  ...
```

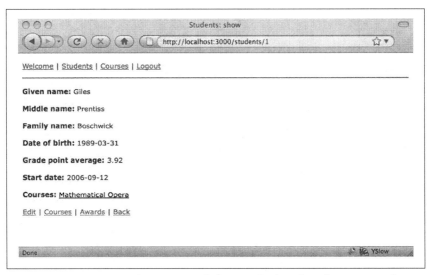

Figure 14-6. Navigation at the top now includes going back to the welcome page or logging out of the application entirely

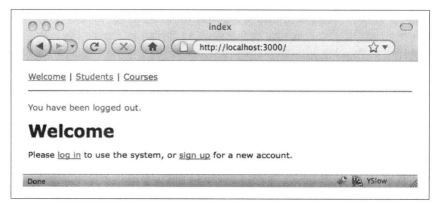

Figure 14-7. After logging out, users are returned to the welcome page, and the Logout option disappears from the navigation menu

to:

```
class CoursesController < ApplicationController
  before_filter :login_required

  # GET /courses
  ...
```

Now, if users visit the students, courses, or awards pages without being logged in, they'll be redirected to the login page.

Classifying Users

Most applications have at least two categories of users—administrators and ordinary users. Many applications have finer-grained permissions, but this is a good place to start. Code for this is available in *ch14/students008*. The first step toward creating an extra category of users is to create a migration with a suitable name:

```
script/generate migration AddAdminFlagToUsers
```

In the newly created migration, under *db/migrate*, change the migration file with the name ending in *add_admin_flag_to_users* so that it looks like Example 14-4.

Example 14-4. A migration for adding a boolean administration flag to the users table

```
class AddAdminFlagToUsers < ActiveRecord::Migration
  def self.up
    add_column :users, :admin, :boolean, :default => false, :null => false
  end

  def self.down
```

```
    remove_column :users, :admin
  end
end
```

This adds one column to the **users** table, a boolean named **admin**. It defaults to **false**—most users will not be administrators—and can't have a null value. Run **rake db:migrate** to run the migration and add the column.

Next, there's a small challenge. The system really should have at least one administrator, but building a complete user administration facility means building another whole set of forms and controller methods. In addition, it probably makes sense to be able to designate an initial user as administrator before locking all nonadministrators out of the user management system.

For this demonstration, there's an easy answer—the Rails console. In addition to its use in debugging, demonstrated in Chapter 11, it's also a great tool for making small direct modifications to databases. Run **script/console** and at the prompt, enter:

```
User.find(:all)
```

Rails will report a list of user records. You need to find the **id** of the one you want to give administrative privileges and assign them with something like:

```
User.find(1).update_attribute('admin', true)
```

This will find the **user** with the **id** value of 1—probably the first user created —and update the **admin** attribute for that record to **true**. You can, of course, pick any **id** value you need for this. If you're feeling paranoid, you can call **User.find(:all)** again to make sure the change is reflected in the record, or just **exit** the console.

Now that users have an administrative flag, and now that there is at least one user with the admin flag set to **true**, it's time to make that flag matter. One of the nicest features of **restful_authentication** is that you can centralize many authentication tasks in the *app/controllers/application.rb* file. Doing that generally requires overriding the **authorized?** method, which is defined in *lib/authenticated_system.rb* quite simply:

```
def authorized?
  logged_in?
end
```

In the examples earlier in this chapter, this was the method that kept out users who hadn't created accounts, thanks to the **before_filter :login_required** at the top of most controllers. (**login_required** is also defined in *lib/authenticated_system.rb*.)

It's time to set this to something stronger. An easy approach would be to add a condition, moving from **logged_in?** to **logged_in? && current_user.admin?**, locking out everyone who isn't an administrator. (It's always best to check *first* that the user is logged in—otherwise, current_user will be null, producing errors when you try to call methods on it.)

Most authentication systems don't limit content to administrators while giving users only the privilege of logging in to a useless system, however. More typically, ordinary users have read access while more privileged users, like administrators, can make changes. In a RESTful application environment, this can be easily implemented by letting users GET anything they want, while only privileged users can use POST, PUT, or DELETE. Rails has a request.get? method that returns true for GET and false for everything else. That makes it possible to write "must be logged and either GETting something or having admin privileges" as:

```
logged_in? && (request.get? || current_user.admin?)
```

First, this checks to see if the user is logged in. If not, Ruby won't bother evaluating the righthand side of the && expression, the part in parentheses, and Rails will reject the request. If the user is logged in, Ruby next evaluates whether the incoming request was a GET. If it was, great—there's no need to evaluate the other side of the || expression, and the user is granted access. If it wasn't, then Ruby checks to see whether the current_user object has its admin flag set. If yes, then permission is granted, because admins can make any kind of HTTP call they want. If not, then permission is denied, because some evil user is trying to make changes they're not allowed to make.

Overriding the method call should look like:

```
protected
  def authorized?
    logged_in? && (request.get? || current_user.admin?)
  end
```

The protected label lets objects of classes that descend from ApplicationController (all your controllers) call the authorized? method, but prohibits other objects from calling it. This can go near the bottom of the *app/controllers/application.rb* file, just above the final end statement. Before closing the file, it also makes sense to uncomment a line just above this, removing the # from:

```
# filter_parameter_logging :password
```

Chapter 11 explained filter_parameter_logging's blocking of certain parameters from the logs, and password information is a good choice for blocking.

At this point you can save the files and call script/server. If you log in with the account you set to be administrator (or don't log in at all), the application works just like it did before. The more interesting case, of course, is to create a new user with fewer permissions, and examine the new user's experience.

Figures 14-8 to 14-11 show how a newly created user steps through the application.

index
http://localhost:3000/
Welcome | Students | Courses | Logout
Thanks for signing up!
Welcome
Hi, zoid.
Done
YSlow

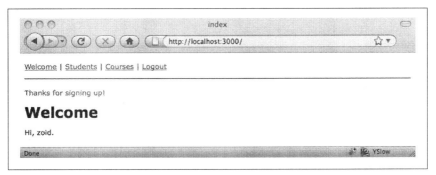

Figure 14-8. A new user, freshly welcomed

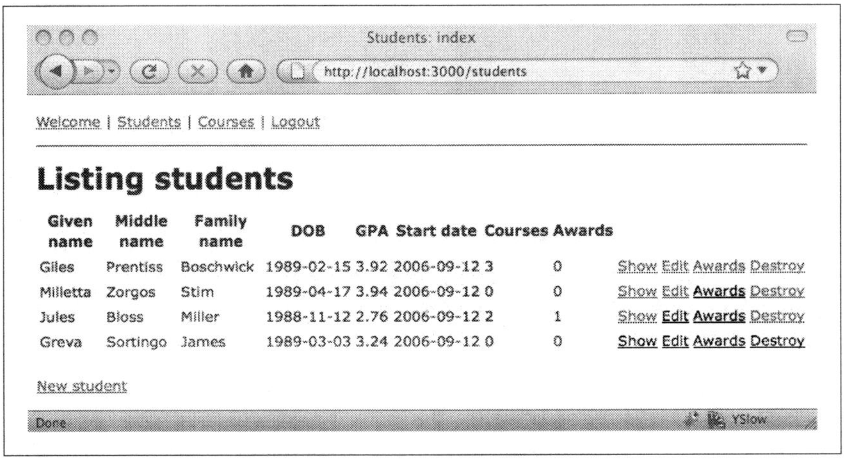

Students: index
http://localhost:3000/students
Welcome | Students | Courses | Logout
Listing students
Given name Middle name Family name DOB GPA Start date Courses Awards
Giles Prentiss Boschwick 1989-02-15 3.92 2006-09-12 3 0 Show Edit Awards Destroy
Milletta Zorgos Stim 1989-04-17 3.94 2006-09-12 0 0 Show Edit Awards Destroy
Jules Bloss Miller 1988-11-12 2.76 2006-09-12 2 1 Show Edit Awards Destroy
Greva Sortingo James 1989-03-03 3.24 2006-09-12 0 0 Show Edit Awards Destroy
New student
Done
YSlow

Figure 14-9. The students page works as planned for the new user

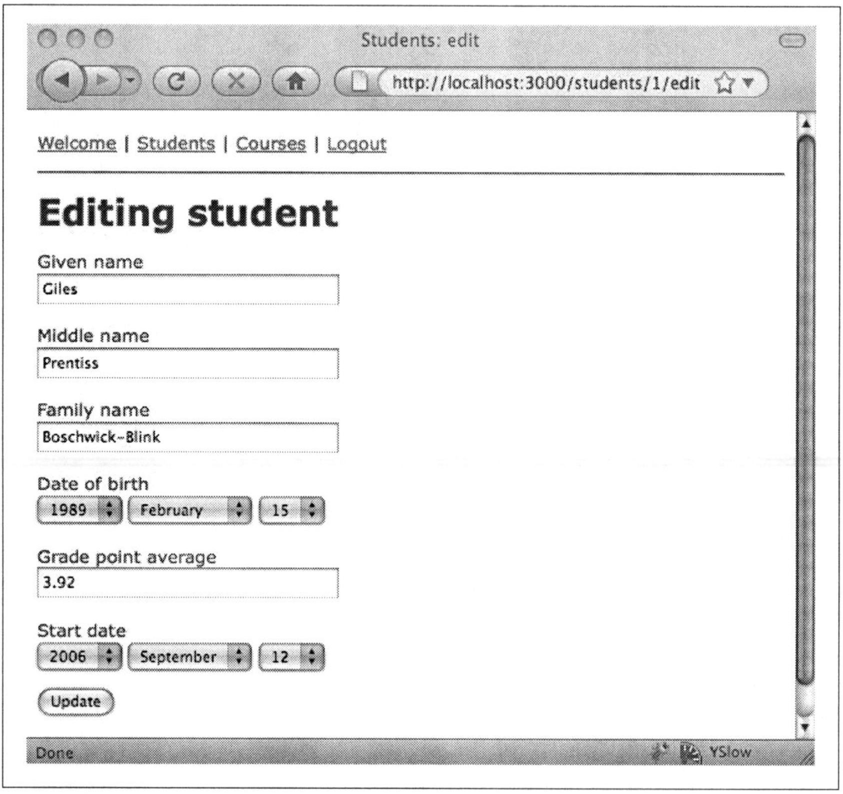

Figure 14-10. The editing page also works for the new user

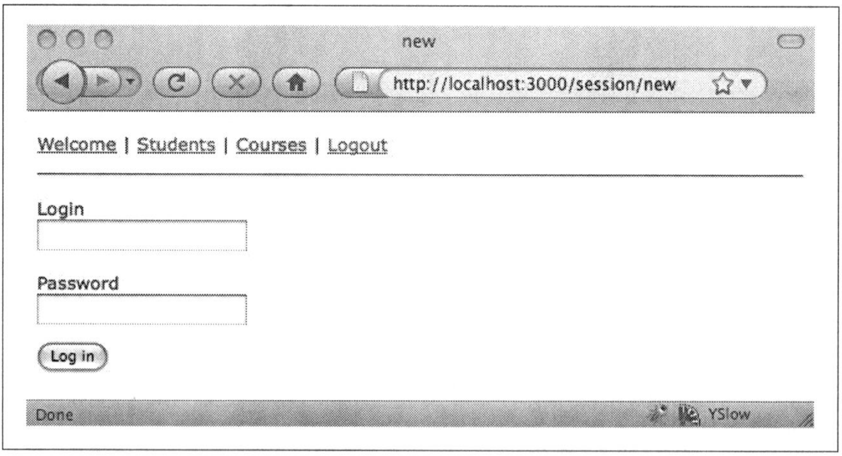

Figure 14-11. The new user's attempt to edit a document is finally blocked and they face a new login screen

The beginning of this user's journey goes as planned. Zoid gets a screen name (14-8), then visits the students page (14-9) where all the data is visible. Feeling curious, though, Zoid tries the Edit link for one of the students and is rewarded with the editing page (14-10). It's only when Zoid tries to submit the edits that the `authorization?` method decides it's time to lock him out (14-11).

From a strictly data security point of view, this is fine. The user can't change data without proper authorization. From the user's point of view, though, the interface is lying, offering opportunities that look like they should be available. As an interface issue, this is a problem with the views and can be solved by checking whether the current user is an administrator before presenting those options. This needs to be checked in each of the *index.html.erb* files for students, courses, and awards—a little repetition is necessary. The changes, though, are just a pair of `if` statements, highlighted in Example 14-5.

Example 14-5. Removing inappropriate choices from a user with limited powers

```
<h1>Listing students</h1>

<table>
  <tr>
    <th>Given name</th>
    <th>Middle name</th>
    <th>Family name</th>
    <th>DOB</th>
    <th>GPA</th>
    <th>Start date</th>
    <th>Courses</th>
    <th>Awards</th>
  </tr>

<% for student in @students %>
  <tr>
    <td><%=h student.given_name %></td>
    <td><%=h student.middle_name %></td>
    <td><%=h student.family_name %></td>
    <td><%=h student.date_of_birth %></td>
    <td><%=h student.grade_point_average %></td>
    <td><%=h student.start_date %></td>
    <td><%=h student.courses.count %></td>
    <td><%=h student.awards.count %></td>
    <td><%= link_to 'Show', student %></td>
    <td><%= link_to 'Awards', student_awards_path(student) %></td>
<% if current_user.admin? %>
    <td><%= link_to 'Edit', edit_student_path(student) %></td>
    <td><%= link_to 'Destroy', student, :confirm => 'Are you sure?', :method =>
:delete %></td>
<% end%>
  </tr>
<% end %>
</table>
```

```
<br />

<% if current_user.admin? %>
<%= link_to 'New student', new_student_path %>
<% end%>
```

This just removes the Edit, Destroy, and New options. (The Awards entry moves up a line, above Edit, to reduce the number of if statements needed.) Now, when Zoid logs in and visits the students page, he'll see Figure 14-12: just the options he's allowed to use.

		Students: index		

http://localhost:3000/students

Welcome | Students | Courses | Logout

Listing students

Given name	Middle name	Family name	DOB	GPA	Start date	Courses	Awards	
Giles	Prentiss	Boschwick	1989-02-15	3.92	2006-09-12	3	0	Show Awards
Milletta	Zorgos	Stim	1989-04-17	3.94	2006-09-12	0	0	Show Awards
Jules	Bloss	Miller	1988-11-12	2.76	2006-09-12	2	1	Show Awards
Greva	Sortingo	James	1989-03-03	3.24	2006-09-12	0	0	Show Awards

Done   YSlow

Figure 14-12. A more limited array of options appropriate to an ordinary user

There are a few other features that need the same treatment, like the link to the form for enrolling students in courses from the *app/views/students/show.html.erb* file. Every reasonably sophisticated application that has moved beyond the basic CRUD interface will have a few of these cases.

It's convenient to check results by keeping multiple browser windows open, logged into different user accounts. Remember, though, that Rails is tracking authentication status through sessions, which use cookies, that apply to the whole browser and not just a single window.

The easy way to deal with this is to open two different browsers and log in to the application separately in each of those, rather than in two different windows in the same browser.

There's still one leftover that may be worth addressing, depending on your security needs. The authorization? method has secured the data, and the view no longer shows the user options they can't really use, but if a user knows the URL for the edit form, it will still open. It's a GET request, after all. This is a good reason to make sure that these forms don't display any information that isn't publicly available through other means. If this is an issue, it may be worth the effort of adding authorization checks to every controller method that could spring a leak.

More Options

A complete application would support many more tasks around authentication. A few of the most notable include:

- An interface for managing users and privileges
- Letting users stay logged into their account on a given browser
- Finer-grained permissions for different categories of users
- Mechanisms that let users reset their passwords
- Email address verification
- Detailed account settings that let users set preferences
- OpenID support

All of these things, however, are projects with details that vary widely across different applications. The `restful_authentication` plug-in supports some of these options, such as connecting the password system to email, but most of this is work that's very dependent on what precisely you want to build. The users model is a model like any other: you can extend it, connect tables to it, and build whatever system you'd like behind your application. The `restful_authentication` plug-in gives you a foundation, and you can build whatever you need on top of it.

Test Your Knowledge

Quiz

1. Where is user and password information stored?
2. Where do you need to `include AuthenticatedSystem` to make authentication available?
3. How you tell a controller that users must be logged in to use that controller?

4. Where do you modify the rules that authorize users to have certain privileges?

5. How do you keep the logs from storing potentially sensitive security-related information?

Answers

1. User and password information is stored in the database, in a model you name when you first generate the authentication mechanisms.

2. You could put include `AuthenticatedSystem` in each of your controllers, but it's no doubt easiest to put it into the `ApplicationController` class in *app/controllers/application.rb*.

3. The `before_filter :login_required` method will block requests by unauthenticated users.

4. You can redefine the `authorized?` method in the `ApplicationController` class in *app/controllers/application.rb*.

5. You can keep sensitive information out of the logs with `filter_parameter_logging`.

## CHAPTER 15

Routing

Rails routing can shock developers who are used to putting their code in files wherever they want to put them. After the directory-based approach of traditional HTML and template-based development, Rails' highly structured approach looks very strange. Almost nothing, except for a few pieces in the *public* folder, is anywhere near where its URI might have suggested it was. Of course, this may not be so shocking if you've spent a lot of time with other frameworks or blogs—there are many applications that control the meanings of URIs through mechanisms other than the file system.

If you prefer to read "URI" as the older and more familiar URL, that's fine. Everything works the same here. (And the core method Rails uses to generate URIs is, of course, url_for, in the UrlModule.)

Rails routing turns requests to particular URIs into calls to particular controllers and lets you create URIs from within your applications. Its default routing behavior, especially when combined with resource routes generated through scaffolding, is often enough to get you started building an application, but there's a lot more potential if you're willing to explore Rails routing more directly. You can create interfaces with memorable (and easily bookmarkable) addresses, arrange related application functionality into clearly identified groups, and much, much more.

Rails 3.0 changes its approach to routing fairly dramatically. While learning what happens in 2.x will still provide a solid foundation, you may want to skip this chapter unless you have actual 2.x routing you need to work on.

What's more, you can even change routes without breaking your application's user interface, as the routing functionality also generates the addresses that the Rails view helper methods put into your pages.

 Changing routing can have a dramatic impact on the web services aspect of your applications. Programs that use your applications for XML-based services aren't likely to check the human interface to get the new address, and won't know where to go if you change routing. Routing is effectively where you describe the API for your projects, and you shouldn't change that too frequently without reason.

Creating Routes to Interpret URIs

Rails routing is managed through a single file, *config/routes.rb*. When Rails starts up, it loads this file, using it to process all incoming requests.

 If you're in development mode, which you usually are until deployment, Rails will reload *routes.rb* whenever you change it. In production mode, you have to stop and restart the server.

The default *routes.rb* contains a lot of help information that can get you started with the routes for your application, but it helps to know the general scheme first. In routing, Rails takes its fondness for connecting objects through naming conventions and lets you specify the conventions. Doing that means learning another set of conventions, of course!

Specifying Routes with map.connect

The easiest place to start is with the default rules, as you've probably already written code using them without having examined them too closely. They are near the bottom of the file and get called if nothing above them matched. You'll always want to put higher-priority routes above lower-priority ones, since the first match wins. The default rules look like:

```
map.connect ':controller/:action/:id'
map.connect ':controller/:action/:id.:format'
```

The `map.connect` method is the foundation of routing, though what it does can be mysterious until you compare it to some actual URIs. (Again, for the purposes of this chapter, if you'd rather read URI as URL, that's fine.) For example, if your Rails server on localhost, port 3000, had a controller named `people` that had an action named show, and you wanted to apply that to the record with the id of 20, this rule would let you do that with a call to:

```
http://localhost:3000/people/show/20
```

When Rails gets this, it looks for a rule that looks like it matches the URI structure. It checks the default rules last, but when it encounters the first default rule, Rails knows from this to set :controller to people, :action to show, and :id to 20. The symbols (prefaced with colons) act as matching wildcards for the routing. Rails uses that information to call the PeopleController's show method, passing it 20 as the :id parameter.

If a request comes in that would match ':controller' or ':controller/', Rails assumes that the next piece would be index, much as web servers expect *index.html* to be a default file. The :action will be set to index. Also, Rails ignores the name of the web server in routing, focusing on the parts of the URI after the web server name.

Routing rules also work in reverse. The link_to helper method and the many other methods link_to supports can take a :controller, an :action, and optionally even an :id, and generate a link to a URL for accessing them. For example:

```
link_to :controller => 'people', :action => 'show', :id => 20
```

would, working with the default rules, produce:

```
http://localhost:3000/people/show/20
```

The second rule is much like the first, with one piece of extra functionality. If a user wanted to request XML specifically, she could write:

```
http://localhost:3000/people/show/20.xml
```

Because these match the second map.connect rule, Rails will set :controller to people, :action to show, :id to 20, and :format to xml. Then it uses that information to call the PeopleController's show method, passing it 20 as the :id parameter and xml as the :format parameter.

If your controller checks the :format parameter—Chapter 5 examined respond_to, the easiest way to do this—and the value is one you've checked for, your controller can send a response in the requested format. This isn't limited to HTML or XML—you can specify other formats through the extension. If your controller supports them, visitors will get what they expect. If not, they might be disappointed, but nothing should break.

You could and probably should also specify the format through the MIME content-type header in the HTTP request, but that doesn't get checked in ordinary Rails routing.

There are many different ways to use `map.connect`. The approach that the default rules take—presenting a string filled with symbols that connect to pieces of a URI—is simple, but a rather blunt instrument. The `map.connect` method offers another approach that lets you specify URIs quite precisely: explicit specification of the URI and directions for where to send its processing. This looks like:

```
map.connect 'this/uri/exactly', :controller => "myController", :action =>
"myAction"
```

Using this rule, if a request comes in to a Rails server at *localhost:3000*, looking like:

```
http://localhost:3000/this/uri/exactly
```

Rails will call the `myController` controller's `myAction` method to handle the request.

 In many older Rails applications and in documentation, you'll often see `map.connect` used with a blank string as its first argument, as in:

```
map.connect '', :controller => "somewhere", :action
=> "something"
```

This tells Rails what to do if the URI points at the top level of the server. It still works, but using `map.root`, covered later in this chapter, is now considered better practice. (You also need to delete *index.html* from the *public* directory.)

While explicitly declaring mappings from individual URIs to particular controller actions is certainly precise, it's also not very flexible. Fortunately, you can mix symbols into the strings however you think appropriate to create combinations that meet your needs. For example, you might have a route that looks like:

```
map.connect ':action/awards', :controller => 'prizes'
```

if Rails encountered a URI like:

```
http://localhost:3000/show/awards
```

Then it would route the call to the `show` method of the `prizes` controller.

The `map.connect` method supports one other important technique. Calls to it aren't limited to the `:controller`, `:action`, `:id`, and `:format` parameters. You can call it with any parameters you want—`:part_number`, `:ingredient`, or `:century`, for example—and those parameters will be sent along to the controller as well. What's more, you can mix those symbols into the URI string for automatic extraction, making it possible to create routes like:

```
map.connect 'awards/:first_name/:last_name/:year', :controller => 'prizes',
action => 'show'
```

Then it would route the call to the show method of the prizes controller, with the arguments :first_name, :last_name, and :year.

A Domain Default with map.root

Often when prototyping, developers (and especially designers) like to start with the top page in a site, the landing page visitors will see if they just enter the domain name. The vision for this "front door" often sets expectations for other pages in the site, and the front door gets plenty of emphasis because it's often the first (or only) page users see. Even in an age where Google sends users to pages deep inside of a site, users often click to "the top" to figure out where they landed.

There are two ways to build this front door in Rails. The first way, which may do well enough at the outset, is to create a static HTML file that is stored as *public/index.html*. That page can then have links that move users deeper into your application's functionality. It's more likely, however, that projects will quickly outgrow that, as updating a static page in an otherwise dynamic application means extra hassle when things change.

The second approach deletes *public/index.html* and uses routing to specify where to send users who visit just the domain name. Before Rails 2.0, this was done by specifying map.connect for an empty string, but Rails 2.0 introduced map.root, a cleaner way of making the connection. The map.root method looks just like map.connect, but doesn't have the first method. If you want visitors to the domain name to receive a page from the entry method of the welcome controller, you could write:

```
map.root :controller => welcome, :action => entry
```

You could also specify :id and any other parameters you want, just as with map.connect.

Route Order and Priority

Using wildcards makes it likely—even probable—that more than one routing rule applies to an incoming URI. This could have produced an impenetrable tangle, but fortunately Rails' creators took a simple approach to tie-breaking: rules that come earlier in the *routes.rb* file have higher priority than rules that appear later. Rails will test a URI until it comes to a match, and then it doesn't look any further.

In practice, this means that you'll want to put more specific rules nearer the top of your *routes.rb* file and rules that use more wildcards further down. That way the more specific rules will always get processed before the wildcards get a chance to apply themselves to the same URI.

Named Routes

While you could use `map.connect` for all of your routes, you'd miss out on a lot of convenience facilities Rails could provide your application. By naming routes, you gain helper methods for paths and URLs, making your application more robust and more readable.

How do you name a route? It's simple—just replace `connect` with the name of your route. For example, to create a route named `login`, you could write:

```
map.login '/sessions/new', :controller => 'sessions', :action => 'new'
```

Once you've done this, you'll have two new helper methods, `login_path` and `login_url`. The first will return `/sessions/new` and the second `http://local host:3000/sessions/new` (if you're running it in the default server). That may not seem that important, but once you have something like this scattered through your views:

```
<%= link_to "Login", login_path %>
```

it's nice to be able to change where those point just by modifying a single line of the *routes.rb* file.

> If you have a lot of named routes pointing to the same controller, you might want to look into `map.with_options`, which sets up a block providing scope to a collection of named routes.

Globbing

While it's useful to have the default route retrieve an `id` value and pass it to the controller, some applications need to pull more than one component from a given URI. For example, in an application that makes use of taxonomies (trees of formal terms), you might want to support those tree structures in the URI. If, for example, "floor" could refer to "factory floor" in one context, "dance floor" in another context, and "price floor" in yet another context, you might want to have URIs that looks like:

```
http://localhost:3000/taxonomy/factory/floor
http://localhost:3000/taxonomy/dance/floor
http://localhost:3000/taxonomy/price/floor
```

The only piece that the routing tool needs to be able to identify is taxonomy, but the method that gets called also needs the end of the URI as a parameter. A route that can process that might look like:

```
map.taxonomy 'taxonomy/*steps' :controller => 'taxonomy', action => 'showTree'
```

The asterisk before steps indicates that the rest of the URI is to be "globbed" and passed to the showTree method as an array, accessible through the :steps parameter. The showTree method might then start out looking like:

```
def showTree
  steps = params [:steps]
  ....
end
```

If the method had been called via *http://localhost:3000/taxonomy/factory/ floor*, the steps variable would now contain ['factory', 'floor']; if called via *http://localhost:3000/taxonomy/factory/equipment/mixer*, the steps variable would now contain ['factory', 'equipment', 'mixer']. Globbing makes it possible to gather a lot of information from a URI.

 Globs can only appear at the end of a match string. You can't glob something and then return to processing something in the URI after the glob has done its work, since everything that appears from the glob marker onward will be put in the array.

Regular Expressions and Routing

While Rails is inspecting incoming request addresses, you might want to have it be a little more specific. For example, you might create a route that checks to make sure that the id values are numeric, not random text, and presents an error page if the id value has problems. To do this, you can specify regular expressions in parameters for your routes:

```
map.connect ':controller/:action/:id', :id => /\d+/
map.connect ':controller/:action/:id', :controller => 'errors',
:action => 'bad_id'
```

The first rule looks like the default rules, but checks to make sure that the :id value is composed of digits. (Regular expressions are explained in Appendix C.) If the id is composed of digits, the routing goes on as usual to the appropriate :controller and :action with the :id as a parameter. If it isn't, Rails proceeds to the next message, which sends the user to a completely different errors controller's bad_id method.

Mapping Resources

If you're building REST-based applications, you will become very familiar with `map.resources`. It both saves you tremendous effort and encourages you to follow a common and useful pattern across your applications. Chapters 5 and 9 have already explored how REST works in context, but there are a few more options you should know about and details to explore. A simple `map.resour ces` call might look like:

```
map.resources :people
```

That one line converts into *14* different mappings from calls to actions. Each REST-based controller has seven different methods for handling requests, and the routing has to handle cases with and without a `:format` property. Table 15-1 catalogs the many things this call creates.

Table 15-1. Routing created by a single map.resources call

Name	HTTP method	Match string	Parameters
people	GET	/people	{:action=>"index", :controller=>"people"}
formatted_people	GET	/people.:format	{:action=>"index", :controller=>"people"}
	POST	/people	{:action=>"create",:controller=>"people"}
	POST	/people.:format	{:action=>"create",:controller=>"people"}
new_person	GET	/people/new	{:action=>"new", :controller=>"people"}
formatted_new_person	GET	/people/new.:format	{:action=>"new", :controller=>"people"}
edit_person	GET	/people/:id/edit	{:action=>"edit", :controller=>"people"}
formatted_edit_person	GET	/people/:id/edit.:format	{:action=>"edit", :controller=>"people"}
person	GET	/people/:id	{:action=>"show", :controller=>"people"}
formatted_person	GET	/people/:id.:format	{:action=>"show", :controller=>"people"}
	PUT	/people/:id	{:action=>"update", :controller=>"people"}
	PUT	/people/:id.:format	{:action=>"update", :controller=>"people"}

Name	HTTP method	Match string	Parameters
	DELETE	/people/:id	{:action=>"destroy", :controller=>"people"}
	DELETE	/people/:id.:format	{:action=>"destroy", :controller=>"people"}

For all of the routes that use HTTP GET methods, Rails creates a named route. As discussed later in the chapter, you can use these to support _path and _url helper methods with link_to and all of the other methods that need a path or URL for linking.

 If your application contains Ruby singleton objects, you should use map.resource rather than map.resources for its routing. It does most of the same work, but supporting a single object rather than a set. (Singleton objects have an include Singleton declaration in their class file, which marks it as deliberately allowing only one object of that kind in the application.)

This map.resources call, its 14 routes, and the supporting seven controller methods are all it takes to support the scaffolding. However, there will likely be times when you want to add an extra method to do something specific. You can do that without disrupting the existing RESTful methods by using the :member or :collection options. :member lets you specify actions that apply to individual resources, whereas :collection lets you specify actions that apply to a set of resources. For example, to add the roll method to the courses resource, Chapter 9 called:

```
map.resources :courses, :member => { :roll => :get }
```

In addition to the 14 methods, the routing now supports two extra. The named routes roll_course and the formatted_roll_course both use the GET method, as the parameter suggests. Both call the roll method on the courses controller, which you'll have to create. The formatted_roll_course route adds a formatting parameter if one was provided.

If you need multiple extra methods, you just list them in the :member options hash:

```
map.resources :courses, :member => { :roll => :get, :history => :get,
:student_attendance => :get }
```

Nesting Resources

Chapter 9 went into extended detail on the many steps necessary to create an application using RESTful nested resources, in which only awards that applied to a given student were visible. Making that change required a shift at many levels, but the change inside of the routing was relatively small. Instead of two routing declarations in *routes.rb*:

```
map.resources :awards
map.resources :students
```

there was only one, combining them:

```
map.resources :students, :has_many => :awards
```

The resulting routes still create 14 routes for `:awards`, but they all look a little different. Instead of names such as `award` and `new_award`, they shift to `student_award` and `new_student_award`, highlighting their nested status. Their paths are all prefixed with `/student/:student_id`, as the award-specific parts of their URIs will appear after that, "below" students in the URI hierarchy.

 The declaration `map.resources :students, :has_many => :awards` is actually an abbreviated form, short for the more verbose:

```
do |students|
    students.resources :awards
end
```

If you need to add extra methods to the `:awards` resource, you'll need to use this longer form, as shown in Chapter 17.

You can also specify multiple resources to nest by giving `:has_many` an array as its argument. If students also have, say, pets, you could make that a nested resource as well in a single declaration:

```
map.resources :students, :has_many => [:awards, :pets]
```

 If you're nesting a `has_one` relationship instead of (or in addition to) a `has_many`, just use a `has_one` parameter on `map.resources`.

Checking the Map

As your list of routes grows, and especially as you get into some of the more complicated routing approaches, you may want to ask Rails exactly what it thinks the current routes are. The simplest way to do this is to use the `rake` routes command. Sometimes its results won't be a big surprise, as when you run it on a new application with only the default routes:

```
/:controller/:action/:id
/:controller/:action/:id.:format
```

If you run it on a more complicated application, one with resources, you'll get back a lot more detail—names of routes, methods, match strings, and parameters:

```
            students GET    /students
{:action=>"index", :controller=>"students"}
   formatted_students GET    /students.:format
{:action=>"index", :controller=>"students"}
                       POST   /students
{:action=>"create", :controller=>"students"}
                       POST   /students.:format
{:action=>"create", :controller=>"students"}
          new_student GET    /students/new
{:action=>"new", :controller=>"students"}
 formatted_new_student GET    /students/new.:format
{:action=>"new", :controller=>"students"}
         edit_student GET    /students/:id/edit
{:action=>"edit", :controller=>"students"}
formatted_edit_student GET    /students/:id/edit.:format
{:action=>"edit", :controller=>"students"}
              student GET    /students/:id
{:action=>"show", :controller=>"students"}
     formatted_student GET    /students/:id.:format
{:action=>"show", :controller=>"students"}
                       PUT    /students/:id
{:action=>"update", :controller=>"students"}
                       PUT    /students/:id.:format
{:action=>"update", :controller=>"students"}
                       DELETE /students/:id
{:action=>"destroy", :controller=>"students"}
                       DELETE /students/:id.:format
{:action=>"destroy", :controller=>"students"}
...
```

And that's just for one resource! Note that Rails lines these routes up on the HTTP method being called, which is not always the easiest way to read it. If you have lots of routes, and especially lots of resources, you'll need some good search facilities to find what you're looking for.

Generating URIs from Views and Controllers

Setting up these routes does more than connect URIs to your application. It also makes it easy for you to build connections between different parts of your application. Code can tell Rails what functionality it should point to, and Rails will generate an appropriate URI. There are many methods that generate URIs (form_for, link_to, and a host of others), but all of them rely on url_for, a helper method in the UrlModule class.

Pointing url_for in the Right Direction

The method signature for url_for doesn't tell you very much about how to call it:

```
url_for(options = {})
```

 Remember, the parentheses around the method arguments are optional, as are the curly braces ({}) around the options hash.

Early Rails applications often called url_for by specifying all of the parts needed to create a URI—:controller, :action, and maybe :id:

```
url_for :action => 'bio', :controller => 'presidents', :id => '39'
```

This would produce a URI like:

```
/presidents/bio/39
```

There's a simpler approach, though, if you just want to point to a particular object, say an @president object that has an id of 39:

```
url_for @president
```

Rails will check through its naming conventions, looking for a named route that matches the object specified. It will then call the named route's _path helper method—in this case, probably president_path. The value returned by that helper will end up in the URI, likely as:

```
/presidents/39
```

To point to nested resources, you need to provide a little more information, two arguments in an array:

```
url_for [@student, @award]
```

And the result would be something like:

```
/students/1/awards/2
```

You can also point to a nested resource by calling its _path helper methods explicitly. For an award nested under a student, you could produce the same result with:

```
url_for student_award_path(@student, @award)
```

Adding Options

The options array is good for more than just specifying the pieces that will go into the URI. It lets you specify how the URI should appear, and add or override details. The available options include:

:anchor
> Lets you add a fragment identifier to the end of your URI, separated by a # sign. This can be very effective when you want to point users to a specific item in a long list.

:escape
> When true (which it is by default), all characters that are problematic for use in an HTML href attribute are escaped. If you just want to see the clean URI—probably for debugging—specify false.

:only_path
> When true (which it is by default), url_for will only return the path part of the URI, the part that comes after the protocol, host name, and port. If you want a complete (absolute) URI, set this to false.

:trailing_slash
> When true, this adds a slash at the end of URIs. While this may meet your expectations for working with directories (or things that look like directories) on the Web, it unfortunately breaks caching, so use it cautiously. This defaults to false.

:host and :protocol
> These let you specify an particular host (including port number) and protocol. If these are specified, the full absolute URI will be returned, regardless of what :only_path was set to.

:user and :password
> These two options must be used together. When present, Rails will incorporate them into the URI for inline HTTP authentication. This is generally not a good idea, as it's not a very secure way to exchange credentials.

Infinite Possibilities

Rails routing is implemented using a DSL—a Domain-Specific Language. Ruby lets developers build all kinds of functionality into a very concise form, but at the same time, DSLs can become pretty mind-bending quickly. Routing in particular can grow extremely complicated if you try to take advantage of too many cool Rails features. There are many, many more possibilities than a *Learning* book can reasonably cover. Among them are:

- Using map.resources with a block

- Custom parameters and conditions
- Abandoning numeric id values in favor of more descriptive unique names
- More precisely defined nested resources with path and name prefixes
- Multiple levels of nesting
- Testing routes with `assert_generates`, `assert_recognizes`, and `assert_routing`
- Debugging routes from the console
- Extending routing

Once you've run out of things to do with the possibilities explored in this chapter, and feel confident that you understand how Rails is routing requests, you can take the next steps forward into deepest Rails.

Test Your Knowledge

Quiz

1. How often does Rails reload the *routes.rb* file?
2. How do you set the routing for the empty URL, which is usually the home or landing page for a site?
3. If there are multiple routes that could match a given URL, how does Rails choose?
4. How do you tell Rails to just "grab the rest of this URL and put it into a parameter"?
5. How many routes does a single plain `map.resources` call create?
6. What's the fastest way to see Rails' list of routes?
7. How do you add a fragment identifier to the end of a URL created with `url_for`?

Answers

1. In development mode, Rails checks to see if the *routes.rb* file has changed and reloads it if it has. In production mode, Rails doesn't check, and you'll need to stop and restart the server to update routes.
2. The `map.root` method lets you tell Rails how to handle requests aimed at the top of your site. You'll also need to delete or rename *public/index.html*.

3. Rails always applies the first route that matches a given URL, starting from the top of *routes.rb*.

4. Globbing, using an asterisk, lets you halt further processing of the URL and send it along to the controller method as a parameter.

5. `map.resources` creates an astounding 14 routes, representing seven different methods built on REST, with and without a format.

6. The `rake routes` command will show you the list of routes Rails believes it has.

7. The `:anchor` parameter lets you specify a fragment identifier, which comes after # at the end of the URL.

## CHAPTER 16

Creating Dynamic Interfaces with Rails and Ajax

Rails emerged at about the same time as Ajax did, and the two technologies can work tightly together. Ajax, a set of technologies for creating much more interactive interfaces in the browser, can connect neatly to Rails' more server-based approach. There's much more than that, though, as the Rails framework includes a number of components designed specifically for making it easier to build Ajax applications from inside of Rails.

 Rails 3.0 improves its Ajax handling pretty tremendously, shifting to an unobtrusive JavaScript approach that can support multiple JavaScript frameworks, including Prototype and jQuery. This chapter will still provide you with an overview of how easy it is to create Ajax applications in Rails, but the underlying details are changing.

 As we mentioned back in Chapter 5, you can download plug-ins, such as `ActiveScaffold` (*http://activescaffold.com*), that provide a lot of built-in Ajax functionality to get you started exploring.

Ajax Basics

If you need to read this section, it's probably a sign that you should find a book devoted to Ajax before building Ajax applications on top of Rails. Rails provides an excellent set of technologies for supporting Ajax development, but you still need to know how to work with the JavaScript browser side of Ajax before you can make effective use of them.

Ajax development is itself worth a book or even a shelf of books, depending on how you want to go about it. Even Rails-based Ajax development has a book: Scott Raymond's *Ajax on Rails* (O'Reilly, 2007). This chapter will get you started, but there's an almost infinite amount of potential complexity around this subject.

Most of what Ajax does today is what used to be called Dynamic HTML, or DHTML. DHTML built on regular HTML by adding JavaScript code that could change the underlying HTML. Change the HTML, and you've changed the page. As browsers became better at and more reliable at presenting those changes, developers created more and more applications offering users a much more interactive experience.

Ajax, which initially stood for Asynchronous JavaScript and XML, took another step toward interactivity. Manipulating the components on a page was useful, a big step forward for user interfaces, but after a while that interface really needed an equally interactive connection to the web server. The old model of loading one page, interacting with it, and then loading another page —shown in Figure 16-1—didn't make very much sense when DHTML could build such powerful interfaces.

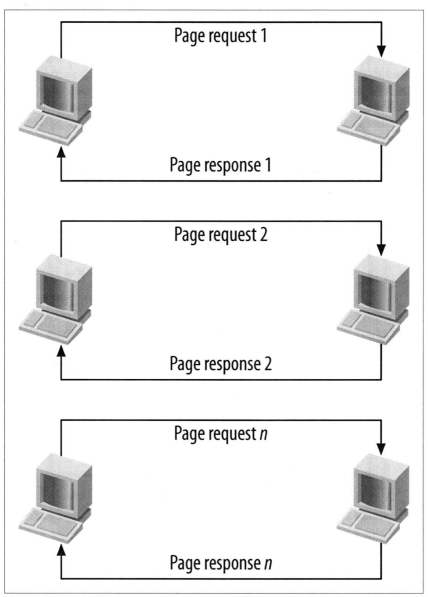

Page request 1

Page response 1

Page request 2

Page response 2

Page request *n*

Page response *n*

Figure 16-1. Traditional HTTP page replacement from the browser

To give those DHTML interfaces a more flexible connection to the server, developers began using the XmlHTTPRequest object. This object let JavaScript make HTTP requests back to the server that the page came from, as shown in Figure 16-2, and the script could then decide what to do with the response.

(The name suggests that the response must be XML, but that's not actually required.)

It took some time for developers to realize that their scripts now had their own powerful communications mechanism, but once the pattern was established, XmlHTTPRequest was popular. So popular, in fact, that developer after developer built library after library to smooth over the odd differences among browser implementations, and programmers with DHTML skills were suddenly back in demand after years of quiet—as long as they rebranded themselves as "Ajax developers."

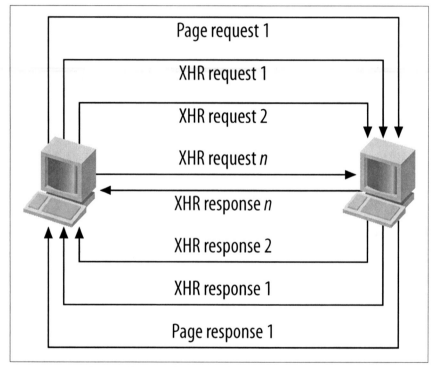

Figure 16-2. Updating only parts of a page with multiple XmlHTTPRequest calls

Using Ajax effectively requires knowing HTML, CSS, and JavaScript, as well as at least a basic understanding of interface design. That takes care of the browser side, but on the server side you can use anything you like—including Rails.

Supporting Ajax with Rails

There are many different ways to provide Ajax support from Rails. Some use Rails itself as a foundation, a provider of web services, while others more tightly bind the Rails application to the details of the client interface.

Rails as a Server API

If a manager comes running down the hallway shouting that you should scrap everything you've built because he's going to replace it with an Ajax application, you may, if you've built your application using Rails' RESTful features, remain pretty calm. If you've built a consistently RESTful API, then Ajax applications issue their requests to it without you needing to tear it down and start over. Some refactoring to let the Ajax application grab smaller pieces might be a good idea, but overall you'll have a solid foundation.

 The RESTful foundation is solid enough, in fact, that anyone who has access to your site could potentially build an Ajax application on top of it. While JavaScript limits XmlHTTPRequest calls to the same server the script came from, anyone who wants to can build a mashup combining your data with their interface if they're willing to set up some creative HTTP proxying.

That doesn't mean the job is done, of course—it just means that most of what you've built will work. You can focus on the clearly Ajax bits, mostly in your views, rather than having to sort through a huge mess of code that used to generate one kind of HTML data structure and trying to figure out how to make it generate another kind of HTML data structure. And if you're panicking now because you didn't build your application in complete—or any—conformance to REST, don't worry. Rails' strict separation between model, view, and controller still spares you work on the model level and below. Instead of having to tear everything down to the database level and start over, you probably have some controller logic and views to reexamine. To get some sense of how rebuilding an application this way works, you might explore Chapters 8 and 9 of *Head First Rails* (O'Reilly, 2008), which creates a mashup from a RESTful Rails application and Google Maps.

Whenever you're developing a Rails application, it's wise to think of the controller structure as an API. Is that API flexible enough to share data outside of your own custom web pages? Is that API clear enough that others can figure it out? Is that API reliable enough that other applications can use it without surprises? Is it stable enough? (Two of the nicest features of REST are consistency and predictability, but you can reach them other ways.)

An API isn't nearly the whole story, though. While you can write an Ajax application in JavaScript on top of Rails' RESTful APIs, it isn't the easiest way to do it—and all that JavaScript takes it beyond the bounds this book can cover. If you want to explore writing Ajax applications by hand, you might explore *Adding Ajax* (O'Reilly, 2007) or *Ajax: The Definitive Guide* (O'Reilly, 2008).

Granularity

One area where you'll probably want to tweak your APIs eventually is granularity. Odds are good that when you built your pre-Ajax Rails application, you organized your controllers so that they produced information in chunks the right size for a given web page.

As you start applying Ajax to your site, each component suddenly has its own needs. It may be helpful to create an API that operates on smaller pieces of information for each call, making it easier to change just one part of a data model with a given interface component. At first, at least, it may seem easier to just have components load a set of data and only make changes to the pieces they need to modify, but this can get unpredictable when multiple components have cached the same data and changed different parts of it.

There isn't a simple rule for addressing this. Just keep in mind that it's something you'll need to consider as you move deeper into Ajax.

Rails and the Client

Even though it's a server-side framework, Rails offers a variety of features you can use to create client-based Ajax applications from within Rails, avoiding the challenge of writing JavaScript by hand:

Helper methods
> Rails' helper methods go well beyond the basic HTML creation, providing support for building more exciting DHTML and Ajax interfaces.

Integration with Prototype and Script.aculo.us
> The Prototype library is a very simple JavaScript library that makes common tasks simpler, like making XmlHTTPRequest calls and retrieving nodes in documents. Script.aculo.us builds on Prototype and provides a wide variety of graphic effects that make it much easier to build a visual interface users can interact with. (Don't like Prototype and Script.aculo.us? There are other options, though they'll take some extra work. For one example,

see jRails, which integrates jQuery with Rails, discussed near the end of this chapter.)

RJS

Remote JavaScript (RJS) is the jewel in Rails' crown when it comes to Ajax development. RJS templates provide a way for developers to specify in Ruby what they want to have happen to the HTML document in the browser. Rails handles all the necessary conversion from the Ruby in the RJS template to the JavaScript actually used by the browser to implement the change.

If you're going to be building Ajax applications specifically with Rails, and everyone involved in the interface development is comfortable working in a Rails environment (rather than the usual Ajax JavaScript client-side approach), using these tools can make it easier to build an Ajax application quickly.

Managing Enrollment through Ajax

The students and courses forms included one slightly complicated form, back in Example 9-4 and Figures 9-17 and 9-18, for adding students to courses and removing them from courses if necessary. It combined showing the list with letting the user change data, and so makes a good candidate for demonstrating Ajax at work. (Code for the demonstration is available in *ch16/students009*.)

Making the Form More Scriptable

As a first step, before actually adding Ajax components, it's a good idea to open up the form a bit so that more components are accessible to JavaScript through id attribute values and so users can see more of what's happening at any given time.

Example 16-1 shows the revised *courses.html.erb* file, with some key changes highlighted. The entire section for adding courses is changed to mirror the section for removing courses, simplifying and manipulating both sections from JavaScript.

Example 16-1. A courses.html.erb file getting ready for some Ajax manipulation

```
<h1><%= @student.name %>'s courses</h1>

<% if @courses.length > 0 %>
  <% form_tag(course_remove_student_path(@student), :html => {:id =>
'removal_form'}) do %>
  <table id="CoursesEnrolled">
    <tr>
      <th>Course</th>
      <th>Remove?</th>
```

```
      </tr>
  <% for course in @courses do %>
    <tr id = "<%= "dom_id(course)" %>">

      <td><%=h course.name %></td>
      <td><%= check_box_tag "courses[]", course.id %></td>
    </tr>
  <% end %>
  </table>
  <br />
  <%= submit_tag "Remove checked courses" %>
  <% end %>
<% else %>
<p>Not enrolled in any courses yet.</p>
<% end %>

<hr />

<h2>Enroll <%= @student.given_name %> in a new course</h2>

<% if @student.courses.count < Course.count then %>
  <% form_tag(course_add_student_path(@student)), :html => {:id =>
'enrollment_form'} do %>
    <% un_courses= @student.unenrolled_courses %>
      <table id="CoursesUnenrolled">
      <tr>
        <th>Course</th>
        <th>Add?</th>
      </tr>
      <% for course in un_courses do %>
        <tr id = "<%= "course#{course.id}" %>">
          <td><%=h course.name %></td>
          <td><%= check_box_tag "courses[]", course.id %></td>
        </tr>
      <% end %>
      </table>
      <br />

  <%= submit_tag 'Enroll in checked courses' %>
  <% end %>
<% else %>
  <p><%=h @student.name %> is enrolled on every course.</p>
<% end %>

<p><%=link_to "Back", @student %></p>
```

The initial list of enrolled courses is unchanged, except that each form and each table row (tr) gains an id attribute. The dom_id(course) is a helper method for creating a string that will uniquely identify this course object.

The list of unenrolled courses changes much more dramatically, shifting from the selection box shown in Figure 9-18 to a list of checkboxes. The structure of the unenrolled courses list is much like that of the enrolled courses, except that it gets its list from `@student.unenrolled_courses` instead of from `@cour ses`, the list of courses the student is taking.

The change to the unenrolled courses interface requires making one change to the `students_controller`, modifying the `course_add` method so that it looks more like the `course_remove` method, as shown in Example 16-2.

Example 16-2. The course_add method, modified to support multiple removals specified by checkboxes

```
def course_add
    @student = Student.find(params[:id])
    course_ids = params[:courses] #was @course = Course.find(params[:course])
    unless course_ids.blank?
      course_ids.each do |course_id|
        course = Course.find(course_id)
        unless @student.enrolled_in?(course)
          logger.info "Adding student to course #{course.id}"
          @student.courses << course
          flash[:notice] = 'Course was successfully added'
        else
          flash[:error] = 'Student was already enrolled'
        end
      end
    end
    redirect_to :action => :courses, :id => @student
  end
```

The new form will look like Figure 16-3, with checkboxes for deleting and for adding courses.

Just as important, underneath the HTML, each row now has its own `id` value:

```
...
<tr id = "course1">
  <td>Reptiles: Friend or Foe?</td>
  <td><input id="courses[]" name="courses[]" type="checkbox" value="1" /></td>
</tr>
<tr id = "course4">
...
```

At this point, if you check a box and click the appropriate Remove or Enroll button, the page will refresh, and the course will move from one list to the other. If you check Mathematical Opera and click "Enroll in checked courses," for example, you'd see Figure 16-4.

In the first Ajax version, that motion will happen without a full page refresh, and will even highlight the changed courses.

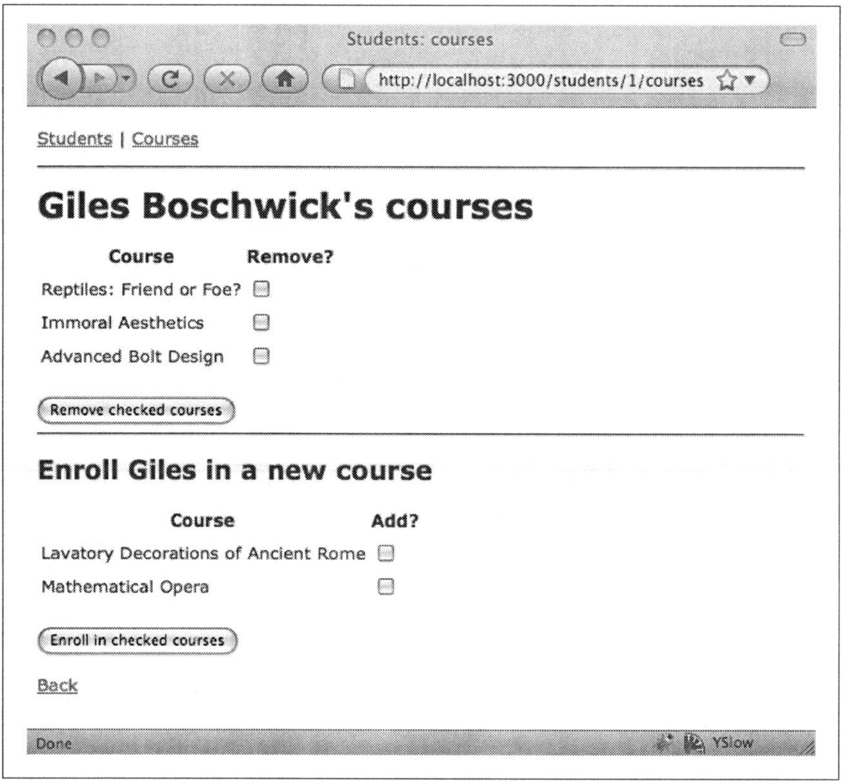

Figure 16-3. A revised form for adding and removing courses for a given student

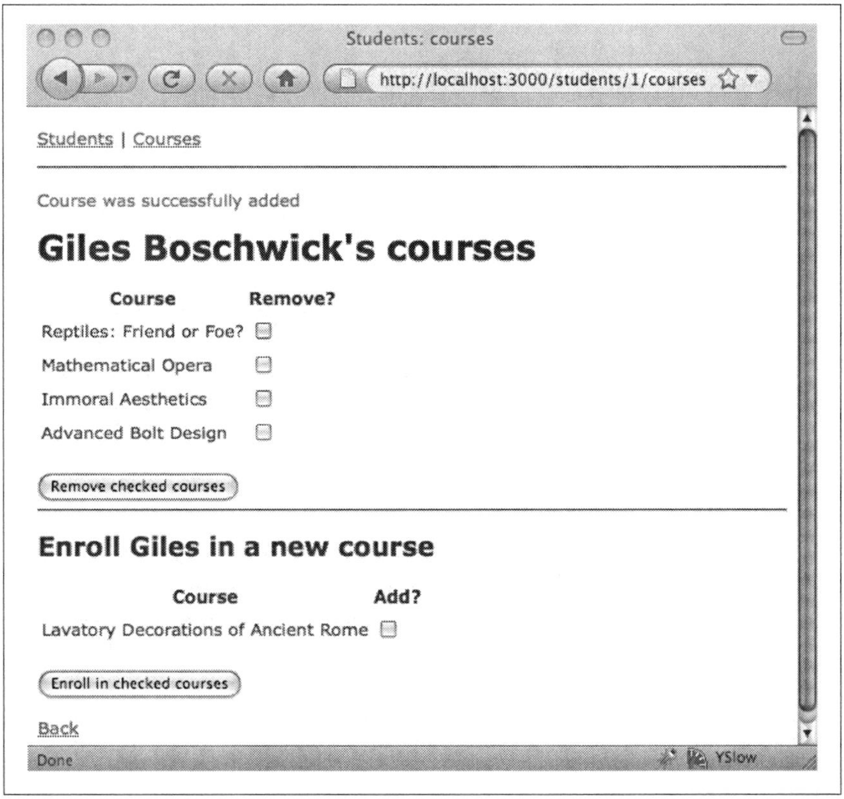

Figure 16-4. Mathematical Opera was shifted from the bottom list to the top by enrolling in it

Changing Courses without Changing Pages

Changing this page to use Ajax rather than a full-page refresh requires one additional line in the layout, two minor changes to the form, a change to each of the underlying controller methods, and the creation of two new view templates. The remarkable part about all of this is just how minor most of it is.

The layout addition, shown in Example 16-3, tells the browser to load the Prototype and Script.aculo.us libraries that Rails will use to make the Ajax work in the browser. In this case, it should go into the *students.html.erb* file under *app/views/layouts*. Adding an `id` attribute to the area where the `flash` is reported also lets RJS change its content.

Example 16-3. Adding the necessary JavaScript links to the students.html.erb layout file

```
<!DOCTYPE html PUBLIC "-//W3C//DTD XHTML 1.0 Transitional//EN"
        "http://www.w3.org/TR/xhtml1/DTD/xhtml1-transitional.dtd">
<html xmlns="http://www.w3.org/1999/xhtml" xml:lang="en" lang="en">
<head>
  <meta http-equiv="content-type" content="text/html;charset=UTF-8" />
  <title>Students: <%= controller.action_name %></title>
  <%= stylesheet_link_tag 'scaffold' %>
  <%= javascript_include_tag :defaults%>
</head>
<body>

<%= render :partial => '/navigation' %>

<p style="color: green" id="notice"><%= flash[:notice] %></p>

<%= yield %>

</body>
</html>
```

This will add a set of **script** tags to your document, such as:

```
<script src="/javascripts/prototype.js?1217725249" type="text/javascript"></script>
<script src="/javascripts/effects.js?1217725249" type="text/javascript"></script>
<script src="/javascripts/dragdrop.js?1217725249" type="text/javascript"></script>

<script src="/javascripts/controls.js?1217725249" type="text/javascript"></script>
<script src="/javascripts/application.js?1217725249"
type="text/javascript"></script>
```

The first of these is for Prototype, and the other four are for Script.aculo.us. If this seems like a lot, you can specify files individually instead.

Next, the forms need to change slightly, using form_remote_tag instead of form_tag. (There is also a form_remote_for method for views that were using form_for.)

```
...
<% if @courses.length > 0 %>
  <% form_remote_tag :url => course_remove_student_path(@student), :html => {:id =>
'removal_form'} do %>
...
<% if @student.courses.count < Course.count then %>
  <% form_remote_tag :url =>course_add_student_path(@student), :html => {:id =>
'enrollment_form'} do %>
```

Note that you need to change from a single parameter in parentheses to an explicit :url named parameter—otherwise, you'll suffer unexplainable Index-Errors. If you look at the form elements this new tag generates, you'll see a lot of JavaScript:

```
<form action="/students/1/course_remove" id="removal_form" method="post"
onsubmit="new Ajax.Request('/students/1/course_remove', {asynchronous:true,
evalScripts:true, parameters:Form.serialize(this)}); return false;">
```

There is still a standard `action` and `method`. If the user's browser has JavaScript turned off, the form will work the way it did before, with a complete page refresh. If, however, JavaScript is enabled, then the JavaScript piled into `onsub mit` will be called instead. The page won't refresh. Instead, the JavaScript will makes its own request, through Prototype's `Ajax.Request`, asking for a Java-Script response.

> The request URL for JavaScript doesn't end in *.js*, but Java-Script is specified deep in the MIME types of the headers. Rails recognizes that as a request for JavaScript, however.

Right now, clicking those buttons will sort of work—the JavaScript call will add or remove the student from a course—but the page won't refresh and the user won't know what changed. Making the page change requires that the controller respond with JavaScript. First, the controller needs to support multiple formats. It can still send a full HTML page when asked for HTML, but send JavaScript when asked for JavaScript. the `Student` controller's actions, `course_add` and `course_remove`, the old concluding line:

```
redirect_to :action => :courses, :id => @student
```

needs to be replaced by:

```
@courses=Course.find(course_ids)
respond_to do |format|
  format.html {redirect_to :action => :courses, :id => @student}
  format.js
end
```

By putting the list of courses from `course_ids` into the `@courses` variable, that information will be available for the view to render. As discussed in Chapter 5, `respond_to` lets controller specify how to handle requests for content in different formats. In this case, requests for HTML will be redirected just as they were before, while requests for JavaScript will be handled—well, it isn't specified. Rails will, however, look for a template in *app/views/students/* whose name matches the controller and whose extension is *.rjs*. In this case, that would be *course_add.rjs* and *course_remove.rjs*, two similar files shown in Examples 16-4 and 16-5. The minor difference is highlighted.

Example 16-4. An RJS file for updating the display when a course is removed from a student's list

```
page.replace_html :notice, flash[:notice]
flash.discard

for @course in @courses do
  page.remove dom_id(@course)
  page.insert_html :bottom, :CoursesUnenrolled, :partial => 'course_row'
  page.visual_effect :highlight, dom_id(@course)
end

page[:removal_form].reset
page[:enrollment_form].reset
```

Example 16-5. An RJS file for updating the display when a course is added to a student's list

```
page.replace_html :notice, flash[:notice]
flash.discard

for @course in @courses do
  page.remove dom_id(@course)
  page.insert_html :bottom, :CoursesEnrolled, :partial => 'course_row'
  page.visual_effect :highlight, dom_id(@course)
end

page[:removal_form].reset
page[:enrollment_form].reset
```

Both of these RJS files are, first and foremost, views written in Ruby. They have access to all of the same variables as regular views, specifically the *@name* instance variables. While they will generate JavaScript, they are not themselves written in JavaScript. The calls to the page object actually create JavaScript, but everything else is ordinary Ruby logic.

> If you want to add your own JavaScript directly to what RJS sends, you can use the << concatenation operator:
>
> ```
> page << "alert('I entered this code myself')"
> ```

The first RJS call in both of these examples replaces the contents of the element with an id of notice (specified here as the symbol :notice) with the current contents of the flash object's :notice. This lets the messages from the controller reach the user. The next line clears the flash object, which is useful in case the user refreshes the page. The flash object's habit of lasting for more than one request, described in Chapter 12, can be weirdly distracting when no redirect was used, so it's best to clear it.

If you want to replace an element completely, not just its contents, use `page.replace` instead of `page.replace_html`.

The loop does the work on the actual deletion and insertion of rows:

```
for @course in @courses do
  page.remove dom_id(@course)
  page.insert_html :bottom, :CoursesUnenrolled, :partial => 'course_row'
  page.visual_effect :highlight, dom_id(@course)
end
```

It's an ordinary Ruby loop, not a JavaScript loop, running over the list of courses that have changed. First, it removes their old entries from what would now be the wrong form, based on their `id` value. Given that `id` values are supposed to be unique, and that it's simply easier to safely delete before adding a new element with the same `id`, removing them first is a good idea.

Next, it inserts a new row. The first argument specifies that the new content should go at the end of the specified target, which is identified by the second argument. `:CourseUnenrolled` means that this content will point to the table with the `id` attribute of `CoursesUnenrolled`.

The content to be inserted is the last argument. That could be specified as a string, but a table row is complicated enough that it makes sense to extract it into a partial, *_course_row.html.erb*, shown in Example 16-6.

Example 16-6. A partial representing a table row

```
<tr id = "<%= dom_id(@course) %>">
  <td><%=h @course.name %></td>
  <td><%= check_box_tag "courses[]", @course.id %></td>
</tr>
```

This could be specified as a very long string with replacements, but debugging those becomes difficult quickly.

Finally, because information is moving from one place to another in the page, a visual effect draws attention to the new rows. The call to `page.visual_effect` highlights the moved row or rows for a second in yellow, making it easy for the user to see what changed, as shown in Figure 16-5.

Highlights are especially useful for giving users a clear sense that something changed, and that they didn't miss it all by blinking while they clicked.

If you want to specify how long the highlight should last, you can add options at the end of the call, like:

```
page.visual_effect :highlight, dom_id(@course),
{:duration => 3}
```

That would make the highlight last three seconds. You can also set startcolor and endcolor, as described at *http://github .com/madrobby/scriptaculous/wikis/effect-highlight*.

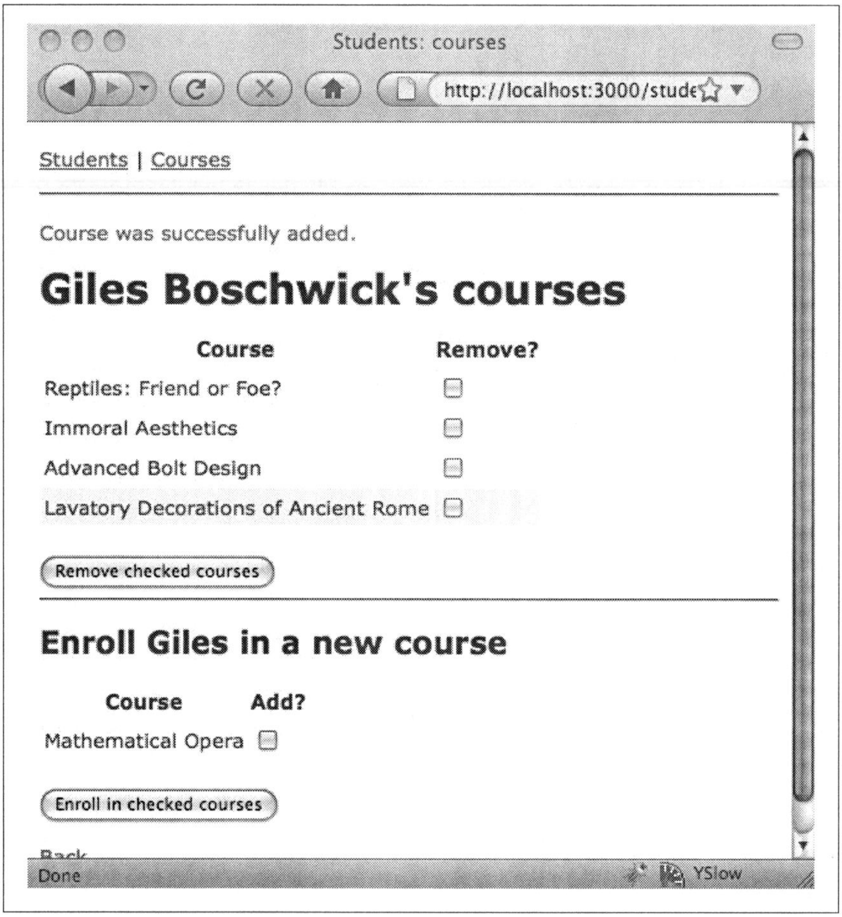

Students: courses

http://localhost:3000/stude

Students | Courses

Course was successfully added.

Giles Boschwick's courses

Course	Remove?
Reptiles: Friend or Foe?	☐
Immoral Aesthetics	☐
Advanced Bolt Design	☐
Lavatory Decorations of Ancient Rome	☐

(Remove checked courses)

Enroll Giles in a new course

Course	Add?
Mathematical Opera	☐

(Enroll in checked courses)

Back

Done   YSlow

Figure 16-5. A highlight effect on a row that moved

The last two lines reset the form.

```
page[:removal_form].reset
page[:enrollment_form].reset
```

This is mostly because Firefox seems to lose track of which boxes were checked and which were not. Safari seemed not to have the problem, but resetting forms when you're done with them is often a good idea in any case.

As Figure 16-5 shows, this works quite nicely. It's not that different from the form reload approach, except for using the highlight, but it does have one advantage: users can add and remove courses and still be a single click of the Back button away from the student record that brought them to the form. While Ajax is often criticized for "screwing up the back button," in this case it actually produces simpler navigation.

Switching to jQuery

Prototype and Script.aculo.us have long histories in Rails, but many Ajax developers are a lot more excited about jQuery (*http://jquery.com/*), a very different (and much larger) set of Ajax libraries. If your plans for Ajax development involve avoiding JavaScript and working only though the tools that Rails provides, you probably don't need to contemplate which Ajax library you want to use. On the other hand, if Rails' Ajax support is only the launchpad for your much grander visions, you may want to look around for more options.

jRails, available from *http://ennerchi.com/projects/jrails*, is designed to make it easier to look around. jRails is "a drop-in jQuery replacement", switching the Ajax support in Rails to use jQuery. You don't have to do very much at all to make the changes happen, so long as you haven't already explicitly written JavaScript that expects to be working with the Prototype and Script.aculo.us libraries.

The example above is a perfect target for this switching. All of the JavaScript used by the forms is generated by Rails, without any hand-coded JavaScript. True "drop-in replacements" are unusual in programming, but in this case it really is that simple. You can take the existing code in *ch16/students009* and run the following command:

```
$ ./script/plugin install http://ennerchi.googlecode.com/svn/trunk/plugins/jrails
```

The jRails installer will add the jQuery libraries it needs to the *public/javascripts* directory, as well as install its libraries for replacing Prototype and Script.aculo.us code with its own jQuery-based code. Because Example 16-3 used javascript_include_tag :defaults, and jRails tweaks the defaults for that, the only thing you need to do to make your application run using jQuery is run it as usual. Everything will look and work just as it did in Figure 16-3 and Figure 16-4.

The only easy way to see the difference is to look at the source code for the Students: courses page. In the older version, running the Rails defaults, the first generated form element looked like:

```
<form action="/students/1/course_remove" id="removal_form" method="post"
    onsubmit="new Ajax.Request('/students/1/course_remove',
    {asynchronous:true, evalScripts:true, parameters:Form.
    serialize(this)}); return false;">
```

The new version, using jQuery, looks like:

```
<form action="/students/1/course_remove" id="removal_form" method="post"
    onsubmit="$.ajax({data:$.param($(this).serializeArray()) +
    '&amp;authenticity_token=' + encodeURIComponent
    ('9e8872df1b25d09bd92011d357506c416b5b7519'), dataType:'script',
    type:'post', url:'/students/1/course_remove'}); return false;">
```

Behind the scenes, jRails will make these kinds of replacements everytime your application uses RJS or the Prototype and Script.aculo.us helper methods. When you feel ready to shift gears and continue your work in jQuery, the work you did in Rails will be much easier to integrate. The only major difficulty might be explaining to other programmers what you have done if you run into trouble. For support, while you could ask in the regular Rails forums and specify that you are using jRails, you might do better to ask in the jRails forum at *http://groups.google.com/group/jrails/topics*.

Alternatively, if you would prefer to work with jQuery and JavaScript more directly in a Rails context, you should probably explore the Railscast at *http://railscasts.com/episodes/136-jquery*. Also, many developers are reconsidering the mix of HTML and JavaScript that Rails and jRails produce in favor of more unobtrusive approaches. Watch for this to be a theme in upcoming Rails releases.

Rethinking Logic

The Ajax form mostly works quite nicely. There are two cases where the logic of the original form breaks down badly for the form updated for Ajax. The first is the case where a student is already signed up for all of the classes before the form is opened. When a user goes to remove them from the classes, they'll get a nasty error. The same error appears when a student hasn't signed up for any classes when the form is initially loaded, as shown in Figure 16-6.

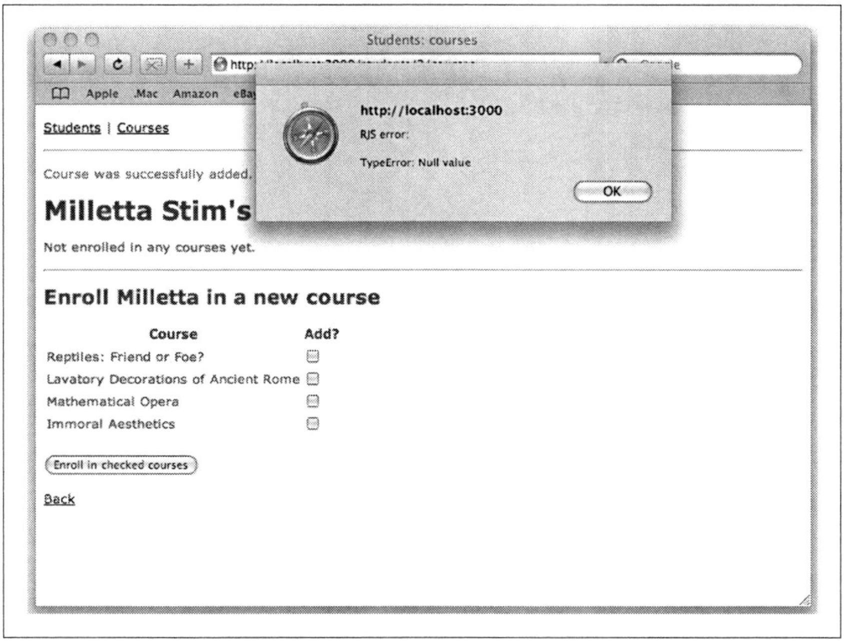

Figure 16-6. Errors produced by trying to register a student for her first class

Underneath the error message (and another message that follows with more JavaScript detail), the course registration actually happened, as the notice in the top left indicates. A refresh would demonstrate that, but it doesn't look right at all. The problem lies in the `if @courses.length > 0` and `if @student.courses.count < Course.count` statements in the *courses.html.erb* file. In a normal HTML context, using these to suppress the form and its table makes good sense, replacing a useless table with an informative message. Unfortunately, that means that the form and table may not actually be there for the Ajax to work on. The easiest solution to this is to remove the `if` statements and accept the empty table, but you can create more complex solutions using JavaScript if you'd prefer.

Moving Further into Ajax

Ajax is a complex subject, and integrating Rails with Ajax opens up many more possibilities. The Prototype and Script.aculo.us functionality supported through RJS provides a foundation on which you can build, but complex interfaces will eventually require you to write JavaScript directly. As you do more with RJS and JavaScript, debugging will become more and more important, and the Firebug plug-in (for Firefox) will likely become a trusted friend.

Test Your Knowledge

Quiz

1. How much JavaScript do you need to write to create Ajax applications from Rails?
2. What is the difference between `form_tag` and `form_remote_tag`?
3. What helper method lets you place identifiers on data on a per-record basis?
4. How do you include the Prototype and Script.aculo.us JavaScript libraries in your pages?
5. Which object lets you create JavaScript using Ruby in RJS pages?

Answers

1. You can create a basic Ajax application using Rails without writing any JavaScript directly. If you want to do complex things in the browser, though, you may find it easier to write some JavaScript.
2. `form_tag` issues an HTTP request that replaces all the content in the browser. `form_remote_tag` issues an HTTP request, but processes the results with JavaScript rather than having the browser render them directly.
3. The `dom_id` helper lets you put identifiers into HTML documents and reference them from your server code as well.
4. Putting `<%= javascript_include_tag :defaults %>` into a view will load the Prototype and Script.aculo.us JavaScript libraries into the resulting HTML document.
5. The `page` object is the bridge between Ruby and JavaScript code.

## CHAPTER 17

Mail in Rails

Rails is mostly a web application framework, but there are many connections that are better made through email. Rails includes a gem, ActionMailer, that lets your application send and receive email messages. Whether email is just something you use to confirm user accounts, or send notifications, or is at the heart of your application, ActionMailer is the key to connecting your Rails application to email.

 ActionMailer was built into Rails, but it has its own way of doing things, dating back to much earlier iterations of Rails. It supports models with views but not controllers, for instance, making it difficult to see how method calls connect to results. The best way to deal with this—for Rails 2.x applications—is to accept that ActionMailer is a somewhat different part of Rails, and keep careful track of where it puts its pieces

Fortunately, Rails 3.0 pretty much tears down and rebuilds ActionMailer. Most of this chapter will, unfortunately, break in Rails 3.0, but that destruction will lead to better things.

Sending Text Mail

Text-based email is a good foundation for sending messages from Rails. Some people simply prefer text email, but in any case it's the simplest way to get going, minimizing the already fairly large set of pieces that need to be coordinated for Rails to send email messages. Awards typically come with certificates to be handed out, so sending an email will be a good way to show Rails' mailing functionality.

Setup

ActionMailer is only one of the components you need to send email to and from Rails. Unfortunately, it's the only part that this book can explain in depth, because every mail setup on every server has its structure and its own quirks. (This example is in *ch17/student010*, but be aware that it may need additional configuration to work with your server.) The key setup for sending mail takes place in the *config/environments/development.rb* file (and in *test.rb* and *production.rb* when you move into testing and production). Near the bottom of *development.rb* you can add a set of options, shown in Example 17-1.

Example 17-1. Options for sending mail, from development.rb

```
# you can normally use sendmail on Mac or Linux
config.action_mailer.delivery_method = :sendmail

# or setup to use your ISP's mail server: omit authentication
# details if they don't require them.

# config.action_mailer.delivery_method = :smtp
# config.action_mailer.server_settings = {
#    :address     => "smtp.myisp.net",
#    :port        => 25,
#    :domain      => "mydomain.example.org",
#    :authentication => :login,
#    :user_name   => "myusername",
#    :password    => "secret"
# }
```

If the sendmail command works on your computer—which doesn't necessarily mean that the sendmail server is installed—you can leave config.action_mailer.delivery_method set to :sendmail. It's certainly simpler than configuring the more detailed options for working with another mail server. If you need to connect to a distant mail server, it may be easiest to test that configuration in a mail client and then copy those details over to these settings. Be sure to comment out the line calling sendmail and uncomment the lines you need for your server's configuration.

Adjusting Routing for an email Method

The next step toward sending email messages when students receive awards is to add an email method to the AwardsController class. Before doing that, though, it's best to ensure that the method will get called by routing. Since AwardsController is a nested resource, as described in Chapter 9, there's a bit of extra work to do. The original routing leading to the :awards controller looks like:

```
map.resources :students, :has_many => [ :awards ],
    :member => { :courses => :get, :course_add => :post,
    :course_remove => :post}
```

There's no place there to declare additional methods for :awards, so it's necessary—as Chapter 15 noted—to change the form of the declaration. The first step is to convert :has_many to the more verbose equivalent form:

```
map.resources :students, :member => { :courses => :get,
    :course_add => :post,
    :course_remove => :post} do |student|
        student.resources :awards
    end
```

Now there's a place to add an additional :member parameter for the email method, which will answer POST requests:

```
map.resources :students, :member => { :courses => :get,
    :course_add => :post,
    :course_remove => :post} do |student|
        student.resources :awards, :member => { :email => :post }
    end
```

Rails' automatic routing capabilities become less automatic when developers add functionality beyond the defaults. It's not hard to fix; it just requires being a bit more specific.

Sending Email

Actually sending an email message from a controller only takes one line of code, though that line of code is, of course, backed up by more code. The email method in *app/controllers/awards_controller.rb*, shown in Example 17-2, is reasonably simple.

Example 17-2. A controller method for sending email

```
def email
    @award = @student.awards.find(params[:id])
    AwardMailer.deliver_certificate(@award, current_user.email)
    flash[:notice] = "Email has been sent"
    redirect_to([@student, @award])
end
```

That doesn't look too bad. There's an AwardMailer object somewhere with a deliver_certificate method on it, and it just needs the award object and an email address to deliver its certificate to. It sounds like a pretty typical request for a controller method—but there won't be an *award_mailer_controller.rb* or anything like that in the *app/controllers* folder.

Instead, this call to action goes to a model, the AwardMailer object defined in *app/models/award_mailer.rb*. Remember, ActionMailer has its own way of structuring things, which doesn't map to the expectations of the rest of Rails. The `AwardMailer` class you need to create to generate the mail message is pretty simple, though, as shown in Example 17-3.

Example 17-3. The AwardMailer model class, which seems to do very little

```
class AwardMailer < ActionMailer::Base

  def certificate(award, email)
    subject       award.name
    recipients    email
    from          'School System <school@example.org>'
    sent_on       Time.now
    body          :award => award
  end

end
```

As you can see, `AwardMailer` has a `certificate` method, but no `deliver_cer tificate` method. The `certificate` method doesn't even seem to do anything —it just defines the contents of some fields that will be in the message. The last of them, `body`, is especially mysterious, setting the `:award` parameter to the `award` argument that came in, but not seeming to call anything.

The `body` information feeds directly into a view, in the file *app/views/ award_mailer/certificate.erb*, without any controller moderating the model– view relationship. The *certificate.erb* file, shown in Example 17-4, is pretty plain, which is fine since it's only generating a text-based email message.

Example 17-4. Generating a plain-text report of an award for emailing

```
<%= @award.name %>

awarded to

<%= @award.student.name %>

<%= @award.year %>

--
Courtesy of the School System!
```

Unlike every other view shown in this book so far, there aren't any HTML tags here. There is an instance variable, `@award`, magically reconstituted by the `:award => award` value given for `body` in the model file. The end of the filename is just *.erb*, not *.html.erb*—when no second format is specified, text is the default.

If there is a *certificate.html.erb* file present, however, Rails will use that, leading to a text message with a lot of HTML tags in it. ActionMailer isn't as smart about formats as the rest of Rails.

The last key component is a means of calling this method. For now, a button from the view that displays awards, *app/views/awards/show.html.erb*, is sufficient, as shown in Example 17-5.

Example 17-5. Connecting to the email method of the awards controller from a view

```
<p>
  <b>Name:</b>
  <%=h @award.name %>
</p>
<p>
  <b>Year:</b>
  <%=h @award.year %>
</p>
<p>
  <b>Student:</b>
  <%=h @award.student.name %>
</p>

<% form_tag email_student_award_path(@student, @award) do %>
  <%= submit_tag 'Email me this award' %>
<% end %>

<p>
<%= link_to 'Edit', edit_student_award_path(@student, @award) %> |
<%= link_to 'Back', student_awards_path(@student) %>
</p>
```

When the user visits an awards page, possibly after creating the award, they'll see an "Email me this award" button, like that in Figure 17-1. Clicking that returns the web result shown in Figure 17-2 and the email shown in Figure 17-3.

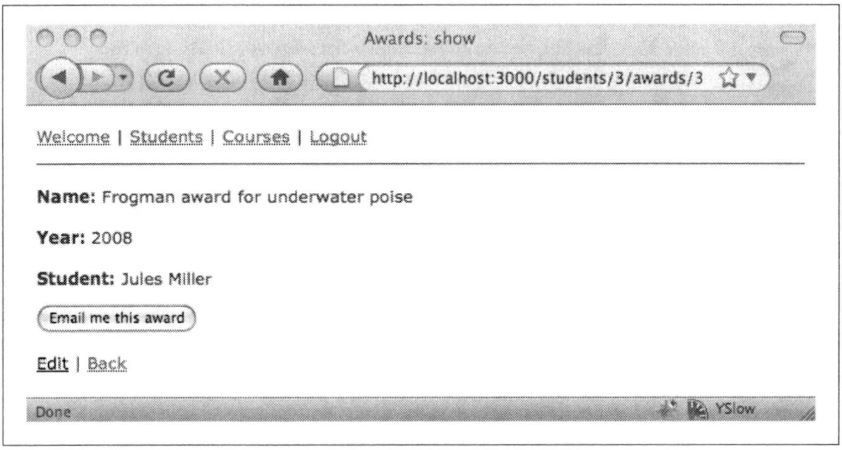

Figure 17-1. An opportunity to send an email

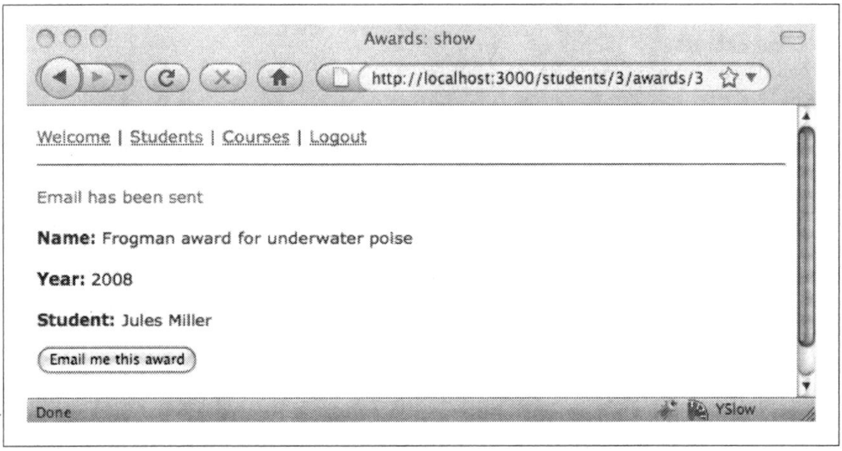

Figure 17-2. A note that the email was sent—always a good idea to report in the interface, rather than waiting for the user to find the email

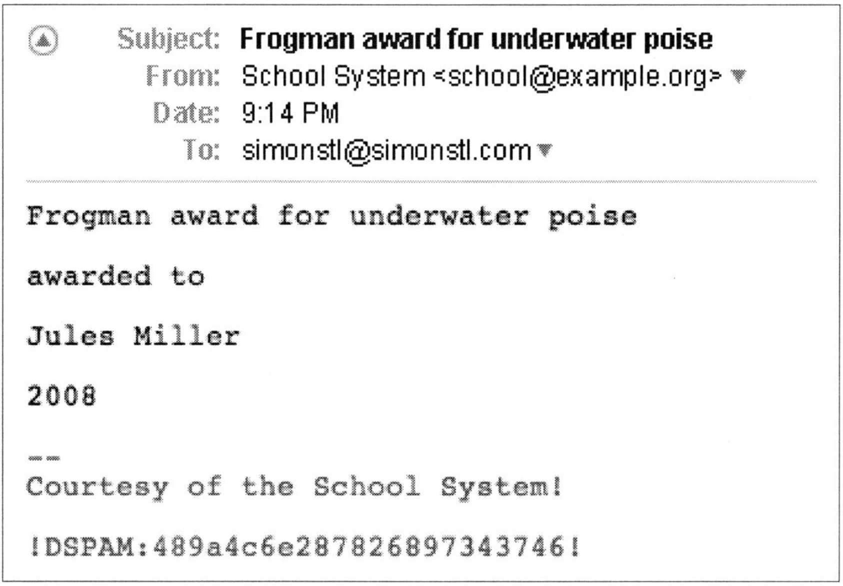

```
    Subject:  Frogman award for underwater poise
      From:   School System <school@example.org> ▼
      Date:   9:14 PM
        To:   simonstl@simonstl.com ▼
─────────────────────────────────────────────────────────
Frogman award for underwater poise

awarded to

Jules Miller

2008

--
Courtesy of the School System!

!DSPAM:489a4c6e2878268897343746!
```

Figure 17-3. The email, received

The log also shows that a message was sent:

```
Sent mail to simonstl@simonstl.com

Date: Wed, 6 Aug 2008 21:14:22 -0400
From: School System <school@example.org>
To: simonstl@simonstl.com
Subject: Frogman award for underwater poise
Mime-Version: 1.0
Content-Type: text/plain; charset=utf-8

Frogman award for underwater poise

awarded to

Jules Miller

2008

--
Courtesy of the School System!
Redirected to http://localhost:3000/students/3/awards/3
Completed in 0.10415 (9 reqs/sec) | DB: 0.00112 (1%) | 302 Found
[http://localhost/students/3/awards/3/email]
```

ActionMailer has its quirks, but it does seem to work. Figure 17-4 shows the flow of data that generated this message.

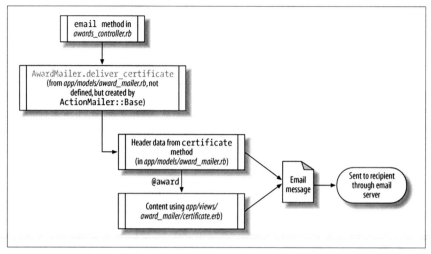

Figure 17-4. Sending mail, from a controller to a model to a view to a message

Sending HTML Mail

Rails is great at generating HTML, so of course ActionMailer can generate HTML. It works almost like generating text messages, but with a few more details. Because some users really prefer text email messages, this demonstration will give them a choice. The form in *app/views/awards/show.html.erb* used to request the email, previously shown in Example 17-5, will have an extra checkbox. This extra component sets a parameter identifying whether to send "rich text" (really HTML) email, highlighted in Example 17-6. (This code is in *ch17/student011*.)

Example 17-6. Adding a checkbox for choosing whether to send HTML or text email

```
<% form_tag email_student_award_path(@student, @award) do %>
  <p><%= check_box_tag :use_html %>
  <label for="use_html">Use rich text?</label></p>
  <%= submit_tag 'Email me this award' %>
<% end %>
```

The `email` method in `awards_controller`, previously shown in Example 17-2, grows a little more complex to support the checkbox's new `:use_html` parameter, as shown in Example 17-7.

Example 17-7. Providing controller support for sending HTML-based email, when desired

```
def email
    @award = @student.awards.find(params[:id])
    if params[:use_html]
      AwardMailer.deliver_html_certificate(@award, current_user.email)
    else
      AwardMailer.deliver_certificate(@award, current_user.email)
    end
    flash[:notice] = "Email has been sent"
    redirect_to([@student, @award])
  end
```

If the checkbox was checked, the user wants rich text, and so the controller calls AwardMailer's deliver_html_certificate method instead of just deliver_certificate. There still isn't really a deliver_html_certificate method in the *app/models/award_mailer.rb* file shown in Example 17-8, but there is a new html_certificate method that looks almost like the certifi cate method from Example 17-3, except that it has a different name and one new field.

Example 17-8. An html_certificate method specifying headers and sending content

```
def html_certificate(award, email)
    subject       award.name
    recipients    email
    from          'School System <school@example.org>'
    sent_on       Time.now
    body          :award => award
    content_type  'text/html'
end
```

The new content_type field is critical if you want the HTML to be rendered in the recipient's mail view rather than show its source. By default, con tent_type will be text/plain, a MIME content type identifier that tells the mailer to render as text. Setting it to text/html tells the mailer to render as HTML. Of course, that means creating a view that will generate HTML, the */app/views/award_mailer/html_certificate.html.erb* file shown in Example 17-9.

Example 17-9. A view that generates the body of an HTML email message

```
<table width="100%" border="1" cellpadding="10">
  <tr>
    <td align="center">
      <br />
      <br />
      <h1><%=h @award.name %></h1>
      <br />
      <br />
      <p>awarded to</p>
      <br />
```

```
      <br />
      <h2><%=h @award.student.name %></h2>
      <br />
      <h3><%=h @award.year %></h3>
    </td>
  </tr>
</table>
<br />
<br />
<hr />

<p>Courtesy of the School System!</p>
```

Now, if users visit an award page, they'll see a checkbox and button like that shown in Figure 17-5, from which they can send a message like that shown in Figure 17-6.

The HTML email sent will also be recorded in the log.

 Through version 2.1 of Rails, ActionMailer had no concept of layouts for its messages. The most recent versions of Rails let you create layouts with filenames that include _mailer_, such as *layouts/award_mailer.html.erb*.

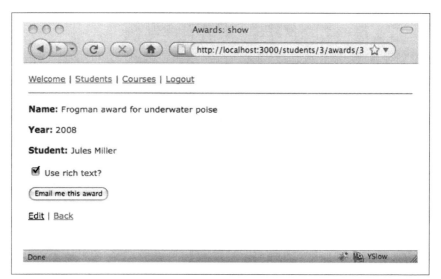

Figure 17-5. An extra option for sending awards email

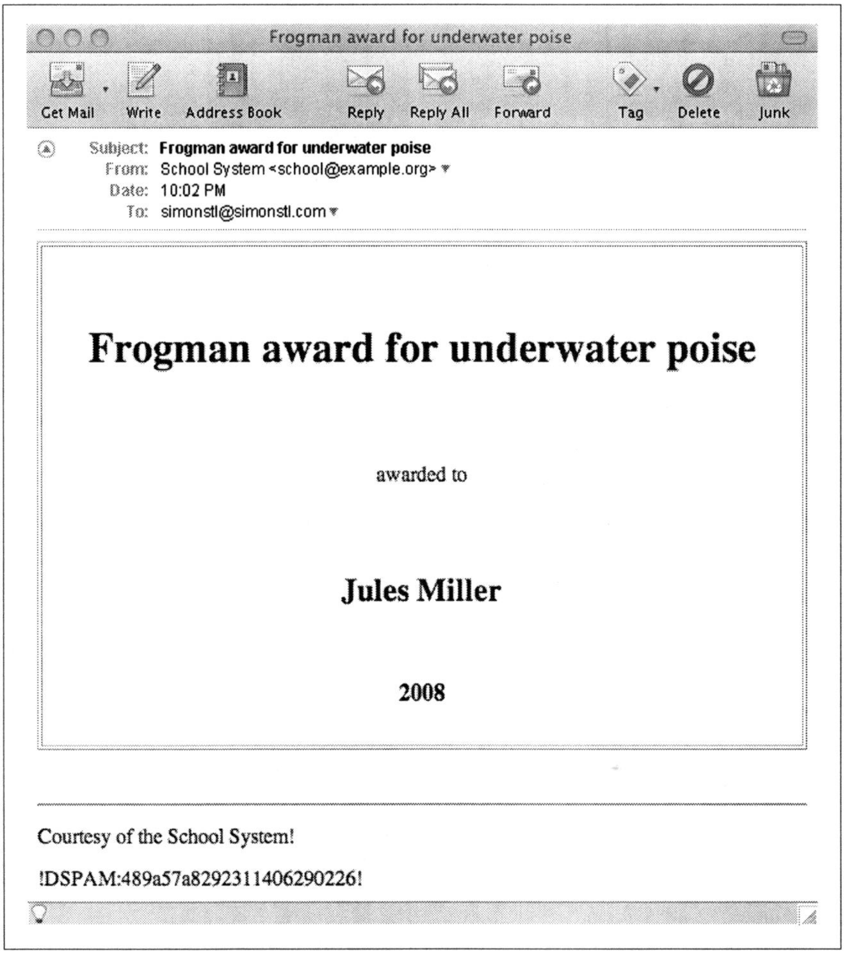

Figure 17-6. A fancier award message

Sending Complex HTML Email

Once you start sending HTML email, odds are good that you'll want to start sending pretty HTML email, complete with graphics. You can include HTML links to resources on your site, but many mail programs block those, because they're potential violations of privacy. Instead, it often makes more sense to send the graphics as part of the email message, as a multipart attachment.

There are fewer and fewer people who deeply object to HTML email, but there are still a lot of people who get annoyed by huge messages that take a long time to download. If you wouldn't feel comfortable sending a message to a relative on dial-up, you probably shouldn't send it to anyone, unless they've specifically requested something they know is large.

ActionMailer can handle most of the logistics for this, using the same tools shown earlier, but it needs one additional library to make it work. From the command line, add the InlineAttachment gem:

```
gem install InlineAttachment
```

One of the nicer features of multipart email is that it can include a plain-text version as well as HTML and graphics, so *app/views/awards/show.html.erb* can revert to the checkbox-free version shown earlier in Example 17-5. Similarly, because the awards_controller no longer needs to evaluate the checkbox, *app/controllers/awards_controller.rb* can revert to the version shown in Example 17-2. (The code for this example is in *ch17/students012*.)

Most of the work needed to send the message now falls into the AwardMailer model, in *app/models/award_mailer.rb*, and two views. The new AwardMailer has a much more complicated certificate method, shown with changes highlighted in Example 17-10.

Example 17-10. A model for sending multipart email messages

```
class AwardMailer < ActionMailer::Base

  def certificate(award, email)

    subject       award.name
    recipients    email
    from          'School System <school@example.org>'
    sent_on       Time.now
    content_type  'multipart/alternative'

    # explicitly enumerate our alternative parts, as we want control
    # for the HTML part

    part :content_type => 'text/plain',
      :body => render_message('certificate.text.plain.erb', :award => award)

    # unique content identifier for the image we'll use - adjust domain for you
    @cid = Time.now.to_f.to_s + "rails.png@example.com"

    part 'multipart/related' do |p|
      p.parts << ActionMailer::Part.new(:content_type => 'text/html',
        :body => render_message('certificate.text.html.erb',
        :award => award, :cid => @cid))
```

```
  p.inline_attachment :content_type => "image/png",
    :body => File.read(File.join(RAILS_ROOT, 'public', 'images', 'rails.png')),
    :filename => "rails.png",
    :cid => "<#{@cid}>"
  end
 end
end
```

This is a very active model, with much more going on than its text or HTML predecessors. The first change, which makes the rest possible, is the shift in content_type from text/plain or text/html to the much more flexible multi part/alternative. When an email client gets a message with a MIME type of multipart/alternative, it will look through the message first before simply displaying it, choosing which part to show the user based on the user's preferences.

 If you just want to send HTML email with multiple pieces, multipart/related is probably a better choice, but the approach outlined here is definitely more appealing if any of the recipients will be reading the message in a plain text viewer. You can also use multipart/mixed to send attachments.

The next few sections define the parts of multipart. The first part call defines the plain text message to send, as the text message normally is, at the start of the message:

```
part :content_type => 'text/plain',
  :body => render_message('certificate.text.plain.erb', :award => award)
```

It specifies a MIME content type of text/plain. The :body parameter calls render_message, explicitly specifying a view and passing it the same :award => award parameter that the older version of certificate had used in Example 17-3. The view, in *app/views/award_mailer/certificate.text.html.erb*, contains exactly the same contents as Example 17-4.

The next part call is much more complicated:

```
@cid = Time.now.to_f.to_s + "rails.png@example.com"

part 'multipart/related' do |p|
  p.parts << ActionMailer::Part.new(:content_type => 'text/html',
    :body => render_message('certificate.text.html.erb',
    :award => award, :cid => @cid))

  p.inline_attachment :content_type => "image/png",
    :body => File.read(File.join(RAILS_ROOT, 'public', 'images', 'rails.png')),
    :filename => "rails.png",
    :cid => "<#{@cid}>"
  end
```

The @cid variable provides a Content-ID header for the attached graphic. Content-IDs are supposed to be unique. The Time object, here called with now to get the current time, to_f to convert that to a number of seconds, and to_s to turn the number into a string, provides a reasonably unique identifier when placed at the front of the string. The next piece is more like a filename. It doesn't have to be the same as the name of the file that's sent, but it's simpler that way. The @ sign separates what is effectively the filename from its source, so you should replace example.com with the name of your own domain.

Once the @cid variable is set, the part call begins, defining a multipart/rela ted part of the message. This represents the actual HTML with graphics combination. It takes a block, using do |p| to set context for the calls which follow. The two calls inside of the block both reference p to add their content.

The first references the p.parts array, part of the TMail library Rails uses to create and process email, and appends (<<) to it a new ActionMailer::Part. The parameters define the contents of the part, setting the content_type to text/html and calling the render_message method again to use the *certificate.text.html.erb* view, shown in Example 17-10, passing it both the award value and the @cid value, which it needs to connect to the graphic.

The second call is to the inline_attachment method, which was the key piece the InlineAttachment gem provided. It also has a content_type parameter, set to image/png in this case to represent the graphic. The :body parameter identifies which graphic. The File.read method takes in a file, at a location identified by the File.join method and its arguments. Why not just write something like *RAILS_ROOT\public\images\rails.png*? Because there are too many different ways to specify file locations on different operating systems, and File.join helps work around that problem. The :filename argument specifies the filename that should be provided for the file—it doesn't have to be the same as the original file. The :cid argument provides the Content-ID for the graphic as well. The HTML, generated by the view shown in Example 17-11, will reference the graphic by Content-ID, not by filename.

Example 17-11. The certificate.text.html.erb view for generating HTML inside a multipart email message, referencing a graphic through its Content-ID

```
<table width="100%" border="1" cellpadding="10">
  <tr>
    <td align="center">
      <p>
        School of Rails<br />
        <img src="cid:<%= @cid %>" />
      </p>
      <br />
      <br />
      <h1><%=h @award.name %></h1>
```

```
      <br />
      <br />
      <p>awarded to</p>
      <br />
      <br />
      <h2><%=h @award.student.name %></h2>
      <br />
      <h3><%=h @award.year %></h3
    </td>
  </tr>
</table>
<br />
<br />
<hr />

<p>Courtesy of the School System!</p>
```

Now, if a user clicks on the "Email me this award" button on an award page, they'll get a message, complete with a graphic, like that shown in Figure 17-7.

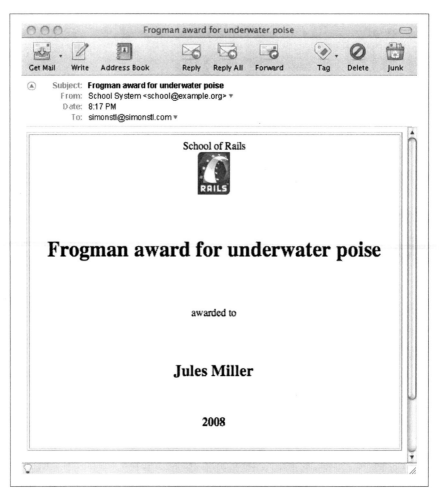

Figure 17-7. A mail message containing a graphic, sent by the fictional School of Rails, whose logo is familiar

The Rails graphic happened to be around, but you can use any images you'd like. Each will need its own Content-ID, and you'll need to specify the path for reaching them. Figure 17-8 illustrates the process of assembling, packaging, and sending this message.

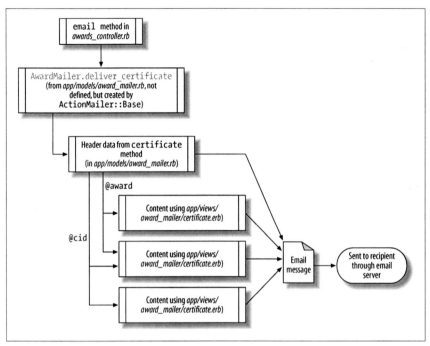

Figure 17-8. Steps in assembling and sending a multipart message

Receiving Mail

While sending email out is probably a more common scenario in most web development, there will also be times when you want your application to process incoming email messages. ActionMailer also supports this, after a setup process that may be more difficult than the Rails-specific part of the work.

Setup

Retrieving email is harder than sending it, because so much depends on the details of how your server delivers it. Servers could use dovecot, getmail, or any of a variety of tools to take mail out of the incoming queue and put it in specific mailboxes. Unfortunately, there's no way for this book to explain configuring mail servers to pass mail to Rails without growing much larger. Instead, you should check out and explore *http://wiki.rubyonrails.com/rails/ pages/HowToReceiveEmailsWithActionMailer*, which offers configuration directions for working with the Postfix, Sendmail, and Qmail servers, as well as regular POP-3 and IMAP connections.

POP-3 and IMAP offer a key advantage—your Rails application is in charge of when and how often it checks mail. That lets you process messages in bulk, making it easier to develop more efficient handling.

All of the setup variations, though, collect incoming messages and send them directly to a class in the Rails application. While Rails does its own routing for incoming HTTP requests, the mail server configuration handles the question of which Rails method will get to receive which email message.

Processing Messages

Once the servers are feeding messages to Rails, the TMail library will help your application process them. The easiest way to do this is to create classes derived from `ActionMailer::Base`, and store them either in *app/models* (if appropriate) or *lib* (which is weird, but a good option if *gmodels* seems wrong).

For a simple, if not particularly secure, demonstration, *ch17/students013* shows how to make this work. The *lib/incoming_scores.rb* file shown in Example 17-13 will process messages formatted like Example 17-12.

Example 17-12. An email message sent to the Rails application to change a student's GPA

```
From: foo@bar.org
Subject: Score

Student: 2
GPA: 3.45
```

Example 17-13. Processing incoming emails to see if they came from an administrator, extracting their content with regular expressions, and then making a change to the student data

```
class IncomingScores < ActionMailer::Base

  def receive(email)
    return unless email.subject =~ /^Score/

    sender = email.from[0]
    user = User.find_by_email(sender)
    if user.nil? or !user.admin?
      logger.error "Refusing scores message from unauthorized sender"
      return
    end

    # we've passed the first test -- email's from an admin user
    # and has a subject starting with 'Score'

    email.body.split(/\r?\n/).each do |l|
      if l =~ /Student:\s*(\d+)/i then
        @student = Student.find_by_id($1.to_i)
      end
```

```
  if l =~ /GPA:\s*(\d+\.\d+)/i then
    @gpa = $1.to_f
  end
end

# if the data's here, make the change.

if @student and @gpa
  @student.update_attribute('grade_point_average', @gpa)
  logger.info "Updated GPA of #{@student.name} to #{@gpa}"
else
  logger.error "Couldn't interpret scores message"
end
  end
end
```

The first few steps check that the message belongs to this processor. First, it checks for a subject line starting with "Score," and just returns, ending this processing, if it doesn't. Then it checks the from address, compares it to the list of emails addresses for users, and again, returns if the user isn't an administrator.

The next part of the method pushes regular expressions hard, first splitting the body of the message on a newline, and then extracting the student's id and their new GPA by testing a match pattern and extracting the matched value, if there is one, from $1. The last part is much simpler, just setting that student's GPA to the one specified.

 When processing email, using logger.info and logger.error is a good idea. No one's going to be seeing a response come back, unless you extend this to emailing an acknowledgment back. Log messages make these kinds of processing much easier to debug.

To try this out, you can send an email message if you've configured your server. If not, there's a complete test message, with headers and content, in the *test.msg* file at the top level of the *students011* directory, which looks like Example 17-14.

Example 17-14. A test message for trying out Rails ability to process incoming email

```
From edd@example.org Wed Aug  6 04:29:56 2008
Return-Path: <edd@example.org>
X-Original-To: edd@example.org
Delivered-To: edd@mail.example.org
Received: from [192.168.250.137] (foo.example.org [192.168.250.5])
   (using TLSv1 with cipher AES128-SHA (128/128 bits))
   (No client certificate requested)
   by mail.example.org (Postfix) with ESMTP id C01F3140040
```

```
    for <edd@example.org>; Wed,  6 Aug 2008 12:32:54 +0100 (BST)
Message-Id: <B3E7FCF0-49E0-4C1D-8547-B5459DB72D69@example.org>
From: Edd Dumbill <edd@example.org>
To: Edd Dumbill <edd@example.org>
Content-Type: text/plain; charset=US-ASCII; format=flowed
Content-Transfer-Encoding: 7bit
Mime-Version: 1.0 (Apple Message framework v928.1)
Subject: Score
Date: Wed, 6 Aug 2008 04:32:54 -0700
X-Mailer: Apple Mail (2.928.1)
Status: RO
Content-Length: 56
Lines: 7

Student: 1
GPA: 3.34
```

A shorter message with fewer headers would do, but this certainly shows ActionMailer's ability to cut through the cruft. Run the Rails application with script/server and then, if you're in Linux, OS X, or another Unix-like operating system, call (in a separate window if necessary):

```
cat test.msg | ./script/runner 'IncomingScores.receive(STDIN.read)'
```

or, if you're in Windows:

```
ruby script/runner 'IncomingScores.receive(STDIN.read) < test.msgs
```

In the log, you'll see the whole message, and then:

```
Refusing scores message from unauthorized sender
```

If you change the from line so that it contains an admin's address, however, you'll get:

```
Updated GPA of Giles Boschwick to 3.34
```

It's a small taste of what Rails can do with email, and it opens up tremendous possibilities beyond the reach of the Web.

 The script/runner command lets you call pieces of your Rails application directly. It's a convenient way to do things like inject content from a shell script, start a long-running process, or, as in this case, test something out.

Test Your Knowledge

Quiz

1. Where do you tell Rails how to send email?
2. How do you specify which variables fit where in a given mail message?
3. What additional field needs to be specified in the model to send HTML email?
4. Can Rails check a POP-3 inbox for messages?

Answers

1. The configuration files in *config/environments/—development.rb, testing.rb*, and *production.rb*—are a good place to specify the settings that Rails should use to send outgoing mail.
2. A model class extending `ActionMailer::Base` containing a method that sets email parameters can handle all of the header information for email messages, and a view can define their content.
3. To send HTML email, the `content_type` must be set to `text/html` for simple HTML email, or to `multipart/alternative` for messages containing images, stylesheets, or other contents beyond the HTML.
4. Yes, Rails can check a mailbox to see whether anything has come in, and retrieve and process messages.

## CHAPTER 18

Securing, Managing, and Deploying Your Rails Projects

When most people think about building a web application, they think about the design, programming, debugging, testing, and all the work that has to happen before an application goes live. Writing the code—while, of course, critical—isn't the only major technology puzzle that has to get solved before an application runs. Bringing that application to the public (or even to an intranet) requires a few more critical steps that are as much about system administration as about code. The Rails framework approach is quite different from the usual CGI or PHP approach, so there are a fair number of Rails-specific issues you need to address.

First, you need to be prepared to battle the hostile nature of the Web. Every publicly exposed application will be tested and tried by a variety of visitors that you may not want or like, and even private applications sometimes face challenges from users. Using Rails isn't particularly dangerous, and a lot of key techniques for protecting your applications from harm have already been covered. Nonetheless, it's worth reviewing some Rails features that can be especially helpful.

Securing Your Application

It's best to consider your application's security before deploying it rather than after. It's much easier to test for security leaks in the relative privacy of development mode, when only the schedule is a likely obstacle, rather than in a publicly available installation with real users who will miss the service if it goes away for a while.

The biggest risk for any application is data coming from outside of your own trusted self. As most applications invite users to put data in, this is an extremely common issue. You shouldn't, of course, seal your application off from outside data—instead, you should always treat the data with suspicion, only trusting it after inspecting it carefully or keeping it in forms where even the worst attacks can cause no harm.

In Rails application building, this means that you should never ever trust any data in parameters (or any other data you didn't write by hand yourself into the code), as it likely comes from outside of your system. There are many different angles where this can be an issue.

SQL Injection

Most applications built on databases rely on Structured Query Language (SQL) to get data in and out. Even if you're relying on Rails to handle all of your database interactions, Rails still uses SQL to communicate with the database.

To understand what's going on, start with a simple `find` call:

```
email = params[:email]
User.find(:first, :conditions => "email = '#{email}'")
```

If `params[:email]` contains `"edd@example.org"`, then the substitution in the double-quoted string used as a value for `:conditions` will produce:

```
email = 'edd@example.org'
```

Using that, Rails executes a SQL statement against the database, like:

```
SELECT * FROM users WHERE (email = 'edd@example.org') LIMIT 1
```

That works nicely. However, imagine if `params[:email]` contained `"' OR 1 --"`. Rails would then execute:

```
SELECT * FROM users WHERE (email = '' OR 1) -- ') LIMIT 1
```

The `--` is a SQL comment, causing everything after it to be ignored. Suddenly, an attacker can retrieve all of the email addresses stored in your database. To avoid this and other serious scenarios, change the way that you pass conditions to a query:

```
User.find(:first, :conditions => ["email = ?", email])
```

Passing the `:conditions` to Rails using the array notation will, as noted at the end of Chapter 4, tells Rails to sanitize the value of `email` before including it in the query. If you're letting Rails create your SQL, that should be all you need to do. If, however, you cannot avoid creating SQL yourself, as you need to use `find_by_sql`, then use the model's `quote` method to do the necessary escaping. That might look like:

```
User.find_by_sql "SELECT * FROM users WHERE email = '#{User.quote(email)}'"
```

It's always best to explicitly ask Rails to check on parameters you don't trust.

Cross-Site Scripting

Cross-site scripting lets users attack other users. The attacking user enters potentially harmful HTML into your system, which is then displayed directly back to other users.

For instance, look at this code from a view:

```
<p>Email address: <%= user.email %></p>
```

This works perfectly well *if* the email address is innocent. But what if a user set his address to be `<script src='http://example.org/my_evil_script.js'>`? When the page is displayed, anybody could fetch and execute the remote JavaScript, which could perform any number of unpleasant functions.

To avoid this you should always escape content on output, as in:

```
<p>Email address: <%=h user.email %></p>
```

Of course, your models should always do the tightest possible validation, which would have noticed that the `script` element wasn't an address. For plain text fields, however, there's not a lot more you can do with validation.

To help you remember and test this, there's a handy plug-in you can use called `safe_erb` (*http://agilewebdevelopment.com/plugins/safe_erb*). It treats any data coming from parameters, the database, or files on the disk as suspect until it's untainted by means of the h escaping in views. Instead of displaying the suspect data, the `safe_erb` plug-in will cause your program to display an error. You will develop good habits very quickly when using this!

 Rails 3.0 automatically applies h to fields unless you tell it not to do so, making it harder for an accidental slip to create an opening for attacks.

There are a few other options for dealing with markup in parameters. Sometimes you do need to display HTML in the output, to allow people to use certain tags such as `<b>` or `<i>` in content, for example. Rail's `sanitize` helper lets you control exactly what can get through or not—allow `<b>` and `<i>` but forbid `<script>`, for instance. Other times you just want to strip all markup and only keep the plain text. Then, you probably want to use `strip_tags`, which removes all HTML tags.

Cross-Site Request Forgery (CSRF)

CSRF is an attack often used for gaining unauthorized access to password-protected websites. If an attacker can persuade you to log into a web app (pretty much everybody leaves themselves logged in all the time these days anyway) and then visit their web page with a malignant JavaScript, that script can fake a form POST to the web app using your existing session and cause destructive behavior.

The way to avoid this problem is to have every form include a special token that guarantees to the application that the incoming POST was in response to a page that came from that web app specifically. Fortunately, Rails has this protection built-in. Open up *app/controllers/application.rb* and you'll see:

```
# Uncomment the :secret if you're not using the cookie session store
protect_from_forgery # :secret => '468e1168cef232cb93c2d56919e9fe4f
```

You should follow the comment and remove the highlighted # if you're using the database or filesystem for your sessions.

If you view the source of a form generated from Rails, you'll see the magic token:

```
<form action="/people" class="new_person" id="new_person" method="post"><div
style="margin:0;padding:0"><input name="authenticity_token" type="hidden"
value="f80a01b9f14d38e0816877e832637e3cc9e668a1" /></div>
```

One thing to note here is that if you're generating your own forms, rather than relying on Rails' help, you'll still need to include the hidden form parameter manually. This can especially be a concern when Ajax code on the browser is generating requests.

URL Hacking

Predictable environments such as Rails leave themselves open to people being able to read more than they ought to. This can be very convenient in development mode, but creates major problems when applications are exposed to real users. Consider the following controller, where show_secret_stuff gives logged-in users (as set up in Chapter 14) a place to see their secret stuff:

```
def show_secret_stuff
  @user = current_user
  @secret = Secrets.find(params[:id])
end
```

Typically, the secret objects will have sequential IDs in the database, like 5, 6, 7, etc. We *assume* that the user will land on this page from a list of possible URLs generated in another page, like:

```
<% @user.secrets.each do |secret| %>
  <%= link_to secret.name, :action => 'show_secret_stuff', :id =>
secret %>
  <% end %>
```

However, there's nothing to stop them from incrementing that id in the URL to explore other people's secrets, too. The controller just shown didn't take any steps to make sure the secrets actually belonged to the current user. The answer is to ensure your finders are always as specific as possible. In our case the controller should instead say:

```
def show_secret_stuff
  @user = current_user
  @secret = @user.secrets.find(params[:id])
end
```

Getting the secrets through the @user object rather than directly will ensure that users can't see other users' secrets. The most important time to watch out for this is always when you're doing resource nesting—i.e., showing anything that's part of a has_many relationship. Never assume that your users are friendly, and always check as much as possible before letting a controller's action do its work.

Other Security Issues

Security is never complete. For a lot more information on potential vulnerabilities, check the Ruby on Rails Security Project at *http://www.rorsecurity.info/* regularly. The other key point to remember, though, is that your code and Rails itself are only two layers of a complex system that makes your application possible. Attackers can assault flaws in your operating system, your web server, or your database, not just your application. Always keep an eye out for security notices and updates, and ensure your operating system stays up-to-date.

Deploying Rails Applications

Deploying a Rails application means switching it from development to production mode and then putting it somewhere the public can see it. That simple switch requires a lot of change.

For vastly more information on this subject than can possibly fit into this book, explore *Deploying Rails Applications: A Step-By-Step Guide* (Pragmatic Programmers, 2008). It doesn't cover Phusion Passenger, which came out right after it was published, but it covers everything else mentioned here and much, much, much more, including other web servers, deploying on Windows, updating deployed applications, and scaling Rails across multiple servers to handle massively busy applications.

Rails 3.0, of course, will be changing the deployment story to some extent, but Phusion Passenger is keeping up.

Changing to Production Mode

Running your application in production mode means that it runs all of its queries against your production database, and that it loads Rails' configuration from *config/environments/production.rb*. Typically, the shift in environments results in changes to the following settings:

`config.cache_classes = true`
Rails doesn't check to see if any code has changed every request, so everything runs a lot faster in production mode.

`config.action_controller.perform_caching = true`
Caching is enabled, letting Rails optimize its performance by minimizing redundant processing.

`config.action_controller.consider_all_requests_local = false`
Verbose error reporting is disabled, so Rails won't confess all to total strangers. Only users coming in from localhost (on the same machine) will see the full report. Instead, most users will get much briefer error messages, and you'll need to check the log files to figure out what's causing those error messages. The logs will also have much more concise reporting, especially of database requests.

You can, of course, configure production mode however you'd like, but the defaults probably make sense for most applications.

Database, Web, and App Servers

Deploying Rails also means changing the usual `script/server` process—known as the application server—you use for development. It isn't suitable for direct deployment because it supports only a single thread of processing. It's not designed to serve content to a large number of users at once.

Also, in development mode you point your web browser directly (and only) at the application server, as shown in Figure 18-1. This setup leaves the app server wasting time doing things like serving static images, stylesheets, and other files that don't require processing.

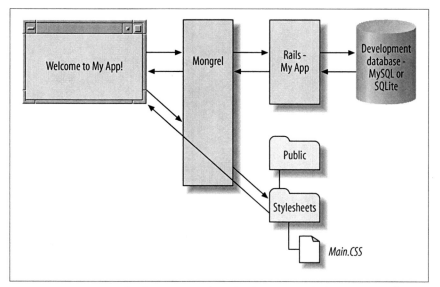

Figure 18-1. How most developers run Rails in development mode

In production setups, you want a program optimized for serving static content —a web server. The web server will serve regular content straight from the file system, as shown in Figure 18-2, and only bother the app server when it needs to. This lets the app server focus on tasks that need its special talents.

Rails deployment comes down to choosing your database server, web server, and app server, and how they're arranged.

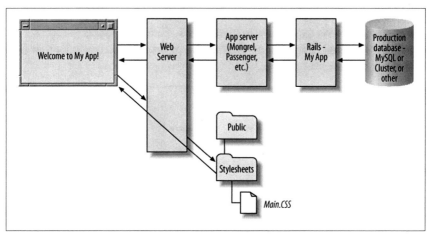

Figure 18-2. A more typical way to deploy Rails in production mode

Database choices

Though SQLite is extremely convenient for development, it is not a good choice for deployment because it isn't designed to handle large numbers of simultaneous requests. Unless you're building a micro-application that will only have a few users, deploying an application using SQLite is asking for trouble. Most Rails deployments use MySQL, though the PostgreSQL database also works well with Rails. Support for all three of these databases is built into Rails.

If you have a boss who says you have to use Oracle, or you're just very fond of it, don't worry—support for Oracle (and many other databases) is just a plug-in away.

Web server choices

Apache has been pretty much the standard web server for large-scale public deployment for years and years, now. It combines scalability, performance, and extensibility in ways that have pretty much kept other servers from developing as competition. However, Rails and Apache haven't always been a good match, so Rails developers have frequently tried out other servers, such as lighttpd (pronounced "lighty") and nginx (pronounced "engine x").

Depending on where you'll be deploying to, you may not have much choice on which web server is used. If you're on Windows, you may need to use Internet Information Server (IIS), though Apache is also available. If you're on a shared machine, odds are good that Apache is the primary web server.

App server choices

If you've been working from a scratch-built install, you've quite likely been using an app server—Mongrel—all the way through this book. Mongrel can operate as a web server, answering all requests on a given address, but it was built to execute Ruby code rather than manage static resources. Mongrel does its finest work when it's behind another web server, able to focus on the unique requirements of answering requests that need Ruby processing. You can also set up a "pack of Mongrels," a cluster of Mongrel servers running behind another web server, maximizing responsiveness. Running Mongrel behind Apache can be done through configuration without changing the Apache install for other users, making it a great option for situations where you don't have complete control.

FastCGI has been another option for Rails development, but it's rapidly fading, at least for Rails use, as Mongrel matures. There's also mod_ruby, an older Apache plug-in for running Ruby programs.

The other app server option is one that doesn't quite look like an app server —mod_rails, also known as Phusion Passenger (*http://www.modrails.com/*), which plugs into the Apache web server. Passenger handles creating processes that run your Rails application as the Apache server passes it requests. Passenger is probably the simplest way to deploy your Rails application if you have complete control over your web server.

Walking Through a Passenger-Based Deployment

While it won't fit all needs, walking through a sample deployment will show at least some of the pieces necessary to get Rails up and running in public.

As a first step, copy your Rails application files to wherever you'll be hosting it. (In the long run, you should be using more sophisticated tools, as described at the end of this chapter.) You'll need to make sure that the correct versions of Ruby, Rails, and any gems your application depends on are also installed. You should also have Apache server set up, and any domain names (DNS) set up that your application needs. You will need access to the command line to make this work.

 You can "deploy" your application to your laptop or another computer first as a test exercise. You don't need to run out and buy fancy web hosting services just to try it out.

Creating the MySQL database

It's almost the last chapter, and it's finally time to look into a MySQL database. If you are running on someone else's MySQL database server and don't have privileges to set up a new database, ask your administrator for a new database. You'll need to specify a name for the database as well as a username and password.

If you have control over your own MySQL installation, you'll need to do a few things by hand to set up the database and account.

 If the server on which you'll be hosting your application doesn't have MySQL installed, visit *http://mysql.com/* for downloads and details, or, if you're on Linux, check your package manager—like apt-get, aptitude, RPM—for information on how best install it.

Once you have MySQL installed, you can create databases from the command line, unless you've set up one of the many graphic interfaces for MySQL administration. To get started, enter:

```
$ mysql -u root -p
Enter password:
```

After you enter your password, you'll see the `mysql` prompt. To create a database, you issue the `CREATE DATABASE` command:

```
mysql> CREATE DATABASE registration;
Query OK, 1 row affected (0.00 sec)
```

 Be sure to end all of your commands with a semicolon (;). Otherwise, MySQL will ask for more information with a -> prompt, which you can dismiss by, of course, entering a semicolon.

Once the database is created, the next step is granting access to it for an account. `GRANT ALL PRIVILEGES` is fairly broad, but is limited to this database, giving Rails the access it needs to create and drop tables, columns, and indexes:

```
mysql> GRANT ALL PRIVILEGES ON registration.* TO 'regrails'@'localhost'
IDENTIFIED BY 't1nker';
Query OK, 0 rows affected (0.00 sec)
```

You have to specify `registration.*` to indicate that the privileges extend throughout the database. The `TO` clause identifies (and actually creates) a username and specifies that it only has access from localhost. The last clause, `IDENTIFIED BY`, is MySQL's way of saying "this is the password."

That's all that you actually need to do in MySQL. The rest is better done in Rake.

Configuring Rails to use the MySQL database

The *config/database.yml* document defines the database connections for the development, test, and production environments. For this deployment, the adapter needs to change to `mysql`, and the username and password need to be specified:

```
production:
  adapter: mysql
  database: registration
  timeout: 5000
  username: regrails
  password: t1nker
```

From the top-level directory of your application, run the database migrations against your new production database:

```
$ rake db:migrate RAILS_ENV=production
```

You'll see all of your migrations go by, just as they did for the development database.

> Rake may report errors—if you have the password wrong, for instance, you'll see something like:
>
> ```
> rake aborted!
> #28000Access denied for user 'regrails'@'localhost'
> (using password: YES)
> ```
>
> If Rake doesn't work, go back to your *database.yml* file and possibly MySQL to figure out what's broken. (And if you get an error about a missing socket file, MySQL probably just isn't running.)

If you want to log back into MySQL and take a look at what it did, you'll see something like:

```
mysql> use registration
Database changed

mysql> SHOW tables;
+------------------------+
| Tables_in_registration |
+------------------------+
| awards                 |
| courses                |
| courses_students       |
| schema_migrations      |
| students               |
```

```
| users                   |
+-------------------------+
6 rows in set (0.00 sec)
```

At this point, MySQL is all ready to go. Rails can handle all of the database work to come.

A quick test

You can check your Rails application in production mode by running:

```
$ script/server -e production
```

You'll be able to connect to it the same way you did during development, but the database is now empty. You may also want to specify -p 80, to have it run on the normal web port, or use the -d option, which has it run as a daemon in the background, no longer connected to the terminal window from which you started it.

For this application, if you remember back to Chapter 14, you'll need to create an initial account and then break into the application through the Rails console to set the administrator flag to true. Rails tools are unfortunately deeply inconsistent in how they switch to production mode, but you can get in and have a session like this one:

```
$ script/console production
Loading production environment (Rails 2.1.0)
>> User.find(:all)
=> [#<User id: 1, login: "simonstl", email: "simonstl@simonstl.com",
crypted_password: "2c1c127100709d98fb26780650ed583d3ddd9a43", salt:
"5572de534481ba9a129d5fe0abcf915c2b921f18", created_at: "2008-08-12 15:38:35",
updated_at: "2008-08-12 15:38:35", remember_token: nil, remember_token_expires_at:
nil, admin: false>]
>> User.find(1).update_attribute('admin', true)
=> true
>> exit
```

You should, of course, be pretty cautious when working from the console on your production setup. At this point, nothing terrible is likely to happen, and it's good to know how to do it, but caution is wise.

 The script/console command has no login, no sense of users or security. You'll definitely want to make sure that the only people with access to script/console are people who should have access to script/console, and have as few of them as possible.

Explore the application, make sure everything works as expected, and then get ready for a more "real" deployment to an application server.

Installing Phusion Passenger

Passenger mostly installs itself, but there's some work you'll need to do along the way, both getting it started and making some configuration changes it requests.

Getting started is simple—install the passenger gem:

```
gem install passenger
```

 If you get an error like:

```
ERROR:  While executing gem ...
(Gem::FilePermissionError)
    You don't have write permissions into the
    /usr/bin directory.
```

then you'll need to use sudo (and give it a password when prompted), as in:

```
sudo gem install passenger
```

If you need sudo for the gem install, you'll also need to use it for the call to passenger-install-apache2-module, coming next.

You should see something like:

```
Building native extensions.  This could take a while...
Successfully installed rack-0.3.0
Successfully installed passenger-2.0.3
2 gems installed
Installing ri documentation for rack-0.3.0...
Installing ri documentation for passenger-2.0.3...
Installing RDoc documentation for rack-0.3.0...
Installing RDoc documentation for passenger-2.0.3...
```

(You may also see some errors about redefined constants in the documentation; at present, it's beta software.)

The next step is installing Passenger—actually, largely having Passenger install itself—into Apache:

```
$ passenger-install-apache2-module

Welcome to the Phusion Passenger Apache 2 module installer, v2.0.3.

This installer will guide you through the entire installation process. It
shouldn't take more than 3 minutes in total.

Here's what you can expect from the installation process:

1. The Apache 2 module will be installed for you.
2. You'll learn how to configure Apache.
```

```
3. You'll learn how to deploy a Ruby on Rails application.

Don't worry if anything goes wrong. This installer will advise you on how to
solve any problems.

Press Enter to continue, or Ctrl-C to abort.
```

The promise of "more than 3 minutes in total" may not come completely true,
but it's pretty close. After you hit Enter, you'll see Passenger checking for required software and proceeding to install if it's all there. Note that the details
of where the files are found and the information it asks you to add to the Apache
configuration files may vary by operating system and local setup:

```
Checking for required software...
 * GNU C++ compiler... found at /usr/bin/g++
  * Ruby development headers... found
  * OpenSSL support for Ruby... found
  * RubyGems... found
  * Rake... found at /usr/bin/rake
  * Apache 2... found at /usr/sbin/httpd
  * Apache 2 development headers... found at /usr/sbin/apxs
  * Apache Portable Runtime (APR) development headers... found at
/Developer/SDKs/MacOSX10.5.sdk/usr/bin/apr-1-config
  * fastthread... found
  * rack... found
--------------------------------------------


--------------------------------------------
Compiling and installing Apache 2 module...
.....
--------------------------------------------
The Apache 2 module was successfully installed.

Please edit your Apache configuration file, and add these lines:

    LoadModule passenger_module /Library/Ruby/Gems/1.8/gems/passenger-
2.0.3/ext/apache2/mod_passenger.so
    PassengerRoot /Library/Ruby/Gems/1.8/gems/passenger-2.0.3
    PassengerRuby
/System/Library/Frameworks/Ruby.framework/Versions/1.8/usr/bin/ruby

After you restart Apache, you are ready to deploy any number of Ruby on Rails
applications on Apache, without any further Ruby on Rails-specific
configuration!

Press ENTER to continue.
```

You should be able to cut and paste the lines highlighted here into your Apache
configuration files. If you have one giant *httpd.conf* file, it can go at the end. If
you have a more fragmented setup, with some configuration for specific sites
and some for Apache in general, this goes into the section on Apache in general,
applying to all sites.

If you receive a warning on Mac OS X that the Ruby headers could not be found, you'll need to install the Xcode tools from your OS X install DVD as described in Chapter 11's section on "The Ruby Debugger" on page 209."

The final instructions are a little more problematic:

```
---------------------------------------------
Deploying a Ruby on Rails application: an example

Suppose you have a Ruby on Rails application in /somewhere. Add a virtual host
to your Apache configuration file, and set its DocumentRoot to
/somewhere/public, like this:

   <VirtualHost *:80>
      ServerName www.yourhost.com
      DocumentRoot /somewhere/public
   </VirtualHost>

And that's it! You may also want to check the Users Guide for security and
optimization tips and other useful information:

   /Library/Ruby/Gems/1.8/gems/passenger-2.0.3/doc/Users guide.html

Enjoy Phusion Passenger, a product of Phusion (www.phusion.nl) :-)
http://www.modrails.com/

Phusion Passenger is a trademark of Hongli Lai & Ninh Bui.
```

You can set up a Rails application with only the two lines in the VirtualHost declaration that this shows, modified for your own site's server name and file location. If you do, however, Passenger may run your Rails application without Apache being able to serve stylesheets, figures, and JavaScript files. A few extra lines will avoid this problem and let Apache reach your static files. (Apache also needs the right permissions to reach those files, of course.)

As a result, a working Passenger installation, customized to address this problem, might look more like:

```
<VirtualHost *:80>
     ServerName rails.simonstl.com
     DocumentRoot /rails/students011/public
   <Directory "/rails/students011/public">
        Options FollowSymLinks
        AllowOverride None
        Order allow,deny
        Allow from all
   </Directory>
</VirtualHost>
```

The added `Directory` directive gives Apache the permission it needs to reach the static content, even if the directory holding the application is outside of the rest of the content Apache serves.

Once you've made these changes, you'll need to restart Apache. On Mac OS X, Windows, and some versions of Linux, you'd use the `apachectl` command. For Mac OS X it might look like:

```
sudo apachectl graceful
```

On Ubuntu, this might look like:

```
sudo /etc/init.d/apache2 restart
```

Unfortunately, this key piece of configuration setting varies from platform to platform.

Results

Once you have Apache restarted, it's time to see if it works. You should see something like Figure 18-3, welcoming you to your application.

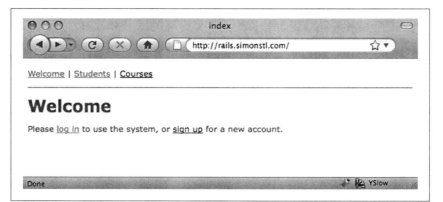

Figure 18-3. A welcome screen from the newly deployed application

You can log in and look around. Because the production database doesn't yet have any students in it, if you click on "Students," you'll find an empty list, like that shown in Figure 18-4.

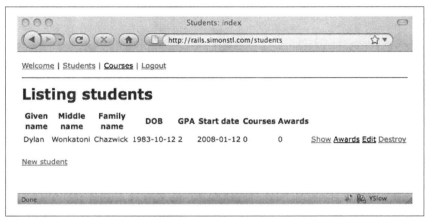

Figure 18-4. An empty list of students

You can try out the application—everything should work the same way as it did when you were running it from `script/server`.

 If you really want to deploy Rails on Windows Internet Information Server, your best source of advice is at *http://wiki.ru byonrails.org/rails/pages/HowtoSetupIIS*, which includes a lot of links to different options for making it work.

If this felt like too much, you may want to look for Rails-friendly hosting options that already do much of this work for you. For a lot more on these options, you might want to explore *http://www.railshosting.org/*, a site with a lot more advice (and strong opinions) on the subject.

Deployment Directions

The deployment approach described earlier is relatively simple and gets your application on the Web. For many situations, it's enough. Small applications that don't change very often will do very well with a simple copying of files, the extra headroom that MySQL provides for multiple users, and an app server managing communications.

However, if you're planning to build applications that change frequently, applications that grow larger and larger over time, or applications with many users, there's a lot more out there which you'll want to learn. Some key tools that haven't been mentioned yet include:

Subversion
> Even if you're a single developer creating applications all by yourself, having version control makes it much easier to fix things when a new idea turns out not quite right. As you move toward larger groups of programmers, version control helps you keep from stepping on each other's code while keeping everyone in sync. Subversion is the most commonly used version control system today, having taken over from the older Concurrent Versioning System (CVS). For more on Subversion, see *http://subversion .tigris.org/*.

Git
> Git is another version control system, slowly taking over many projects from Subversion. Rails itself is now hosted in Git. For more on Git, see *http://git.or.cz/*.

Capistrano
> Rake lets you manage tasks involved in building a Rails application, safely and repeatably. Capistrano provides similar management capabilities for Rails deployment, automating many of the steps involved. For more on Capistrano, see *http://www.capify.org/*.

Monitoring tools
> It's wonderful to have your application running, but you probably want to check up on it periodically, especially as it grows. Which monitoring tools are appropriate will vary depending on the specific choices you make in your deployment, but you will quickly want to move beyond checking up on log files. Depending on the setup you choose, monitoring (and sometimes pruning) is a critical part of keeping the application running.

All of these are, unfortunately, beyond the scope of this book, but you should definitely investigate your options.

Test Your Knowledge

Quiz

1. How can you sanitize information being passed to a SQL query so it can't harm your database?
2. What's the simplest way to keep user-entered data from attacking other users' browsers?
3. How does switching to production mode affect caching?
4. Where do you make changes to Rails' production database configuration?

Answers

1. Specifying the `:conditions` parameter as an array makes Rails take a closer look at incoming data to ensure that isn't potentially damaging SQL.

2. Applying the h method to all outgoing content is the simplest way to ensure that nothing awful gets through, though stripping all HTML tags is another similarly effective option.

3. Rails caches heavily in production mode, helping you to maximize throughput while minimizing processing time.

4. The *config/database.yml* file is the place to specify database information, including the type of database, where to connect to the database, and any authentication information.

## CHAPTER 19

Making the Most of Rails— And Beyond

At this point, Rails should seem much less mysterious. You should understand how to build fairly sophisticated Rails applications, the magic of assembling applications by naming convention, and the challenges involved in deploying an application. As much as you've learned, though, there's much farther that you could go.

Keep Up with Rails

Rails 2.1 was the latest and greatest when this book was originally written, but Rails continues to evolve, and is currently at 2.2 with 2.3 on the way. An easy way to keep an eye on Rails is to visit Riding Rails, the website for core Rails development announcements, at *http://weblog.rubyonrails.com/*. Their "This Week in Rails" series catalogs new Rails articles and software releases, while "Living on the Edge" explores what's coming (and sometimes going) in Edge Rails, the cutting-edge version of Rails that occasionally turns into the next release.

If you'd like to talk rather than read, the #rubyonrails IRC channel on *http:// irc.freenode.net* is usually busy. You can find more information and logs of past conversations at *http://wiki.rubyonrails.org/rails/pages/IRC*. In email, the ru-byonrails-talk list on *http://googlegroups.com* churns through 100 or more messages a day, at all levels of difficulty.

Screencasts and podcasts are another good way to learn more about Rails. You can find free tutorial screencasts at *http://railscasts.com/*, for example, or screencasts for a fee (usually $9.00) at *http://peepcode.com/*. To keep up with Rails ongoing evolution, you may also want to listen to the weekly Rails Envy podcast, which is available at *http://www.RailsEnvy.com*.

Plug-ins

One of the fastest ways to add functionality to your applications is to install Rails plug-ins. Chapter 9 showed off `validates_existence_of` and Chapter 14 used `restful_authentication`, but those are only two of the most common ones. You can find a directory of many more—1,129 at this writing!—at *http://agilewebdevelopment.com/plugins*.

Installing plug-ins is a quick way to make Rails do more for you. One especially nice feature of Rails is that when you install a plug-in, you only affect the project in which you install it. None of your other Rails applications are affected at all. This makes it easy to install plug-ins, try them out on experimental projects, and add them to more complicated projects later if you decide they proved worthwhile.

Eventually, you may also be ready to package your own code as a plug-in. When you reach that point, *Advanced Rails* (O'Reilly, 2008) or *The Rails Way* (Addison-Wesley, 2007) can show you how to make that work. When you distribute your plug-ins, remember to provide two key things that will help people use your plug-in: a test suite and detailed documentation. It may be harder to use a great plug-in that comes with only a brief API sketch than to code functionality from scratch.

 If you reach the point where you'd like to change Rails, becoming a contributor, that's an option Rails' creators would like to encourage. For details on how to do that, see *http://railscasts.com/episodes/113*.

Ruby

Ruby is an immensely powerful and flexible language. It makes it possible, even sometimes easy, to perform complicated tasks in a few lines of code. Its metaprogramming capabilities and facilities for creating Domain-Specific Languages (DSLs) allow developers to create frameworks optimized for particular tasks. Rails takes full advantage of these features and offers an opportunity to learn how they can simplify application development.

At the same time, though, these features can be among the most confusing, as they don't look quite like the normal Ruby programming you'd find in an ordinary tutorial. They can make reading documentation and source code difficult when you're not familiar with the techniques being used.

Once you've gotten comfortable in Rails, learning more Ruby is probably the best way to jump-start your learning process. A thorough understanding of

Ruby will let you write more efficient and sometimes even more readable code. It will help you to look through the Rails source code when documentation isn't quite clear enough about what something is supposed to do. It will let you repackage your functionality as libraries or plug-ins, making it easier to reuse your code.

Part of the promise of Rails is that you don't need to write a lot of code to get things done, but once you've started applying Rails, you'll want to know a lot more about Ruby. When you're ready to explore deeply, try *The Ruby Programming Language* (O'Reilly, 2008), *The Ruby Way* (Addison-Wesley, 2006), *Programming Ruby* (Pragmatic Programmers, 2004), or the *Ruby Cookbook* (O'Reilly, 2006). For an approach more specific to Rails, try *Ruby for Rails* (Manning, 2006).

Web Services

Although this book started out by examining how to use Rails to generate HTML, you can create Rails applications that are meant to be used by other programs as web services. The RESTful scaffolding already provides a foundation, if those other programs can work with a RESTful approach. However, some environments demand SOAP (or the much simpler, older, XML-RPC). For those situations, you'll want to use the ActionWebService plug-in, or a newer version that was released as the datanoise-actionwebservice gem (*http://www.datanoise.com/articles/2008/7/2/actionwebservice-is-back*).

ActionWebService provides a generator and framework that works much like the rest of Rails, except that it works with the SOAP, WSDL (Web Services Description Language), and XML-RPC protocols. Compared to a RESTful application, these have simpler routing to a given URL, but more complicated interior processing, which ActionWebServices handles through an additional layer of dispatching.

If your Rails application needs to consume SOAP services, you can use Ruby's built-in Soap4r library and the built-in XMLRPC library for XML-RPC services. For more information, see *Web Services on Rails* (O'Reilly, 2006).

To reliably generate custom XML for consumption by other programs in a more precise way than to_xml or render :xml permit, you'll want to explore Builder view templates.

Explore Other Ruby Frameworks

If you made it all the way to the end of this book, you probably have developed some level of fondness for Rails. Nonetheless, you may find that Rails is more than you need, not quite appropriate for the work you want to do, or otherwise annoying. You may even want to supplement your Rails application with something written using a different framework. If you're interested in exploring further, these are a few of the available options:

Rack (http://rack.rubyforge.org/)

A very minimalist piece of middleware, more of a web server interface, that mostly provides a way to connect servers with other Ruby frameworks. It implements a simple direct connection to HTTP requests, and supports handlers that connect to different web servers, letting you switch servers however seems convenient.

Rails 2.3 will actually use Rack as its foundation, and will likely offer "Rails Metal", a toolkit that lets your Rails applications include quick and tiny bits of code that run without all of the overhead of Rails routing and Action Controller. If your application includes functionality that needs constant polling, for example, the performance savings can add up quickly!

Merb (http://merbivore.com/)

Originally Mongrel plus ERb, Merb started out as a simple tool for supporting file uploads alongside Rails, but developed into a very different framework. Merb provides a few packages for key things, but the basic gem is deliberately minimal. There is an object-relationship manager, but that's a separate plug-in, as are view helpers, object-relational mappers, etc. Merb builds on Rack. Routing lets you choose different kinds of handling—event handling to optimize for requests that last a short time or threaded server to optimize longer requests.

Merb very deliberately avoids the "magic" of Rails' naming conventions, which makes it harder to build quickly, but also makes it easier to build exactly what you want and nothing more.

And, as it turns out, the Merb and Rails communities have decided to bring the Merb approach to Rails 3.0, which will also be Merb 2.0. Goals for the merger include making Rails more modular, complete with a defined public API against which people can write components. If you only need part of Rails, you'll be able to use just the pieces you need, and swap in other components. Don't like Active Record? You'll have more options. Merb's emphasis on performance should bring more speed, even when you're still using Rails as usual.

Camping (http://camping.rubyforge.org/)

Camping is a "microframework," with a core under 4K of code. It's meant for developing small applications or rapid prototyping. Camping applications are all in one file, which puts some natural limits on size. Intriguingly, multiple Camping applications running on the same server share the same database, which could be cool for connecting the applications or could be disastrous if applications overwrite each other's data. Output is defined using Markaby, generating HTML from within Ruby block syntax.

Sinatra
A tiny RESTful framework, with minimal dependencies beyond Rack. Sinatra defines routes with simple syntax and return responses.

The common element across all of these is that they are simpler frameworks that do less than Rails. If you feel Rails is doing too much for what you need, these are great tools to explore. You can run them along or in place of Rails, and you can even use some Rails pieces (like ActiveRecord) with them if you'd like.

Migrating Legacy Applications to Rails

It's much easier to use Rails for new applications than to try to layer Rails on top of existing applications and their underlying databases. That said, once you're comfortable in Rails, there are many times when you'd like to replace an old system but keep the underlying data. If by some chance the creators of the tables followed Rails' conventions for names that are singular, for names that are plural, and for identifying primary and foreign keys, it might not even be that painful. Here are a few alternate paths forward you'll need to consider:

Export all the data into Rails
If the legacy application already has a web service interface of some kind, you may be able to write some transfer code that sends all of that data to a new Rails application, which then structures it however is needed. This avoids any tinkering with the existing database, but may present challenges all its own. If you need to make substantial changes to the data structure anyway, though, it may not be too much extra work.

Modify the database to work with Rails
If you're comfortable renaming tables and columns inside your database, you may be able to modify the database so that it follows the conventions Rails expects. For a small project with just a few tables, this might be an acceptable path, but it could be a lot of work for an application with many tables. You'll still, of course, have to write a Rails application that knows how all of the database tables are connected, as Rails won't pick that up automatically.

Configure Rails to work with the database
Rails was built to work on naming conventions, but if you have to fall back to configuration, you can write model classes that override the usual con-

ventions. A model can specify, for example, that it works on a table other than the one its name suggests by setting a value for `self.table_name('table_name')`, or it can specify that the primary key is a specific field with `self.primary_key('column_name')`. The `ActiveRecord::Base` class offers a lot of control.

All of these paths require you to do some extra work, but they can certainly be your next steps for learning Rails.

Keep Exploring

Rails may not directly meet all of your web development needs, but the community and capabilities are growing fast. At this point you're probably not a Rails expert, but hopefully this book has given you the foundation you need to become one.

An Incredibly Brief
Introduction to Ruby

Fortunately, you don't need to know a whole lot of Ruby to get real work done with Rails. The creators of Rails have used many of Ruby's most advanced features to make Rails easy to work with, but fortunately you can enjoy the benefits without having to know the details. This appendix explains the basics you'll need to perform typical tasks in Rails and should help you get started. For a lot more detail on Ruby, try *Learning Ruby* (O'Reilly, 2007), *The Ruby Programming Language* (O'Reilly, 2008), the *Ruby Pocket Reference* (O'Reilly, 2007), or *Programming Ruby* (Pragmatic Programmers, 2004).

If you've never worked with a programming language before, this appendix may go too fast for you. It's hard to be incredibly brief and cover the basic basics at the same time. However, if you've worked with JavaScript before, you should be able to get started here.

Ruby is a beautiful but sometimes mystifying language, and probably a better choice as a second language to learn rather than a first language.

Because this is a Rails book, examples will work inside of the Rails framework, in a Rails view and controller, rather than from the command line. If you haven't touched Rails before, it makes sense to read Chapter 1 first and get Rails installed, and then come back here for more instruction.

How Ruby Works

Ruby is an object-oriented language. Although it's often compared to Perl, because Ruby code often looks like Perl, Ruby's object-orientation goes much deeper. Practically everything in Ruby is an object.

What does that mean?

Objects are combinations of logic and data that represent a (usually mostly) coherent set of tasks and tools for getting them accomplished. Programming objects aren't quite as concrete as objects in the real world, often created and destroyed (or at least abandoned for cleanup later) in fractions of a second. Nonetheless, in those brief moments—or in the hours, days, or years they could also exist—they provide a practical means of getting things done.

In some sense, a program is a big toolchest filled with these objects, and programming is about assembling objects to put into the chest. Ruby provides some starter objects and a means of creating new objects and, of course, ways to start these objects interacting with each other so that the program actually runs.

There are a few other important things to know about Ruby. They're probably most important if you're coming to Ruby from other programming languages that have different expectations, but they all affect the way you'll write Ruby programs:

- Ruby is an *interpreted* language, meaning that Ruby reads through the code and decides how to execute it *while it's running*, rather than reading it and turning it into a highly optimized set of instructions before it actually runs. (There are a few people working on ways to create a compiled Ruby, but that's unusual.) While that slows things down, it also adds a lot of flexibility.

- Ruby also has really *flexible syntax* expectations. Most of the time this makes things easier—you don't need to type parentheses around method parameters most of the time. Other times, however, you'll find yourself facing mysterious error messages because you didn't include parentheses and the situation is slightly ambiguous. (This book tries to warn you about these kinds of situations when they appear in Rails.)

- Ruby uses *dynamic typing*.* Some languages (notably Java, C, and C++) expect that the programmer will always know, and always specify, the kind of information they expect to store in a given information container, a *variable*. Locking that down in advance makes it easy to do some kinds

---

* Sometimes this is called "duck typing" because when Ruby processes information, "if it looks like a duck and quacks like a duck, it's a duck."

of optimization. Ruby has taken another path, leaving variables open enough to contain any kind of information and be created at any time. Again, this allows for a much more flexible approach, in which operations can change what they do based on context. Sometimes, however, it means that things can go wrong in strange and unpredictable ways if something unexpected is in a variable.

- Ruby supports *blocks* and *closures*. You don't need to know how to create methods that work with blocks or closures in order to use Rails, but you definitely do need to know how to call methods that expect a block of code as an argument. At first, your best choice for dealing with these features will be to look at sample code and use it as a foundation rather than trying to step back and figure out how this should work in the abstract.

- Ruby lets advanced developers perform *metaprogramming*, even creating *Domain Specific Languages* (DSLs), which are kind of like their own miniature programming language focused on a particular task. You don't need to know how to do metaprogramming to use Rails, but you should be aware that Rails uses these techniques. Sometimes you'll encounter something that claims to be Ruby but seems very strange and too specialized to be part of the Ruby language. Odds are good that metaprogramming is involved. As with blocks and closures, it's often best to start out by emulating sample code to work toward figuring it out.

Ruby is a very powerful language. It's not hard to get started in Ruby, but you should at least be aware of these powerful techniques so you can recognize them when you encounter them. Knowing that these possibilities exist may help reduce your frustration when you encounter mysterious difficulties.

How Rails Works

Rails is a set of Ruby objects that together make up a *framework*. Installing Rails is a first step toward building an application, but while it gives you many useful objects that can run happily in a web environment, there's a lot missing, a lot you have to provide.

You can buy a beehive—a set of boxes with frames that the bees will inhabit and fill with honey. It'll have a top, a base, an entrance, a number of useful architectural features, and a nice coat of paint. It looks like a beehive when it's set up. Unfortunately, setting up a beehive is just the first step. To make a beehive work, you have to add bees, who will finish building their home, collect useful nectar and pollen, and make the hive interact with the world.

Rails gives you an empty beehive. You don't add bees, exactly, but you do populate it with your own logic. That logic turns Rails from an empty container into a dynamic application, connected to the outside world and performing the tasks you define.

The rest of this chapter will teach Ruby within the Rails framework, explaining the language in the context you'll likely be using it.

If you haven't installed Rails yet, take a look at Chapter 1. It might be easiest to use Heroku, a web-based implementation that will spare you having to really install Rails before getting started. On the other hand, if you want to stay at the command line, you can also run much of this code in irb, the Ruby command-line interface described in Chapter 11.

Getting Started with Classes and Objects

Most of the Rails files you'll work with and create define classes. (They do so even when they don't have explicit class definitions, as Rails performs some of its magic in the background.) The clearest place to work with objects in Rails is in the controller classes. To get started, therefore, go to the command line and create a new application and a new controller:

```
rails testbed
...
cd testbed
...
ruby script/generate controller Testbed index
```

If you're using Heroku, instead of going to the command line, log in to Heroku and click on the Create A New Application button from the My Apps page. You can rename it "testbed" if you want, but the application name doesn't matter much. What does matter is that when the application editing screen opens, you click on the gear menu near the bottom left, choose Generate, and enter `controller Testbed index`. That will set things up for the rest of these examples.

For the rest of this appendix, there are only two files that matter: *app/views/testbed/index.html.erb* and *app/controllers/testbed_controller.rb*. For right now, replace the contents of *app/views/testbed/index.html.erb* with:

```
<%= @result %>
```

That will make it easy to see the results of the code in the controller, which is a clearer place to explore Ruby. (`@result` is a variable whose value various examples will set.)

If you open *app/controllers/testbed_controller.rb*, you'll see the code below. It doesn't yet do anything, except tell the programmer what it is and what it derives from:

```
class TestbedController < ApplicationController
  def index
  end

end
```

The first line, `class TestbedController < ApplicationController`, tells you two important things. First, it tells you that this file contains a class definition, for a class named `TestbedController`. Second, it tells you—you can read `<` as "inherits from"—that this class is descended from `ApplicationController`. Even though this file is basically empty, it inherits a lot from `ApplicationController`. Well, actually, even though `ApplicationController` is almost as empty (see *app/controllers/application.rb* if you're curious), it inherits from `Action Controller::Base`, a key part of the Rails framework that provides a lot of functionality for connecting controllers with requests and data.

 Fortunately, one of the benefits of Rails is that you almost never need to worry what's actually done in the superclasses, as these ancestors are called. It's strange to say "don't look" in a tutorial—but you really don't have to look, and certainly not at first.

The next two lines define an empty method, `index`, which the next section will improve on. Finally, the closing `end` brings the definition of the `TestbedCon troller` class to its conclusion.

So, this is a class. What's an object?

An object is an *instance* of a class. This class defines what a `TestbedControl ler` looks like. When Rails gets a request that it thinks requires a `TestbedCon troller`, it reads the class definition and creates an object that will perform as that class specifies. If necessary, Rails will create places to store the object's data as well as connections to call its methods. Rails may create many different `TestbedController` objects at the same time (one per request), but all will use the same definition. The process of creating an object from a class definition is called *instantiation*.

Comments

While they don't actually do anything in a Ruby program, comments are critical for making code readable, especially complicated code. Ruby comments start with a # character and continue to the end of that line. If a line starts with #, then the entire line is a comment. If a line starts with code and then includes a # (outside of a quoted string or regular expression), then everything to the right of the # is considered a comment and ignored. For example:

```
# This whole line is a comment
x = 2  # x is assigned the value 2, and the comment is ignored.
```

Comments are useful for humans, especially when you read someone else's code or return to a project after a long while away, but Ruby will just ignore them.

Variables, Methods, and Attributes

TestbedController is a pretty dull class so far. If you start Rails (with ruby script/server, the >> button in Heroku, or whatever does it in the environment you've installed), and visit *http://localhost:3000/testbed/*, you'll get a mostly blank response. (In Heroku Garden, you may need to add testbed right after the URL that Heroku Garden sends you to when you've pressed >>.) There's nothing in @result, because TestbedController's index method doesn't actually do anything.

That's easily fixed. Change the definition of index to:

```
def index
    @result = 'hello'
end
```

Now, when you load the page, you'll see "hello" as the result. (This is not exciting enough to deserve a screenshot.)

Variables

@result is a variable, a container for information. Because the name of the variable started with @, it is an *instance variable*, connected to the object in such a way that other objects can see it. That let the view retrieve it to shows its value. The new line of code assigned (=) an expression to the @result variable, the string hello.

The string was surrounded with single quotes (') to indicate that it was a string, a series of characters, rather than another variable name or something else entirely. If you need to include an apostrophe or single quote inside of a single-quoted string, just put a backslash (\) in front of the quote, as in 'Hello! Ain \'t it a pretty day?'. This is called *escaping* the quote, hiding it from normal processing.

Ruby also lets you surround strings with double quotes. Double-quoted strings offer a lot more escaping functionality, but single-quoted strings are simpler and faster to work with. If you're used to putting double quotes around strings, that will still work, but you may want to explore the documentation to learn what you're getting yourself into.

@result could take a variety of different kinds of values; Ruby isn't picky about what goes into its variable containers. You can assign it numbers, objects, boolean values—pretty much anything that comes to mind in Ruby work. Ruby will do its best to figure out what to do with the values you assign to your variables. For example, you could write:

```
def index
  one = 1
  two = 2
  @result = one + two
end
```

The value of @result would be 3, what you get for evaluating the expression one + two, which leads to adding 1 and 2. (Note that one and two are *local variables*—they don't have an @ in front of their names, and are only available within the index method.) If, however, you'd written:

```
def index
  one = 'one'
  two = 'two'
  @result = one + two
end
```

The value of @result would be onetwo, because the plus operator (+) combines strings sequentially (also called *concatenating* them) instead of adding their numeric values. When Ruby runs that line of code, it checks to see what types are in the values before deciding how the operator will behave.

Ruby isn't as flexible as some other dynamically typed languages. If you set one to 'one' and two to 2, you'd get the error message "can't convert Fixnum into String." Ruby may not keep close track of what types your variables have, but effectively it's your responsibility to do so.

While programmers often think of their code as determining the main flow of logic through an application, from a user's point of view most of what's interesting is what happens to the variables. Does data go to the right place? Is it stored properly? What are the results of calculations on that data?

Variables are the places you store that data as they follow these paths through your applications. You can assign values to variables and change those values. You can perform operations on those values (like +, -, *, /, and much, much more), and pass variables to methods as arguments.

Arrays and hashes

Sometimes a variable should hold more than just one value. It needs to contain a list, a list of lists, or even a collection where values are connected to names. Ruby supports these needs with arrays, which are simple lists, and hashes, which are collections of named data.

Arrays start out simple. While you can create arrays more programmatically with the **Array** object, it's easiest to create an array by surrounding a comma-separated list of values with square brackets:

```
my_array = [1, 2, 'tweet']
```

The values can be any Ruby expression. This one happens to mix two numbers and a string. You can reference specific items by number. For example, you might redefine the index method to look like:

```
def index
  my_array = [1, 2, 'tweet']
  @result = my_array[2]
end
```

If you've done a lot of programming, you might not be surprised that the @result variable ends up containing tweet. Why? Because Ruby counts arrays from zero, not from one. my_array[0] is 1, my_array[1] is 2, and, of course, my_array[2] is tweet.

Sometimes you'll want to have lists containing lists. Ruby supports this by letting you put arrays inside of arrays:

```
myNestedArray= [ [1, 2, 'tweet'], [3, 4, 'woof'], [5, 6, 'meow'] ]
```

If you wanted to reach the meow, you'd go to item 2 of the overall array, and then item 2 of the array inside of item 2, as in:

```
def index
  myNestedArray= [ [1, 2, 'tweet'], [3, 4, 'woof'], [5, 6, 'meow'] ]
  @result = myNestedArray[2][2]
end
```

You can mix arrays of any size you'd like inside of another array, or even mix in ordinary values. There's no requirement that the array structure must be consistent.

Hashes are just a little more complicated. Hashes, also called maps or associative arrays, contain keys and values. Keys are effectively names that correspond to values. Within a given hash, all of the keys have to be unique. (Values can duplicate as necessary, though.) The easiest way to create a hash is with a hash literal:

```
myHash={ 'one' => 1, 'two' => 2, 'three' => 'tweet' }
```

To retrieve items from the hash, just call for them by name, as in:

```
def index
  myHash={ 'one' => 1, 'two' => 2, 'three' => 'tweet' }
    @result = myHash['two']
  end
```

In this case, @result will contain 2, as that corresponds to the name two. As with arrays, you can also create hashes through the Hash object and its methods.

Both the key and the value can have any type: you can use numbers, or strings, or, as Rails often does, especially in method calls, symbols.

Symbols

Rails uses symbols—names preceded by a colon, like :courses or :students—practically everywhere. They get used like variables, to refer to models. They get used as labels for options in method calls. When you're first starting out in Rails, your best option is to study the examples and see where symbols are used and where other kinds of variables are used. Then, just follow the established pattern.

Why does Rails use symbols? The short answer is efficiency. Ruby handles symbols with less processing than strings. The long answer is a lot more complicated than that, involving the metaprogramming glue that holds the framework together. When you're ready to extend the Rails framework yourself, you'll need to learn the details. Until then, you don't need a deep understanding.

Methods

So far, all of the action in these examples have taken place in one method: index. You may have the occasional controller with just one method, but most classes contain more than one method. Methods can call each other, passing each other data, establishing program logic through these many interconnections. A simple demonstration in the same testbed controller can show how this works:

```
class TestbedController < ApplicationController
  def index
    @result = addThem (1, 2)
  end

  def addThem (firstNumber, secondNumber)
    firstNumber + secondNumber
  end

end
```

When `index` is called, it sets a value for `@result`. The expression it uses, however, is a call to another method, `addThem`, which is given two arguments, 1 and 2.

 The arguments are shown here in parentheses because most other languages use them, and it's a little easier to imagine what happens. However, the parentheses are optional in Ruby and often omitted.

The `addThem` method specifies that it takes two parameters, named `firstNumber` and `secondNumber`. The expression on the second line, `firstNumber + secondNumber`, will be evaluated, yielding 3. Ruby methods return the last value they produced, so `addThem` will tell `index` that its answer is 3. `@result` will be set to 3, which will be presented through the view.

 If you prefer, you could write `return firstNumber + secondNumber`, making it explicit that the value is the return value for the method. However, you won't see this done frequently in other people's Ruby code.

Privacy, please

Because of the way Rails routing works, the `addThem` method is currently exposed to the public—though there isn't a view for it, it won't get useful arguments, and so on. Fortunately, Ruby offers a way to hide such methods from public view while keeping them accessible to other methods in the same class. Just add the keyword `private` before `addThem` is defined:

```
class TestbedController < ApplicationController
  def index
    @result = addThem (1, 2)
  end

  private

  def addThem (firstNumber, secondNumber)
```

```
    return firstNumber + secondNumber
  end
end
```

Methods that follow the **private** are still available to the other methods in the class, but can no longer be called from outside of it.

 Ruby also offers **public** and **protected** keywords for specifying access to methods, but they aren't frequently needed in Rails programming.

super

The methods explicitly listed in the TestbedController class are only a subset of the methods the class actually contains, because of the opening declaration:

```
class TestbedController < ApplicationController
```

All of the methods that are defined in ApplicationController will also be available in TestbedController. If you want some different behavior in Test bedController, you can *override* methods—defining new methods with the same name and arguments.

Chapter 8 shows how overriding methods can work, but there's frequently one small problem. As often as not, the new method wants to do what the old method did, plus something additional. For example, this was a method overriding the text_field method from ActionView::Helpers::FormBuilder:

```
class TidyFormBuilder < ActionView::Helpers::FormBuilder
....
def text_field(method, options={})
    label_for(method, options) + super(method, options)
end
```

The text_field method here wants to create a label, and then call the original method that it was overriding. The call to super isn't to a method called super —it's to the text_field method specified in the ActionView::Helpers::For mBuilder class. This is a common technique when you need to tweak the functionality the framework provides.

Calling methods: advanced options

While you probably won't be writing methods as sophisticated as the ones in the Rails framework itself for a little while, there are a few techniques you should understand for calling those methods.

The first, simpler one, is Rails' frequent use of methods that take an options hash as an argument. While reading the Rails API documentation, you might encounter something like:

```
text_field_tag(name, value = nil, options = {})
```

The method name is `text_field_tag`, and it takes a `name` argument and a `value` argument which has a default value of `nil`. But what is `options = {}`, especially since most calls to `text_field_tag` don't even use { and }?

`options = {}` provides a way for methods to accept named parameters, taking hash with named values specified elsewhere in the documentation. In a more formal world, the named parameters would form a hash literal inside of { and }, but Ruby doesn't require that level of formality. You could write:

```
text_field_tag 'Name', 'Jim', {:maxlength => 15, :disabled => true}
```

But more typically you'll see:

```
text_field_tag 'Name', 'Jim', :maxlength => 15, :disabled => true
```

In general, named parameters go at the end of the method call, and the curly braces are optional. There are times, however, when the braces are necessary, as noted in the "Creating Checkboxes" on page 92" section in Chapter 6.

The second, harder one, is Rails' use of methods that take an unnamed block of code as an argument. This happens frequently with the helper methods listed in Appendix D, as well as in the migration code explored in Chapter 10, but it's a pattern that can appear anywhere. Sometimes, as in the layout issues discussed in Chapter 2, the block-passing is just a quiet part of the framework, and you only notice it because of a `yield` call.

The key to recognizing a method that takes a block as an argument is the `&proc` or pair of curly braces at the end of the list of arguments, and examples that show the method wrapping around other code, usually with do. The typical form looks pretty similar, whether in straight Ruby code or in ERb view markup. For example, `create_table` in a migration looks like:

```
create_table :awards do |t|
    t.string :name
    t.integer :year
    t.integer :student_id
end
```

A `form_for` call, meanwhile, looks like:

```
<% form_for([@student, @award]) do |f| %>
  <%= f.error_messages %>
  <p>
    <%= f.label :name %><br />
    <%= f.text_field :name %>
  </p>
```

```
<p>
  <%= f.label :year %><br />
  <%= f.text_field :year %>
</p>
<p><%= f.submit "Create" %></p>
<% end %>
```

Each of these calls does something when it is first called. `create_table` orders the creation of a database table, while `form_for` creates an HTML form element. They don't just complete and disappear, however—they create a context, using `do`, that applies until the `end` statement. The `t` variable and the `f` variable provide information that makes it possible for the calls inside of the `do` to be much shorter (and much less repetitive) than would otherwise be necessary.

 When you're working in Ruby code you'll often use { and } in place of `do` and `end`. It's easier to read `do` and `end` amidst the < and > of the HTML markup, though.

Rails uses blocks for other purposes as well. Chapter 2 explains how the `yield` statement lets a method execute code passed to it as a block when it seems convenient, and Appendix D lists some helper methods (notably `bench mark` and `cache`) that use blocks for their own purposes.

 If you want to become a Ruby pro, studying techniques for using blocks as arguments is a good way to familiarize yourself with ways that Ruby makes amazing things happen in a very compact amount of code.

Attributes

Ruby attributes lie somewhere between methods and variables. Well, actually, attributes are methods, but when used, they feel like variables. Attributes are methods that end in =, and they get called whenever you assign a value to the property with that name. Chapter 8 used a `photo=` method to capture incoming data when the `photo` field arrived from a form. You may find use for them eventually in your Rails development, but at the beginning, it's mostly useful to know the technique exists.

Logic and Conditionals

Classes, variables, and simple methods may carry some basic applications a surprisingly long way, but most applications need more logic. This quick tour through Ruby's control structures will give you more tools for building your applications.

Operators

Your program logic will depend on combining variables with operators into expressions. Those expressions then get resolved into results, which may be used to assign values to variables, or to give an answer about whether a test passed or failed. Most Ruby operators should look familiar if you've ever used a programming language before. The following table shows an abbreviated list of operators you're likely to encounter in your first forays into Rails.

Operator	Use(s)
+	Addition, concatenation, making numbers positive
–	Subtraction, removing from collections, making numbers negative
*	Multiplication
/	Division
%	Modulo (remainder from integer division)
!	Not
**	Exponentiation (2**3 is 8, 10**4 is 10000)
<<	Shift bits left, or add to a collection
<	Less than
<=	Less than or equal to
>=	Greater than or equal to
>	Greater than
<=>	General comparison—less than yields –1, equal returns 0, greater than 1, and not comparable nil
==	Equal to (note that a single = is just assignment and always returns true)
===	Tests to see whether objects are of same class
!=	Not equal to
=~	Tests a regular expression pattern for a match (see Appendix C)
!~	Tests a regular expression pattern for no match
&&	Boolean AND (use to combine test expressions)
||	Boolean OR
and	Boolean AND (lower precedence)
or	Boolean OR (lower precedence)
not	Not (lower precedence)
..	Range creator, including end value

Operator	Use(s)
...	Range creator, excluding end value
defined?	Tests variable definition, returns details

Nearly all of these can take on other meanings, as Ruby lets developers redefine them. Usually they'll behave as you expect, but if they don't, you may need to examine the context you're programming in.

if, else, unless, and elsif

The if statement is pretty much at the heart of all computer programming. Though it might be very painful, nearly all code could be rewritten as if statements. The basic approach looks like:

```
if expression
  thingsToDo
end
```

To create a simple example again, return to the TestbedController:

```
class TestbedController < ApplicationController
  def index
    @result = 'First is greater than or equal to last.'
    first=20
    last=25
    if first < last
      @result = 'First is smaller than last.'
    end
  end
end
```

Because the value of first is less than the value of last, the first < last expression will evaluate to true, and @result will be set to First is smaller than last. For evaluation purposes, anything except for false or nil will evaluate to true. Definitely try changing the values of first and last and reloading.

The if statement has a simple opposite: unless. It performs its tasks if the expression returns false. While you don't really need it, it can make some code more readable:

```
def index
  @result = 'First is smaller than last.'
  first=20
  last=25
  unless first < last
    @result = 'First is greater than or equal to last.'
  end
end
```

The unless first < last statement means exactly the same as if !(first < last).

Sometimes you want to do something more when your first test fails. This calls for the else statement, which lets you do things instead of what you had planned if your if or unless succeeded. You could rewrite these two little methods as:

```ruby
def index
  first=20
  last=25
  if first < last
    @result = 'First is smaller than last.'
  else
    @result = 'First is greater than or equal to last.'
  end
end
```

and:

```ruby
def index
  first=20
  last=25
  unless first < last
    @result = 'First is greater than or equal to last.'
  else
    @result = 'First is smaller than last.'
  end
end
```

Using an else can both make your code's results more explicit for later developers who have to maintain it, and support your efforts to do different things based on a single test.

There's one last option in regular if statements: elsif, which combines an else and an if. You can only use it with if, not with unless, but you can have as many elsifs as you want. A simple example that extends the logic of the previous code is:

```ruby
def index
  first=20
  last=25
  if first < last
    @result = 'First is smaller than last.'
  elsif first == last
    @result = 'First is equal to last.'
  else
    @result = 'First is greater than last.'
  end
end
```

Note that it's elsif, not elseif, and that the double equals sign (==) tests for equality rather than assigning a value. Using a single equals sign in a comparison is a common mistake for new arrivals from other languages. Not only does it assign the value, it always returns true, satisfying the conditional test.

There is still one other variation on if that you might encounter. Instead of:

```
if expression
  thingsToDo
end
```

it looks like:

```
somethingToDo if expression
```

It's more concise and sometimes more readable, but it can certainly confuse you if you're looking for neatly indented logical statements. If you want, though, you can write:

```
@result = 'First is greater then last' if first > last
```

?:

The ?: operator isn't precisely a statement, but it works like an abbreviated if/else statement. It's mostly used in cases where you need to return a slightly different result for one of two cases. It starts with a test expression, then has a question mark (?), then the value returned if the test expression is true, then a colon (:), and then the value returned if the test expression is false. You could rewrite the earlier if/else example as:

```
def index
  first=20
  last=25
  @result = (first < last ? 'First is smaller than last.' : 'First is greater than
  or equal to last.')
end
```

Again, the message reported would be that First is smaller than last., but you can try changing the values to see what happens.

case and when

If your if statements start sprouting elsifs everywhere, it may be time to switch to case and when statements. These let you specify an expression in the case, and then test it against various conditions. You could rewrite the earlier test as:

```
def index
  first=20
  last=25
  case
    when first < last
      @result ='First is smaller than last.'
```

```
    when first == last
        @result ='First is equal to last.'
    when first > last
        @result ='First is greater than last.'
  end
end
```

There are actually many ways to write case statements. If you want to reduce repetition, you might try:

```
def index
  first=20
  last=25
  @result =case
    when first < last
        'First is smaller than last.'
    when first == last
        'First is equal to last.'
    when first > last
        'First is greater than last.'
  end
end
```

This works because case returns a value, and the when clauses just set that value. You can also add an else clause to the end of your case statement, to catch the situation where none of your when clauses matched.

Loops

Evaluations are useful, but sometimes you want to just go around and around until you've tested something a set number of times, a particular condition is met, or you just plain run out of additional data to process. Ruby offers all kinds of ways to go around and around.

while and until

The while and until methods let you create loops that run until the specified condition is true (while) or false (until). Both of these take a do...end block that will be run until the loop decides to stop. A simple example that demonstrates this is counting. With while, counting from 1 to 10 might look like:

```
def index
  count=1
  @result =' '
  while count <= 10 do
    @result = @result + count.to_s + " "
    count= count + 1
  end
end
```

The first time through the loop, count starts out with a value of one, and the condition count <= 10 evaluates to true, so Ruby proceeds into the loop. The string value of count gets tacked onto the end of @result, with a space for clarity, and then the value of count is increased by one. When the end corresponding to the do is reached, the loop goes back to its start at while and evaluates the condition. If the condition is still true, it goes through the loop again; if not, it ends the loop and goes forward. In this case it hits the end at the end of the index method, and we're done. The view reports @result, which is "1 2 3 4 5 6 7 8 9 10."

 The to_s method on count converts its numeric value to a string. The to_s method is a general facility for turning Ruby objects into strings. You may want to support this in your own programming, as it is often easier to see the state of something when it can be expressed as a string.

You could write the same thing with until, except that the condition would be reversed:

```
def index
  count=1
  @result =' '
  until count > 10 do
    @result = @result + count.to_s + " "
    count= count + 1
  end
end
```

You will doubtless have more exciting conditions than incrementing variables, but remember: Rails can do many things for you, but it won't protect you from an infinite loop. If your conditions aren't met (or refused for until), your code will go on and on until you halt it or it runs out of resources. Always make sure that the loop will come to a halt by itself, no matter what you feed it.

Just Counting

If you know how many times you want something to go around in a loop, you can use the times method on any numeric variable. times takes a block, marked with {}, which it will run that many times. For example:

```
def index
  count=3
  @result =''
  count.times {
    @result = @result + "count "
  }
end
```

will produce "count count count" as the loop goes around three times.

for

A for loop takes a variable and a collection. In its simplest counting approach, the collection is a range, specified with a starting value, then two periods (..), and then an end value. The variable will be set to a value from the range as the loop proceeds, and will advance one step every time the loop hits end until it's done:

```ruby
def index
  count=13
  @result =' '
  for i in 1..count
    @result = @result + i.to_s + " "
  end
end
```

Of course, like most things Ruby, the for loop has greater powers than just this. You can use it to iterate over an array:

```ruby
def index
my_array= [5, 4, 3, 2, 1]
@result =' '
  for i in my_array
    @result = @result + i.to_s + " "
  end
end
```

The loop will go through the array to produce "5 4 3 2 1." You can do even fancier things with hashes, extracting both the key and the value:

```ruby
def index
my_hash= { 'one' => 1, 'two' => 2, 'three' => 3, 'four' => 4 }
@result =' '
  for key,value in my_hash
    @result = @result + "key: " + key + " - value: " + value.to_s + "<br />"
  end
end
```

As always, don't expect the hash to be reported in any given order. Ruby reserves the right to present hashes however it wants. You'll see a result something like:

```
key: three - value: 3
key: two - value: 2
key: one - value: 1
key: four - value: 4
```

These are a few of the simpler ways to use loops in Ruby. There's much more to explore.

Many More Possibilities

Ruby offers, and Rails can use, a variety of other structures for passing control through a program:

- `return`, `break`, `next`, and `redo` statements for moving through or from loops
- `throw` and `catch` statements for breaking out of code
- Iterators that go beyond loops
- `raise`, `rescue`, `retry`, and `ensure` statements for exceptions

Rails doesn't allow the use of Ruby's `BEGIN` and `END` statements, however, or its support for threads.

An Incredibly Brief Introduction to Relational Databases

"I thought the whole point of Rails was that it hid the database and just let me write Ruby code! Why do I need to know about these things?"

Rails has all kinds of features for building web applications, but its foundation component is the way that it lets you get information into and out of relational databases. You *can* build simple applications without knowing much about databases, just telling Rake to do a few things and making sure you gave Rails the right data type for each field. You *don't* need to know Structured Query Language (SQL), the classic language for working with databases.

Building a more complex Rails application, though, really demands at least a basic understanding of how relational databases work. It helps to think about tables and their connections when defining Rails models, at least when you first set them up.

Tables of Data

The foundational idea underneath relational databases is a simple but powerful structure. Each table is a set of sets, and within a single table all of these sets have the same data structure, containing a list of named fields and their values. For convenience, each set within a table is called a row, and each field within that row is part of a larger named column, as shown in Figure B-1. It looks a lot like a spreadsheet with named columns and unnamed rows.

id	given_name	middle_name	family_name	date_of_birth	grade_point _average	start_date
1	Giles	Prentiss	Boschwick	3/31/1989	3.92	9/12/2006
2	Milletta	Zorgos	Stim	2/2/1989	3.94	9/12/2006
3	Jules	Bloss	Miller	11/20/1988	2.76	9/12/2006
4	Greva	Sortingo	James	7/14/1989	3.24	9/12/2006
...	...	...	...	...	...	...

Figure B-1. The classic row–column approach to tables

The resemblance to a spreadsheet is only superficial, however. Spreadsheets are built on grids, but those grids can have anything in them that any user wants to put in any given place in the spreadsheet. It's possible to build a spreadsheet that is structured like a database table, but it's definitely not required. Databases offer much less of that kind of flexibility, and in return can offer tremendous power because of their obsession with neatly ordered data. Every row within a table has to have the same structure for its data, and calculations generally take place outside of the tables, not within them. Tables just contain data.

You also don't normally interact with database tables as directly as you do spreadsheets, though sometimes applications offer a spreadsheet-like grid view as an option for editing them. Instead, you define the table structures with a *schema*, like that shown in Table B-1, and move data in and out with code.

Table B-1. A schema for the table in Figure B-1

Field name	Data type
id	:integer
given_name	:string
middle_name	:string
family_name	:string
date_of_birth	:date
grade_point_average	:float
start_date	:date

Depending on the database, schemas can be very simple and terse or very complicated and precisely defined. Rails isn't that interested in the details of database schema implementations, however, because its "choose your own database backend" approach limits how tightly it can bond to any particular one. As a result, Rails takes the terse and simple approach, supporting only these basic data types:

```
:string
:text
:integer
:float
:decimal
:datetime
:timestamp
:time
:date
:binary
:boolean
```

Rails won't create a database schema much more complicated than the one shown in Figure B-2, though it will probably add some extra pieces to the schema that you don't need to worry about. There are timestamps, which Rails adds even when you don't ask for them, and IDs, which you don't control but which come up in URLs all the time. The Rails ID serves another function inside the database: it's a *primary key*, a unique identifier for that row in the table. Databases can find information very rapidly when given that key.

id	given_name	middle_name	family_name	date_of_birth	grade_point _average	start_date
1	Giles	Prentiss	Boschwick	3/31/1989	3.92	9/12/2006
2	Milletta	Zorgos	Stim	2/2/1989	3.94	9/12/2006
3	Jules	Bloss	Miller	11/20/1988	2.76	9/12/2006
4	Greva	Sortingo	James	7/14/1989	3.24	9/12/2006
...	...	...	...	...	...	...

id	username	password_hash	role
763	Demetrius	ASVUQP8AZV8	administrator
845	Sharon	8WEROCPA387	class_admin
973	Wilmer	S3DO3VP3A8AS	class_admin
1021	Nicolai	SDF83NC9A2F2J	data_analyst

Figure B-2. Multiple but unconnected tables in a database

Limitations of Tables

There is a huge amount of data out there that doesn't fit neatly into tables. Most of the time, in web applications, you can just put the pieces that do fit into tables, and put the pieces that don't fit easily (like pictures, or XML files) in the filesystem somewhere.

If you get into situations where little of the information you're working with fits neatly into tables—lots of hierarchical information, for instance—you may want to go looking for other kinds of tools. You might need a different kind of database, an XML store maybe, and you probably won't find Rails to be your best option. Rails bindings for XML databases *could* be very cool—`ActiveDocument?`—but certainly aren't a mainstream tool at present.

Connecting Tables

You can build many simple applications on a single-table database, but at some point, working within a single table is just way too constraining. The next step might be add another table to the application, say for some completely separate set of issues. A users table that identifies users and their administrative roles might be the next thing you add to an application, as shown in Figure B-2.

With these tables, you can write an application that checks to see if users have the rights to make changes to the other table. You could add lots of other disconnected tables to the database as well (and sometimes you'll have disconnected tables), but at the same time, this isn't taking advantage of the real power of relational databases. They're much more than a place to store information in tables: they're a place to manage related information effectively and efficiently.

So, how does that work? Remember the primary key? Rails uses it to get to records quickly, but the database can also use it internally. That means that it's easy for data in one table to refer to a row in another using that same primary key. That yields structures like the one shown in Figure B-3.

id	Award	Year	Student_id
1493	Best Handwriting	2007	1
1657	Nicest Smile	2007	3
1831	Cleanest Desk	2007	3
1892	Most likely to win the lottery	2008	4

id	given_name	middle_name	family_name	date_of_birth	grade_point_average	start_date
1	Giles	Prentiss	Boschwick	3/31/1989	3.92	9/12/2006
2	Milletta	Zorgos	Stim	2/2/1989	3.94	9/12/2006
3	Jules	Bloss	Miller	11/20/1988	2.76	9/12/2006
4	Greva	Sortingo	James	7/14/1989	3.24	9/12/2006
...	...	...	...	...	...	...

Figure B-3. Connected tables in a database

Establishing connections between tables is simple—one just has to reference the other using its key. When you link to a record in another table by storing the key for that record in your own table, that key is called a *foreign key*. By using foreign keys to connect to primary keys, databases can assemble related information very quickly. Whose "2007 Best Handwriting" award was that? Student 1, who we can find out is Giles Boschwick by checking the other table.

You can link tables to tables to tables. You might, for example, have a table that lists who presented each award, which links to the award table the same way that the award table linked to the students table, as shown in Figure B-4.

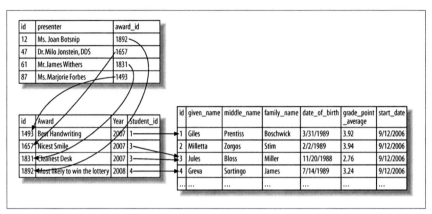

Figure B-4. Connected tables in a database

With tables linked this way, you can ask questions like, "Which presenters gave Jules Bloss Miller awards in 2007?" and get the answer of, "Dr. Milo Jonstein, DDS" and "Mr. James Withers." You—or more likely a program— can follow the IDs and the links to those IDs to come up with the right answer.

Using Tables to Connect Tables

These kinds of links allow the table doing the pointing to establish one connection per row. That might lead to no connections to some rows in the targeted table, one connection to a row, or even many connections to given rows in the targeted table. You can constrain those options, but there's one kind of connection that isn't supported by this simple mechanism. It doesn't allow for many-to-many relationships.

A classic many-to-many relationship is students and classes. Often, each student takes many classes. Each class contains many students. The mechanism shown in Figures B-3 and B-4 isn't very good at this. You *could* create multiple fields for holding multiple links to the same table, but any time you have more than one field pointing at the same table, you're setting yourself up for some complicated processing. It's hard to know how many pointers you'll need, and all of your code would have to look in multiple different places to establish connections. None of this is fun.

It's fine, even normal, to have multiple foreign keys in a table, as long as they all reference different tables.

There is, however, a convenient way to represent many-to-many relationships without creating a tangle. Instead of putting pointers from one table to another inside of the table, you create a third table that contains pointers to the two other tables. If you need to represent multiple relationships between different rows in the two tables to be joined, it's easy—just add another row specifying the connection in the table representing connections.

Figure B-5 shows the students table, a new courses table, and a new table connecting them. (For convenience of drawing, the courses table has its ID values on the right side, and the join table has its mostly useless ID in the middle, but it doesn't really matter. You can leave IDs out of join tables entirely if you want.)

course_name	id
Reptiles: Friend or Foe?	1
Lavatory Decorations of Ancient Rome	2
Mathematical Opera	3
Immoral Aesthetics	4
Advanced Bolt Design	5

course_id	student_id
2	3
3	3
3	4
3	1
1	2
5	2

id	given_name	middle_name	family_name	date_of_birth	grade_point_average	start_date
1	Giles	Prentiss	Boschwick	3/31/1989	3.92	9/12/2006
2	Milletta	Zorgos	Stim	2/2/1989	3.94	9/12/2006
3	Jules	Bloss	Miller	11/20/1988	2.76	9/12/2006
4	Greva	Sortingo	James	7/14/1989	3.24	9/12/2006
...	...	...	...	...	...	...

Figure B-5. Connected tables in a database

If you work through the connections, you can see that course 5125, Mathematical Opera, is popular, at least in these tiny fragments of what is probably a larger data set. It has Jules Miller, Greva James, and Giles Boschwick in it. Working the other direction, you can also see that Jules Miller is taking both Mathematical Opera and Lavatory Decorations of Ancient Rome. Using this approach, students can have many courses, and courses can have many students, and all our queries need to do is ask for all of the connections.

Remember, in Rails, you never want to name a table (or other object) "class." Rails has a lot of reserved words that can lead to very strange errors.

Granularity

In addition to linking through keys, there's one other critical aspect of database table design that you should know before embarking on writing applications: data granularity matters! If you read traditional explanations of relational databases, you'll see a lot about *normalization*, which is the process of creating tables that can be easily manipulated through code.

Much of normalization is about reducing duplication, which is usually best done by breaking data into multiple tables, as shown earlier. Another key part, however, is deciding how small (or large) each field in a table should be.

In the students table, shown originally in Figure B-1, each piece of a student's name had a separate field. Why? Well, it's pretty ordinary to want to sort a list of students by last name. It's also normal to leave out middle names in most correspondence. That's much easier to do when the pieces are already broken out, and avoids the problem of figuring out which part of a name is which algorithmically. In the presenter's table in Figure B-4, it probably wasn't worth breaking out those pieces—the name would go on a certificate once and never be examined again.

Doubtless, some purists would want those presenters' titles and names broken into smaller pieces, and you could do that. The question, though, is always going to be what you want to do with the data. If you're not interested in sorting the presenters' names, it may not be worth the extra effort on your part of fragmenting them. Similarly, if you only use street addresses for mailing, it might make sense to keep them as one field rather than separating house number from street number.

Problems, of course, arise when you realize that you really did need to sort a list of addresses by street or presenters by last name. Splitting existing data into smaller pieces once you've already built an application can be extremely annoying. For your first few applications, you may want to err on the side of breaking things up, as it's easier to recombine separate fields than to split them out again.

 Rails makes combining those fragmented fields easier with the composed_of method.

Once these structures are built, you can write queries that look for those connections—in SQL or in Rails. (Rails will effectively write the SQL query for you.)

Databases, Tables, and Rails

For more than a decade, most web applications that used a database used Structured Query Language (SQL) to move information into and out of databases. SQL is a powerful tool for creating and manipulating database structures, as well as for moving information in and out of those structures, but it's tightly focused on database projects only. You can't build a complete web application using SQL, so historically developers have written the bulk of their applications in another language, and then made SQL calls against a database. Developers needed to know both SQL and the other language.

Rails changes all of this, taking the position that it's better to manage data and logic in the same language, in this case Ruby. ActiveRecord abstracts the SQL calls away, though they still exist if you look through the development logs. At the same time, Rake and migrations handle the care and feeding of the database, defining and creating (or removing) tables. You define the tables in Ruby, and call `rake db:migrate` to make things happen.

If you already know SQL, you have a bit of an advantage when it comes to debugging Rails applications by checking logs and tinkering inside of the database. You may, however, have a disadvantage in getting started with Rails, as Rails pretty much expects developers to put the SQL toolkit away. There may be times when SQL is still actually necessary, so Rails supports a `find_by_sql` method, but in general, if you find yourself writing SQL, odds are good that you just haven't found a better way to do things in Rails itself.

You do have one critical choice to make regarding databases, however: which database to use with Rails. By default, since Rails 2.0.2, SQLite is the default database. It's easy to use with minimal configuration, keeps its information in a single (easily transferred) file, and is widely available.

For many applications, though, you will want to consider heavier-duty options that can handle more simultaneous connections. For many people, MySQL will be the right choice—heftier than SQLite, but not as intimidating as PostgreSQL. Bindings for all three are built into Rails by default, so that part's relatively easy, and bindings for many other databases are available as plug-ins.

You don't need to be a database expert to learn Rails. You will want to have administrators who know how to manage, optimize, and backup whatever database system you choose to use for deployment—but those issues should get addressed after you've finished learning Rails. You may want to pick up

Learning MySQL (O'Reilly, 2006) if you're new to relational databases and you want to take your knowledge to the next level.

An Incredibly Brief Guide to Regular Expressions

Ruby, like many other languages, contains a powerful text-processing shortcut that looks like it was created by cats walking on the keyboard. Regular expressions can be very difficult to read, especially as they grow longer, but they offer tremendous power that's hard to re-create in Ruby code. As long as you stay within a modest subset of regular expressions, you can get a lot done without confusing anyone—yourself included—who's trying to make sense out of your program logic.

For a much more comprehensive guide to regular expressions, see Jeffrey E. F. Friedl's classic *Mastering Regular Expressions* (O'Reilly) or Tony Stubblebine's compact but extensive *Regular Expression Pocket Reference* (O'Reilly).

What Regular Expressions Do

Regular expressions help your programs find chunks of text that match patterns you specify. Depending on how you call the regular expression, you may get:

A yes/no answer
Something matched or it didn't

A set of matches
All of the pieces that matched your query, so you can sort through them

A new string
If you specified that this was a search-and-replace operation, you may have a new string with all of the replacements made

Regular expressions also offer incredible flexibility in specifying search terms. A key part of the reason that regular expressions look so arcane is that they use symbols to specify different kinds of matches, and matches on characters that aren't easily typed.

Starting Small

The most likely place that you're going to use regular expressions in Rails is the `validates_format_of` method demonstrated in Chapter 7, which is shown here as Example C-1.

Example C-1. Validating data against regular expressions

```
# ensure secret contains at least one number
  validates_format_of :secret, :with => /[0-9]/,
    :message => "must contain at least one number"

# ensure secret contains at least one upper case
  validates_format_of :secret, :with => /[A-Z]/,
    :message => "must contain at least one upper case character"

# ensure secret contains at least one lower case
  validates_format_of :secret, :with => /[a-z]/,
    :message => "must contain at least one lower case character"
```

These samples all use regular expressions in their simplest typical use case: testing to see whether a string contains a pattern. Each of these will test `:secret` against the expression specified by `:with`. If the pattern in `:with` matches, then validation passes. If not, then validation fails and the `:message` will be returned. Removing the Rails trim, the first of these could be stated roughly in Ruby as:

```
if :secret =~ /[0-9]/
  #yes, it's there
else
  #no, it's not
end
```

The `=~` is Ruby's way of declaring that the test is going to compare the contents of the left operand against the regular expression on the right side. It doesn't actually return `true` or `false`, though—it returns the numeric position at which the first match begins, if there is a match, and `nil` if there are none. You can treat it as a boolean evaluator, however, because `nil` always behaves as `false` in a boolean evaluation, and other non-`false` values are the same as `true`.

There isn't room here to explain them, but if you need to do more with regular expressions than just testing whether there's a match, you'll be interested in the $~ variable (or Regexp.last_match), which gives you access to more detail on the results of the matching. A variety of methods on the String object, notably sub, gsub, and slice, also use regular expressions for slicing and dicing. You can also retrieve match results with $1 for the first match, $2 for the second, and so on, variables created by the match.

There's one other feature in these simple examples worth a little more depth. Reading them, you might have thought that /[0-9]/ was a regular expression. It's a regular expression object, but the expression itself is [0-9]. Ruby uses the forward slash as a delimiter for regular expressions, much like quotes are used for strings. Unlike strings, though, you can add flags after the closing slash, as you'll see later.

If you'd prefer, you can also use Regexp.new to create regular expression objects. (This usually makes sense if your code needs to meet changing circumstances on the fly at runtime.)

The Simplest Expressions: Literal Strings

The simplest regular expressions are simply literal strings. There are plenty of times when it's enough to search against a fixed search pattern. For example, you might test for the presence of the string "Ruby":

```
sentence = "Ruby is the best Ruby-like programming language."
sentence =~ /Ruby/
# => 0 - The first instance of 'Ruby' appears at position 0.
```

Character Classes

Example C-1 tested against letters and numbers, but there are many ways to do that. [a-z] is a good way to test for lowercase letters in English, but many languages use characters outside of that range. Regular expression character classes let you create sets of characters as well as use predefined groups of characters to identify what you want to target.

To create your own character class, use the square braces: [and]. Within the square braces, you can either list the characters you want, or create a set of characters with the hyphen. To match all the (guaranteed) English vowels in lowercase, you would write:

```
/[aeiou]/
```

If you wanted to match both upper- and lowercase vowels, you could write:

```
/[aeiouAEIOU]/
```

(If you wanted to ignore case entirely in your search, you could also use the i modifier described earlier: /[aeiou]/i.)

You can also mix character classes in with other parts of a search:

```
/[Rr][aeiou]by/
```

That would match Ruby, ruby, raby, roby, and a lot of other variations with upper- or lowercase R, followed by a lowercase vowel, followed by by.

Sometimes listing all the characters in a class is a hassle. Regular expressions are difficult enough to read without huge chunks of characters in classes. So instead of:

```
/[abcdefghijklmnopqrstuvwxyz]/
```

you can just write:

```
/[a-z]/
```

As long as the characters you want to match form a single range, that's simple —the hyphen just means "everything in between."

There's also a "not" option available, in the ^ character. You can reverse /[aeiou]/ by writing:

```
/^[aeiou]/
```

Regular expressions also offer built-in character classes, listed in Table C-1, that can make regular expressions more readable—at least, more readable once you've learned what they mean.

Table C-1. Regular expression special character classes

Syntax	Meaning
.	Match any character. (Without the m modifier, it doesn't match newlines; with the m modifier, it does.)
\d	Matches any digit. (Just 0–9, not other Unicode digits.)
\D	Matches any nondigit.
\s	Matches whitespace characters: tab, carriage return, newline, form feed.
\S	Matches nonwhitespace characters.
\w	Matches word characters: A–Z, a–z, and 0–9.
\W	Matches all nonword characters.

Escaping

Of course, even in simple strings there can be a large problem: lots of characters you'll want to test for are used by regular expression engines with a different meaning. The square braces around [0-9] are helpful for specifying that it's a set starting with zero and going to nine, but what if you're actually searching for square braces?

Fortunately, you can "escape" any character that regular expressions use for something else by putting a backslash in front of it. An expression that looks for left square brackets would look like \[. If you need to include a backslash, just put a second backslash in front of it, as in \\.

Some characters, particularly whitespace characters, are also just difficult to represent in a string without creating strange formatting. Table C-2 shows how to escape them for convenient matching.

Table C-2. Escapes for whitespace characters

Escape sequence	Meaning
\f	Form feed character
\n	Newline character
\r	Carriage return character
\t	Tab character

Modifiers

Sometimes you want to be able to search for strings without regard to case, and you don't want to put a lot of effort into creating an expression that covers every option. Other times you want to search against a string that contains many lines of text, and you don't want the expression to stop at the first line. For these situations, where the underlying rules change, Ruby supports modifiers, which you can put at the end of the expression or specify through the Regexp object. A complete list of modifiers is shown in Table C-3.

Table C-3. Regular expression modifier options

Modifier character	Effect
i	Ignore case completely.
m	Multiline matching—look past the first newline, and allow . and \n to match newline characters.
x	Use extended syntax, allowing whitespace and comments in expressions. (Probably not the first thing you want to try!)

Modifier character	Effect
o	Only interpolate #{ } expressions the first time the regular expression is evaluated. (Again, unlikely when starting out.)
u	Treat the content of the regular expression as Unicode. (By default, it is treated as the same as the content it is tested against.)
e, s, n	Treat the content of the regular expression as EUC, SJIS, and ASCII, respectively, like u does for Unicode.

Of these, i and m are the only ones you're likely to use at the beginning. To use them in a regular expression literal, just add them after the closing \:

```
sentence = "I think Ruby is the best Ruby-like programming language."
sentence =~ /ruby/i
# => 8  - "ruby" first appears at character 8.
```

If you want to use multiple options, you can. /ruby/iu specifies case-insensitive Unicode matching, for instance.

Anchors

Sometimes you want a match to be meaningful only at an edge: the start or the end, or maybe a word in the middle. You might even want to define your own edge—something is important only when it's next to something else. Ruby's regular expression engine lets you do all of these things, as well as match only when your match is *not* against an edge. Table C-4 lists common anchor syntax.

Table C-4. Regular expression anchors

Syntax	Meaning
^	When at the start of the expression, means to match the expression only against the start of the target (or a line within the target, *when* multiline matching is on).
$	When at the end of the expression, means to match the expression only against the end of the target (or the end of a line within the target, *when* multiline matching is on).
\A	When at the start of the expression, means to match the expression only against the start of the target string, *not* lines within it.
\Z	When at the end of the expression, means to match the expression only against the end of the target string, *not* lines within it.
\b	Marks a boundary between words, up against whitespace.
\B	Marks something that isn't a boundary between words.
(?=expression)	Lets you define your own boundary, by limiting the match to things next to *expression*.

Syntax	Meaning
(?!expression)	Lets you define your own boundary, by limiting the match to things that are *not* next to *expression*.

These make a little more sense if you see them in action. For example, if you only want to match "The" when it's at the start of a line, you could write:

```
/^The/
```

If you wanted to match "1991" when it's at the end of a line, you could write:

```
/1991$/
```

If multiline matching was on, and you wanted to make sure these matches apply only at the start or end of the string, you would write them as:

```
/\AThe/
/1991\Z/
```

The \b anchor is really useful when you want to match a word, not places where a sequence falls in the middle of a word. For example, if you wanted to match "the" without matching "Athens" or "Promethean," you could write:

```
/\bthe\b/
```

Alternately, if you wanted to match "the" *only* when it was part of another word, you could use \B to write:

```
/\Bthe\B/
```

The last two items in Table C-4 let you specify boundaries of your own—not just whitespace or the start or end, but any characters you want.

Sequences, Repetition, Groups, and Choices

Specifying a simple match pattern may take care of most of what you need regular expressions for use in Rails, but there are a few additional pieces you should know about before moving on. Even if you don't match something that needs these, knowing what they look like will help you read other regular expressions when you encounter them.

There are three classic symbols that indicate whether an item is optional or can repeat, plus a notation that lets you specify how much something should repeat, as shown in Table C-5.

Table C-5. Options and repetition

Syntax	Meaning
?	The pattern right before it should appear 0 or 1 times.

Syntax	Meaning
*	The pattern right before it should appear 0 or more times.
+	The pattern right before it should appear 1 or more times.
{number}	The pattern before the opening curly brace should appear exactly *number* times.
{number,}	The pattern before the opening curly brace should appear at least *number* times.
{number1, number2}	The pattern before the opening curly brace should appear at least *number1* times but no more than *number2* times.

You might think you're ready to go create expressions armed with this knowledge, but you'll find some unpleasant surprises. The regular expression:

`/1998+/`

might look like it will match one or more instances of "1998", but it will actually match "199" followed by one or more instances of "8". To make it match a sequence of 1998s, you would write:

`/(1998)+/`

If you wanted to specify, say, two to five occurrences of 1998, you'd write:

`/(1998){2,5}/`

The parentheses can also be helpful when specifying choices, though for a slightly different reason. If you wanted to match, say, 2013 or 2014, you could use | to write:

`/2013|2014/`

The | divides the whole expression into complete expressions to its left or right, rather than just grabbing the previous character, so you don't need parentheses around either 2013 or 2014. Nonetheless, if you wanted to do some thing like match 2013, 2014, or 2017, you might not want to write:

`/2013|2014|2017/`

You could instead write something more like:

`/201(3|4|7)/`

 Parentheses also "capture" matched text for later use, and that capturing may determine how you structure parentheses. It's probably not the first place you'll want to start, though.

Greed

There's one last feature of the repetition operators that can cause unexpected results: by default, they're *greedy*. This isn't a question of computing virtue, but rather one of how much content a regular expression can match at one go. This is a common issue in things like HTML, where you might see something like:

```
<a href= "http://example.com" >Example.com</a>
```

You might think you could match the HTML tags simply with an expression like:

```
/<.*>/
```

But instead of matching the opening tag and closing tag separately, that expression will grab everything from the opening < to the closing > of </a>, because it can. If you want to restrain a given expression so that it takes the smallest possible matching bite, add a ? behind any of the repetition operators:

```
/<.*?>/
```

Greed matters more when you use regular expressions to extract content from long strings, but it can yield confusing results even in supposedly simple matching. If you have mysterious problems, greed is a good thing to check for.

More

Regular expressions have nearly infinite depth, and this appendix has barely begun to scratch the surface, either of expressions or the ways you can use them in Ruby and Rails. A few of the things this incredibly brief guide hasn't been able to include are:

- Using expressions to fragment a string into smaller pieces
- Referencing earlier matches later in an expression
- Creating named groups
- Commenting regular expressions
- A variety of special syntax forms using parentheses

Again, for a much more comprehensive guide to regular expressions, see Jeffrey E. F. Friedl's classic *Mastering Regular Expressions* or Tony Stubblebine's compact but extensive *Regular Expression Pocket Reference*. For more on using them specifically with Ruby, see *The Ruby Programming Language*, by David Flanagan and Yukihiro Matsumoto (O'Reilly).

A Catalog of Helper Methods

Everyone who has used Rails for a while has their own set of "commonly used" helper methods. Many times, though, those commonly used sets are different. Some people use `FormHelper` for all of their forms, while others prefer `FormTagHelper`. Some people use `AssetTagHelper`, while others handcode links to static resources like stylesheets and images.

Rather than provide a comprehensive reference to these methods—the API documentation does that—this appendix provides a catalog you can browse to decide which methods might actually prove useful to your own needs. Much of the difficulty in using helpers is in finding them before you reinvent the wheel yourself.

All of these classes are subclasses of `ActionView::Helpers`.

> The easiest place to find API documentation, in a friendlier form than usual, is at *http://rails-doc.org/*. The search boxes give you choices as you type, and the explanations are presented in smaller pieces. You can also find the documentation at *http://www.railsbrain.com/* and *http://www.gotapi.com/rubyrails*. They're all a little different, but hopefully one of them will prove comfortable for you.

Calling Helper Methods

Every helper method has its own set of parameters, and often it's not clear from the documentation which parameters it will accept. How do you interpret the following?

```
label(object_name, method, text = nil, options = {})
```

The first few parameters at least take simple values. The `object_name` parameter will take a symbol pointing to an ActiveRecord object, like `:person`. The method parameter, though—what method does it take? It actually wants a symbol, say :name, for an attribute from the object specified in the previous parameter. Why would the Rails documentation call that a method? Because it'll use a method to access the attribute.

The next parameter, text, is shown with its default value, nil. Any time you see a parameter listed as equal to something, that value is the default.

And options? What is options? It looks like lots of methods must have the same options, because they all have the same entry in the documentation, but it's really just a convention. The actual options, named parameters, are listed below in the documentation for the method. Sometimes the options just create HTML attributes—use the name of the attribute to create an attribute, like :id => 'myIDvalue'. Other times the helper methods take more specific options that fit their particular needs. You don't generally need to surround the options in {}, either.

> For more on a case where the curly braces ({}) are necessary, see "Creating Checkboxes" on page 92" in Chapter 6.
>
> There's also a case—with FormHelper methods in particular— where some of the parameters disappear into a context object. See the section "Form As a Wrapper" on page 88" in Chapter 6 for more information on how this works.

Sometimes you'll also see parameters listed that begin with an asterisk, like *sources. This means that you can supply multiple values for that parameter.

Parameters and named parameters are enough for most helper method calls, but every now and then you'll see a method whose arguments end with &block. form_for is one of the commonly used ones that does this, but some methods take this as an option and others require it. When you call a method with a block, however, the block doesn't look quite like part of the arguments:

```
<% benchmark "It took this long:" do %>
  <%= my_long_method %>
<% end % >
```

In this case, the benchmark method is taking two arguments. The first, a string, is "It took this long:"; this will be text incorporated in the log. The second argument starts with do and closes with end, and includes everything in the middle. That's the block. (Blocks can also be marked with { and } in normal Ruby code, but in the ERb where you'll be writing helper methods, do and end are a better choice.)

Because benchmark is keeping track of how long it takes some code to run, it needs that code included as an argument. The cache, capture, and con tent_for methods have similar needs, as do form_for and fields_for, which surround a group of methods and provide them context.

For developers coming from less flexible languages, Ruby's creative use of blocks can be very difficult to figure out. If you're feeling stuck, your best option is to work from examples until you're ready to move forward with your own experiments.

ActiveRecordHelper

The ActiveRecordHelper class seems intent on providing the fastest possible path from an ActiveRecord object to an HTML representation. These methods may be useful for putting together very quick demonstrations or for debugging purposes, but they aren't likely to be your best choice for application-building. (In general, FormHelper and FormTagHelper are better choices for building forms.)

error_message_on
> Returns a div containing the error message for a given object and method. You can add text before or after the message.

error_messages_for
> Returns a div containing all the error messages for a given object. (The documentation suggests that you look at the code and make your own method if you need something more specific.)

form
> Creates a POST-based form based on the ActiveRecord object, all in one call. You can add extra pieces to the form through a block, but mostly this is good for quick-and-dirty instant forms.

input
> Creates an input element based on the type of the object and method it's passed. It's kind of like a field-by-field version of form.

AssetTagHelper

In Rails terms, an *asset* is something static that you want to include on a web page that isn't controlled by Rails. These include things like stylesheets, Java-Script libraries, and sometimes images.

When working on a small scale, assets are stored in the *public/* directory of your Rails application, but you can put them on a separate server and tell Rails where to find them through ActionController::Base.asset_host. A separate server can speed delivery, let you share assets with other applications, or just reduce the amount of work your Rails application has to do itself.

The methods in `AssetTagHelper` will assume files are in your *public/* directory unless you've specified otherwise. Most of them generate HTML tags for you, though a few let you specify ways to generate tags in the future.

The methods you should probably focus on initially include:

`auto_discovery_link_tag`
Lets you specify the location of an RSS or Atom feed.

`image_tag`
Returns an HTML img tag for the specified image name.

`javascript_include_tag`
Returns a `script` tag for the JavaScript files you identify as parameters. If one of the parameters is `:defaults`, the *application.js* file will be included, bringing in the Prototype and Script.aculo.us libraries. You can provide full paths to your scripts, even scripts on other servers, or you can just provide the file's name. If you're feeling fancy, you can define groups of styles with `register_javascript_expansion`, and reference them with symbols.

`stylesheet_link_tag`
Returns a `link` tag for the CSS stylesheet files you identify as parameters. You can provide full paths to your stylesheets, even stylesheets on other servers, or you can just provide the name of the file. The `:all` symbol will link all of the stylesheets in the *public/stylesheets* directory. As with scripts, if you're feeling really fancy, you can define groups of styles with `register_stylesheet_expansion`, and reference them with symbols.

There are other methods in `AssetTagHelper`, but they're mostly internal or only used in special cases:

`image_path` (*or* `path_to_image`)
An internal method used to calculate where to point for an image.

`javascript_path` (*or* `path_to_javascript`)
An internal method used to calculate where to point for a JavaScript file.

`register_javascript_expansion`
Lets you register a symbol that can reference JavaScript files. Useful if you consistently use a group of script files together.

`register_javascript_include_default`
Lets you add JavaScript files to the `:defaults` symbol used by the `javascript_include_tag` method.

`register_stylesheet_expansion`
> Lets you register a symbol that can reference style files. Useful if you consistently use a group of stylesheets together.

`stylesheet_path` (*or* `path_to_stylesheet`)
> An internal method used to calculate where to point for a stylesheet.

AtomFeedHelper and AtomFeedHelper::AtomFeedBuilder

Atom feeds started out as more or less the next generation of RSS syndication feeds. RSS can stand for Really Simple Syndication, Rich Site Summary, or RDF Site Summary, which is part of why Atom's developers decided to start over with a new name. Syndication feeds make it easy for sites, especially news sites and weblogs, to share their content with other websites and consumers, offering a simpler format for articles than full HTML pages. Atom, especially its REST-based Atom Publishing Protocol (AtomPub), has grown beyond just exchanging lists of articles, but Rails' built-in helper functions focus on fairly traditional feed applications.

`AtomHelper` is mostly used in Builder templates for creating XML:

`atom_feed`
> Takes a block, creating an `atom:feed` element and giving the block an AtomFeedBuilder object that child components can use for context. It also accepts parameters for `:language`, `:root_url`, `:url`, and `:schema_date`.

`entry`
> Creates an `atom:entry` element. Accepts parameters for `:published`, which represents the time when the entry was first published, `:update`, which represents the time of the latest changes, and `:url`, where to find the entry.

`updated`
> Takes a time and converts it to the right format for Atom feed times.

BenchmarkHelper, CacheHelper, and CaptureHelper

All three of these classes contain methods that wrap around content in your templates. `BenchmarkHelper` is a class you'll mostly want to use during development, when it may help you isolate code that's taking the view a long time to run. `CacheHelper` and `CaptureHelper` are both for advanced development. While `CacheHelper` allows you to specify fragments of your views that will be stored for future reuse, and applied when the same call comes through, Cap tureHelper lets you manually grab content that needs to be used again in the same view, probably to share content from the template with the layout:

benchmark

The benchmark method takes an optional message argument and an optional logging level argument (:debug, :info, :warn, or :error). It records how long the wrapped code takes to run. It requires a block argument, so it usually looks something like:

```
<% benchmark "It took this long:" do %>
  <%= my_long_method %>
<% end % >
```

The message and the length of time it takes to run will end up in the logs.

cache

The cache method lets you flag fragments of your view to be kept for caching. Like benchmark, cache wraps around the view code it's meant to work on with a block argument:

```
<% cache do %>
  <%= my_repetitive_method_that_should_be_cached %>
<% end % >
```

You should only cache information that doesn't change very often, but many HTML components are pretty stable.

capture

The capture method wraps around view code and stores its output to a variable. You can then reference the variable and have that content appear wherever you need. In operation, it looks like a variable assignment to a method:

```
<% @trapped_content = capture do %>
  <%= content_to_put_in_there %>
<% end % >
```

Once you've captured it, you can reference @trapped_content wherever it is convenient.

content_for

The content_for method is much like capture, but instead of putting the content in a variable, it lets you create a named block you can yield to in order to include the content.

DateHelper

The DateHelper class contains two kinds of helper methods. There's a small set of methods for expressing times in somewhat more human-friendly forms:

distance_of_time_in_words
> Takes two time values and expresses how far apart they are in rough word descriptions rather than precise time notation—e.g., "2 days," or "about 1 month," or "less than a minute."

distance_of_time_in_words_to_now *or* time_ago_in_words
> Like distance_of_time_in_words, but with the to_time always set to now.

Most of DateHelper's methods, though, create form fields for specifying times and dates. They're kind of clunky, but they may be useful for when you're getting started or when you feel like overriding them. Three of them are bound to particular objects of type :date, :time, or type :datetime:

date_select
> The date_select method creates drop-down year, month, and day select fields bound to a particular ActiveRecord object of type :date.

datetime_select
> The datetime_select method creates drop-down year, month, day, hour, minute, and second select fields bound to a particular ActiveRecord object of type :datetime.

time_select
> The time_select method creates drop-down hour, minute, and second select fields bound to a particular ActiveRecord object of type :time.

The rest of DateHelper's methods create HTML form fields, but aren't bound to any particular ActiveRecord object:

select_date
> The select_date method creates drop-down year, month, and day select fields.

select_datetime
> The select_datetime method creates drop-down year, month, day, hour, minute, and second select fields.

select_day
> The select_day method creates a drop-down field for day of the month (1–31).

select_hour
> The select_hour method creates a drop-down field for hours (0–23).

select_minute
> The select_minute method creates a drop-down field for minutes (0–59).

select_month
> The select_month method creates a drop-down field for month (1–12).

select_second
> The select_second method creates a drop-down field for seconds (0–59).

select_time
> The select_time method creates drop-down hour, minute, and second select fields.

select_year
> The select_year method creates a drop-down field for year. By default it uses five years on either side of the current or selected year, but you can set start and end years through parameters.

DebugHelper

The DebugHelper class isn't exactly a powerful debugger, but its one method lets you do something that's often useful in development mode—report an object's contents:

debug
> The debug method takes an object as its argument. It then serializes the object into YAML, and wraps the YAML output (and any errors) in pre tags so you can inspect it.

FormHelper, FormTagHelper, and FormOptionsHelper

These three classes of helper methods offer different approaches to building forms and some different pieces for creating forms. Much of the time you'll want to use either FormHelper or FormTagHelper, but you might mix FormOptionsHelper with either of the other two.

The FormHelper methods create form fields bound to particular attributes of ActiveRecord objects. They are easiest to use within a form_for method that sets their context, as described in Chapter 6. If you don't like that approach, you can supply an object and attribute name as the first two parameters when calling them. (The documentation for each method shows the parameter approach.)

check_box
> Creates a checkbox field bound to an attribute from the object specified in form_for or in the parameters. (It also creates a hidden field bound to the same attribute for use if the checkbox isn't checked.)

fields_for
> fields_for is like form_for, except that it doesn't create the actual form tags.

---

file_field
> Creates a file upload field bound to an attribute from the object specified in form_for or in the parameters. (You'll need to modify the form_for call as described in Chapter 8 to use this method.)

form_for
> Creates a form element and sets the context for the other helper methods in FormHelper.

hidden_field
> Creates a hidden field bound to an attribute from the object specified in form_for or in the parameters.

label
> Creates a label for a field created with the other methods of FormHelper.

password_field
> Creates a password field bound to an attribute from the object specified in form_for or in the parameters.

radio_button
> Creates a radio button bound to an attribute from the object specified in form_for or in the parameters.

text_area
> Creates a larger multiline text area bound to an attribute from the object specified in form_for or in the parameters.

text_field
> Creates a single-line text field bound to an attribute from the object specified in form_for or in the parameters.

The FormTagHelper class does similar work but provides no automatic binding to a single shared object for a form. It lets you build forms where each component is specified separately:

check_box_tag
> Lets you create checkboxes. Unlike check_box, it doesn't automatically create a hidden field for use if the box is unchecked.

field_set_tag
> Creates a fieldset tag for grouping form elements. You can set the legend for the fieldset as an argument.

file_field_tag
> Creates a file upload tag. To use this, you also need to give the form_tag method a :multipart => true parameter.

form_tag
> Creates a form tag that wraps around other form elements but does not set context like form_for.

`hidden_field_tag`
: Creates a hidden form field.

`image_submit_tag`
: *Not* for submitting images, but rather for creating submit buttons that are presented as images.

`label_tag`
: Creates a label.

`password_field_tag`
: Creates a password field.

`radio_button_tag`
: Creates a radio button.

`select_tag`
: Creates a drop-down select or multiselect list.

`submit_tag`
: Creates a submit button with a text caption.

`text_area_tag`
: Creates a larger multiline text area.

`text_field_tag`
: Creates a single-line text field.

The `FormOptionsHelper` methods are complementary to the methods in the other two form-related helper classes. Some of the methods (`collection_select`, `country_select`, `select`, and `time_zone_select`) take the same arguments as the field-creating methods in `FormHelper` and can be used the same way, with a context set by `form_for` or without. The other methods are focused on creating options for those methods, and may also be used to create option lists for the `FormTagHelper`'s `select_tag` method:

`collection_select`
: Creates a select list from a specified object or array.

`country_options_for_select`
: Creates `option` tags for an alphabetical list of countries, accepting arguments to indicate which should be selected and which should appear first in the list.

`country_select`
: Creates a complete `select` list of countries including `option` tags. Also accepts arguments for a selected default and for giving countries higher priority in the list.

`option_groups_from_collection_for_select`
: Creates `option` tags structured with `optgroup` tags based on an object or array.

`options_for_select`
> Creates option tags based on a hash or array.

`options_from_collection_for_select`
> Creates option tags based on a collection object.

`select`
> Creates a complete select list including option tags.

`time_zone_options_for_select`
> Returns option tags for time zones across the planet.

`time_zone_select`
> Returns a complete select list for time zones across the planet.

JavaScriptHelper

Sometimes your Rails code will need to generate JavaScript, and not always in the context of RJS, as described in Chapter 16. These helper methods make it simpler to add basic JavaScript functionality to your pages, and remove the need to code some kinds of simple JavaScript by hand:

`button_to_function`
> Creates a button that will call a JavaScript function using its onclick handler. It accepts a block of code, which works like RJS.

`define_javascript_functions`
> Creates a link to Prototype and other JavaScript files, but is best avoided. Use javascript_include_tag instead.

`escape_javascript`
> Reformats JavaScript containing carriage returns and quotes so that it can safely be put into HTML attribute values.

`javascript_tag`
> Creates a script tag. Again, javascript_include_tag may be a better option.

`link_to_function`
> Creates a link that will call a JavaScript function. Like button_to_function, it also can take a block that works like RJS.

NumberHelper

The NumberHelper class provides convenience methods for formatting numbers:

number_to_currency

Turns a number into a currency representation. You can select the :unit (denomination), :separator (normally .), :delimiter (normally ,), :for mat (whether the currency comes before or after the number), and :preci sion (normally 2).

number_to_human_size

Turns file-size byte counts into more typical human representations, like 12 GB.

number_to_percentage

Turns a number into a percent value. You can select the :precision (normally three digits after the decimal), and the :separator (normally .).

number_to_phone

Turns a number into an American-style telephone number. You can specify a country code, extension, delimiter, and whether or not the area code has parentheses, but you can't specify how the numbers are broken down.

number_with_delimiter

Formats a number with a given :delimiter between thousands (, by default) and decimal :separator (. by default).

number_with_precision

Formats a number to present as many digits after the decimal point as are specified in the second argument (three is the default).

PrototypeHelper

The Prototype JavaScript library simplifies many common Ajax tasks, but these helper methods make it even more convenient to incorporate calls to Prototype in Rails templates:

evaluate_remote_response

Evaluates the JavaScript response from a remote service using the JavaScript eval method. The eval method opens JavaScript applications up to attack, so be certain that what you're processing is free of potentially harmful code.

form_remote_for

Same as remote_form_for, described later.

form_remote_tag

Creates a form element that uses an XmlHttpRequest call to submit form data. This allows the page to handle the response rather than reloading an entirely new page.

link_to_remote
: Creates a link that issues an `XmlHttpRequest` call, again allowing the page to handle the response rather than replacing the current page with a new destination.

observe_field
: Watches the content of a given field and makes a remote call (or a JavaScript function call) when the content of that field changes. Useful for components like text fields that provide suggestions.

observe_form
: Watches the content of a given form and makes a remote call (or a JavaScript function call) when the content of that field changes.

periodically_call_remote
: Makes an `XmlHttpRequest` call every so often, according to a duration specified in seconds set as the `:frequency` option.

remote_form_for
: Works like `form_for`, except that submitting the form triggers an `XmlHttpRequest` call that gets handled by Ajax in the browser instead of the usual form submission process.

remote_function
: Returns the JavaScript needed to make an `XmlHttpRequest` call to a remote function.

submit_to_remote
: Creates a button that will submit a form using an `XmlHttpRequest` call.

update_page
: Creates the context for RJS calls, allowing a block of code to update multiple elements on the same page.

update_page_tag
: Creates JavaScript, wrapped in a `script` tag, using the same mechanisms as creating RJS code.

RecordIdentificationHelper

These methods make it easier for views to identify components referring to Rails objects when building HTML or RJS:

dom_class
: Creates a value suitable for a `class` attribute that is the singular form of the object name.

dom_id
: Creates a value suitable for an id attribute that is the singular form of the object name plus _ and the object's id value.

partial_path
: Creates a value containing *plural/singular* form of an object's name, like turtles/turtle or people/person.

SanitizeHelper

The SanitizeHelper methods support a variety of approaches to escaping HTML and CSS. They complement the h method (short for html_escape, part of the ERb:Util class) by providing other approaches to escaping markup or letting it pass:

sanitize
: The sanitize method provides a customizable approach to removing attributes and markup that you don't want to pass through. The customization can be specified through the :tags and :attributes parameters, or set by default through initializer code.

sanitize_css
: The sanitize_css method removes features from CSS that the creators of sanitize felt were too dangerous. This is used by sanitize on style attributes.

strip_links
: The strip_links method leaves markup other than links intact, but removes all links from the argument.

strip_tags
: The strip_tags method removes all HTML markup from the argument. (The documentation warns that it may not always find all HTML markup, however.)

ScriptaculousHelper

Like the PrototypeHelper methods, ScriptaculousHelper methods provide ready Ruby-based access to JavaScript components in the browser. While Prototype focuses on basic Ajax communications, Script.aculo.us focuses more on actions and special effects:

draggable_element
: Identifies an HTML element, specified by id attribute value, as supporting user efforts to drag it around the screen and potentially drop it on a receiving element.

drop_receiving_element

Identifies an HTML element, again by `id` attribute value, as a container where users can drop draggable objects and expect a response. When the drop happens, the code this creates can make a remote Ajax call or a local JavaScript call, and supports `class`-based constraints on which objects to accept. It also supports changing the `class` of the receiving element to give users visual feedback when they've positioned a draggable object over a container that could accept it.

sortable_element

Identifies an HTML element, again by `id` attribute value, as a collection users can reorder, making an Ajax call when changes occur.

visual_effect

Provides access to the Script.aculo.us library's collection of visual effects, applying them to an HTML element specified by `id`.

TagHelper

`TagHelper` may be of use when you want to create explicit XHTML markup using ERb templates, or want to create view logic that lets the data determine which markup is used. On the one hand, these methods are somewhat obscure; on the other, they may be exactly what you need if clean XHTML is your goal:

cdata_section

As its name suggests, the `cdata_section` method lets you create CDATA sections wrapping the content specified in the argument. (CDATA sections let you mark sections of an XML document as not containing any markup, so you can use <, >, and & to your heart's content.)

content_tag

The `content_tag` method is a generic tag building method. You define the name of the tag, the attributes, and the content of the tag through the arguments.

escape_once

The `escape_once` method is extremely convenient when you have content that needs <, >, and & escaped—but you might already have done some of the escaping. This method is smart enough to escape markup text that needs escaping, while leaving the ampersands that are part of prior escaping alone.

tag

The `tag` method creates an empty tag (like `<br />`).

TextHelper

The `TextHelper` methods offer a variety of tools for formatting, manipulating, and presenting plain text. If you're building blogs or other software where users are entering content, this class is worth a close look:

`auto_link`

   The `auto_link` method is a simple way to make links live without requiring people to use HTML. Its first argument is a block of text. By default, it will turn all URLs and email addresses in that text into live links. The `link` parameter defaults to `:all`, but also accepts `:email_addresses` and `:urls` as options if you just want one or the other. The `href_options` parameter lets you add attributes.

   (If you want to get really fancy, you can supply a block of code that will be executed for every link that gets added, letting you control processing precisely.)

`concat`

   Used for those obscure times when you want to generate output inside of a `<% %>` ERb code block instead of the usual `<%= %>` block.

`cycle`

   Creates an object that lets you alternate different values for each member of an array. This lets you do things like alternate formatting to reflect even and odd rows, or mark every 10th element.

`excerpt`

   Finds a given phrase in a given text and returns the phrase with surrounding context.

`highlight`

   Finds a given phrase in a given text and marks all occurrences with `<strong class="highlight" >`.

`markdown`

   When used with the BlueCloth plug-in (*http://www.deveiate.org/projects/BlueCloth*), lets you convert text containing Markdown codes (*http://daringfireball.net/projects/markdown/syntax*) into HTML.

`pluralize`

   Lets you apply Rails' inflector (the same code that manages singular and plural for ActiveRecord objects) to any text you'd like.

`reset_cycle`

   Starts a `cycle` (described earlier) over again.

`simple_format`

   Adds HTML line breaks and paragraph marks to plain text.

textilize
> When used with the RedCloth plug-in (*http://whytheluckystiff.net/ruby/ redcloth/*), lets you convert text containing Textilize codes (*http://www .textism.com/tools/textile*) into HTML.

textilize_without_paragraph
> Just like textilize, but with one fewer surrounding paragraph mark (`<p>...</p>`).

truncate
> Cuts off the end of a string after a specified number of characters and adds a truncate string, usually ....

word_wrap
> Wraps text to a specified line width, breaking on whitespace when possible.

UrlHelper

The UrlHelper class provides methods for creating links inside of your Rails application, letting you take advantage of the routing functionality Rails uses to manage addresses. (And even though the REST world frequently talks about URIs rather than URLs, URLHelper is the place to go to create both.)

button_to
> Generates a form containing a single button that links to the specified controller. (It's the same as url_for, but wraps the result in a button.) You can ask users to confirm their interest after clicking the button.

current_page?
> Returns true if the current page has the same URL as the URL created by the options listed.

link_to
> Creates a link (a) element linking to the specified controller. (It's the same as url_for, but wraps the result in an HTML link.)

link_to_if
> Like link_to, but lets you specify conditions.

link_to_unless
> Like link_to, but lets you specify prohibitions.

link_to_unless_current
> Like link_to, but won't link if the link is to the current page.

mail_to
> Creates a mailto: link to a given email address.

`url_for`

Creates a URL based on the options provided and the Rails application's routing table.

Glossary

Speaking in Rails

Rails, like many communities, has developed its own language. You need to know a lot of that language to understand what other people are saying, even when those people are trying to be helpful. This glossary gives you a quick guide to some common terms used in Rails that aren't obvious to outsiders and provides the extra Rails meanings for words used elsewhere that have acquired additional meaning in Rails. Hopefully this will make it easier for you to understand Rails documentation and conversation, but of course, new terms will emerge over time:

37signals
> The company where Rails was born, emerging from their Basecamp product.

ACID
> Atomicity, Consistency, Isolation, Durability. A set of principles, usually implemented with relational databases and transactions, that are intended to ensure data reliability. Rails is not designed with ACID as a priority, though transactions are available as a plug-in. (In a different meaning, there are also a variety of "Acid" tests for CSS implementation conformance.)

ActionController
> The part of the Rails library that directly interacts with incoming HTTP requests, including routing, parameter passing, session management, and deciding how to render a response. Controller objects are the main way in which Rails developers interact with ActionController.

ActionMailer
> The part of the Rails library that manages incoming and outgoing email.

ActionPack

The combination of ActionController and ActionView, which provides a complete package for dealing with and responding to HTTP requests.

ActionView

The part of the Rails library that generates responses to HTTP requests, based on information received from ActionController.

ActiveRecord

The Rails library that handles mappings between the database and Ruby classes. ActiveRecord is pretty much the foundation of Rails, but it can be used outside of Rails as well.

ActiveSupport

A collection of classes that were developed for Rails, but that can be used in any Ruby environment.

acts_as

A common naming convention used in Rails, typically with plug-ins, to indicate that part of a model operates using code provided elsewhere.

adapter

Code, usually Ruby or Ruby and other languages, that connects Active-Record to a specific database.

aggregation

Often used to describe collecting RSS or Atom syndication feeds, but has another meaning in Rails. Aggregation lets you create simpler ways to access combinations of data using the composed_of method. You might do this to combine first and last names, or address parts, or other pieces that can be broken down but that are often conveniently used together.

Agile

A variety of software development techniques that tend to focus on smaller-scale iterative development rather than on top-down "waterfall" design and implementation.

Ajax

Originally Asynchronous JavaScript and XML, this former acronym now refers more broadly to web development where methods within a page call back to the server and make smaller changes to a page rather than calling for a complete refresh every time. Ajax applications often resemble desktop applications more closely because of this added flexibility.

assertion

Claims made in test methods whose results will be reported.

assets

In Rails parlance, assets are information outside of your application and its database—images are a classic example—that are incorporated by reference. Assets don't need to be entirely outside of the application, however. Chapter 8 shows how to have Rails manage the arrival of image assets.

association

A relationship between fields in a database.

Atom

An XML-based format originally used for syndicating information from blogs, but now moving into many applications where data needs to flow from site to site.

attributes

Attributes are information about an ActiveRecord model class, such as what fields it contains, what types they hold, and so on. Usually, Rails figures out what the attributes are directly from the application database, which knows what they are because they were set by migrations.

authentication

The process of making sure that a user (or other process) has the privileges they claim to have. Usernames and passwords are classic authentication mechanisms, but many others are possible.

Basecamp

A collaboration tool (*http://www.basecamphq.com/*) developed by *37signals* and *DHH*. DHH realized while building Basecamp that the underlying framework could be reused for a lot of other projects, and that became the foundation of Rails.

benchmark

Code used to determine and compare performance. Generic benchmarks used to test things like CPU performance are the most common usage, but you could create your own benchmarks to test performance specific to your application.

block

Chunks of code that can be passed among Ruby methods. Rails uses blocks to implement much of its view functionality, using this technique to connect code from different files into a coherent program.

Builder

An API used to generate XML files from Ruby objects.

business rules

Logic that is specific to a given application, and often specific to a given business. They specify rules for data that go beyond the computer-specific "This variable must be a string" to more complex rules like, "This date must be no earlier than x and no later than y" or "All expense reports must come with explicit and authenticated approval before consideration for payment."

CamelCase

Rails does not do CamelCase, except in class names. CamelCase uses uppercase letters to identify the beginnings of new words. Rails more typically keeps everything lowercase, using underscores (_) to separate the words.

Capistrano

A Ruby tool for automating running scripts on remote computers, typically used to deploy Rails applications and their updates.

class

A collection of methods and properties that together provide a definition for the behavior of objects.

component

A bad idea that disappeared in Rails 2.0, becoming a plug-in. Components mixed rendering and controller logic, and created applications that were both messy and slow.

console

A command-line interface to Rails applications, which is accessible through `script/console` (also see *irb*).

Content type

In HTTP requests (and network requests generally), content types are used to identify the kind of content being sent. Content types are often called MIME types, from their original development as Multipurpose Internet Main Extensions.

controller

The switchboard for Rails applications, controllers connect information coming in from requests to appropriate data models and develop response data that is then presented through views.

cookie

A small (typically less than 4 kilobytes) chunk of text that is stored in a user's browser and sent to the server that created it along with requests. Cookies can be used to track users across multiple requests, making it much simpler to maintain state across requests. In general, however, you should never store any significant information in cookies.

cron

A Unix approach to scheduling tasks that need to run on a regular basis. "Cron jobs" are managed through the crontab configuration file, and the cron daemon makes sure they get executed as requested. (Rails itself doesn't use cron, but you could use cron to manage periodic background housekeeping on a server, for instance.)

CRUD

Create, Retrieve, Update, and Delete (sometimes Destroy). The basic functions needed by most data manipulation programs. *SQL* is very CRUD-like, as is *REST*.

CSS

Cascading Style Sheets, a vocabulary for specifying how precisely web pages should be displayed on screen, in print, or in other media. In a Rails application, a CSS stylesheet is typically an extra file or files kept in the *public/stylesheets* directory, referenced from each view that uses it.

CSV

Comma-separated values, a common if basic method for sharing tabular data.

CVS

Not the American pharmacy/convenience store, but the Concurrent Versioning System, used to manage different versions of programs and related files. In Rails, CVS has typically been replaced by *Subversion* or *Git*.

DELETE

An HTTP verb that means what it says—to delete the resource the DELETE request is addressed to.

deployment

Putting something out in the "real world," typically moving an application from development to operation.

development

The mode in which you'll most likely modify and create code. In Rails, development uses a different database and settings from the test or production modes.

DHH

David Heinemeier Hansson, the creator of Rails and its lead developer. For more DHH, see his blog, *http://www.loudthinking.com/*.

DOM

Document Object Model, the standard API for manipulating HTML documents in a web browser. (It's also used for XML and HTML outside of the browser.)

DRY

Don't Repeat Yourself—a central principle of Rails development.

duck typing

"If it walks like a duck and quacks like a duck, it's a duck." A way of determining what type an object has by looking at what it contains and how it behaves, rather than by looking for an explicit label on it. Duck typing is built into the Ruby language.

dynamic scaffold

Automatically generated HTML that would let you tinker with a model and the underlying data without actually creating any views. Discontinued in Rails 2.0 in favor of *static scaffolding*.

dynamic typing

See *duck typing*, described earlier.

Edge Rails

The latest and (sometimes) greatest version of Rails, Edge Rails lets you develop with the most recent updates to the framework. Exciting for advanced developers, but potentially explosive for beginners. (Note that you can *freeze* Rails versions if one goes by that you really liked or, worse, a new one appeared that broke your code.)

ERb

Embedded Ruby, the syntax used for Rails views and layouts. ERb lets you mix HTML (or other text-based formats) with Ruby code.

Erubis

An implementation of ERb that is both faster and offers several extensions to ERb. For more information, see *http://www.kuwata-lab.com/erubis/*. You can use Erubis with or without Rails.

exception

A signal sent by a method call as it terminates (using `raise`) to indicate that things didn't go correctly. You can deal with exceptions using `rescue`.

filter

Controller code that lets you wrap your actions with other code that will get run before, after, or around your actions' code.

Firebug

A Firefox plug-in for debugging JavaScript and a wide variety of other aspects of web development.

fixture

Data created for the explicit purpose of using it to test your Rails applications. Fixtures are specified in YAML and provide a customizable set of data you can use to check the functionality of your Rails code. They are stored in the *test/fixtures* directory.

flash

> While you can include Adobe Flash content as external *assets* in your Rails application, `flash` in a Rails context more frequently refers to a method for passing objects between actions. You can set a message in the controller using `flash` and then retrieve and display that message in a view, for example.

form builder

> A class containing methods for creating HTML forms. Form builders are typically used to create consistent-looking interfaces across an application and to present complex aspects of your models that need additional interface support.

fragments

> Pieces of views that you've asked Rails to cache so that they will be available on subsequent requests.

freezing

> Locking your Rails application down so that it runs on a particular version of Rails, no matter what version of Rails you install on your computer more generally. For production applications, this provides a much more reliable running environment. You freeze and unfreeze through the Rake tool.

gem

> A package for a Ruby program or library that makes it easy to install across systems. Rails is distributed as a gem.

generate

> Generate, or `script/generate` as it is called from the command line, is a program you can use to have Rails create a wide variety of different types of code for you. In general, when creating new functionality, you should let Rails generate much of the code and then customize it, rather than writing from scratch.

GET

> The most commonly used HTML request, which has the general meaning of "retrieve content from the specified URL." GET requests are supposed to be *idempotent* and, despite the availability of query parameters, should not be used to change information in an application.

Git

> An application for sharing code and code development across many computers and developers. Ruby on Rails itself is now developed using Git to store and manage the code.

h

A commonly used method for escaping potentially dangerous content, removing HTML content that could create security problems.

hash

An unordered collection of name-value pairs. You can retrieve the values by asking for them by name. (You need to know the name to do that, of course!)

HEAD

An HTTP verb that is very similar to GET, but that only retrieves the headers, not the body of the request.

helper method

Provides support for commonly performed operations in view code. Helpers are a little less formal than *form builders*, which typically have more understanding of the context in which they work. Rails provides a wide variety of helper methods for common tasks like generating HTML, and you can add your own helper methods as well.

HTML

HyperText Markup Language, a common language used to present information over the web. HTML files define web pages, including content, formatting, scripts, and references to external resources.

HTTP

HyperText Transfer Protocol, along with HTML, is the foundation on which the Web is built. HTTP supports requests that include a verb (like GET, POST, PUT, or DELETE) along with a variety of supporting information. Those requests are then answered by a responding server, which reports a [Response Code] and hopefully some information useful to whoever initiated the request. HTTP is itself built on top of TCP/IP, typically using port 80 to receive requests.

HTTPS

Like HTTP, but encrypted. Technically, the HyperText Transfer Protocol over Secure Socket Layer. HTTPS works much like HTTP, except that the web server adds a layer of encryption using public key certificates, it runs on port 443, and browsers are typically much more cautious about caching information that arrived over HTTPS.

id

An identifying value. In Rails, usually the primary key from a table of data, used for quick access to a particular row or object. In HTML, a unique identifier for one element in a document, often used for styling.

idempotent

A fancy word for a specific meaning of reliable. If an action is idempotent, you can perform that action repeatedly without changing the result.

irb

A command-line shell prompt for interacting with Ruby directly, irb lets you try out code in a much simpler environment than Rails.

IRC

Internet Relay Chat, a key part of the communications that hold the Rails community together. You can find a lot more information on Rails and IRC, including servers, channels, and clients, at *http://wiki.rubyonrails .org/rails/pages/IRC*.

iterator

A method that loops through a set of objects, working on each object in the set once.

JSON

JavaScript Object Notation, a text-based format for exchanging objects. Douglas Crockford "discovered" it already existing inside of JavaScript and made it a popular interchange format. It's often seen as a more programming-oriented complement or competitor to *XML*. (It's also a subset of *YAML*.)

layout

A file containing the beginning and end of the HTML documents to be returned by views, allowing views to focus on the content of documents rather than on the headers and foots.

Leopard

Mac OS X 10.5, notable mostly for improvements to its Ruby support, which make it much easier to use and update Rails. (Rails comes preinstalled now, though in an old version.)

lighttpd

A new web server designed to be smaller and more efficient than Apache. If you want to run Rails through FastCGI, lighttpd is a good option.

linking

Rails supports traditional HTML linking, but in many cases you'll want to use a helper method to create links between the components in your applications.

Matz

Yukihiro Matsumoto, creator and maintainer of the Ruby language. "Matz is nice, and so we are nice" (MINASWAN) is a key principle of Ruby culture.

Merb

Originally "Mongrel plus ERb," Merb is a Ruby-based MVC framework that is not Rails.

method

A unit of code that accomplishes a task.

migration

Instructions for changing a database to add or remove structures that Rails will access. The Rake tool is used to apply or roll back migrations.

mock object

A technique for testing Rails applications that creates objects that expect particular methods to be called, and that exposes more information on the objects for easier debugging.

mod_rails

See Passenger.

model

Code that handles the interactions between Rails and a database. Models contain data validation code—code that combines or fragments information to meet user or database expectations—and pretty much anything else you need to say about the data itself. However, models do *not* contain information about the actual structure or schema of the data they manage —that is kept in the database itself, managed by *migrations*.

Mongrel

A Ruby-based web server now used as the default server for Rails applications when run from the command line. In production, a "pack of mongrels" often runs behind an Apache web server, connecting HTTP requests to Rails.

MVC

Model-View-Controller, an architecture for building interactive applications that lies at the heart of the Rails framework. (See Chapter 3 for a lot more information.)

MySQL

A popular open source relational database, commonly used to store data for larger Rails applications.

naming conventions

The glue that holds Rails together, letting applications figure out which pieces connect to which pieces without requiring a formal mapping table. Rails makes naming conventions feel more natural by supporting features like *pluralization*.

nil

A value that means "no value." Nil also evaluates to `false` in comparisons.

object

    An instance of a class, combining the logic from the methods of the class with properties specific to that particular object.

ORM

    Object-Relational Mapping, the hard part of getting object-oriented languages and relational databases to work together. Rails addresses this using *ActiveRecord* and makes it (mostly) transparent through *naming conventions*.

pagination

    Chopping up long lists of data into smaller, more digestible chunks. In Rails 2.0, pagination moved out from the core framework into plug-ins, most notably `will_paginate`.

partial

    A piece of view code designed to produce part of a document. Multiple views can then reference the partial so that they don't have to repeat the logic it already contains. Partial names are prefixed with _.

Passenger

    An Apache module, also called *mod_rails*, for deploying Rails applications behind an Apache web server.

Pickaxe book

    Programming Ruby, the first major book on Ruby, published by the Pragmatic Programmers. Its third edition covers Ruby 1.9.

plug-in

    Additional code, often packaged as a *gem*, that you can use to provide additional functionality to Rails.

pluralization

    A feature of *ActiveRecord* that generates much controversy. Models have singular names, like person, while views and controllers use plurals of those names, because they work with many instances of the models. Rails has a set of defaults that handle both standard English pluralization and some common irregulars, like person and people, child and children. There are cases where pluralization doesn't work in English, but fortunately they rarely affect programming.

POST

    An HTTP method that sends information to a given URI. POST is mapped to CREATE in REST-based Rails applications, though POST has been used as a general "send-this-stuff-over-there-via-HTTP" method in the past.

Postfix

    A commonly used mail server on Unix and Linux computers.

PostgreSQL

A more powerful but somewhat more daunting open source database that is frequently used by developers who want more control than MySQL provides, or access to specific extensions, like the geographic data work in PostGIS.

Pound

A proxying load balancer designed to pass HTTP requests from a web server to other servers in the background.

Pragmatic Programmers

The Pragmatic Programmers, Dave Thomas and Andy Hunt, and their publishing company (*http://www.pragprog.com/*). They've written and published a wide variety of books on Ruby and Rails, and run related training courses.

private

Private methods and properties appear in Ruby classes after the `private` keyword, and are only accessible to other code in that same class.

Prototype

A basic JavaScript library for Ajax development that reduces the amount of redundant code needed to build an application.

proxy server

Proxy servers (or proxies) receive requests on one end and then resubmit them to other servers. Proxies can be used to manage performance, to provide caching, to hide servers from users (and vice versa), for filtering, or for pretty much anything you want to do with an HTTP request between the request and the response.

PUT

An HTTP method used to send a file to a URI. In Rails RESTful routing, PUT maps to UPDATE, replacing content that was previously there with new content.

quirks mode

A technique used by several browsers to support web pages formatted with older (broken) browsers in mind, while still allowing developers to specify that their pages should be processed using newer and generally more correct standards.

RailsConf

A conference focused on Rails, usually once a year in North America and once a year in Europe. For more information, see *http://railsconf.com/*.

Rake

A command-line tool that originally was Ruby's replacement for the *make* build tool commonly used by Unix applications. Thanks to its scriptable extensibility, it has turned into a one-stop toolkit for applying *migrations* to databases, checking up on routes, *freezing* and unfreezing the version of Rails used by a given application, and many more tasks.

RDoc

The documentation generator used by most Ruby applications, including Rails. The Rails API documentation all gets built through RDoc.

redirect

Responding to a request to one URI by telling the requester to visit a different URI.

regex

Regular expression, a compact if sometimes inscrutable means of describing patterns to match against targeted text.

render

To convert data from one form to another, usually to present it. Web browsers render HTML into readable pages, while Rails views render data from Rails into HTML that gets sent to users' web browsers.

request

In HTTP, a request is a message sent from a client to a server, identifying a resource (a URI) and providing a method—usually GET, PUT, POST, or DELETE.

resource

For Rails development purposes, it's probably easiest to think of a resource as code identified by a URI (or URL). It's the code that will get called once Rails routing has examined the request and decided where to send it. (Outside of Rails, it can be a deeply philosophical notion at the heart of web architecture and infinite debates about web architecture.)

response

In HTTP, a response is a message sent from a server to a client in response to a request. It generally includes a status code as well as headers describing the kind of response, and data to present the client.

REST

Not a vacation. Technically, "Representational State Transfer," but really just a sane way to handle interactions on the Web in a way that takes full advantage of the underlying web architecture instead of chucking it and building something entirely different. Rails 2.0 includes a lot of features designed to make building REST-based applications easier. (See Chapter 5 for a lot more detail.)

REXML

An XML parser built into Ruby.

RJS

A kind of Rails template used to generate JavaScript, typically for Ajax applications.

RMagick

A *gem* that lets Ruby applications manipulate graphics using the Image-Magick library.

route

To send from one place to another. In Rails, the routing code examines requests coming to the server from various clients and decides based on their URIs which controller should respond to them.

RSS

An acronym of various meanings that refers to several different XML formats for syndicating information from one site (typically weblogs, but also newspapers, periodicals, and others of sites) to clients and other servers that might be interested.

RubyForge

A site (*http://rubyforge.org*) that hosts a wide variety of open source Ruby software projects in development. You can use it as a place to share code you write or to find code others have already created.

scaffold

Code that gets you started, much as scaffolding on a construction project lets workers get to the parts of a building they need to modify. Rails can *generate* scaffolding code for a wide variety of different project needs, though in Rails 2.0 scaffolding most frequently refers to the REST-based set of models, views, and controllers created by `script/generate scaffold`.

scale

Scale reflects size. If a program scales, it can survive growing rapidly from serving only a few simultaneous users to serving thousands or even millions of users.

Script.aculo.us

A JavaScript library, built on top of *Prototype*, for creating Ajax applications and effects, often used in Rails-based Ajax development.

session

A series of HTTP interactions between a single client and the web server. Sessions are usually tracked with *cookies* or with explicit logins.

singleton

An object that has only one instance in a given application. You shouldn't (and generally can't) create more than one of it.

SOAP

Originally the Simple Object Access Protocol, it proved not very simple, not necessarily bound to objects, and not exactly a protocol. SOAP is the foundation of most web services applications that don't use REST, taking a very different approach to communications between applications.

SQL

The Structured Query Language is a common foundation used by databases to create and destroy structures for holding data, and to place and retrieve data inside of them. While SQL is extremely useful, Rails actually hides most SQL interactions so that developers can work with Ruby objects only, rather than having to think in both Ruby and SQL.

SQLite

A simple database that stores its information in a single file. (In Rails, that file is kept in the *db* directory.) SQLite is extremely convenient for initial development, but slows down dramatically as the number of users grows.

Subversion

A program used to manage different versions of programs and related files across many computers and developers. Many developers building Rails applications use Subversion, but the Rails code itself is now managed in *Git*.

symbols

Ruby identifiers prefaced with colons that Rails uses for pretty much every variable that gets passed from model to view to controller, as well as for named parameters. Symbols look and behave like variables for most ordinary programming purposes, but they give Rails tremendous flexibility.

template

Templates are files used to generate output. In Rails, views are written as templates, typically *ERb* or *Builder* templates, though a variety of other template formats are available as extensions.

test

Code designed to put a particular application piece through its paces. Rails comes complete with support for creating your own unit tests (does a model behave predictably?), functional tests (does a method do what it should?), integration tests (do these methods work together?). You can also create performance tests (how fast does this go, anyway?), and use stubs and mock objects to isolate components for testing.

threads

If you came to Rails from Java or a similar language, you may be looking around for threads. Ruby has threads after all—why doesn't Rails? Well, Rails is single-threaded, handling requests in a single thread. There are lots of ways around this, including having multiple instances of Rails servers all accessing the same database.

Tiger

Mac OS X 10.4, notable mostly for including an old version of Ruby that made it hard to install and use Rails.

UDDI

Universal Description, Discovery, and Integration, a supposedly magical but now largely forgotten piece of the *web services* picture. It was designed to help developers and programmers find *SOAP*-based web services.

Unicode

The industry-standard way to identify characters. Originally, Unicode mapped one character to each of 65,535 bytes, but as that space filled, it became clear that things were more complicated. Ruby's Unicode support improved substantially in version 1.9, but most things will work fine in 1.8.6.

URI

Uniform Resource Identifier, a slightly polished up and abstracted version of the old *URL* that can be used to identify all kinds of things, no longer bound to a few protocols. In REST-based Rails applications, URIs connect to applications in a generally unsurprising way.

URL

Uniform Resource Locator, the identifers that hold together the web. URLs specify a scheme (like http, ftp, or mailto) that maps to a particular protocol, and the rest of the URL provides information that, used with software supporting the scheme, gets you to the information the URL points to. (Or, if the information is gone, an error message.)

UTC

Coordinated Universal Time, formerly known as Greenwich Mean Time (GMT) or Zulu Time. Time zones are generally expressed as offsets from UTC. (UTC is a "compromise abbreviation" between English and French.)

UTF-8

A common encoding for Unicode characters. Old ASCII files are naturally UTF-8 compliant, but characters outside the ASCII range are encoded into multibyte representations. UTF-16 uses two bytes for most commonly used Unicode characters (on the Basic Multilingual Plane) and encodes characters outside of that range into multibyte sequences.

validate

Checking that something is what it's supposed to be. In Rails, data validation should be performed in the model, though some checks may also be performed in view code—for example, in Ajax applications that do as much on the client as possible.

view

The aspect of a Rails program that presents data and opportunities for interaction to users, whether those are users of web browsers getting HTML or other programs using XML or JSON or something else entirely.

Web 2.0

What happens when the world finally "gets" the Web instead of treating it as a place to present brochures and catalogs, recognizing that the interactions among millions of people are creating new and (often) useful things.

web developer

A generic term for people who build applications or sites for the Web. Also, a Firefox plug-in that makes it easy to inspect various aspects of client-side website functionality as well as turn them on or off.

web service

Using the Web for program-to-program communication, rather than the classic model of a human at a web browser interacting with a server. Web services development has largely bifurcated into SOAP-based (or WS-*) development and REST development. Rails 2.0 took a decisive shift toward REST, though you can still write SOAP web services in Rails if you want to.

WEBrick

A Ruby-based web server that is built into standard Ruby distributions since version 1.8.0. Recent releases of Rails typically use *Mongrel* instead.

why (the lucky stiff)

Author of "Why's Poignant Guide to Ruby" (*http://poignantguide.net/ ruby/*), and much more at *http://whytheluckystiff.net/*.

WSDL

The Web Services Description Language, used most frequently by SOAP-based (or WS-*) web service developers, provides a way of describing a web service that programs and humans can use to develop code for interacting with it.

XHTML

Extensible HTML—basically HTML with XML syntax. If you're doing a lot of Ajax work, using XHTML can simplify some of your debugging, but it hasn't exactly caught the world on fire.

XML

Extensible Markup Language is a widely used format for storing information. It insists on precise syntax, but can support a very wide and customizable set of data structures.

XMLHttpRequest

A JavaScript method that lets a program running in a web browser communicate with the server that delivered the page, using the full set of verbs in the HTTP protocol. It is supported by all of the major graphical web browsers, though implementation details are only recently becoming consistent across implementations. `XMLHttpRequest` is at the heart of *Ajax* development.

XML-RPC

An early web services protocol that let developers make remote procedure calls using a particular (and very verbose) XML vocabulary sent over HTTP requests.

XSS

Cross-site scripting is a security hazard that allows crackers to interfere with your program's logic by inserting their own logic into your HTML. The main means of ensuring that your applications don't encounter it is to treat content that might have originated from outside of your immediate control as hostile, accepting as little HTML as your application's needs can tolerate. The `h` method makes it generally easy to escape any HTML that does come through.

YAML

Yet Another Markup Language, YAML was originally developed as a more programming-centric alternative to XML. Ruby supports YAML for object persistence. Rails uses YAML for configuration information. (And as it turns out, largely by coincidence, JSON is a subset of YAML.)

yield

A sometimes mind-boggling Ruby feature that lets methods take a block of code along with the rest of their parameters and then call that code with `yield` when needed. Among other things, this is how Rails implements the relationship between views and layouts.

Index

dynamic interfaces with Ajax (see Ajax)
dynamic scaffolds, defined, 422
dynamic typing, 358 (see duck typing)

E

-e option (script/server), 216
Edge Rails, 422
edit method, 69, 75
    functional testing, 229
else statement, 372
elsif statement, 372
email, 309–329
    HTML-based mail, sending, 316–324
    receiving and processing messages,
        325–328
    text-based, sending, 309–315
empty URL, routing for, 277, 286
enctype attribute (form element), 130
end statements, 17
:end_year parameter (date_select and
        datetime_select), 100
enforcing model relationships, 158, 188
entry method, 403
environment.rb file, 8
    settings for Rails modes, 216
    storing session data, 252
environments for running applications,
    215
    deploying applications, 335
equality operator (==), 372
:equal_to parameter
        (validates_numericality_of
        method), 123
ERb (Embedded Ruby) syntax, defined,
    422
.erb filename extension, 13, 312
:error key, flash messaging, 253
:error parameter (assert_response
        method), 230
errorExplanation div element, 116
error_messages_for method, 85, 401
error_message_on method, 401
Erubis, defined, 422
:escape parameter (url_for method), 285
escape_javascript method, 409
escape_once method, 413
escaping characters, 393
evaluate_remote_response method, 410

:even parameter
        (validates_numericality_of
        method), 123
:except parameter (layout declaration),
    33
exceptions, defined, 422
excerpt method, 414
execute method, 201
existence testing (validation), 124
    for model relationships, 158
exists entries, 12
exit command (irb session), 206
:expires option (cookies object), 247, 253
Extensible HTML (see XHTML)
external data storage, 133–136
external stylesheets, 26, 37

F

FastCGI server, 339
fields, creating new, 202
fields_for method, 406
fieldWithErrors div element, 117
field_set_tag method, 407
file uploads in forms, 129–140
    model and migration changes, 131–
        136
File.join method, 322
File.read method, 322
file_field method, 407
file_field_tag method, 407
filing unit tests purposefully, 223
filter code, defined, 422
filter_parameter_logging method, 205,
    266
find method, 52, 54–56, 57, 74
    :conditions parameter, 332, 349
find_all_by_given_name method, 56
find_by_given_name method, 56
find_by_sql method, 332, 386
Firebug plug-in, defined, 422
:first parameter (find method), 54, 58
fixtures, 216–220
    defined, 422
fixtures directory, 217
flash messaging, 76
    defined, 423
    session state and, 252
flash method, 177

S

safe_erb plug-in, 333
--sandbox option (script/console), 205
sanitize method, 21, 333, 412
SanitizeHelper class, 412
sanitize_css method, 412
save method (Base class), 50
save method (console), 207
scaffold argument (ruby script/generate),
    59, 80
scaffolding, 46, 59–63
    ActiveScaffold, 78
    creating functional tests, 227
    fixtures, creating during, 217
    generating HTML forms with, 83–87
    making changes and, 83
    self.up and self.down methods, 197
scaffolds, defined, 430
:scale parameter (:decimal type), 198
scales, defined, 430
scaling applications, 78
schemas, 380
SchemaStatements class, 201
:scope parameter
        (validates_uniqueness_of
        method), 122
screencasts on Rails, 351
script folder, 15
Script.aculo.us library, 294, 430
script/console command, 205
    classifying users, 265
    security, lack of, 342
script/destroy command, 13
script/generate command, 12
    to create migration files, 193
    creating models, 47
    scaffold argument, 59, 80
script/runner command, 328
script/server command, 7
    -d option, 342
    deployment and, 336–339
    -e option, 216, 342
    -p option, 342
ScriptaculousHelper class, 412
searching for records (see find method)
secret information, not logging, 205, 266
secrets, validation of, 118–123

:secure option (cookies object), 247
securing applications, 331–335
securing views from controllers, 20
select method, 96, 142, 409
    creating lists from related collections,
        154
:select parameter (find method), 56
selected attribute (HTML option
        elements), 99
:selected parameter (select method), 99
selection lists in HTML forms, 96–99
select_date method, 405
select_datetime method, 405
select_day method, 405
select_hour method, 405
select_minute method, 405
select_month method, 405
select_second method, 406
select_tag method, 408
select_time method, 406
select_year method, 406
self-referential joins, 187
self.down method, 48, 192, 194, 202
    as generated by scaffolding, 197
    remove_index and, 200
self.errors.add method, 126
self.up method, 48, 57, 192, 194
    add_index and, 200
    as generated by scaffolding, 197
sending email
    HTML-based messages, 316–324
    text-based messages, 309–315
sendmail command, 310
sequences in regular expressions, 395
server API, Rails as, 293
server, running Rails applications on (see
        Mongrel server)
Session class, 207
session object, 247–253
:session_secure option (session object),
    251
sessions, HTTP
    cookies, 239–247
    defined, 430
    storing data between, 247–253
    user authentication and, 257
SessionStore class, 252
show method, 69, 73

text fields in HTML forms
    creating, 90–91
    labels for, 101–102
text layouts, turning off, 33
:text type, 81
    :limit parameter, 198
text-based email
    receiving and processing messages,
        325–328
    sending, 309–315
text/html content type, 317, 329
TextHelper class, 414
textilize method, 415
textilize_without_paragraph method, 415
text_area method, 85, 90, 407
text_area_tag method, 408
text_field method, 90, 407
    automation with (example), 144
text_field_tag method, 41, 408
37signals, 417
threads, defined, 431
:through parameter (has_many method),
        176, 187
Tiger operating system, defined, 432
time selection fields (HTML forms), 86,
        99
:time type, 81
times constructs, 23
times method, 375
:timestamp type, 81, 198
timestamps method, 198
time_ago_in_words method, 405
time_select method, 100, 405
time_zone_options_for_select method,
        409
time_zone_select method, 409
time_zone_select selection field, 99
timing information, logging, 204
title element, layouts and, 30
TMail library, 326
tmp folder, 16
to_json method, 72
to_s method, 375
TRACE requests (HTTP), 65
tracking users (see user management)
trailing newlines, stripping, 24
:trailing_slash parameter (url_for
        method), 285

truncate method, 415
type-checking, 127
types (see data types)

U

UDDI (Universal Description, Discovery,
        and Integration), defined, 432
unchecked value (checkboxes), 93
Unicode standard, defined, 432
:unique parameter (add_index method),
        200
uniqueness validation, 121
unit testing, 220–226
    reasons for, 226
:unless parameter, validation methods,
        125
unless statement, 371
unsaved migration files, 194
until method, 374
update method, 69, 76
    functional testing, 229
updated method, 403
update_attributes method, 77
update_page method, 411
update_page_tag method, 411
uploading files using forms, 129–140
    model and migration changes, 131–
        136
URIs (universal resource identifiers)
    defined, 432
    fragment identifiers in, 285, 287
    generating from views and controllers,
        283–285
    interpreting with routing, 43, 274–283
        default domains (map.root), 277
        leveraging taxonomy in (globbing),
            278, 287
        with map.connect, 274–277
        named routes, 278
        nested resources, 282
        regular expressions with, 279
    trailing slash, 285
URL hacking, 334
_url helper method, 278, 281
:url parameter (form_for method), 89
URL processing, 45
UrlHelper class, 415
UrlModule class, 284

About the Authors

Simon St.Laurent is a senior editor at O'Reilly and a web developer. His books include *Programming Web Services with XML-RPC* (O'Reilly), *XML: A Primer* (Wiley), and *Office 2003 XML* (O'Reilly). In his spare time, he tends to his family's ducks, chickens, dogs, cats, and rabbits, and sometimes the garden when he is done with the animals. His wife Angelika and new daughter Sungiva keep him well entertained.

Edd Dumbill is co-chair of O'Reilly's Open Source Convention. He is also chair of the XTech web technology conference. Edd conceived and developed Expectnation, a hosted web service for organizing and producing conferences. Edd has also been managing editor of XML.com, a Debian developer, and a GNOME contributor. He writes a blog called Behind the Times (*http://times .usefulinc.com*).

Colophon

The animals on the cover of *Learning Rails* are tarpans (*Equus ferus ferus*). The tarpan was a wild horse that lived in Europe and Asia and died out in the 19th century. Smaller and stockier than a modern domestic horse, it was mouse-gray in color with a dark mane and a black stripe down its back. The breed was known to be intelligent, curious, and independent.

The ancient tarpan ranged from southern France and Spain to central Russia. Its decline was caused by the growth of the European human population in the 17th and 18th centuries, which encroached on the tarpan's natural habitat. Tarpans were also hunted for their meat. The last wild tarpan died in the Ukraine in 1879, and the last pure tarpan died in a Russian zoo eight years later, at which point the species officially became extinct.

However, you can still see a tarpan today, thanks to two German zoologists who succeeded in genetically recreating the breed in the 1930s. Heinz and Lutz Heck began a breeding program while working at a Munich zoo, believing that genes still present in the gene pool of an overall species could be used to re-create extinct breeds. They combined the genes of living horses who showed similar characteristics to the ancient tarpan, and bred the first modern tarpan at the zoo in 1933. This new form of tarpan, known as the Heck horse, is a phenotypic copy of the original wild breed, meaning that it resembles the ancient tarpan but is not exactly the same genetically. Today, there are about 50 tarpans in North America, all of which trace back to the original project in Munich. Most of them are owned by private breeders who are trying to increase the tarpan population. There are not many more than 100 tarpans in the world.

The cover image is from Richard Lydekker's *Royal Natural History*. The cover font is Adobe ITC Garamond. The text font is Linotype Birka; the heading font is Adobe Myriad Condensed; and the code font is LucasFont's TheSansMonoCondensed.

LaVergne, TN USA
23 November 2010
206076LV00011B/30/P

9 781449 383138